American Sublime

Landscapes are formed by landscape tastes. People see their surroundings through preferred and accustomed glasses and tend to make the world over as they see it. Such preferences long outlast geographical reality.
David Lowenthal, "The American Scene"

"Approaching Cozzens' " from: "Views of New York State,"
A Scrapbook of Post Cards and Other Views, New York Public Library Collection.

American Sublime

Landscape and Scenery of the Lower Hudson Valley

Raymond J. O'Brien

Columbia University Press • New York

Raymond J. O'Brien is associate professor of geography and environmental studies at Bucks County Community College, Newtown, Pennsylvania

Columbia University Press
New York   Guildford, Surrey

Library of Congress Cataloging in Publication Data

O'Brien, Raymond J.   1945–
    American sublime.

    Bibliography
    Includes index.
    1. Hudson Valley—Description and travel.
2. Hudson Valley—History.   3. Geology—Hudson
Valley.   I. Title.
F127.H8O27   974.7'3   80-21827
ISBN 0-231-04778-9

c 10 9 8 7 6 5 4 3 2

To Mom and Dad

They gave me life where the river flowed,
I grew and we travelled . . .
And she died . . .

. . . on the banks of the Hudson.

Contents

Illustrations

Acknowledgments

IT IS ALL but impossible to properly acknowledge all those who over the course of the years aided me in the process of research and writing. The various stages of work leading to the conclusion of this manuscript have spanned the better part of a decade, while the Hudson itself as an area of interest and field work has been a lifelong preoccupation.

There were very many people who either in a personal way or in their professional capacity, or both, helped bring this manuscript to a successful completion. Of those whose assistance and support were essential are the following: Frank Innis for instilling in me the very beginnings of interest in historical geography; David Lowenthal for his initial interest in the project and the time he took to correspond and discuss it with me while he was at the American Geographical Society; at Rutgers University: Professors Brush, Boxer, and Holcomb for their constructive criticisms and encouragements; Peter Wacker for his concern and advice at the personal and academic levels; and a very special debt of gratitude to Cal W. Stillman: as advisor and friend from the very early days of my research into the Hudson, he gave far more in terms of time, carefully thought-out personal insights, and hospitality than were ever asked of him.

I am indebted too to John Orth of the Palisades Interstate Park Commission for his interest in my research; to Ina Alterman of Lehman College for her assistance in editing the chapter on the physical setting. Thanks too to all the anonymous staff at the local history, map, and manuscript divisions of the New York Public Library for taking time to find things, and in a pleasurable way.

Thanks to Brother Jim and Manny for help with the photographic copy work, and to family and friends who accompanied me through the hard years and good, especially Aunt Betty, Uncle Charlie and Stevie. For their friendship, and the support it gave this work, you made the task lighter: Charlie T., Robert and Tania, Jack and Anita, Tom, Joe M., and Joe D. And thanks to Tina for helping with the manuscript.

RO'B
Newton, Penn.
January 1981

American Sublime

Part I
Time and the River Valley
*Ideas of Landscape
and the Physical Reality*

Chapter 1
"America's River"

*When conservation of the environment is broadened to include
what people have* thought *about it as well as its actual condition, the potential of conservation history is increased. . . .
inextricably involved are ideas about national identity and
purpose as well as a society's aesthetic, religious, and ethical
convictions.*

Roderick Nash, "The Potential
of Conservation History"

IN 1961 THE WRITER and landscape critic Paul Shepard proposed the concept of the "Cross Valley Syndrome" to describe
how and why mountainous landforms were popularized and
sanctified in nineteenth-century America; he wrote that mountains were idolized as sublime scenery when situated at water
gaps or at places where rivers cut across mountain ranges. At
these locations the clearly dramatic orogenic forces of nature and
the handiwork of God conspire to produce landscapes of very
high aesthetic value. The following year, the Consolidated
Edison Company proposed the concept of a gravity flow,
pumped-storage power plant to generate electricity for the New
York area; the plant was to be carved out of Storm King Mountain in the highlands north of the City. Here, two concepts

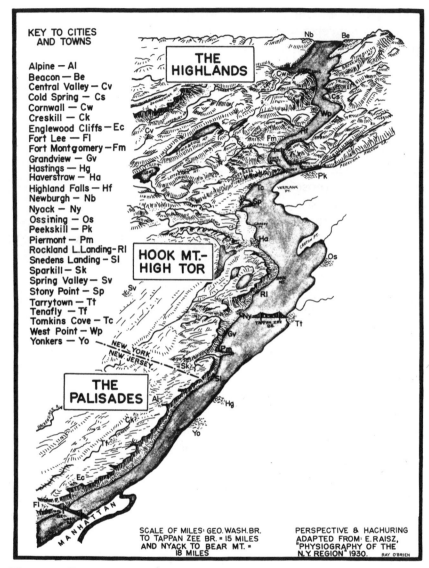

KEY TO CITIES
AND TOWNS

Alpine — Al
Beacon — Be
Central Valley — Cv
Cold Spring — Cs
Cornwall — Cw
Creskill — Ck
Englewood Cliffs — Ec
Fort Lee — Fl
Fort Montgomery — Fm
Grandview — Gv
Hastings — Hg
Haverstraw — Ha
Highland Falls — Hf
Newburgh — Nb
Nyack — Ny
Ossining — Os
Peekskill — Pk
Piermont — Pm
Rockland L.Landing — Rl
Snedens Landing — Sl
Sparkill — Sk
Spring Valley — Sv
Stony Point — Sp
Tarrytown — Tt
Tenafly — Tf
Tomkins Cove — Tc
West Point — Wp
Yonkers — Yo

THE HIGHLANDS

HOOK MT.-HIGH TOR

THE PALISADES

SCALE OF MILES: GEO. WASH. BR.
TO TAPPAN ZEE BR. = 15 MILES
AND NYACK TO BEAR MT. =
18 MILES

PERSPECTIVE & HACHURING
ADAPTED FROM: E. RAISZ,
"PHYSIOGRAPHY OF THE
N.Y. REGION" 1930.   RAY O'BRIEN

Figure 1. The Lower Hudson River Valley with Settlements and Surface Features

ultimately clashed in a two-decade-long battle that resulted in landmark national environmental legislation. Appropriately, the area was surely that one American valley most exemplative of "Cross Valley" aesthetics—the Hudson; and the cause was that great, brooding, ancient river sentinel, "scenic" Storm King. There is a conceptual continuity from nineteenth- to twentieth-century American environmental thought. We draw upon it; we use it to win our preservation battles; and nowhere is it more clearly and potently alive than in the lower valley of this, "America's River."

No region of America or the world is more representative of the manner in which changing cultural attitudes toward landscape helped to shape and reshape the society's aesthetic consciousness than the lower Hudson. It is true that other river valleys, such as those of the Mississippi, Ohio, and St. Lawrence, were said to possess an appealing "Rhenish" quality; but the Hudson "more than any other locale had inspired a new American attitude toward nature."[1] The Hudson is consequently the quintessential North American example. The interplay of attitudes and ideas about mountainous riverscapes in nineteenth-century America unfolded most dramatically in the lower valley. The period guidebooks touted this region as "nature's greatest panorama." It was an integral part of any "Grand Tour," birthplace of the nation's first school of landscape painting, and home of successive generations of aristocratic and landed patrons of culture and conservation. That section of the valley characterized by mountainous or highland topography was visually accessible to the greatest number of travelers and was universally agreed to be a prime source of aesthetic inspiration and national pride.[2] It is by no means coincidental that in the 1800s a series of rocky landforms in this area of the valley were considered scenic, that those same landforms were brought under the banner of the Palisades Interstate Park Commission at the turn of the century, and that so publicized and tumultuous a campaign to save Storm King was undertaken here.

Along the west side of the valley is a nearly uninterrupted shoreline and hinterland of mountainous or clifflike scenery from the Palisades to the highlands. The area is often treated as a distinct and interrelated scenic and geologic entity.[3] For a distance of some 40 miles the eye is regaled with a succession of landforms renowned for nearly two centuries as "picturesque," "sublime," or at the least "beautiful": the Palisades, Hook

Mountain, High and Low Tors, Stony Point, and the highland peaks of Dunderberg, Bear Mountain, Crows Nest, and Storm King.

It is largely with society's collective conceptual images of these topographic features (now mostly contained within the administrative boundaries of the Palisades Park as shown in fig. 2),[4] and with the varying uses to which they have been put in the social and economic history of the region, that explanations are found for the origins of a Hudson River aesthetic, the genesis of an interstate park, and the continued vitality of the environmental movement in the valley (and nation) today.

During the nineteenth century, national parks were established in the American West. Much attention was given to the reports of explorers on the Colorado (for example, John Wesley Powell's *Report on the Lands of the Arid Region of the United States*) and in the Rockies. Landscape artists such as Albert Bierstadt and Thomas Moran and their Western subjects proved very popular on canvas. American thought was, to a large degree, drawn to visions of primitively beautiful Western scenery. The struggle to preserve the natural and curious wonders of this region generated much national political interest.

However important the Trans-Mississippi West was in terms of natural beauty and the movement to save that beauty, it was the Eastern Seaboard that was most often evaluated in verse and on canvas by Americans and foreigners alike.[5] Nineteenth-century conceptions of the picturesque and sublime landscape found their source of financial and aesthetic inspiration in the East, where a sophisticated, educated elite in New York, Philadelphia, and Boston functioned as both innovators and interpreters for national environmental values. The overwhelming number of artists were located there, and it was in the Middle Atlantic and New England states that various concepts of scenery were first explored and elaborated upon.

In this region there were innumerable "picturesque" localities which were said to be "innately romantic": the St. Lawrence,

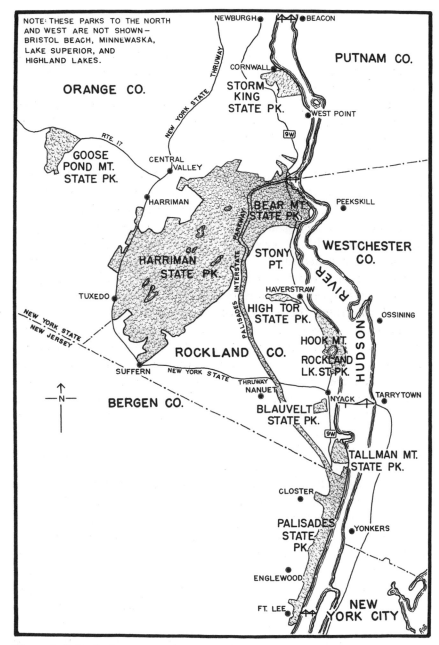

NOTE: THESE PARKS TO THE NORTH
AND WEST ARE NOT SHOWN —
BRISTOL BEACH, MINNEWASKA,
LAKE SUPERIOR, AND
HIGHLAND LAKES.

NEWBURGH
BEACON

PUTNAM CO.

CORNWALL

ORANGE CO.

STORM
KING
STATE PK.

WEST POINT

9W

RTE. 17

GOOSE
POND MT.
STATE PK.

CENTRAL
VALLEY

HARRIMAN

PEEKSKILL

BEAR MT.
STATE PK.

WESTCHESTER
CO.

STONY
PT.

HARRIMAN
STATE PK.

TUXEDO

HAVERSTRAW

HIGH TOR
STATE PK.

OSSINING

HOOK MT.
ROCKLAND
LK. ST. PK.

ROCKLAND CO.

NEW YORK STATE
NEW JERSEY

SUFFERN

NEW YORK STATE

THRUWAY

NANUET

—N—

BERGEN CO.

BLAUVELT
STATE PK.

NYACK

TARRYTOWN

TALLMAN MT.
STATE PK.

9W

CLOSTER

PALISADES
STATE
PK.

YONKERS

ENGLEWOOD

FT. LEE

NEW
YORK CITY

Figure 2. Palisades Interstate Park system today
Base map from: PIPC, Administration Headquarters, Bear Mountain, N.Y., 1965.
(Scale: 1″ ≈ 3.5 miles)

Schuylkill, Connecticut, and Potomac Valleys, and such "curiosities of nature" as Virginia's Natural Bridge and the falls at Niagara and at Paterson, New Jersey. But the landscape most talked about, admired, and frequented was without doubt "romantic" highland scenery. It was mountainous or hilly areas and associated watergaps and falls that became the delight of foreign and American traveling writers and painters. Consequently, it is the function of mountainous or highland areas in the nation's aesthetic imagery that is critical to so many theories and concepts of art. Furthermore, regions such as the White and Green Mountains, the middle Delaware River at its watergap through the Kittatinny Range, the misty Catskills and Taconics, and even the less accessible Adirondacks, were all frequented by the romantic-minded traveler and fawned over and dressed with an idealized vocabulary before being preserved as park areas.

By mouthing the guidebook rhetoric and following the lead of the artistic, literary elite and what they perceived to be reflective of the "Cross Valley Syndrome," such featuresque locations were given an aesthetic soul, a status or designation that proved ultimately effective in their preservation. The epitome of "grand scenery," where the relationship between the panoramic and titanic powers of landscape aesthetics and preservation worth is seen to work most effectively, is where the granitic and bouldery highlands of New York State and the sheer clifflike Palisades close in upon the Hudson's valley.

This work looks at the manner in which ideas about landscape affect the way the Hudson Valley appears today. Attitudes and concepts of what is beautiful or not-so-beautiful are seen in this instance as the basis of human life and action; or as the late cultural geographer Jan Broek once said, "the manner of the utilization of the land finally rests on ideas."[6] Scholars have examined various interpretations of American reaction to nature and American society's adjustment to romantic ideas imported from Europe. Such interpretations involve relationships between groups within the society at different times, as well as the evolution of landscape concepts and patterns. Neither have these theories and interpretations dealing with the interaction of man's aesthetic values and nature been actually tested in much depth, nor have such concepts been directly applied to the rise of a preservation ethic in specific places. The existence of a regional aesthetic, its root causes in the nineteenth century and its consequences in this century, is valuable to an overall understanding of the historical progression of land use in the United States from romanticized, idealized wildscape to its tamed use for recreation. A clearer and thus far undigested understanding of the myriad forces that have been influential in the preservation of the still-much-fought-over and debated precious landscape of the lower valley of the Hudson can accomplish this synthesis. In a broader sense, at the level of national historical attitudes and *isms,* the origins and growth of the "impulse" to preserve, fired by mental images of topographic excellence, are documented.

Despite the many essentially physical, photographic, and historical works dealing with the Hudson Valley[7] that have appeared over the years (the best of which are cited in the bibliography) there is no detailed study that has explored the way changing patterns of land use and thought conflicted and in time coalesced constructively in the creation of a scenic-recreational landscape appreciated by millions of people. Because of such neglect, this work adds to the permanent historical record of an area lacking not at all in primary documentation by collecting and organizing that material in such a way that the region's history takes on a deeper meaning.

More importantly perhaps, those cultural forces which led to the establishment of an urban-fringe recreational entity, the Palisades Interstate Park in New York and New Jersey, are documented. The park's formation—and indeed the origins of the American park and preservation movement—are viewed in terms of environmental concepts and landscape attitudes that were cultivated throughout the nineteenth century and seized upon as a *modus operandi* by groups and individuals in the twentieth century. The reasons for a preservation "impulse" have been very popular topics of literary investigation, but few have looked at how that "impulse" was generated in a specific place and how it is both formative to and reflective of the movement to create national or state parks and forests—as it has been in the Hudson.[8]

Today, the lower Hudson Valley of course has serious problems inherent in its location within the reach of the Seaboard megalopolitan corridor: pollution, planning battles, continuous need to expand recreational facilities, and related demands that place great pressure upon its hearty yet delicate ecology. The nature of these current problems is better comprehended if seen in the context of theories of land use and landscape evaluation advanced by historians, geographers, and others in the past few decades.

Paul Shepard's concept of the Cross Valley Syndrome has already been alluded to. When so viewed, much of the lower Hudson has truly been memorialized and placed on a lofty aesthetic pedestal that seems to make it a "framed" piece of the world, above and isolated from surroundings that are so less endowed with scenic quality. But, depending on how they are viewed, the perception of areas as finished, varnished landscape paintings from another era is either an obstacle to progress or a confirmation of aesthetic strength. Storm King is inherently and with reason the symbol of Cross Valley aesthetics in the Hudson; ergo, it must not be tampered with by power companies or others who would abuse its scenic integrity whatever the local economic needs or regional power demands. In a local newspaper column, Grant Jobson expressed the concern that recreational value too might be diminished because so much of the valley has been scenically or historically "monumentalized."[9] The Hudson has always possessed that contradictory duality of aesthetics and industry: the nation's first great highway of commerce—whose history is written in smoke, brick, steam, and rail—yet somehow a river of constant beauty. This duality, this balance of necessary economic activity and the scenic, is sometimes lost sight of by environmentalists who emphasize only the river's aesthetic side. In many instances society's baser economic furnishings are perfectly fitting pieces of the landscape, when held in proper check by the aesthetic impulse and its implied recreational values.

A Soft Nostalgic Glow

Nostalgia is a commodity that colors our view of the past (e.g., seeing the 1950s as innocent "Happy Days") and, when we draw upon and recycle elements from that supposedly more preferable past, it often conditions the way we deal with the present. This nostalgic evocation of an idealized past can be a powerful catalyst to the preservation of what is perceived to be environmentally aesthetic.

David Lowenthal has recognized the importance of this strategy in environmental issues and in the Hudson Valley. In his 1962 essay, "Not Every Prospect Pleases," and again in his "The American Scene" of 1968, Lowenthal found that society has constantly idealized the past and used it as a "sanctuary from the awful present." And "that past includes not only historic buildings and places, but also a pastoral countryside and a sublime wilderness."[10] In times of rapid social change, when everything appears to be unsettled or unfixed, people grasp for the ordered and enduring regularities of nature and simultaneously "turn to a time that seems more substantial. . . . What we want to see is something better, more solid, more beautiful."[11] Or as the old joke goes: nostalgia is like a grammar lesson; you find the present tense and the past perfect! When the present is threatening or insecure, the past is evoked. The early romantics turned to Walter Scott, distant empires, classical times, and biblical shepherds. These devices provided a form of escapism from technology, and also had consequence for the Hudson Valley in that the riverscape was infused with a sense of history—at least on canvas and in thought, if not entirely in fact.

It is ironic that the one great "deficit" of American landscape always deplored by nineteenth-century commentators—the appalling absence of historical connotations at specific places—should by 1900 have proved to be one of the strongest and most persistently useful assets in viewing places as scenic. In the twentieth century, as Robert Frost has said, the land could no longer remain "still unstoried, artless, unenhanced."

In the Hudson Valley not only was the past evoked, it was

actually used as an aesthetic enhancement (i.e. viewing the world through lace-curtained windows or a rose-tinted rearview mirror). Or, "when something is about to go, it has its sunset. It has its most beautiful colors and then disappears. When the railroads are coming in, people write poems to trees."[12] Fortunately, many of the scenic landforms in the lower Hudson Valley were rescued in time, but the body of "sunset aesthetics" they inspired while threatened was so solidly constructed that it has been recycled again and again to thwart attacks in every decade.

The use of a growing national nostalgia for the vanishing countryside, along with the resurrection of the Revolutionary War heritage, had invested the landscape with an historical linkage to simpler and more glorious times. Nostalgia and adulation for a landscape enhanced by ancient and therefore scenically romantic ruins repeatedly availed itself of the geographic artifacts of the War of Independence. If the Hudson was to be conceived of as aesthetically pleasing, it was important for example that old Fort Putnam, "a gray and veteran ruin of '76," wear "the appearance of a ruined castle upon a mountain crag."[13] Weathered over the course of time and sentimentalized by generations, the ruins of the old highland military works on Constitution Island and the forts along Popolopen Creek added immeasurably to the picturesque landscape. The Hudson was found to be not without its time-worn ruins, and "these ruins and their many associations," in the words of the traveler deDamseaux, "spring from the period of the American Revolution."[14] The visualization of the valley as teary-eyed nostalgic ground was used to great effect in the preservation movement in the latter part of the nineteenth century.

Now, the use of this same nostalgia for different purposes is no less the case. The *National Geographic* magazine wraps a gauze of "pastoral" nostalgia about the "Mighty Hudson" and valley realtors claim to have "captured the life you used to love" at the nostalgic "Arcadia Hills" housing tract.[15] In the late 1960s and 1970s, the paintings of the old Hudson River School were in vogue again; various exhibitions were mounted and the price tags on the works of Church and Cropsey greatly inflated. Involved here is an appeal to a regional sublimity made all the more valuable through an exhortation of the past. Lowenthal expressed the mood and intent of one such exhibition:

A recorded commentary urged visitors to remake the river as it used to be. No one questioned whether the nineteenth-century Hudson Valley really conformed to the painters' view of it; no one seemed to doubt that the present scene was one of unmitigated blight.

As the Federal Power Commission hearings examiner noted in the Storm King case: "Storm King does not exist in an environment of untouched natural beauty as in the idyllic past, but rather is all but irrevocably associated with the present realities."[16] But many, it seems, would prefer that idealized past.

A sham nostalgia may in part explain this renewed interest in cracked and yellowed landscape paintings, but there's more. That the Hudson is still grand and evocative scenery today is evident in the continued symbiotic relationship between painter and landscape. Artwork and the valley intertwine now as before; the region's beauty gives life to the artist's vision and the artist in turn—through his works and public involvement in conservation and preservation—gives back to the valley a chance at life. This idea was well illustrated when Rockland County artists donated their works for auction at the Parke-Bernet Galleries ("Art for the Mountain") to raise money to save Clausland Mountain. It was very appropriate too that in the mid 1970s the Palisades Park system was selected as the first interstate park in the nation to be memorialized on canvas and in other media through the America the Beautiful Fund's "Artists in Residence" program. To "harvest" the beauty of that parkland, to provide the public with a sense of land-derived spiritual and aesthetic uplift, and to show visitors that parks exercise minds as well as muscles, were in the words of the park manager the reasons for the program.[17]

That aesthetic "harvest" is never exhausted here; the Hudson is a great well of scenic refreshment that whether viewed through the last century's "Light of Distant Skies," or the "Artists in Residence" program of today exudes that near spiritual awareness of the natural environment; beauty is its hallmark, but without a strong national and local societal commitment to visual quality it would be lost. And artwork, now as then, feeding upon the aura of pure beauty as well as the more formulated beauty of which nostalgia is a part is a means to the realization of that commitment.

Nostalgia—the sticky pervasiveness of this nineteenth-century "geographical disease"—was once raised to the status of a major "sociological complaint" according to Lowenthal,[18] but the memory of scenes past did in itself become a recreational resource and a justification for defending the valley from change.

Today, nostalgia engulfs much of the valleyscape, placing landforms like Storm King and the Dunderberg "off limits." But conversely, it is nostalgic imagery, too—whether based on fact or fantasy—that produces a "hands on" situation for tourism: Come see the romantic valley of history where the Headless Horseman hounded Ichabod Crane and hear the highlands echo with the thunder of bowling balls hurled by Henry Hudson's ghost crew! Tourist literature, real estate come-ons, and the everyday news story all hinge upon retrospect to gild that soft, vanished time:

> Congers: A Trip Down a Quiet Memory Lane
> Tomkins Cove Still Strides to a Pace of Another Time
> Jones Point—it Isn't What it Once Was

Whatever it once was, it is now firmly and usefully entrenched as part of our culture's great preserved landscapes of nostalgia: Wordsworth's Lake District, Hardy's Wessex, Twain's Mississippi, and Irving's misty Hudson.

But Whose River?

The Hudson has, from the early nineteenth century, been regarded as something more than just a regional river or part only of a local landscape, which leads to a further consideration of the valley's mental role best stated again by Lowenthal: that the tourists'-eye view and understanding of the world being traveled through is ignorant, artificial, and therefore of little consequence. "We disdain the mere onlooker and dismiss his opinion of the landscape. What right has a passive spectator to impose his judgment?" asks Lowenthal. Mark Twain and Henry James are quoted to the effect that a spectator's opinion is superficial, possessing no truth as to the real nature of the environment. In short, scenery—a cultural device at best and not the genuine, rugged face of the real world—is perceived by "outsiders." But the landscape's "ultimate critics are its residents, not its visitors, however unappreciative the former, however learned or perceptive the latter."[19] Decisions affecting the use and appearance of the land ought then to be left in their hands.

The use of this "outsiders versus insiders" dichotomy and seeing travelers or valley tourists as uninitiated and ill-informed intruders raises serious questions about the current and future use of the land. In the Hudson a neat categorization between residents and visitors ("insiders and outsiders") is difficult; the line is blurred between those who live in the valley and those whose views and opinions actually bear weight in terms of land-use decisions. It has in fact been this way historically. The river was esteemed as a symbol of national pride by American travelers— an attitude commented upon by Europeans. The Hudson was "our river" to Virginia planters ensconced in the local mountain house retreats, to the New York City–based literary and journalistic elite, and to the itinerant landscape artists. The shad fishermen working their nets below the Palisades and the rock farmers in the Orange County highlands had no particular claim to a region that transcended the bounds of parochialism. There could be nothing local about "America's River." It might thus be argued that the only real "outsiders" were perhaps, and only perhaps, the European visitors.

The sublime, scenically pleasing countryside of the valley and its spectacular uplands was shaped, popularized, and transmitted through time by a handful of individuals: Irving, Cole, Willis, Downing, and a few others. But are these generators of popular taste insiders or outsiders? Although a part of the New York City and European cosmopolitan elite, they were no less residents of the Hudson Valley than the fishermen and farmers. From their homes at Irvington, Catskill, Cornwall, and Newburgh they interpreted the valley to others from a uniquely local, yet international perspective. Likewise, the local "mountain people," who lately formed a core of opposition to Con Edison's Storm King project, are in no sense hardscrabble Appalachian Folk types, but actually well-to-do New York City businessmen and attorneys with private weekend retreats in the highlands. Yet, the line blurs because many of them may truly be "insiders"—families whose vested property interests there go back generations.

It might be concluded that, in a very real sense, the Hudson, as "America's River," had and has no "outsiders." The river flows deep in our national consciousness—and even beyond if the Scenic Hudson Preservation Conference's designation, "Humanity's River," is used. However jealously guarded by those who consider themselves privileged fifth or more generation "valley folk," the river is such that appreciation and criticism of its landscape and of policy decisions affecting its use are of regional and national scope. *The New York Times* and other outside newspapers such as *The Boston Transcript* had become involved in exposing visual blight on the Palisades as early as the 1890s; city-based entrepreneurs beautified the Rockland County, New York, and Bergen County, New Jersey, hillsides and cliffs with landscaped properties and drained "malarial" marshlands; the picnic groves and mountain houses were built for and patronized both by the diarist G. T. Strong's "immigrant hordes" and by his wealthy suburbanite acquaintances; the building stone quarries, wood slides, and ice houses were operated for and by Manhattan's townhouse society; the eventual preservation of what was aesthetic was effectuated by a combination of urban-based interest groups, wealthy "local" landowners who were anything but local in outlook and place of permanent residence, and distant state legislatures.

Throughout the course of its evolution from a settlement

frontier to recreational entity, the highland areas of the lower Hudson Valley have been interpreted and modified through the agency of outsiders, but in the regional or national sense in which the Hudson must be viewed there are in fact no outsiders. The status achieved by the river valley in the national graphic and literary iconography has elevated it above the control of those who live within it. National aesthetic attitudes and the appraisal of the valley as merely a scenic mask—a prerogative supposedly the domain of nonresidents—has had more lasting impact upon the spatial transformation of the land than all the local decisions concerning what crops to plant, where to place a road or mill, or which town supervisor to elect. This perhaps is a fact seldom appreciated or conceded to by the "residents" when conflicts of land use or resource allocation arise today.

Debt to the Nineteenth Century

The various ideas and influences that have reacted to create a valley aesthetic form the core of the chapters which follow. These ideas and influences were conditioned by events between roughly 1783 (the end of the Revolutionary War) and 1909 (the tricentennial of Hudson's upriver voyage in 1609 and the Centennial of Fulton's experimental voyage of the *Clermont*). During this period, the romantic concept achieved its greatest effect, culminating in the birth of the Palisades Interstate Park and the preservation of so much of the valley's landscape.

With the birth of the nation came an almost immediate patriotic and nostalgic appreciation of the hallowed battlegrounds of the Revolution, and for the Hudson, this translated into a quicksilver aesthetic and mode of scenic appreciation. This was abetted by the essentially favorable and pleasurable attitudes coming in with the European romantic movement, which reached the shores of America in the latter part of the eighteenth century. Only then did description of places become a "religion," a social grace, a precise scenic science, a painterly preoccupation, and a philosophical passion.

The great emotional and legal struggle for supremacy between aesthetic regard for the land and the exploitation and economic development of the landscape was characteristic of the period. By 1910, dramatic changes in attitude and action marked the way Americans viewed themselves and their relationship to the land and nature. The frontier had closed, and with it what Frederick Jackson Turner called the era of free and unlimited horizons.[20] Tourism and recreation had widened to become the domain of the common man. The ecstatic outdoor ramblings and jottings on "romantic" nature became passé, along with the Hudson River school of painting. And perhaps most importantly, the preservation movement had gained momentum in the Eastern United States by 1900, as witnessed in the changeover from reckless and wasteful attitudes toward ideas of at least controlled exploitation in vanguard areas like the Adirondacks and Hudson Valley.[21]

As a result of these value changes, by the late nineteenth century the Hudson Valley began to be regarded with an environmental concern, much as the poets and painters of an earlier era had hoped. In the 1880s and 1890s, newspaper editorials began to scold the public for tolerating a billboard blight on the Palisades and the movement for scenic and historic preservation snowballed. At that time, many of the quarries were forced to cease their operations. Also, the Palisades Interstate Park Commission began to assemble properties deemed worthy of preservation along the Hudson's western shore. "The western shore was to be viewed and the eastern shore to be lived along" became the unwritten rule.[22]

Stony Point: The World in Microcosm

The interplay of events and attitudes occurring within this timespan that effectuated the changeover in attitudes toward land and nature in the Hudson valley from abusive and usative to sanctifying and idolizing are nicely seen with the aid of one small illustration. The forces that shaped the social imagery and

molded the physical landscape at Stony Point—a minor headland
that projects into the Hudson three miles south of Haverstraw
(fig. 3)—encapsulates in miniature the broader system of symbols
and imagery simultaneously affecting the preservation of the Palisades and highlands to the south and north.

A part of the Palisades Interstate Park system since 1906,
Stony Point is not strictly a highland or clifflike landform and
does not, as claimed by Colt's *Traveller's Guide* of 1871, "command the waters of the Hudson." Still, the rocky headland does
provide a welcome intrusion onto the flat Haverstraw Plain and
is, in the period travel literature, considered a part of "the great
hills of grandeur and beauty."[23] From the deck of the riverboat,
this steep-sided conical hill does jut quite prominently into the
river and draws the traveler's attention. Therefore, it becomes a
subdued but nonetheless apparent "Cross Valley" presence.

The ingredient necessary to light the fires of scenic rapture
was provided this "little Gibraltar" when General Anthony
Wayne attacked the point's small British garrison, and captured
this "eminence of fame" in the summer of 1779. A "humble
crag" had been converted "into a mountain peak of liberty." To
paraphrase William Cullen Bryant's comments to river travelers
a century later, how can a true American pass this granite hill
without tears and thoughts of the exploit associated with the
place! If somewhat weak in topographic sublimity, the call to nationalism and historical pride more than compensated. Wallace
Bruce put it to verse:

> From Stony Point to Bemis Height,
> From Saratoga to the sea,
> We trace the lines, now dark, now bright,
> From seventy-six to eighty-three.[24]

Clothed in fittingly dramatic human associations, the little
peninsula was regarded as picturesque or sublime throughout the
nineteenth century. The point, linked to the mainland by a
"morass, deep and dangerous," and where "the rocks lay in wild
confusion," lured travelers to its summit to view "the classic

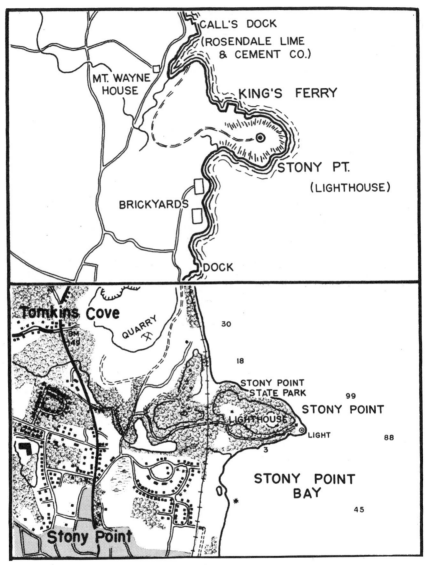

Figure 3A. Stony Point in the 1850s and 1960s

Top: Detail from: O'Connor's map of "Rockland County, New York," 1854
Bottom: Detail from: U.S.G.S. Haverstraw topographic sheet, 1967
(Scale: 1″ ≈ 2000′)

Figure 3B. The Day Liner Passing Stony Point.
Hudson River Day Line Magazine, New York: Robert Stillson Co., 1903. (New York Public Library Uncatalogued Collection of Pamphlets and Books Pertaining to the Hudson River and Valley)

ground" surrounding the headland.[25] Almost with the same frequency as the Dunderberg and West Point, Stony Point appeared in winter and summer, in sunlight and shadow, in its share of period lithographs.

The landscape of hurry and suburbanization, so feared by the writers and painters, was always very close to Stony Point. The brickyards, lime kilns, quarries, and docks of the Haver-straw–Tomkins Cove area were disturbingly near. Summer homes and country mansions lined the mainland shore by 1890. The forest around the point was badly cut over for fuel and building material, and a never-developed magnetite mine on the peninsula's northern side did for a time raise fears of development.

Befitting its rise to scenic fame and the desire to preserve "unchanged in form and feature" the historic ground, Stony

Point was conserved for reasons of recreation, Revolutionary remembrances, and aesthetic contemplation. Indeed, the utilization of the area for purposes of recreation dates at least back to the 1850s, when picnics on the battlefield, Sunday walks to the lighthouse, and a week's stay at the Mount Wayne House, were common pastimes.

J. Pierpont Morgan, as vice president of the American Scenic and Historical Preservation Society, helped get the state legislature to appropriate $25,000 for the purchase of the Stony Point battlefield as a state park in 1897. The Wayne memorial was dedicated by Governor Odell in 1902, the battle site became part of the Palisades Park system in 1906, and on "Stony Point Day" in October of 1909, as part of the Hudson-Fulton celebrations, a memorial arch was dedicated by the Daughters of the American Revolution.

The elements necessary to scenic preservation had fused successfully: historical connotations, aspects of nationalism, salvation from an imminent industrial and technological tidalwave, enshrinement in lithograph and verse, and in this case a gentle but compelling natural sublimity. These same preconditions were being met and the same events were occurring all along the Hudson's lower shores, only on a much grander scale.

A Timeless Relevancy

The enlistment of the concepts and stratagems that were effectively employed at Stony Point and throughout the larger "Cross Valley" region did not of course end in 1909; they have become the underlying philosophy at many times since of those concerned with "saving" what is aesthetic in the valley. Consequently, the significance of these nineteenth-century symbols and maneuvers goes beyond a pure research interest: timeless relevancy is inherent through a continued application of these same devices in the cause of good environmental planning and policy decade after recent decade. The dictates of poetic and artistic romanticism have endured in such a way as to influence the thought and actions of succeeding generations. Importantly, the pattern set for the aesthetic evaluation of the Palisades, the Tors, and the highland peaks—so solidly established before 1909—was repeatedly summoned forth in the decades that followed.

Threats Old and New in the 1930s

After a sleepy hiatus of sorts between 1909 and the coming of the New Deal, a second national wave of conservation consciousness, characterized by Franklin Roosevelt's creation of the various three-letter agencies, found fertile ground along the Hudson. Carl Carmer's classic and flowing account, *The Hudson,* appeared as part of the "Rivers of America" series. The concept of the picturesque, precious landscape was firmly rooted here and perhaps for the first time a public concern for river pollution was noted. With a pessimism that was to re-echo in the 1960s and 1970s, the pollution of the west shore bathing beaches was decried. In the 1930s defenders of the Palisade and highland regions also became alarmed with what were seen as the dire changes caused by the construction of the George Washington Bridge and the long-envisioned Palisades Parkway. Since the opening of the Bear Mountain Bridge and Storm King Highway in 1923–24, 5 million recreationists per year were pouring into the highlands. They also feared that a prime suburban real estate zone would be developed atop the Palisades, but in 1935 John D. Rockefeller buried that fear with a gift of 700 cliff-top acres to the Park Commission.

At a time when the strength of Cross Valley aesthetics was perhaps at its lowest ebb, the great horizontal scar of the Storm King Highway was cut, and the mountain's unimpaired river face sacrificed to the CCC for jobs. But, as in the past, the most blatant assault upon the landscape was posed by the quarrymen who were actively gouging away the slopes of Little Stony Point and Mount Taurus, crushing, grading, and barging the stone downriver. Unabashedly, the stone quarry companies proclaimed the benefits of steam shovels and pulverized rock in the souvenir program issued at the New York World's Fair in 1939.[26] The reaction to quarrying, as gleaned from the charter of the Hudson River Conservation Society (1936) and a succession of *New York Times* editorials and stories from the late 1920s to World War II, was an appeal to preservation in terms of the river's romantically sublime scenery and historical content.[27] It was only natural in such circumstances that the paintings of the old Hudson River School should be dusted off for an exhibition in January of 1932, and that *The New York Herald Tribune* should editorialize ("A River with Friends") on how the "hand of the despoiler" had befouled this ancient and sublime stream, in a manner befitting "the American genius for taking beautiful things and making them ugly."[28]

"Happy Days"?

By the 1950s, a potentially lethal threat was posed to the valley's scenery.

The first "sample mile" of the Palisades Interstate Parkway opened as a noncommercial component of the metropolitan area's highway system in 1951, but its function, originally conceived as a landscaped-scenic drive, was quickly superseded by its role as a major commuter artery. A "skyscraper invasion" threatened the uninterrupted silhouette of the Palisades, but Rockefeller money again poured into the breach, and headed off proposals for high rise developments at Fort Lee by buying up the site of the Revolutionary War fort for the Palisades Interstate Park Commission. Only the already gritty, industrial landscape of the lower Palisades would be further "violated" by the invasion of thirty-story glass and concrete condominium towers in the decades to come.

As elsewhere on the New York suburban fringe, post Korean war population growth was dramatic in Rockland County. Here, a shadow was cast upon the survival of the northern Palisades and Tors when the 3-mile-wide Tappan Zee was spanned by the newly opened Thruway Bridge in 1955. The

2200 cars that poured across the giant cantilever bridge in its first two hours of operation signaled an era of incredible population growth for suburban Rockland—from 89,000 in 1950 to 230,000 by 1970. But in the 1970s, with population growth slacking off, the Park Commission emerged as the largest landowner in the county (27%), effectively guaranteeing a green, open space environment for the future.

The quarry-weakened crags and visual scars on the back side of the Tors were (and continue to be) a problem, but on other fronts the pockmarked legacy of the quarrymen yielded to the mending impulses of aesthetic man. Before his death the industrial designer Russel Wright, who had devised plans for the conversion of the quarry pit on the face of Mount Taurus into an open air amphitheatre, sought successfully to heal the "open wound" that was the old King Company granite quarry in the highlands at Garrison. Referring to the "spiritual integrity of the land," he, in the course of 35 years, wove about that ancient pit a blanket of landscape design in tune with the sacred geography of the Orient and the theology of the American Indian. In a harmony with nature that would be understood by Thoreau and Burroughs the quarry has become the centerpiece of a nature sanctuary, "Manitoga"—the place of the Great Spirit in the local Algonquin vocabulary. Here, where one feels deeply embedded within the surrounding woodland confines of the highlands, the enjoyment of nature and art together has again become the theme and visitors are encouraged to interpret the cycles of forest and pond ecology through the medium of music, dance, and photography.

Into the Age of Ecological Consciousness

The renewed interest in Hudson River aesthetics today is perhaps an outgrowth of the ecology movement of the 1960s, when the noble but noxious Hudson was to be expurgated of its worsening accumulation of watery filth. But river pollution, aside from the physical danger it poses to human and aquatic life in the valley, ruins the image of the river so painstakingly created by artists and writers over the years and detracts from its recreational value. Thermal discharges from atomic reactors, sewage injection, and chemical waste (PCBs) have all been cited by ecologists for damage done to food chains and habitats, but much of the condemnation comes in the form of comments aimed at damage done to the purely scenic quality of the area. Rotting fish, fish crucified on power plant intake screens, eutrophic scum, and smelly and oily water are matters of both biology and beauty. The use of aesthetics—the use of Hudson Valley aesthetics—to fight pollution is certainly implicit in arguments leveled against Con Edison's plants and plans for electric generation by the Hudson River Fishermen's Association. The weaving together of a concern for landscape aesthetics and marine life is symbolized too in the career of the Hudson River sloop *Clearwater*. Launched in 1969 to promote public concern for a cleaner river (Pete Seeger: "Her cargo now is a message: We can clean up this polluted stream"), she now sails to a tune of beauty as eloquent as any ever penned or painted: "savor the sound of water lapping against the hull and appreciate the magic of a tall, white sail slipping past a bluff."[29] Employing the lure of nostalgia, as Seeger says, to make it "the way it was on the river a hundred years ago—and maybe could be again."

Various organizational and governmental efforts in recent years have created a river said to be less polluted than in the recent past. The oxygen level in the lower Hudson has apparently regained something of its nineteenth-century level, the danger of marshland eutrophication is reduced (the Iona Island salt marsh, for example, received protection as a registered national landmark in 1976), "edible" shad and sturgeon are again more plentiful, clams have been seen in the river for the first time in more than fifty years. The legacy of three decades of toxic PCB accumulation, which reached unprecedented deadly proportions in 1975–76, will be partially mitigated through a costly and difficult cleanup effort. Author and fisherman Robert Boyle, however, paints the river pollution problem in a much more sombre hue in his expanded 1979 edition to *The Hudson River: A*

Natural and Unnatural History. Although he admits to "some advances of the anti-pollution front," the role of the state government and its Department of Environmental Conservation are criticized unreservedly ("just about worthless" . . . having "sinned against the Hudson River for years by commission, omission, and emission . . .") and recent instances of pollution are cited: cadmium waste dumping, landfill projects in the river shallows, and toxic chemical contamination.[30] Whatever the truth, one would hope that the worst is over and that optimism is warranted, as expressed in recent headlines: "The Hudson: That River's Alive," and "Despite Abuse, Hudson Remains a River of Life."[31]

Now, concern for the river valley environment must take into account as well the less scientifically measurable, the less tangible, the more elusive and misty river aesthetic. And nowhere has a more solid, elaborate aesthetic base been laid than along the Hudson. "Equal rights" for aesthetic values and the social feelings conducive to legislation dealing with environmental quality are more than at home in this valley; they were born here. Recent issues and events continually draw their philosophical and emotional vitality in large part from that extensive body of aesthetic lore that has become the birthright and signature of the Hudson.

Very explicitly, the aesthetic heritage has served as the taproot for legislation and organizations currently involved in scenic preservation and enhancement. The adverse effect upon scenic and historic values was cited by national and local conservation groups in the 1960s as a reason not to build the proposed East Bank Expressway along the Westchester shoreline. How can an expressway "designed to carry trucks and buses with their roaring speed, fumes, and inexorable pressures on the flow of traffic," asked *The New York Times,* "make a positive contribution to natural beauty?" The idea of a "Hudson Valley Scenic and Historic Corridor," as proposed by Governor Rockefeller in 1965 to preserve and beautify the valley, would surely have pleased the like of Irving and Cole. That concept came closer to reality in 1979, when the state Commissioner of Environmental

Conservation urged that the Hudson shoreline be preserved because of its spectacular scenic uniqueness. In designating the Hudson Highlands a "scenic area" he cited the role of these mountains in the "evolution of America's literary and artistic heritage" and the related "tangible economic benefits" brought to the valley by tourism.[32]

Birth and Death of the Hudson River Valley Commission

Although the driving legacy of history, regional literature, and art have proved strong stimulants to cleanse the river physically, there is more still that our present draws from the river's past. More than can possibly be reflected in all the "coffee table" picture volumes, shad fishing, and river revivals dedicated to the river's rebirth. Our culture has had transmitted to it those psychic or spiritual values best expressed as the awe and deep-down-inside-you euphoria that comes from being alone on a mountaintop, for instance. The Cross Valley syndrome is alive and well along the Hudson and is as acutely felt now as in the years before the Civil War. To clean the river's waters is good but insufficient to fully satisfy this feeling—one that demands a larger effort to secure the integrity of the overall scenic package that sparks such euphoria.

Perhaps in no one instance is the recent concern for the scenic and historic integrity of the valley better seen than in the short but active life of the Hudson River Valley Commission. Created by the state legislature in 1966, the commission was charged with the enhancement and preservation of landscape within one mile of the river's edge (two miles when the land within that distance was visible from the river). Although its powers were largely advisory, through its newsletters, annual reports, and special publications (e.g. its *Inventory of Historic Resources of the Hudson*) the agency's 66 staff members gave due credence to aesthetic standards and values that were incorporated into project reviews—a technique that the staff pioneered in developing—and designs for comprehensive land use within its jurisdictional area. The need for such a coordinating body was, however, thrown into question and, whether due to economics or politics (a "weak and ineffective . . . puppet of Nelson Rockefeller"), it foundered. It trampled on the toes of insiders, eluded delicate political control, and was probably not single-minded enough for the more ardent outside environmentalists. With its demise in 1974 (the commission was gutted and "stuffed into a closet somewhere in the bureaucracy"[33]) this generation's attempt to explain, enumerate, and preserve that which we have come to regard as aesthetic on the face of the land has most surely been blunted.[34]

Storm King Aesthetics

Although an aesthetic rootline to the past can be seen in various other ways—the concern with "visual blight" caused by the Bowline Point power plant at Haverstraw (more compelling than the sulfur dioxide emissions?) and the intent to visually restore some of the lost elegance and grandeur to the economically decayed but reviving river towns like Nyack—perhaps that link with the past is seen most clearly in the Storm King controversy.

For two decades the Scenic Hudson Preservation Conference fought a delaying battle against Con Edison's proposed Storm King pumped storage hydroelectric plant. It cited especially the issues of water contamination, possible damage to the Catskill aquaduct, decimation of Atlantic fishery resources, and the non-necessity of the facility in terms of projected regional power needs. Although technical and scientific considerations were eventually drawn into the legal fray, the original concept was to save natural splendor; implicit in the organization's title and in its use of nineteenth-century highland lithographs in its publicity brochures was the idea of "Scenic Preservation"—saving land-forms that were beautiful today, still beautiful in fact because they were sanctified and mythologized in our romantic past.

This direct or implied use of romantic lore at Storm King—arguments based on the premise that beauty itself is an essential public resource, far outweighing economic advantages—eventually became a basis for the National Environmental Policy Act (NEPA) of 1969. The concept that federal actions, like licensing power plants, should take into account the irretrievable loss of natural beauty draws largely on the groundwork laid in the Storm King case.

The possibility that Storm King would be gouged out into a "giant flushable Port-o-San" to satisfy an appetite for electric energy, an appetite which had by the late 1970's diminished nationally, was killed in December 1980 in what *The New York Times* hailed as "A Peace Treaty for the Hudson." The nearly two decade-long dispute ended with Con Edison surrendering its license to build at Storm King and donating the 500-acre site for park use.

The Grand Old Lady of River and Highland Aesthetics

The geographer James Vance, in an article entitled "California and the Search for the Ideal," has postulated that our nation's collective cultural vision of what we regard as aesthetic migrated westward (along with the population) to the Pacific or "handsome side of the continent" after it had played itself out in areas such as the Hudson.[35] But it must also be stressed that arcadian and sublime imagery mellowed and lingered on in the East as a sometimes tired but always latently explosive tradition, to be donned like an old plate of thick armor upon those things the society had come to know as beautiful when the need to protect arose. The search for a "beneficent, edenesque" landscape had shifted West by the late nineteenth century, but was never fully abandoned in the East. Without this dormant layer of aesthetic awareness for local scenery, the Palisades might well have been reduced to traprock.

From the Cross Valley Syndrome to the China Syndrome, people have always recorded their impressions of the Hudson's highland landforms in accordance with popular social and aesthetic imagery. That imagery's intensity has fluctuated over time, but the form has changed little. There was and is a body of recognizable and compounded aesthetic conception applied to the landscape that has sometimes conflicted with an economic reality. More than any other factor, that imagery, clothed in and even concealed beneath the vocabulary of romanticism, nationalism, and the formulas of sublimity, effectuated the rise of a national conservation awareness, and finally, the protection of the Hudson's scenery via the creation of the Palisades Interstate Park. The application of that sublime formula embracing within it elements of both human and earth history and aesthetics, now fused with an ecological awareness, is abundantly clear in the rhetorical questions posed by Donald McNeil in a 1980 *New York Times* essay, "The Hudson is Forever":

What is left of the Hudson River? Is it a slag heap, floating the broken shards of Bear Mountain down to the sea in yellow barges and drugging the flesh of fish racing toward their spawning grounds with chlorinated hydrocarbons?

Is it still Ichabod Crane's stomping ground and the namesake of a school of canoe-paddling artists who fell in love with its abrupt hills shot full of orange in November and striped with landslides of snow and black tallus in January?[36]

The lower Hudson Valley, "the resplendent main link of the American geographical chain,"[37] stands before us today worn and tattered in places, but largely as preserved and sanctified national landscape. It is a continually evolving document of past and present social and political struggle and ultimate survival fought out in the arena of environmental conflict. Writing on the "violence" wrought against the Hudson by the threat of superhighways and the displacements caused by more and more auto traffic, Arthur Schlesinger made a strong appeal to "the aesthetic mood and ideals of another time . . . the beauty of the past—a legacy . . ." The invaluable role of the Hudson on our nation's doorstep, "this organic part of American History," is a priceless contribution of no less significance today than in the past. The visual grandeur of the Hudson is a "tonic for the nation" Schlesinger wrote: "it is precisely a perception of [its] impalpable values that our confused and turbulent society needs most today."[38]

Chapter 2
From the Palisades
to the Highlands

An open book with the river
as a crystal book mark.
The Hudson River by Daylight, 1914.

THE AREA FROM the Palisades to the highlands contains—by common agreement—some of the best scenery in the world. And although what is scenic, what is romantic, is of course subjective, to understand how cultural values evolve we must first examine the area objectively. We shall take a look at the raw, physical "stage" that has become filled with what has proven to be politically effective aesthetics. What follows, therefore, is a geologic and topographic primer to that rocky ribbon of landforms that constitutes the region of the lower Hudson.

The Palisades

The Palisades "front" is an extensive rock formation that stretches for 30 miles along the western side of the Hudson from Hoboken, New Jersey, to Haverstraw, New York. As a visually distinct topographic feature with similar patterns of land use, however, it is desirable to limit the Palisades to that 12.5 mile stretch of river "wall" from Fort Lee, New Jersey, north to Sparkill Creek, New York, where an apparent "structural sag" causes the cliff to swing away from the river and the crest to drop from more than 500 to less than 100 feet.[1]

Bluff Point at Fort Lee (one half mile south of the George Washington Bridge) is usually regarded as the southern terminus of the Palisades proper (see figs. 1 and 4). The composition of the cliff-face north and south of Fort Lee was seen as visually and structurally distinct by commentators throughout the nineteenth century. The period guidebooks remarked upon the rather abrupt physical transition in the vicinity of Fort Lee, while others traced the almost unbroken "columnar range" south to this point.[2] The cliff-face itself dips away from the shore and becomes less elevated and less precipitous, and therefore less scenically spectacular. Van Vorst commented on this in *Harpers* magazine in 1905: "At Fort Lee [the Palisades] come to an abrupt stop on the Jersey shore, and with it ends the natural grandeur of the Hudson's banks"[3] (fig. 5). South of Fort Lee the landscape of the lower Palisades was junked and violated by industrial blight long ago. The Edgewater, Guttenberg, West New York area, is—topographically and aesthetically—quite separate from the Palisades proper.[4]

The manner in which the dark gray to blue gray crystalline diabase or traprock evolved into the Palisades has been described in detail by several writers.[5] The geomorphologic processes are best summarized in a section of the *New York Walk Book,* a source which was used by Lobeck (fig. 6); it is the standard explanation for the evolution of the cliff:

The rocks of the Palisades section . . . are almost exclusively of two kinds—the Newark sandstones and the intrusive Palisades diabase. For millions of years there accumulated in the [Triassic] lowlands, of which a broad belt of this part of the present state of New Jersey then consisted, layer upon layer of sand and mud [Cambrian and Ordovician in age] washed down from the higher lands in times of high water and spread out over wide areas thousands of feet deep. Solidified, partly by

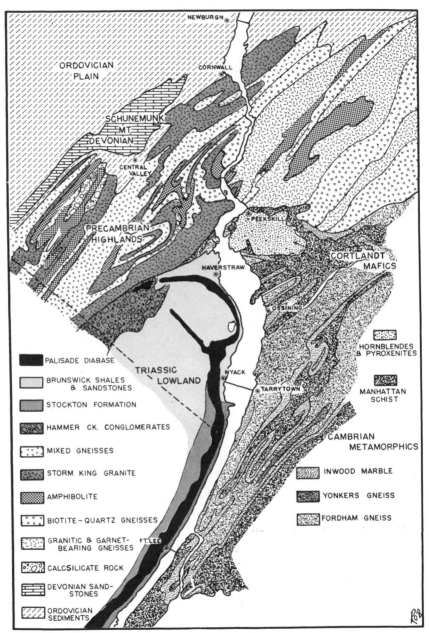

Figure 4. Surface Geology of the Lower Hudson Valley
Adapted and simplified from: "Geologic Map of the State of New York," 1970
(Scale: 1″ ≈ 4.5 miles)

RT LEE HOTEL·   SITE OF OLD FORT LEE

Figure 5. Fort Lee Transition on the Palisades

TOP. Wallace Bruce, *Panorama of the Hudson Showing both sides of the Hudson River from New York to Poughkeepsie,* Bryant Literary Union, 1901 (1906 edition).
BOTTOM. Today

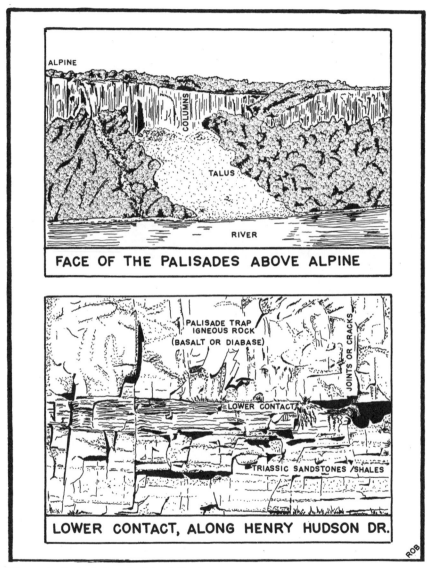

Figure 6. Geologic Detail of the Palisades
From: A. K. Lobeck, "Panoramic View of the New York Region," 1952.

pressure but in great part by the deposition of mineral matter which penetrated the porous mass and cemented its particles together, these deposits became the so-called Newark sandstones. Today they lie under the Palisades and beneath the Hackensack meadows [fig. 2]. After these sandstones had been formed, sometime in the ages that followed, molten rock was forced upward through the rifts in them, forming immense dykes and sills or sheets 700 to 1000 feet thick. . . . When the molten mass cooled, contraction broke the sheets into great crude vertical columns; these now form the Palisades.[6]

Palisades diabase, the meat of this great "primeval sandwich," is a heavy rock composed primarily of the minerals feldspar and pyroxene (and sometimes small amounts of greenish olivine); long-exposed surfaces are colored a dirty gray, while fresh rock surfaces weather to brown.[7] The red sedimentary layers of shale and sandstone, which create a distinct zone of contact with the diabase above (fig. 6) and overlie the great Triassic basin on the lowlands to the west, constitute the Stockton and Brunswick formations of the Newark Group or Series (fig. 4). These strata dip or tilt west toward the Hackensack Valley. The exposed surface of the Palisades averages one and one half to two miles in width.[8]

The erosive action of continental glaciation stripped away the upper layer of Triassic sediments which once capped the diabase formation. The summit of the cliffs was smoothed "and the planed surfaces bear numerous striae caused by pebbles being gouged along the rock by the ice foot."[9] Apart from the innumerable striations (anywhere from several inches to a foot deep and five feet wide), glaciation littered the Palisades' surface with sandstone erratics and boulders of granite and gneiss brought from the highlands to the north and west. The cliff-top is locally veneered with a thin sheet of glacial till, but in other places the diabase sill lies exposed and striated. Soil as such is nonexistent and nowhere attains a depth greater than four inches.[10]

What is today Palisades traprock gushed up through crushed sandstones to form an intrusive lava sill perhaps 195 million years ago.[11] This injection of primeval lava appears to have been contemporaneous with the formation of other lava beds on the sedimentary lowlands of Connecticut, New Jersey, and Pennsylvania; a Palisade-like basalt forms the first range of the New Jersey Watchungs, and similar structures are found in the Hanging Hills of Meriden, Connecticut, at Mounts Tom and Holyoke in Massachusetts, and at Coffman Hill in Bucks County.[12]

Over the course of time the Palisades cliff-face has attracted much curiosity and geological speculation. An exhaustive descriptive vocabulary developed in the nineteenth century from the many attempts to formulate a word-picture of this skyline of ancient volcanic rock: "massive stone logs," "titanic pickets," "a great wall of posts," "an uninterrupted columnar front," "a bold rocky bluff." It is the rather rare combination of these large usually prismatic columns and talus slope that gives the face of the Palisades its distinctive appearance (fig. 6).[13] The peculiar vertical jointing is the result of both the cooling and contracting of igneous materials and weathering:

> The columnar effect of the cliffs is due to weathering. . . . The trap cooled in hexagonal or pentagonal prisms, and the joints were lines of weakness which were affected by frost and rain causing blocks to be pried off to fall and to make the heavy talus slope at the bottom.[14]

Rock-falls often leave scars on the cliffside, tearing loose vegetation and exposing fresh rock. The cliff-face is also characterized by overhanging rock forms and leaning columns created by jointed and weathered diabase pillars exhibiting human-like façades; several of these landmarks (e.g., Washington Head and Man-in-the-Rock) were blasted away by quarrymen early in this century. A further irregularity is given the Palisades front by recesses and stream coves (created along lines of weakness, mainly joints and faults),[15] complemented by "hooks" and headlands (Bombay Hook, Allison Point, Ruckman's Point). Between Clinton Point and Alpine Landing the cliff top achieves its greatest width in the Greenbrook Sanctuary near Buttermilk Falls.[16]

The base of this great traprock formation is sometimes devoid of a beach zone or "talus apron," and "there is often neither beach nor platform. . . . the river bathes the solid wall of rock." [17] But more often a "foot-slope of fallen fragments" [18] has accumulated over the centuries into a well-defined talus zone of mass-wasted broken rock, now largely covered with vegetation. The talus zone is today dotted with such recreational facilities as boat docks, hiking trails, automobile approaches, and park buildings—all constructed for the most part with native Palisade diabase.

Clausland Mountain and the Nyack Terrace

North of the state line and along the Rockland County shore the Palisade cliff continues, but in less precipitous and less elevated form. This area of the Northern Palisades contains the Tallman Mountain Section of the Palisades Interstate Park—a headland averaging 150 feet in height that descends rather abruptly toward Sparkill Creek on its northern flank. The creek itself, the only natural approach to the Hudson between Weehawken and Nyack, rises 2.5 miles to the west in the vicinity of Tappan and drains into the Hudson via a series of meanders in the Piermont salt marsh. The notch in the Palisades at Sparkill was probably a water gap in pre-Cenozoic times through which coursed the channel of the "ancestral" Hudson, which originally flowed west of the Palisades and down through the Newark Basin to Raritan Bay. When, through headward erosion and stream "piracy" or capture, the Hudson assumed its present course, the water gap at Sparkill, left high and dry by downcutting of the river channel, became a wind gap reoccupied by the smaller channel of Sparkill Creek. [19]

Although from Piermont to Nyack the "more gentle swell" of the Palisades is less evident, the sandy shore and its mountain backdrop serve to link the Palisades with the highlands. In this area the Palisades lose their wall-like character and break away into a series of hills and ridges ("the little hills of Rockland"). The generally uninterrupted ridge that parallels the river from Piermont through Upper Grandview to South Nyack attains elevations greater than 680 feet; known locally as Clausland Mountain, it demarcates the scenery and settlements of the Hudson Valley from the rolling countryside to the west. This mile-wide ridge, which peaks at Mount Nebo, in part consists of the Blauvelt section of the Palisades Interstate Park, a 536-acre addition created in 1913 (fig. 2).

Before the Palisades formation again sweeps back to the shoreline to reemerge as Hook Mountain, a semicircular mountain-rimmed terrace or shelfland occurs along the river edge where the Tappan Zee is widest. This platform is the site of Nyack, "the gem of the Hudson" situated upon a confined but fertile "champaigne country."[20] Encompassed by the gently rising Nyack hills (400 to 670 feet), the river town occupies what many writers have described as a natural amphitheatre with its open side facing the river.

Hook Mountain and the Tors

Between the Tappan Zee Bridge and Haverstraw Bay the Palisade traprock again attains clifflike proportions, with average elevations of above 500 feet along the Rockland County shore. Surfacing through the surrounding Triassic sandstones and shales, the 11-mile-long ridge curves west just south of Haverstraw and plunges beneath the conglomerates of the Hammer Creek formation near the Mahwah River at Mount Ivy (fig. 4).

The "bold headland" has always quite properly been regarded as a portion of, as indeed the topographic highpoint and culmination of, the Palisade range.[21] Whether because of the boulder strewn beaches below the talus slope, the economically exploitable diabase, or the fractured volcanic columns, this section was regarded as the aesthetic equal and geological continuation of the Palisades, an ideal scenic link between the Bergen shore and the Hudson Highlands (figs. 32 and 40). An area of volcanic rock, the Hook Mountain section is a continuation of the Palisade sill that curves away from the river and cuts across the adjoining sedimentary layers.[22]

Hook Mountain (*Verdrietige* or "tedious" hook to the

Dutch)[23] is that section which forms the river wall from Upper Nyack to Snedekers Landing south of Haverstraw; this headland which "juts into the river like an enormous buttress"[24] averages 500 to 700 feet in elevation and peaks at 736 feet on its southeastern wall. Like the Palisades, Hook Mountain's cliff-face is scarred by quarries, broken in places by "transverse cracks," displays columnar flutings, and has below it a precipitous talus cone. Sandstone and shale appear in the cliffs, overlaid with traprock talus. Along the tidal beaches below are bouldery "landings" and derelict docking facilities that date from the ice harvesting and rock quarrying period.

Hidden from the river view and atop Hook Mountain (now crossed by highways 303 and 9W) is an area of swamp and lake which constitutes the headwaters of the Hackensack River system. Congers, Swartwout, and Rockland Lakes are on higher ground immediately to the west of Hook Mountain. Rockland Lake is the largest and most historically important of the headwater lakes (fig. 22); at 150 feet above the level of the Hudson, it is spring-fed and usually remains unfrozen after the Hudson itself ices up.[25]

The north end of Hook Mountain is set apart from the Tors by "fault cloves," one natural and the other artificially cut. The Long Clove is a natural declivity which carried the original transmountain highway and today route 9W; the West Shore Railroad is tunneled beneath this part of the ridge. Farther north is the man-made Short Clove, which is significant for two reasons: it carries highway 304 to a junction with 9W, and it is through this hollow that the Appalachian Stone Company's traprock conveyor descends to the river's edge.

From the Short Clove north-northwest to Mount Ivy is the five-mile ridge designated "South Mountain" on the Haverstraw topographic sheet (fig. 32). High Tor State Park, which occupies most of the ridge, is the northernmost portion of the Palisade cliff. The range "is much broken in outline, consisting of craggy masses of rock, but all connected, sweeping west in general trend."[26] The range is dominated by High Tor (827 feet and apparently deriving its name from Hey Tor peak in Dartmoor) and

Low or Little Tor (710 feet).[27] Some 300 feet higher than any section of the Palisades proper, High Tor peak was vividly described by Maxwell Anderson in a three act play of that title:

the broad flat trap-rock summit of High Tor, from which one . . . might look down a sheer quarter mile to the Tappan Zee below. A cluster of hexagonal pillared rocks marks the view to the left and a wind-tortured small hemlock wedges into the rock floor at the right.[28]

The Haverstraw Delta

From the base of South Mountain six miles north along the river to the Highland gate at Dunderberg Mountain is a triangular area of sand and clay deposits, derived of the Brunswick sandstones and shales (fig. 4). This is known as the Haverstraw "flats" or delta. The town of Haverstraw is built upon a delta of unconsolidated sediments deposited by glacial meltwater streams in the late Pleistocene period when the surface of the Hudson was at least 100 feet higher than it is today.[29]

This area is ringed by mountains to the west and north (the Ramapos and Highlands) and is dominated by the towns of Haverstraw, Stony Point, and Tomkins Cove. The topography is rolling to hilly, with low isolated mountains and outlyers of the Ramapos in the western parts (Cheesecote Mountain, Rider Hill, Buckberg Mountain, and others).[30] The sandy lowland is drained by Cedar Brook and Minisceongo Creek, streams which rise in the Ramapos and enter the Hudson at Grassy Point and Bowline Point (Haverstraw) respectively. Here, reddish Triassic sandstones were extensively quarried for use as "brownstone" in the nineteenth-century New York City building trade.

The Haverstraw shoreline is very irregular, and characterized by low, rocky promontories (Grassy Point and Stony Point)[31] that, but for artificial linkages, would be isolated from the mainland at high tide. Much of the riverline is underlain with clay beds which have been worked in connection with the famous Haverstraw brick industry.

The Haverstraw delta, at the northern end of the great

Triassic Lowland, finally terminates in the Tomkins Cove area against a wedge of marble and schist (fig. 4). These rock formations constitute almost the entire eastern side of the lower Hudson Valley and appear on the western shore only between Tomkins Cove and the Dunderberg. The dolomitic marble has historically been described as a "great limestone cliff outcropping two hundred feet high" [32] and has been much reduced by quarrying.

The Hudson Highlands

The Ramapo fault line is a fracture along which there have periodically been minor earth tremors, a fact producing some anxiety because of the nearness of atomic reactors at Indian Point just to the south. This fault trends northeast-southwest between the Triassic lowlands and the crystalline highlands in Bergen and Rockland Counties and serves to demarcate the southern perimeter of the highlands. [33] From here north to the Cornwall Plain is a 10-mile-wide belt of heavily glaciated granites and gneisses that has elicited perhaps the strongest display of scenic sentiment and commentary of any region in America: "the billowy swells of rock-ribbed, cloud-capped earth;" "the rocky and precipitous bluffs;" "hill upon hill till lost in the loftiest peaks." [34]

The highlands ("the high lands" on early maps) trend northeast-southwest across southeastern New York State and northern New Jersey. This exposed Precambrian "basement rock" constitutes the Reading Prong of the New England Upland, a geologic subdivision which cuts diagonally across New York State from the Berkshires and Taconics to Reading, Pennsylvania. [35] These landform regions are contained within the greater Appalachian physiographic area which extends from the Atlantic Provinces of Canada to Georgia. The highlands' pronounced topographic linearity (i.e. the strong northeast-southwest trend) is reflected in the arrangement both of physical and of cultural landscape features such as drainage pattern and road network.

The highlands are studded with boulder fields; weathered pits and furrows are common on the surface of the granites and gneisses. The roundness of many highland summits (as in the Adirondacks) is due to the "unloading" or "shelling-off" of exfoliation sheets.[36]

The geomorphologic evolution of this region of bare rocks and "craggy" summits is very complex and, as geologists of this very active research region have observed, the details are still sketchy; shrouded in the mists of Precambrian times and hindered by a lack of good post-Cambrian studies, the rock record and its episodes of uplift and erosion, folding and faulting, remains to be analyzed further.[37] It is generally agreed, however, that the Precambrian rocks are more than 1 billion years old.

Although the flanks of the mountains are buried beneath more recent sedimentary deposits and glacial till has filled in the clefts and valleys, these "Crystalline Highlands" are everywhere composed of metamorphics, the most pronounced of which are granites and coarsely foliated gneisses with a characteristic streaked or banded appearance. Variations within the bedrock composition of the several divisions of the highlands are diagrammed below.[38]

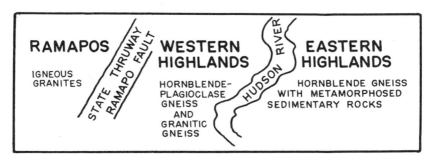

In the highlands west of the Hudson the higher peaks are composed of Storm King granite, a pinkish, gneissic, hornblende granite (fig. 4); this rock of uncertain age constitutes the bulk of Storm King Mountain itself, Crows Nest, the ridges to the rear of the West Point Plateau, Bear Mountain, and the Dunderberg. "In some places one finds bands or lenses of granite and gneiss alternating, or bodies of one kind of rock grading into the other."[39] The lower elevations of these highlands generally exhibit Precambrian gneisses; Storm King Clove, Washington Valley, and Doodletown Hollow are composed of a variety of granitic and leucogranitic gneisses, and biotite-quartz gneisses. The West Point platform or "terrace" south through the Popolopen Creek–Hessian Lake area consists largely of gneiss and amphibolite. While some of these same rock formations reappear east of the Hudson (e.g. the Storm King granite at Breakneck Ridge, Mount Taurus, and Manitou Mountain), that highland division possesses a markedly different bedrock composition. Garnet-bearing gneisses and biotitic and feldspar gneisses occur more frequently than the granites, and infolded limestones, slates, and quartzites are also more prolific here than west of the river.[40]

Throughout, the highlands are riddled with thrust and tear faults, dykes, and veins of metallic ore. Kurt Lowe, in his study of the Bear Mountain vicinity, has documented the location and importance of these fault zones,[41] while the effect produced upon the mountain profiles by basaltic dykes and joints is clearly seen in Thompson's photographic interpretation of the highlands (figs. 7 and 8). Veins of zinc, copper, silver, and even gold have been reported in the highlands, but none apparently of commercially exploitable size.[42] The most important mineral ore associated with the highlands is magnetite iron ore. The Storm King and Canada Hill granites are discolored in places where veins of iron have been exposed to weathering. Fortunately these granites ("which would make superior building stone")[43] have ironically been spared extensive quarrying because of this imperfection. The iron ore itself is found in zones not sharply defined and consists of short parallel veins that usually crop out of ridges.[44]

The highest elevations and the most spectacular relief occur in the northern highlands, where the river has scoured a deep and narrow fiord-like passage between Storm King (1463 feet) and Crows Nest (1403 feet) to the west and Breakneck Ridge, the Beacons (North Beacon at 1531 feet and South Beacon at 1640 feet), and Bull Hill (1420 feet and with its name romanticized to

Figure 7. Physical Geography of Iona Island and Anthony's Nose

TOP: Iona Island. Probably a remant of Anthony's Nose, severed from main ridge by glacial enlargement of a notch. Old channel, right: present channel, left. Playfield (left foreground) represents Albany erosion level. Dunderberg in right distance.

BOTTOM: Anthony's Nose. Steep, triangular, faceted front is apparently the result of truncation by a tongue of ice in the gorge. Ravine (straight down from summit) represents postglacial differential erosion along a basic dike in the granite.

From: *Bulletin of the Geological Society of America, vol. 47.*

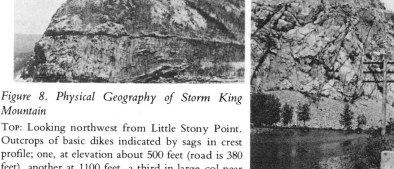

Figure 8. Physical Geography of Storm King Mountain

TOP: Looking northwest from Little Stony Point. Outcrops of basic dikes indicated by sags in crest profile; one, at elevation about 500 feet (road is 380 feet), another at 1100 feet, a third in large col near extreme left, between Storm King proper and Buttermilk Hill.

BOTTOM LEFT: Looking southwest from Breakneck. Large cross joint surface (lower left) parallel with river. Rise of structure along overthrust on lower right. Ravine (center) marks longitudinal basic dike. Dark line of trees (right) indicates basic dike cutting across the ridge.

BOTTOM RIGHT: Joints in granite of Storm King. Most prominent joints dip steeply southwest. Basic dike at the left.

From: *Bulletin of the Geological Society of America,* vol. 47.

Mount Taurus by N. P. Willis) to the east. The western highlands have their greatest topographic expression to the north of
the line formed by Washington Valley and Long Pond Hollow;
this is in the Storm King area, a rugged upland with a dozen
summits over 1400 feet. The region is largely contained within
the Palisades Interstate Park, the U.S. Military Academy, and
Harvard's Black Rock Forest (fig. 2).

The Hudson River itself is narrowest (1400 feet) and deepest
(202 feet) between the West Point glacial terrace and Constitution
Island. The river channel, however, attains its greatest depth beneath Storm King Mountain, where more than 700 feet of sand,
clay, and boulders rest atop the bedrock. Here, with an overall
relief of 2100 feet, the valley is truly a fiord, a very rare occurrence in the eastern United States: "a river valley deepened below
sea level by glaciation, then filled by the sea as the ice melted."[45]

The River Islands

There are several islands of note whose "position in the
[highland] waterscape," as one historian emphasized, "entitles
them to recognition in [the] topography."[46] These islands are in
most cases backed by salt marsh and approachable from the
mainland only at low tide.

Iona Island in Doodletown Bight and Constitution Island in
Foundry Cove are very similar in this respect. Iona, as seen on
O'Connor's 1854 map and on the Peekskill topographic sheet in
fig. 26, is actually a series of hills and ridges 20 to 100 feet in
elevation; they resemble individual islands when the Salisbury
Meadow and its adjacent marshes are inundated. This marshy
area consists primarily of recently deposited muds which formed
"the Iona Island Delta" at the mouth of Doodletown Brook.[47]
Thompson believes that this 200-acre "island" was a "remnant of
Anthony's Nose severed from the main ridge by glacial enlargement" and straightening out of the present river canyon (fig. 7);
according to this explanation, the course of the "ancestral" Hudson was through what is today Doodletown Bight and the Salis-

bury Meadow.[48] Constitution Island, somewhat larger and more regular in form, approaches 140 feet on its western side and is crossed by the tracks of the Penn Central Railroad, to the east of which lies a half mile stretch of tidal flat and salt marsh.

There are other insular-like features along this section of the river (Little Stony Point and Con Hook) which are of minor significance, but the only other island of note is Pollepel's Island, situated off the Dutchess County shore opposite Cornwall at the northern entrance to the highlands (see fig. 1). The island, because of the Bannerman family's castle-style arsenal, is sometimes termed Bannerman's Island; in the last 200 years, however, the island has had at least a half dozen names.[49] Described by the traveler Timothy Dwight as a "mere bird's nest,"[50] it is best described quite briefly: it consists of almost seven acres of rock lying one thousand feet from the river's eastern shore from which it is separated by shallow-water flats deep enough for small craft.[51]

In Dutchess County, the northern side of the highlands, formed by Breakneck and the Beacons ("the Fishkill Mountains"), is marked by a "great fault"[52] below which courses the Fishkill Creek. A similarly abrupt topographic fault occurs on the northern slopes of Storm King, where the elevation plunges from 1300 feet to Cornwall Landing. This fault parallels the northern perimeter of the highlands in Orange County and forms a line through Cornwall-Mountainville-Highland Mills-Central Valley-Harriman.[53] From Mountainville to Central Valley the fault valley is occupied by Woodbury Creek, a tributary of the Moodna, which separates the highlands from the Schunemunk Mountain formation to the west.[54] Erratics from Schunemunk are common on the highlands' surface.

North of these fault lines are the rolling interior uplands of Orange and Dutchess Counties, an expansive region of well-drained sands and glacial tills historically exhibiting a prosperous farmscape of field crops and orchards.[55]

Part 2
The Hudson Valley in Colonial Times

FROM THE PERIOD when "the eyes of discovery" first looked upon the American landscape until the start of the Revolutionary War, negative or at best dull topographic attitudes were generally the rule in appraising the appearance of the land. And although the lower Hudson was relatively neglected, bypassed for settlement in favor of choicer areas, something in the way of "consciousness of place," especially the beauty of place, seems integral to at least a few of the Dutch settlement accounts. Precisely to what extent a landscape aesthetic evolved is difficult to judge, thanks to the historical and literary mongrelization of that cultural period by later writers, especially Washington Irving. It would appear, however, that neither the English Yorkers or Yankee immigrants had much esteem for the niceties of landscape, as they were very likely conditioned to the tradition of what has been called European "mountain gloom." The land was still too raw and threatening to be much appreciated, but in the gradual domestication of the valley we may glimpse the dawning of that cultural artifact known as "scenery"

Chapter 3
The European Landscape in the Valley

DESPITE THE NONEXISTENCE or vagueness of colonial descriptions and settlement accounts of the lower Hudson Valley during the Dutch and English administrations (1609–1776), enough information emerges out of the mist to establish at least some general patterns.[1] For example, maps of pre-Revolutionary settlement reveal that the occupation as well as the cultural and economic development of much of the lower valley occurred remarkably late. Where settlement was present, it was mostly in the western and northern interiors, and appears to have avoided the immediate valley. Orange County, which in colonial times included what is present-day Rockland, is described by one of its chroniclers as "at the time of its erection [in 1683] . . . a howling wilderness with scarcely a single settler located within its territory. Nor . . . was its early growth rapid. By 1693 the total population amounted to about 20 families . . . to the North of the Orangetown patent stretched the primeval wilderness." [2]

While figures of speech such as "howling" and "primeval" are classical Cotton Mather, they do convey a sense of uninhabited wilderness. This is confirmed by population data: only 268 persons were said to be here in 1702—very probable in view of the figure of 200 persons in Governor Bellmont's census of 1698.[3] The county is described by another of its compilers as "a district in the wilderness with boundaries upon paper." [4]

Retardation of Settlement

At the end of the Dutch regime there was not a single Dutch Reformed Congregation on the Hudson for 100 miles north of New Amsterdam. A relative settlement vacuum seems to have existed in the valley. Village patterns were slow to evolve, the Dutch scattering individual *"bouweries"* or farms throughout the valley. No cultural or economic factor tended to induce a concentrated population. By 1664 there was but one village north of New Amsterdam, that of Esopus (later Kingston).[5]

Similarly, no substantial population impact was apparent before 1700 along the river in northeastern New Jersey. Although by 1640 there were settlements on Bergen Neck in the Hoboken and Secaucus area, and on "plantations" around Snake Hill and Communipaw (near Jersey City in what is now Hudson County), until 1643 no village—not even a house—was established in the area of Bergen County.[6] There continued to be Indian hostilities in the 1660s and 1670s, when plantations spread northward between the Hackensack and Hudson Rivers to Saddle River and Old Bridge. As late as 1709, there were at most 70 families in Bergen.[7]

That settlement in the region should be so spotty and ill-advanced is rather remarkable in that "no other colony had anything like a Hudson River to allow such easy penetration into the interior, yet [settlers in other colonies] had made much further advances" before the Revolution; "New York's [interior] growth appear[ed] to be relatively slow in pace and restricted in area."[8] Why did such a settlement lag persist for so long in the region of the lower Hudson, and what were the consequences for subsequent periods of growth?

Military and political factors presented a formidable barrier both to early and to permanent settlement in the lower Hudson. For example, the ill-fated De Vries colony near Sparkill Creek (1640) was utterly destroyed by the Indians in 1643—a bloody enough caution to end "all attempts to colonize this County for a period of six and forty years." [9] Settlements were repeatedly devastated by Indian raids while an additional depressant to up-valley colonization was the threatening presence of the French, always somewhere to the North. Later, of course, national rivalries and their colonial wars exerted even more repressive force on New York State's colonization. Between 1689–1708, 1754–63, and 1776–83 ("The Reign of Mars") the Hudson-Champlain corridor, as the "Key to Empire," was the foremost theatre of colonial conflict. It must certainly be concluded that such conflict was not conducive to furthering the orderly and permanent settlement of civilian populations.

Another factor delaying the evolution of a cultural landscape in the region was the policy of the Dutch colonial government. The Metropole's land policies and narrow, mercantilist interests did little to further actual settlement in the colony. Conditions in Holland were said to have contributed to this situation, but apart from the short term interest in the fur trade, ultimately "the concentration of landed wealth in the hands of a small group . . . greatly retarded the expansion of the upstate area. Most of the great patents remained virtually uninhabited." [10] Commencing in the late Dutch period (with the Rensselaer patroonship) and continuing into the English period (with the Philipse, Van Cortlandt and Livingston patents) much of the valley was blocked out into a series of great manorial grants (fig.9). The various dimensions of this system are well documented by the historians and there is no need to pursue its fine points here. What is pertinent is the effect the system had upon the overall settlement pattern.

Since all the patents and grants were on the eastern side of the valley (with Rensselaerswyck occupying both banks of the river, but farther north where the Hudson affords a less formidable line of division), the spread of settlement here by small patentees and individual freeholders was successfully held in check. Nor did manorial or any other type of agriculture take root on

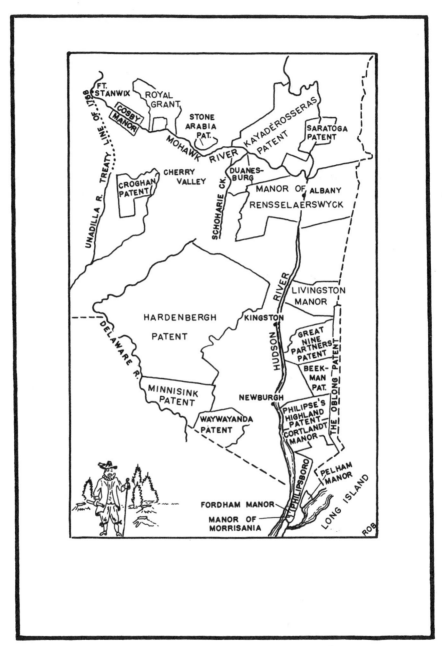

Figure 9. Major Land Grants and Patients in Colonial New York
From: Ellis, Frost, et al., *A Short History of New York State*, p. 72.

the western side of the valley. Since individual settlement was discouraged by the Dutch government, which provided no protection to such settlers, "the more forbidding cliffs and headlands on the western shore remained for the most part unsettled." [11] The very reliable Cadwallader Colden remarked in his journals upon the dearth of settlement in the western part of the valley as late as the mid-eighteenth century. [12] Free of both manorial grants and freehold farms, the shore of present day Orange and Rockland Counties remained an area of abundant vacant land which attracted yeoman farmers slowly and haltingly. Substantive and permanent occupation of lands on both sides of the lower valley, by all but a few manor lords and their disenfranchised tenants, was suppressed for political and administrative reasons. What had been described by many visitors to the valley as the aroma of cedar wood and the aromatic scent of a luxuriant carpet of vegetation that wafted far out to sea was not yet destroyed by the groundclearing of civilization.

Deflection of Settlement

After the hesitant start, settlement did come to the several counties of the lower Hudson, and by the Revolution the region was at least nominally occupied and mainly to the rear of the frontier. This pattern and the spread of pre-Revolutionary settlement are graphically portrayed by Donald Meinig in the *Geography of New York State*. [13] But the population was by no means evenly distributed and a persistent theme in this period is the general avoidance of the Hudson's shoreline and the related deflection of settlement to the more fertile interior and northern hinterlands.

The Palisades and highland precincts were bypassed by the Dutch and early English settlers in favor of the Hackensack and Wallkill Valleys further west. The Dutch in the Jersey City area moved northward into the Hackensack Valley, avoiding the Palisades, while others penetrated the Tappan and Orangetown areas through the Nyack and Haverstraw lowlands. By 1600 New

Barbados and Old Bridge were well established in the Hackensack Valley—the principal line of communications ("the King's
Highway") between Nyack Bay and the Tappans.[14] Tappantown
(Tappan), the oldest village in Rockland and the original county
seat, and Orangeburg, along the western base of the "Nyack
Hills," prospered in the seventeenth century as "western" trading posts connected with the Hudson via the then navigable
Sparkill Creek. By the 1720s the settlers in the Hackensack Valley had begun moving up to occupy farmland on the extensive
western slope of the Palisades. But, as the historian Carl Nordstrom has pointed out, Rockland County was very damp and
swampy, and such meager farming as was possible was probably
limited to some of the hillsides.[15]

By 1690 settlement in the northern part of the Esopus District had expanded into the Wallkill Valley, a leading agricultural
area, long before permanent settlement was achieved on the
Orange County shore. After 1700 Wallkill pioneers penetrated
down into the western highlands, arriving at the town of
Blooming Grove by the 1720s. They, and others moving north
from the Bergen area, were in the Ramapos by the 1740s. Occupation of the Newburgh-Beacon Plain to the north of the
highlands came somewhat later. Although the village of New
Windsor dates from around 1749, the land about was already patented and cultivated in the 1720s. There is, furthermore, a
strong indication that the area north of the highlands was
stripped of timber in the seventeenth century.[16] As one traveler
observed of the area in 1749, "the farms become more numerous
and we had a view of many grain fields." [17] This would indicate
a pattern of permanent villages and a probable road network on
the interior and northern plains, with the immediate western
shore stagnating in vacant or scantily occupied tracts of forest
land.

Patterns of Settlement

At the Palisades. Throughout the seventeenth century the
Palisades cliff was referred to as "the King's Woods," i.e. timber

reserved for the crown.[18] This in itself probably hindered settlement along the ridge for many decades. Piermont, at the north end of the ridge proper, is said to date from the late-seventeenth century, but who the settlers were, and precisely when they arrived, is not clear.[19] The hamlet of Palisades, less than one mile to the west of the ridge (and today west of highway 9W), claims to have the oldest building in the area, the "Big House" which dates from 1685. Westervelt contends that Huguenot settlers arrived in the late 1600s, but Clayton states emphatically that there was no settlement here before 1700.[20]

A ferry was in operation at Sneden's Landing by 1700, and a mill and possibly several houses located there by 1710.[21] Whatever the date of initial settlement along and atop the Palisades cliff, the development of the area was slow. Peter Kalm, the extraordinarily observant Swedish naturalist, reported the cultural and physical details of the Hudson Valley in 1749 and saw "the tops of these mountains [the Palisades] covered with oaks and other trees. A number of stones of all sizes lie along the shore." [22] Two decades later Richard Smith, a New Jersey lawyer and diarist, noticed on his journey up the Hudson that "the lofty rocks" of the Palisades were "thinly overspread with Cedars, Spruce and Shrubs. . . . hardly any houses appear on the Bergen side from Paulus Hook to the line of Orange County." [23] These observations are sustained by Governor Pownall's topographic view of the northern Palisades, "sketched on the spot by his excellency" in 1768. In this view the towering and heavily wooded cliffs are densely covered with vegetation from top to bottom; the ridge top, cliff face, and talus slope are mantled in foliage, and not a single structure appears along the river.[24] It also seems likely that uncertainty as to the exact location of the New Jersey–New York boundary (not surveyed and marked until 1769) kept potential settlers away from the northern region of the Palisades.

On Hook Mountain and the Tors. No doubt a similar history of meager development is true of the Hook Mountain–High Tor section. While the Nyack and Haverstraw lowlands housed an ethnic mosaic of Dutch, German, Huguenot, and perhaps Danish and Flemish by the 1720s, it was not until after this decade that the polyglot mixture was supplemented by the great wave of New Englanders coming across the valley.[25] This movement largely affected the villages, since the rural districts were already claimed if not in fact cultivated by Yorkers. By the 1750s Connecticut migrants, and especially Long Islanders (second-generation Yankees) were prevalent in Haverstraw, where settlers "were erecting homes along the riverfront from the Long Clove to Dunderberg," and at Stony Point and Tomkins Cove; but between Nyack and Haverstraw, the brooding highland formation of Hook and Tor Mountains appeared "scarcely inhabited at all." [26] By the Revolution some settlers had no doubt penetrated the wooded upland, but the pattern of field and farm was embryonic at best.

The Highlands. The Hudson Highlands were purchased from the Indians as a unified tract in 1685 and patented to a Captain Evans. The Captain retained the tract for speculative purposes and the region was not subdivided until after 1710. Most of the highland patents were granted between 1710 and 1730; [27] the stained-glass-like mosaic produced by the metes and bounds of these patents was later mapped by Simeon deWitt and are shown in fig. 10.

Some of the patents were held by speculative companies, and actual settlement in many cases lagged by several decades more. When settlers arrived in the mid-eighteenth century, they were likely Yankees moving across from Westchester and Long Island. Highland Falls and Cornwall date from this period and their origins are related to small Yankee-run sawmill operations.

In 1749 Kalm described the rolling and wooded highland precincts:

The country was unfit for cultivation, being so full of rock, and accordingly we saw no farms. . . . In one place on the western shore we saw a wooden house painted red, and we were told that there was a saw mill further up. But besides this we did not see a farm or any cultivated grounds all forenoon.[28]

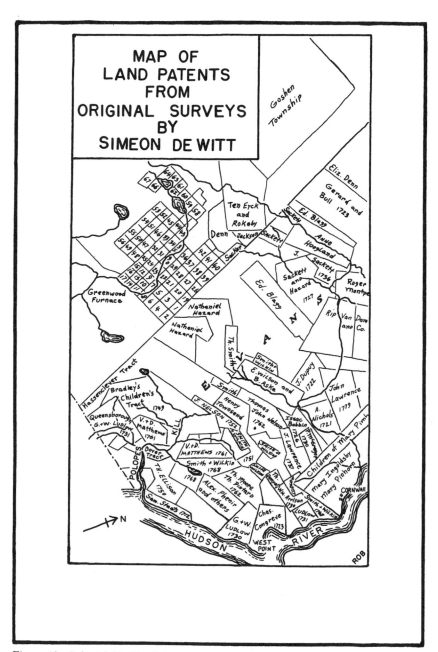

Figure 10. Colonial Highland Patents west of the Hudson River
From: Ruttenber and Clark, *History of Orange County,* p. 18. (no scale)

Certainly there were some farm families on the upland slopes by the eve of the Revolution, for as Smith reported in 1769: "On the west side among the Highlands are a few houses seated in the small vallies [sic] between the Mountains." [29] Smith visited one of these "miserable farms" and was convinced that the owner and his neighbors were desirous of leaving the infertile mountains. The Hudson Highlands (as well as the Ramapo Mountains in northern New Jersey) were, as Kury states, evaluated negatively by prospective settlers and consequently avoided:

. . . the imposing slopes and infertile soils of the Highlands appeared rather inhospitable, were thought to be wholly incapable of improvement, and were wholly without transport facilities. . . . agriculture consequently met with only limited success and the pace of early Highlands settlement was exceedingly slow. [30]

Because of the better historical documentation associated with the establishment of the military academy at West Point, a somewhat more exact knowledge of the ownership and utilization of these highland acres is available for the period immediately preceeding the Revolution. Captain Horace Reeve, in his history of the West Point area, says that: "Until the American troops began to cut timber for military purposes and to crown the surrounding hills with forts and redoubts, West Point and the neighboring highlands were little else than a wilderness of rugged hills and virgin forests." Major Boynton's account of West Point corroborates this: "The probabilities are that, beyond a settlement made to secure a site or grant, West Point, being in a region of stratified [sic] rocks, heavily covered with drift deposits, and without a suitable soil for cultivation, remained a mere woodland tract." [31]

The "Virgin woodland" of the highlands referred to by Reeve and Boynton was composed largely of mixed hardwoods; the natural or supposed "climax" vegetation for this region consisted of the deciduous oak-hickory and the since-blighted chestnut forest. [32] The colonial highland forest also had a small percentage of scrub oak and pitch pine interspersed with "blasted" or barren areas of rock outcroppings where vegetation could not take root. Any more specific detailing of the extent and composition of the pre-Revolutionary forest would be inaccurate in view of the available maps—maps often ornamented with "decorative" vegetation by engravers in their London workshops. Such patterns of vegetation were not indicated on the initial manuscript drafted in the field by the cartographers and surveyors.[33]

As to adjacent areas, the Eastern highlands in Putnam County likewise attracted little settlement before the Revolution. A rugged topography and a narrow marsh-fronted shoreline had little to offer settlers. North of the highlands, the Beacon Plain was well cultivated with farms and orchards on the eve of the war. Scores of "tenants" were farming the area north of Breakneck Ridge, and their numbers were augmented when the Philipse patent was divided into farmlots in the 1750s. By the 1770s village patterns had begun to coalesce north of the highlands.[34]

Patterns of economic activity and the progress of settlement in the valley from the Palisades to the highlands were then minimal. A brisk commerce did not develop at very many river landings since the best profits were being turned with the Indians in the interior fur trading settlements (e.g. Tappan) along the headwaters of the Hackensack, and further north along the Wallkill.[35] A lean subsistence argiculture at best characterized the scattering of farms on the lower slopes of Hook Mountain and the highlands.

The river Highlands were also bypassed because of the discovery of magnetite iron deposits in the Ramapos and the interior highlands. Kury states that by the Revolution every highland ore body known today had been opened, but apart from the Forest of Dean furnace and an iron "plantation" on Popolopen Creek, every facility associated with the colonial charcoal iron industry was located in the Ramapo Valley, Ringwood, and Sterling areas.[36] The Palisades and Hook Mountain sections had no apparent mineral wealth, and were, along with the highland shores, steep and inaccessible barriers to commerce.

The avoidance of settlement, or at best its late beginnings, along the western shore of the lower Hudson Valley had at least one positive aspect: the area remained free of the blight of land-lordism, a social condition deriving from the early system of patroons and manor feifs that was to curse both the northern and eastern sections of the valley for nearly two hundred years. Furthermore, a differentiation in land usage or nonusage had been established. Although something of a generalization, the argument can be made that the western shore of the Hudson, unlike the eastern side, developed less fully and less rapidly. The mostly rocky and precipitous shores of Bergen, Rockland, and Orange Counties, because they were less desirable as settlements, achieved an early status as something to be regarded with the eye rather than to be lived in. This is without doubt the most significant pattern evolved in the colonial period, a pattern of land use and conception solidified in the course of the next century. What the eye beheld in colonial times might be regarded as economically unattractive, but it would later be regarded as scenic.

Chapter 4
The Seeds of a Less Hostile View of Nature

Consciousness of place had already begun to grow . . .
John Howatt, *The Hudson River
and its Painters*, p. 23.

ARE ANTECEDENTS TO nineteenth-century romantic thought found in the attitudes and beliefs of colonial Yorkers and Yankees? Are the seeds of a later-day will to preserve the scenic beauty of the lower Hudson Valley traceable to this early era? Did the lateness and deflection of original settlement away from the western shore have an effect upon popular images of this area? Should it be assumed that the colonial period in the Hudson Valley was one of physical action only—pressing the frontier, battling the forest "heathen," struggling to ward off hunger—rather than one of mental reflection? Was it a period in which the settlers, so feverishly engaged in resolving the problems of day-to-day existence, had no time to even consider an environmental aesthetic? [1]

Answers to these questions are important if the evolution of appreciative attitudes toward nature expressed in the Revolutionary and post-war eras are to be seen in their proper context.

Despite the obvious overriding importance of nineteenth-century Romantic-Nationalist sentiment in awakening a public to the need for landscape preservation, more than "a few crude suggestions of conservation"[2] may indeed have been indicative of the colonial Dutch and English response to the scenery of the Hudson Valley.

Although interplay between conception and actual land use and the utilization of specific aesthetic formulas is negligible in this period, the Dutch New Netherlanders are significant in two ways: first, it is in the years of initial contact between this culture and the valley that the faint beginnings of an aesthetic delight are witnessed; secondly, the supposed Dutch view of and relationship with the local landscape became an integral part of Romantic rhetoric in the period 1820–1850.

Alleged Dutch Topophobia

One encounters several inherent and related difficulties when studying the Dutch and early English settlers in the Hudson Valley. While the documents on which to construct a fairly precise record of settlement are available, indications of the way the Dutch viewed the landscape must unfortunately be deduced from the more general evidences of the ways they viewed the entire Hudson Valley region and the New World at large.[3]

Compounding this problem is a rather thick and crusty layer of contradiction and misconception about the Dutch culture's attitudes toward landscape. A lack of agreement is apparent in most interpretations of Dutch mentality, society, and settlement.[4] Furthermore, the power of misconception concerning the Dutch population and its relationship with nature has led to a pervasive stereotype, which is one of the few things writers seem to agree on. If representative phrases and terminology from several generations of popular writers and social historians are formed into a composite impression of the New Netherlanders' relationship with their environment, the following picture emerges:

The Dutch who settled on the banks of the Hudson River were a super-stitious, devil-fearing, folk culture. A sense of fear and mystery, derived from Norse and Teutonic forest demonology, conditioned their response to the psychologically repulsive and unnerving forests of the New World. They harbored an unspeakable fear not only of the seem-ingly infinite forests, but also of the wild men and wild and unclassifia-ble beasts lurking upon the unfamiliar—and therefore terrifying—ter-rain. Being semi-literate peasants, novel variations of local weather were believed to be the work of the supernatural. From Fort Amster-dam to Fort Orange on the Hudson, and from Fort Nassau on the Del-aware to Fort Good Hope on the Connecticut, the land they settled was haunted, and the land beyond was a vast and brooding *terra incognita.*

This impression of Dutch cultural response to the Hudson's landscape has permeated much historiography. The classic ap-praisal of their reaction to the environment of New Netherland appears in Maud Goodwin's 1919 work, *Dutch and English on the Hudson:* the Dutch at Rensselaerswyck (or one might substitute Bergen or Tappan) are pictured sitting "by their lonely hearths in a little clearing of the forest, listening to the howl of wolves and fearing to see a savage face at the window." Throughout the valley, while the parents kept an anxious vigil in the night, the children "fell peacefully to sleep, oblivious of the wild beasts and wilder men lurking in the primeval forests around the little clear-ing." The rhetorical question was posed as to why the Dutch, so phlegmatic and unimaginative by reputation, reacted with so much fear to their new environment, and why they began to endow the river valley with terrifying creatures of their collective imagination:

Does the explanation perhaps lie in the fact that the Dutch colonists, coming from a small country situated on a level plain where the land-scape was open as far as the eye could see, and left no room for mys-tery, were suddenly transplanted to a region shut in between overhang-ing cliffs where lightning flashed and thunder rolled from mountain wall to mountain wall, where thick forests obscured the view and strange aboriginal savages hid in the underbrush? Was it not the sense of wonder springing from this change in their accustomed surroundings

that peopled the dim depths of the hinterland with shapes of elf and
goblin, of demon and superhuman presences?[5]

Goodwin's line of inquiry appears to be quite popular to
judge from the number of times it reappears in the secondary accounts of Dutch settlement in New Netherland. Paul Wilstach
rephrased it slightly in his 1933 work, *Hudson River Landings:*
"The Dutch imagination, frightened by the unfamiliar heights,
with their ominous night shadows, has peopled [this area] with
its own share of the specters which are attached to the river."
Robert Boyle too quoted it verbatim in his 1969 *The Hudson
River, A Natural and Unnatural History.*[6]

Maud Goodwin was not, however, the first to take this line
of thought. In 1909 Clifton Johnson in *The Picturesque Hudson*
had the Dutch cowering in their mud hovels while the "primeval
wilderness . . . resounded nightly with the growl of bears, the
wail of panthers, and the yelps of wolves, while serpents lurked
in the dense underbrush."[7] Serious historical inquiry as well has
been colored by such attitudes. Merle Curti in *The Growth of
American Thought* considered the fanciful and fearful response of
the Dutch to the natural world the "intellectual legacy" of a
"simple . . . and superstitious people."[8]

Perhaps no writer since Washington Irving has done more to
perpetuate the aura of uncertainty and foreboding in the Dutch
view of the Hudson Valley than Carl Carmer. Through a literary
evocation of landscape mood in *The Hudson River,* he has done
for the region in this century what Irving did for it in the nineteenth. Through Carmer, the fears of the Dutch have been transmitted through innumerable generations and diverse cultures. In
1939, he found the lower valley under the spell of witchcraft
(there had indeed been trials for witchcraft in New Netherland)
and peopled with cultural leftovers of obscure origin and more
obscure beliefs: "the atmosphere here is murky with fear of the
supernatural . . . the [mountain people] live in terror. . . . The
woods they live in frighten them and the people who live outside
the woods frighten them even more."[9]

Today, this element of fear, long attributed to the Dutch,

echoes as resoundingly as highland thunder on the dust jackets of recently published river histories, which trumpet "mysterious" and "unknown" landscapes. Furthermore, newspaper stories refer to the mid-Hudson area as full "of mystery . . . like a nightmare fantasy . . . a heavy silence hangs over everything," whereas the Boscobel "Light and Sound Show" seeks to evoke "ghosts," and the *National Geographic* warns of multitudinous anxieties, hidden fears, and dark expectations to be encountered in today's highlands. [10]

Whether this brooding sense of topophobia accurately portrays Dutch cultural conception of the river region is very questionable. The significance of this alleged relationship between the Dutch and a landscape of fear which has been developed over the centuries lies in the fact that this interpretation has provided, and continues to provide, a visual filter which subsequent generations feel obliged to use. The employment of a sense of fear and mystery, retroactively applied to supposed Dutch beliefs, contributes in a very powerful way to the conception of the valley as romantic in the nineteenth and scenic in the twentieth centuries. The manifestation of how others thought the Hudson Valley Dutch viewed their physical milieu is a persistent environmental attitude arising from the colonial period.

True Dutch Landscape Attitudes

Historical analysis suggests that the real relationship between Dutch culture and the environment is somewhat different from the traditional view. [11] The Dutch were likely a rational and realistic people with a practical and useful attitude toward what they confronted in their environment. They seem to have been in no great way addicted to supernatural beliefs and fears. Indeed, they appear to have had a proclivity for outdoor amusement, outdoor dining, and in general, much communion with nature.

The first New Netherland accounts, those rare but succinctly written chronicles of discovery, offer suggestions along these lines. The value of this type of topographically descriptive material has often been questioned, and much of it might well be dismissed as the initial fascination or euphoria of the fact of discovery itself.[12] However, it may well be true that "our first impression of a place is also our last, and it depends solely upon the weather and the food."[13] Is it any surprise then that the impression of a howling and bitter land encountered in mid-winter by an ill-fed crew of Pilgrims survived so long? Or that what Cartier described as the "Land God gave Cain," the rocky and barren shores of the lower St. Lawrence, still holds such a grim impression today? First impressions of the land are important— however slanted—and they endure. The Hudson Valley and Manhattan Island were first explored in late summer and settled in the spring; the impression at both times must have been one of majestic and solemn beauty.

Writers have taken it upon themselves to reinterpret what the early explorers probably thought of the area: historians such as Bacon and Johnson presented Henry Hudson with a land of "mysterious possibilities" and geographic unknowns; Codman *thought* that "there must have been always something forbidding about the western shore."[14] But the accounts of Hudson and Verrazano emphasize the commercial possibilities and the landscape's beauty. Although, of course, not a Dutchman, Verrazano in 1524 initiated a long aesthetic tradition: "We passed up [the Hudson] river, about half a league, where we found it formed a most beautiful lake. . . . This region . . . seemed so commodious and delightful."[15]

The geographer Richard Hakluyt preserved the logbook of Robert Juet, one of Hudson's mates, who in the autumn of 1609 found a "pleasant [land] with grass and flowers," trees far better than those of the old world, an omnipresent sweetness in the air, and a "loving" people.[16] The river was full of fish, the rocks suggested gold and silver, and the land was laced with streams and offered delightful prospects for future towns. Such was the initial conception recorded by the "Eyes of Discovery."

Promotional writings, aimed at luring settlers to the newly claimed lands, quickly followed; these tracts, surfacing throughout the period of Dutch sovereignty, were aimed at recruiting tenants for Rensselaerswyck and later freeholders for the Esopus area. Again, the value of this genre of material, often used as evidence of environmental conception, might be questioned. Much of it was written in Europe by those who had never seen the land they described. One illustration, engraved in Holland, depicted the animals and vegetation of New Netherland: palm trees, undescribable creatures, and a playful unicorn. (The unicorn symbol, popular in Medieval tapestries, was associated with the innocence of the Garden of Eden.) [17]

But there may be a deeper content to promotional literature than the obvious deceptions caused by partiality and bias. "Aesthetic imagining is merely a sub-species of promotional imagining," and despite the often fictitiously and fancifully created conceptions, much of it "is a result of realistic subjectivity." [18] A certain degree of realism and descriptive truthfulness may then be contained in promotional tracts, especially when they are the work of those who had actually been in contact with the land described. Adrian Van Der Donck and Cornelius Van Tienhoven were such publicists.

Van Der Donck, the sheriff (or *schout*) of Rensselaerswyck, had lived in New Netherland for ten years before writing an official promotional tract addressed to the Dutch in Europe. Van Der Donck is described as "one of America's most literate chroniclers" whose works had "a tremendous impact on Dutch thinking." [19] His writing, perhaps somewhat hyperbolic, shows how the valley around Albany appeared to him and is indicative of how later-day romantics would search out scenic overlooks:

We sometimes in travelling imperceptibly find ourselves on high elevated situations, from which we overlook large portions of the country, the neighbouring eminence, the surrounding valleys and the highest trees are overlooked and again lost in the distant space. Here our attention is arrested in the beautiful landscape around us, here the painter can find rare and beautiful subjects for the employment of his pencil. [20]

Van Tienhoven, Peter Stuyvesant's Provincial Secretary, was less poetic, but painted an equally golden and prosperous picture of the agricultural prospects of the colony in 1650. The land, the soil, and the climate were particularized and found highly favorable and far better than that of the homeland.[21]

Apart from the promotional literature and the accounts of discovery, a fairly considerable body of poems, letters, and travel pieces, does exist and further hints at a form of aesthetic awareness. Because of the late development of the Hudson Valley, most of the material pertains to other regions within New Netherland, but is indicative nonetheless of prevailing cultural attitudes about the region in general.

Jacob Steendam, for example, wrote poetry for other than promotional purposes. In 1659 he reveled in "all the blessings" that this "Great River strew" and favorably contrasted the people and land of New Netherland with the uncouth minions of New England's soil, whom he allegorically depicted as swine. Other New Netherland poets such as Nicasius DeSille and Henricus Selyns described a sunshiny and nourishing world, better than any they had ever known.[22]

Unfortunately, most writers on New Netherland would probably accept the description of a stone age person's reaction to the shadow world beyond the cave as applicable to the Dutch mentality: i.e. "their 'known world' was only a pool of light in the midst of a shadow, limitless, for all that was definitely understood and proven."[23] While it is true that the territory to the west and north of the highlands was a geographic unknown before the 1690s, mention of it did not necessarily bring forth a sense of fear. It was referred to quite matter-of-factly as "the undefined Minisink Country." As Van Der Donck put it: "to the north-west is still undefined and unknown. . . . we know not how deep, or how far we extend inland."[24] Lions and other strange creatures were rumored—by the Indians—to inhabit this area as well as the highlands, but Van Der Donck was skeptical.

In sum, regions in the valley and beyond its borderland may have been viewed cautiously for fear of intruding Frenchmen or Yankees, but the demons and shadows were not of Dutch creation. These remote areas were in fact sought out and colonized more rapidly than the Hudson Valley itself.

Copious descriptions were also written by Jasper Danckaerts; though somewhat of a religious fanatic, his biographer described him as "an intelligent man, and a keen-eyed and assiduous note-taker." No writer until the Puritan Jonathan Edwards found nature so appealing—appealing as the abode of God, but nonetheless aesthetically appealing.[25] The landscape of New Netherland was seen as beautiful through its association with godliness. It is not surprising then to find the Reverend Megapolensis in 1657 describing the Esopus region as "exceedingly fine country," and the pastor of the Dutch church at Kingston writing in 1681 that the "land is flowing with milk and honey."[26]

Men of the cloth were not the only ones from which aesthetic beginnings are gleaned. The diarist of the Creiger expedition against the Indians in 1663 remarked upon the beauty and fertility of the Wallkill Valley and the Rosendale area. The settlers who were approaching the highlands from the rear found, in Ulster County, an "exceedingly beautiful land," and a region of great "beauty and apparent fertility."[27]

There is the occasional literary passage that tempts one to place the beginnings of the whole conservation-preservation ethic in the seventeenth century. Van Der Donck, for example, mentions that "there are some persons who imagine that the animals of the country will be destroyed in time, but this is an unnecessary anxiety."[28] An "unnecessary anxiety" for him perhaps, but apparently a concern of someone in the colony. And then there is the curious petition submitted to the government by the Rhenish Palatines of New Paltz to preserve, it seems for reasons of beauty and Indian remembrances, a natural feature within their patent, the Mohonk spring below Skytop Mountain.[29]

The oral tradition should be of much significance for a culture group such as this;[30] but surprisingly, there seems to be very little actually Dutch-derived folklore preserved. It is known that "by Washington Irving's time, the Valley had a unique folklore and this mythical and historical background opened the way for artistic and aesthetic discovery of the Hudson."[31] But what was the source of, and the content of, this folklore? Was it in essence Dutch? Investigation of two of the standard works on

Hudson Valley folklore, *Legends and Poetry of the Hudson* (1868), and *Teacup Tales—Folklore of the Hudson* (1958), reveals that most of the material is based on Indian legends, Revolutionary War episodes, and early-nineteenth-century remembrances. The odd bit of supposed Dutch folklore usually comes from Irving.[32] However interesting the folkloric tradition, it provides little or no evidence on how the Dutch viewed their environment. Its importance is in demonstrating how the romantic imagination of the nineteenth century both recorded and created a folk world with a geographical basis in the lower Hudson Valley, characterized by the exaggerated and supernatural.

The literary and folkloric evidences have been stressed above, but the landscape tradition in art and the ordering of the settlement pattern are other channels of investigation that shed further light onto the Dutch colonial environmental relationship. Again, in contrast with the Puritans, an obvious love of painting and decorative work was much apparent in New Netherland. Landscape had been popular in Holland, a nation with a claim to "the first modern landscapes" and more than two centuries of landscape tradition.[33]

By the time Hudson sailed on the Tappan Zee, "pictures were so cheap [in Holland] that every middle-class home could have them in every room."[34] Landscapes and seascapes are prominent in the huge New Netherland inventories of household effects. Of course, painters in the colony, such as Evart Duychinck and the DePeyster painter, were artist-craftsmen working (when not on fire buckets and stained glass windows) in portraiture. Yet this is an indication of financial necessity more than anything else, and faint landscapes *do* find their way into the backgrounds of the portraits. Danckaerts, traveling freely and with no economic restraints, claimed to have sketched parts of the valley in 1679—out of sheer delight.[35]

Given the pattern of occupation and settlement, it might be inferred that, because of the dispersed, non-nucleated layout of individual plantations and *bouweries,* the Dutch—far from having anxieties about being alone in the "savage" regions of the New World—preferred to labor in distant fields and even invite Indians home for supper. That is a curious attitude taken by the settlers, entirely unexpected of people presumably so fearful of the forest and the "wild people." Indeed, the degree of fraternization with the "infidels" was so great that the government made it a criminal offense to harbor natives in the house after dark.[36] Expediency, the preference for good soil, the location of patented lands, situation with respect to trade possibilities, and avoidance of topographically deficient areas such as the highlands and the Palisade crest, appear to have been the settlement determinants. Personal security and the alleviation of fear apparently were not important in the pattern of settlement; nor did they help to shape environmental attitudes.

The English and Yankee View of the Land

While the Dutch influence in the Hudson Valley was very pervasive and, as in South Africa, long outlasted the homeland's political suzerainty (indeed Dutch was commonly spoken in Rockland County until at least the 1820s), the last hundred years of the colonial period must of course be regarded as one of English and Yankee ascendancy. By the Revolution, cultural attitudes attested to "the more complete subordination of Dutch tradition to fashionable preferences derived from the English element of the population."[37]

The New England Puritan-derived population that flowed across the Taconics and into the Hudson Valley in the late seventeenth and early eighteenth century was probably little concerned with, and less aware of, the aesthetic qualities of the region. Despite its ever-loosening grip on the immigrants, orthodox Puritanism still formed the conceptual basis for many of their cultural attitudes. Puritan society was dominated by three lines of thought, which ultimately governed their relationship with whatever environmental situation confronted them: rejection of everything in nature not of immediate value; disregard for the aesthetic qualities of nature; a strict scorn for outdoor activities and pleasures.[38]

This may be somewhat of a generalized overstatement. Daniel Denton, for example, in 1670 described the Raritan Valley in decidedly positive terms. And yet the minions of Increase and Cotton Mather were, in the phrase used by Perry Miller, on God's "Errand into the Wilderness" and had neither time nor inclination for emotional releases found in nature. It was this culture group, not the Dutch, who initiated the large-scale civilizing and Christianizing assault upon the New World environment; with them, "progress became synonymous with exploitation." [39]

Whether the Puritan attitude was one of outright hostility or simple indifference toward what would later be regarded as pleasurable landscapes, the feelings of New Englanders (like the Dutch) entering the Hudson Valley were conditioned by ideas older and perhaps stronger than Puritan practical ethics. Mountain landscapes were surrounded by "superstitious awe" since the Dark Ages and nature itself was a "haunted and gnomed mire" filled with "malign and awful presences and powers." To English travelers of the time (inheritors of a Judeo-Christian tradition of repugnance for landscape) the mountains of Scotland and Wales and the Alps were viewed as "the rubbish of the earth, swept away by the careful housewife Nature—waste places of the world, with little meaning and less charm." [40] Rather than even endure such repulsive mountain scenery, English gentlemen often drew the stagecoach blinds when traveling through such regions of horror.

This sense of "mountain gloom," when alloyed with negative Puritan attitudes, resulted in the use of a package of conventionally distasteful adjectives that were handed down from generation to generation, from Europe to America. As the Derbyshire Highlands were damned for their "ugliness, solitude and inaccessibility" in the seventeenth century, so the mountainous and forested realms of the New World colonies were condemned for their barren, uncouth, unfrequented, forsaken, sky-threatening, pathless nature in the eighteenth century. [41] John Josselyn, a botanist who climbed Mount Washington, depicted New England's highlands in a manner similar to the way he would have described the Hudson Highlands—had he seen them: "Dauntingly

terrible, full of rocky hills and clothed with infinite thick woods
. . . a tract of land God knows how many miles full of delfs and
dingles and dangerous precipices, Rocks and inextricable difficulties." [42]

   This is the expected assortment of cultural concepts carried
in by the Anglo-Saxon population, but relatively little documentation actually exists as to what an English or New England population thought of the landforms in the lower Hudson Valley
before the mid-eighteenth century. The Yankee vanguard who
arrived in the seventeenth century were yeoman farmers, traders,
and small entrepreneurs seeking out mill sites on Sparkill Creek
and Murderer's Creek (the Moodna). They might well have been
influenced by Puritan and Old World–derived environmental
images, but, largely inured to village life in places like Nyack and
Cornwall, they left no written record of the countryside beyond.
It can only be assumed that they operated within the same frame-
work of repugnance for landscape that was put ashore with the
Mayflower. As had the Dutch, many of these immigrants avoided
direct contact with raw highland nature, opting for the more
economically profitable and fertile lowlands and valleys to the
west and north. For this reason, the highland precincts were not
commented upon as a rule by (illiterate?) settlers, for there were
few of them anyway. As regards the society's "elite," as gleaned
from Nevin's *American Social History as Recorded by British Travellers,* the region simply had not yet become a magnet for traveling
gentlemen, wandering essayists, or itinerant military men. [43]

   It was a rare and highly sentient observer who in the early
1700s could have equated a Hudson River landscape with things
of beauty, and more incredible still if that observer was a Puritan
metaphysician with strong ties to the orthodox New England
ministry of the previous century. But Jonathan Edwards appears
to have leapfrogged a century of aesthetic evolution when in
1723 he found God's beauty reflected in nature along the banks of
the lower Hudson: "I very frequently used to retire into a solitary place, on the banks of Hudson's River . . . for contemplation on divine things and secret converse with God: and had
many sweet hours there." [44]

A Less Hostile View of Nature

Apart from such an unexpected confession as this, in the decades immediately preceding the American Revolution something of a general change in attitude seems slowly to have infiltrated environmental thought: not the dramatic aesthetic transitions that would be the hallmark of succeeding periods, but a gradual and subtle shift in emphasis toward a less hostile view of nature. Perhaps it was somehow fostered by the kinder Dutch regard for landscape, a changing aesthetic attitude in Europe, or by the fact that the region of the Hudson was, through the accumulation of knowledge, becoming less and less a *terra incognita*. Whatever the reasons, conceptions of the valley were no longer unconditionally negative.

Cadwallader Colden, an early American product of the age of reason and scientific achievement, in his voluminous letters and papers dating from the 1750s, had corresponded with the Swedish botanist and traveler Kalm and with Franklin and other learned colonials. "Our mountains," "these Highlands" were described objectively by him as to botanical and zoological species as well as to the advisability of surveys and availability of maps.[45] The individual landforms were never described as picturesque or beautiful, but at least they no longer evoked a rhetoric of horror and the allegories of fear. Kalm himself quite objectively and dispassionately described the course of the lower Hudson (1749) as did Smith (1769). To the latter, the highland landforms were neither threatening nor appealing, but merely "aspiring mountains."[46]

Landscape-like paintings too began to appear in the colonies before the Revolution, and most importantly the scenes depicted real American subjects. Virgil Barker in his *American Painting* traces the "obscure beginnings of esthetic consciousness and broadening [artistic] taste" to the few topographic prints and "birds-eye views" of the New York and Boston areas executed between 1720 and 1770.[47] With the perspective views of gentlemen's estates in the Hudson Valley, faint scenic backgrounds for portraiture, and Governor Pownall's topographically accurate sketch of the Palisades, "consciousness of place had already begun to grow," for now the landform had become the subject of the sketch pad.[48]

It is important to understand the contrast in attitudes toward the land that evolved among the Dutch and English settlers in the Hudson Valley. In light of evidence presented by literary tradition, and perhaps indirectly by settlement patterns, the supposition that the supernatural, the mysterious, and the fearful were endemic to Dutch culture cannot be maintained. A respect for nature and an elemental appreciation of the lands they found in New Netherland seem more in keeping with their world vision.[49]

It has furthermore been suggested that "Europeans coming to America feared and disliked the forest" and that elements of the "wild man mythology" were transferred intact to New Amsterdam, and that the "dark and mysterious qualities of the New World forest" made it a setting in which "the prescientific imagination could place a swarm of demons and spirits."[50] That the New Netherland Dutch were conditioned by elements of this mythology is speculative and cannot be supported by literary or other tradition. It seems *more* likely that, as Kenneth Clark believes, these old Germanic fears had been tamed by the Dutch.[51] That "tradition of repugnance" possibly characterizing the Puritan relationship with nature (at least on the "elitist" level) seems closer emotionally to the medieval Anglo-Saxon ethic of forest fear.[52] The sense of religious mission and cultural antipathy reflected in such terminology as howling, dismal, baffling, gloomy, and terrible are absent from the Dutch conception of the wilderness and mountains. To the contrary, the settlers of New Netherland, unlike the "raw-boned . . . peddlers and strapping corn-fed wenches" of New England who descend upon the valley after the Dutch, seem to have been liberated from Old World suspicion and raised to "the gentler world [wherein] God might be manifested in nature."[53]

Why such differences exist can only be hinted at. More unequivocal statements regarding man's relationships with nature in the Hudson Valley cannot really be postulated for this period, given the sources available. For example, folk response to the great northeastern earthquake and meteor shower of 1663 would shed further light on the cultural-environmental equation, but recorded reactions are wanting. Great fear and millennial commotion appear to have been occasioned in Lower Canada and New England by these simultaneous natural occurrences, but in the Hudson Valley (where the river also overflowed, ruining the harvest) it was viewed only as an omen of probable political change. This might well suggest differing views of nature's might, but substantiation is difficult.[54]

On the whole, it appears that the Hudson Valley Dutch were characterized by a perceptive and well-balanced view of natural phenomena and landscape; that they had a direct line of influence upon subsequent aesthetic environmental theory is more difficult to accept. The negative attitudes which arrived with the Yankee invasion likely created a hiatus between Dutch landscape tradition and the evolution of nineteenth-century romantic thought. For their part, the English settlers in the Hudson Valley contributed little to the evolution of an aesthetic tradition; as frontiersmen with a not-too-distant Puritan strain, they had neither time nor respect for nature's beauty. What was true of the French explorers in the Great Lakes country, and of the first English to penetrate Australia, applies here: i.e., they became so used to the landscape that they no longer bothered to describe it or their feelings about it.[55] These "folk" were so "profoundly in transaction"[56] with nature and the physical world so much a part of their daily routine, that the need for expressing so intimate and personal a relationship was unapparent. Backwoods "campfire opinion" went unrecorded and fireside talk in the settlers' cabins likely focused on the realities of hunger, cold, work, ailments, and Indians. Aesthetic values were not the pioneer's realities. Perhaps the kindest that can be said of their cultural vision was expressed by R. L. Duffus: "Nature was not then admired—there was altogether too much of it."[57]

By the 1770s, however, an ambivalence had become apparent that would be more fully accentuated after the disruptions of war were mended. A sense of fear and hate may have still been present, but it was tempered—especially among the educated elite—not yet by a love of nature, but by a growing respect for it in areas such as the Hudson Valley. Such areas were no longer on the "cutting edge" of the frontier and no longer a "threat" to the survival of the settlers. Although somewhat discontinuous in time and uneven among the various cultures, there is evidence enough to suggest a definite linear growth of scenic appreciation and aesthetic imagining from colonial times.

Part 3
Americans Doing, Europeans Observing
The Valley from the Revolutionary War to the 1820s

THE AMERICAN REVOLUTION served as a stimulus to both increased use of land in the valley and to a deeper appreciation of the landscape itself. A pattern of rural and village economics—including quarrying, shipbuilding, farming, iron manufacturing, and recreation—was established by the early nineteenth century. With it, however, came the seeds of future discord: competition between quarrying and recreation.

The conception of landscape as a scenic, human asset made important strides in these decades. Many writers and travelers preferred either to ignore the attractiveness of the Hudson's landforms or to report upon them in a rather mechanical, objective way; tourists still enjoyed seeing artillery practice tear chunks of rock off the Crows Nest, while others inaugurated a long era of Hudson Valley grafitti by painting or carving their names on the cliffs and rocks. Yet a growing use of aesthetic concept was apparent. Some Americans, displaying an ambivalent fear of or enthrallment with features such as the Palisades and Storm King Mountain, reflected the inroads of English romanticism. What might be called a more harmonious or ecological manner of relating to nature became the technique of the traveling scientist-artist. Much in the manner set by Alexander von Humboldt, these visitors brought to American river and mountainscapes a geological curiosity complemented by aesthetics.

Chapter 5
A Busy Valley, A Young Republic

A critical point in the geographic development of New York [the Revolution] would markedly reshape the regional patterns of settlement.
D. W. Meinig, "The Colonial Period" [1]

IN 1777 THE TWENTY year old Marquis de Lafayette first saw the Valley of the Hudson at the head of a Continental regiment in Washington's Army; in 1824, as an old man wishing once more to see the Hudson before he died, he triumphantly and ceremoniously toured the river he had known 47 years before. In the intervening years, the valley had begun to evolve as a major industrial area and transport facility for the Eastern Seaboard, although patterns of economic growth and population increase had not yet dramatically changed the face of "Father Hudson" in a way such that Lafayette would not know it.

Out on the rapidly closing New York frontier, conditions of life were especially frenetic as villages and towns proliferated almost daily, creating "a whole new array of areal patterns." [2] While campaigning in various parts of New York, Continental soldiers, particularly New Englanders, favorably evaluated the region's potential and later returned to help settle the upper Hudson, the Oneida–Mohawk region, and the upper Delaware and Susquehanna drainage basins.

But these same decades were something less than hectic for the lower Hudson Valley. It was mostly a time of "filling in," searching out, and occupying "every nook and corner suitable for habitation,"[3] and often places not suitable. Population for the river counties climbed into the thousands; Rockland had slightly more than 6000 people by 1800. Rural areas became more fully developed and evenly spread with houses and farm fields.

It was also a time of social reorientation and economic recovery. The war was followed by a depression and an especially unsettled state of affairs in the lower valley. As a principal theatre of war,[4] the valley was plundered for materiel, and its fields, villages, and hamlets burned. Bergen and Westchester, as "neutral" ground between the opposing armies in the highlands and in New York City, were badly ravaged. The postwar period was also characterized by problems involving the disposition of confiscated Tory estates, which were sometimes parceled out to small farmers, but more often resold intact.

Origins of the Resort and Recreation Industry

Significantly, resort and recreational facilities on the banks of the lower Hudson trace their origin to this period. Until the construction of the Erie Canal in 1825 it was the East River rather than the Hudson which was preferred for commercial purposes.[5] Probably because of northwesterly winds and the fear of winter ice, warehouses and docks were located on the east or lee side of Manhattan while gardens, pleasure parks, and esplanades were built along the Hudson. Even in Dutch times the Governor's Gardens and the village of New Haarlem (Harlem), New Amsterdam's rural "place of amusement," had marked the Hudson's shores with greenery.

A continuity of recreational land use was provided by the Vauxhall Gardens (on Warren Street), which were at the height of their vogue in the 1780s; elsewhere, picturesque carriageways led down to the Hudson's edge, where beyond the salt meadows the sun set "in golden glory behind the Jersey Hills."[6] Later, when ferry service opened the New Jersey shore to weekend tourists, the Elysian Fields between Hoboken and Weehawken became a very popular and crowded resort.[7] It is significant that an important social pattern had been established at a very early date. It is a pattern that not only survived through time, but assumed a more dominant role in the decades to come, as the shorelands along the Palisades, the Tappan Zee, and the highlands to the north were pre-empted for recreation.

The Agricultural Landscape

Agriculture remained the most prevalent and essential activity in most of the valley until after the 1820s. "At the close of the Revolution the Hudson River Valley [as a whole] was known as 'the Bread Basket of the Nation,' and it is this post-war era that has been characterized as "the heroic age of farming in New York State."[8]

The construction of turnpikes and public roads was common in this period and was an activity closely related to the rise of agricultural commerce and farm villages. In 1790 a public road was put through from the farms at Nyack to those at Piermont, while the beginnings of a complex road network through the interior farmlands from Newburgh to Bergen is indicated on the Erskine (1778) and DeWitt (1802) maps.[9] Although a river road was not completed until later, spur roads did connect ferry landings (the King's Ferry at Stony Point, Sneden's, and the Fort Lee area) and river landings with the hinterland. These river landings, such as Piermont and Caldwell's below the Dunderberg, functioned as market towns for the produce of farm, forest, and mine. "Each river market built up a hinterland, the size of which was fairly definitely circumscribed by the crucial factor of transportation."[10]

Subsistence agriculture was prevalent throughout the region

before the 1830s, and it appears that farming was geared to the growing of wheat on the river bottomlands and in the generally more productive hinterlands. Because of wars and other disruptions in Europe there was a world-wide demand for wheat between 1783 and 1824, which New York wheat farmers partially filled.[11] Although wheat was the principal commodity grown, rye, barley, and other crops were important: "A plot of wheat, another of corn, a patch of flax, a meager garden, perhaps a few fruit trees, a yoke of oxen, a few cattle and hogs were the common elements." Intensive regionalization in the form of dairying and horticulture had not yet developed.[12]

The Palisades and Its Peopling

During the Revolutionary War the Palisades was both a strategic obstruction and a tactical strongpoint, and much descriptive material was compiled in the form of sketchbooks and journals in the course of maneuvers and skirmishes along the Bergen shore. From these sources it appears there were only three settlements along the ridge by the 1770s: Fort Lee with its ferry landing and perhaps a few houses and tavern surrounded by a "vast" forest; Liberty Pole (Englewood) which was the site of a "public house" and apparently not much else; and Sneden's Landing, a major river crossing.[13]

Elsewhere the region of the Palisades was one of "woods and open spaces, broken by an occasional farm house, grist mill or country manor."[14] The roads (or more precisely trails) which zigzagged their way down the defiles to the river landings were flanked by dense woods. One can vicariously experience the great physical exertion required of Cornwallis's troops in Lord Rawdon's famous watercolor of the British Army scaling the heavily timbered cliff-face above Closter Dock in 1777.[15] Rawdon and others who sketched and mapped the Palisades (such as Dominic Serres and Thomas Davies) are in accord in their rendition of a densely wooded shoreline, both cliff-face and talus slope.[16]

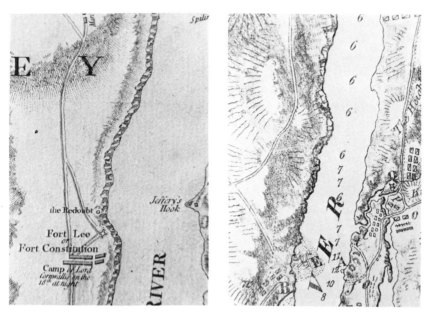

Figure 11. The Palisades in the Revolutionary Period

LEFT. Detail of the Palisades from: "A Plan of the Operations of the King's Army under the Command of Gen. Sir Wm. Howe in New York and East New Jersey etc," by Claude J. Sauthier. Engraved in London by Wm. Faden, 1777. New York Public Library Map Collection.

RIGHT. Detail of the Palisades from: "A Sketch of the Operation of His Majesty's Fleet and Army Under the Command of Vice Admiral the Right Honorable Lord Viscount Howe," by J.F.W. Des Barres, London, Jan. 1777. New York Public Library Map Collection.

From the sketches drawn by British officers, the ridge-top appears to have been rather fully vegetated. Artist and engineer Archibald Robertson composed a topographic view of the Bergen shore above Sneden's Landing showing a tree-lined ridge. The infamous Colonel John Simcoe composed a sketch map depicting the activities of his Queen's Rangers in the Fort Lee–Fort Washington area and chose to show the Palisades in close hachuring and with the wooded cartographic symbol on top.[17] However, other sources indicate that the ridge summit immediately to the west of the cliff-face (something of course not observable from the river or the heights of upper Manhattan) was probably farmed to some extent. A pattern of open woods and farmland was likely, along with a scattering of taverns, wayside houses, and mills.[18]

Farming was certainly practiced along the Palisades ridge during the Revolution; indeed, local farms were repeatedly sacked by the British Army, which made off with much livestock and grain. Major André composed a poem warning the Americans that the British would "drive away the cows" from your Bergen shore; such an incursion is documented in the minutes of the Council of Safety for Bergen County.[19] The shore from Fort Lee to Piermont was "much exposed to [these] depredations of foraging forces from the enemy's ships,"[20] and "shore guards" were instituted to protect the farms. Since the area was furthermore "infested" with Tories, countermeasures by the Patriots resulted in the devastation of much Loyalist property.

The Palisades front did not escape the inflictions of war. Designated as the "King's Woods" in pre-Revolutionary times, the composition and extent of the forest was not greatly affected since the primary source of masting timber, the white pine, was absent from the Palisades crest.[21] It remained for the contending armies to utilize much of the growth for firewood. During the bitter-cold winter of 1779–80 the Hudson froze over and the British drove sleds across from Manhattan to strip the Bergen woods for fuel.[22] In all likelihood the area was largely cutover by 1783.

While the war itself was quite obviously a potent and destructive force upon the landscape of the Palisades, the postwar record of land use is somewhat hazy. When the armies departed, so too did the many knowledgeable observers and cartographers, and in the terminology of the county historians, the region enjoyed a "sleepy existence."

In the early national period, it appears that "farming activities . . . crept up the western slope of the Palisades, but may have been later curtailed on the slope."[23] The local genealogies recount the entry of new families into the area atop the Palisades, and since the cartographic sources indicate no river hamlets or villages,[24] it can be assumed that this was a rural-based farm population, either "yeomen" or "gentlemen" farmers. It has been suggested that the slope of the Palisades was pastured while "the Ridge top [was] left as a source of wood for fuel or lumber."[25] The regenerated forest on the summit was again employed as a source of firewood, this time for the growing needs of New York City. The many "pitching places" from which cordwood was thrown down the slope to be shipped to the city by sloop have their origin in this period.[26]

While farming and forest-cutting were conducted on the back slope and the ridge top, the river shore has its own history. Soon after the war, Closter Dock and Sneden's Landing were joined by other small communities below the cliffs. Huyler Landing, originally a collection point for cordwood pitched from the ridge top, was probably the largest of these. The use of Palisades cordwood and associated shoreline collection points assumed an even greater importance by the 1820s, when large numbers of steamboats began plying the river, stopping at the landings to take on wood for their boilers.

With some exaggeration perhaps, the landing basin below Englewood Cliffs was described as the "first seaport" along the Bergen shore: "from hamlets, farms, and orchards in the Hackensack Valley to the west, farmers brought their produce on carts and wagons over bumpy roads and trails to the [Englewood Landing] for shipment to New York markets."[27] At the northern terminus of the Palisades, Piermont (or "Tappan Slote" before the 1820s) functioned as the main shipment point for farm produce originating in the interior of Rockland and north Bergen. "The mouth of the Sparkill . . . offered facilities for landing, and the valley of that stream gave easy access to the [Hudson] river." Piermont, larger than Nyack at that time, improved upon its landing site in the 1820s by partially filling in a salt marsh at the entrance to the creek, then navigable inland some distance.[28] Nicholas Gesner, a farmer and diarist in the northern Palisades, described in some detail the subsistence and cash crop production of apples, raspberries, and potatoes he engaged in. The latter were sent to New York via the nearby river landings.[29]

Many period topographic views show settlement details in

the undercliff area. A variety of wooden structures and boat houses (some with fencing and gardens) are depicted in the "Iconography of New Jersey" collection compiled by the New Jersey Historical Society. William Guy Wall's classic "Palisades," done for the *Hudson River Portfolio* in 1820, locates several houses along the base of the talus slope.[30] These post-Revolutionary hamlets of wood collectors and fishermen were located where the shore was least rocky and wide enough to erect houses and industry; these settlements, peopled by the descendants of Dutch and Huguenot farmers from the Hackensack Valley, were described by Crèvecoeur and other travelers in the early nineteenth century.[31]

Finally and most prophetically, the quarrymen made their appearance. These bogeymen of the nineteenth century may have begun work on the Palisades formation as early as 1736, but unquestionably traprock was being quarried shortly after the Revolution: "Boat building and quarrying at the base of the cliffs began and small homes of fishermen, woodcutters and stonecutters sprang up under the cliffs."[32] This is verified by the presence of large quarry holes in the northern Palisades on John Eddy's 1818 map of the Bergen and Rockland shores.

Activities on the Nyack and Haverstraw Lowlands

Nyack and Haverstraw were little more than primitive river landings at the time of the Revolution. The immediate countryside had been devastated by the war and in 1810 "the Nyack neighborhood was still very rural. . . . Only seven houses were within the limits of what is today the incorporated village of Nyack. . . . Abram Tallman operated a store at the landing. Otherwise, there was little to indicate that the neighborhood was on the verge of a vigorous expansion."[33]

Haverstraw, serving as the ship landing for the Ringwood iron works, contained but one house as late as 1794. On the DeWitt map of 1802, Nyack (Niak) is the only settlement indicated on the Rockland shore. Haverstraw's first street was not laid out until 1803.[34]

At this time, however, the geography of the Rockland shore was radically realigned and its reportedly bucolic landscape devastated by the coming of the quarrymen and brickmakers. Observe one man's reminiscences of Haverstraw as it was in 1794 and as it was to be:

the fields all around were sown with rye. The river bank was the handsomest I ever saw. From Grassy Point down to where James Wood first set a brickyard, was a beautiful row of large chestnuts and oak trees, growing all along the banks. It was a beautiful walk. How different now! A large village, and also a village of brickyards! [35]

The rapidity and totality with which the high cedar-covered banks of the Hudson were obliterated in Haverstraw is testimony to the thoroughness of the industrial development in this area of Rockland County.

As in the northern Palisades, the Hudson's hilly shore from Grandview to Nyack was exploited for building materials needed for paving and docking in New York and other growing cities in the Hudson Valley. The red sandstone underlying the Palisades formation was also exploited for building blocks. [36] The War of 1812 provided impetus for the industry here, much stone being needed for the construction of forts in New York harbor. The building stone business, however, peaked in the 1820s, a period in which as many as twelve vessels at a time hauled stone from the Rockland shore. But the traprock quarries continued to prosper throughout the century.

At Haverstraw, as the traveler Milbert observed and sketched (fig. 32):

[the] harbor was nicely located, with a basin formed by two projecting jetties where boats can load and unload their merchandise beside the large warehouses. Several houses on the cultivated slopes have views both of the river and the mountains surrounding this amphitheatre. [37]

In the Haverstraw area quarries were of importance too; limestone was being extracted from Tomkins Cove by 1790. Yet it was brickmaking that became the mainstay of this town's economy. Attempts to establish brickmaking were made on the banks of the Minisceongo before 1810, but the first successful operation dates to 1815. Bricks became synonymous with Haverstraw and the industry thrived (it eventually employed over 2400 workers) because of the resources available in the immediate vicinity: brick clay and vast amounts of wood for charcoal. James Wood's inventive process of mixing anthracite coal dust (brought into the Hudson Valley via the Delaware & Hudson Canal and Kingston) with the clay to produce stronger bricks permanently established Haverstraw as the brickmaking capital of the lower valley.[38] The scale and persistence of the valley's brick industry is evident even today in the ubiquitous presence of the old broken bricks that are everywhere washed by the tides in the river shallows.

Activities on Hook Mountain and the Tors

While the coming of quarries and brickyards provided Nyack and Haverstraw with commercial impetus, the brooding crescent-shaped upland of Hook Mountain and the Tors was slowly changing. As with the Palisades in Bergen, the British had raided inland from Nyack to Haverstraw and inflicted much damage upon the region. Slaughter's Landing (Rockland Lake Landing) is a place name that dates from Revolutionary times, denoting the point where British foraging parties slaughtered cattle they had rounded up in the countryside about the lake. Immediately after the war, the area appeared "devastated and scathed . . . [fields] now lay a waste rankly o'ergrown with weeds . . . a few charred, blackened fragments of the [farm] buildings."[39]

Although most of the mountain area had been deeded and nominally occupied after the war, there was no apparent rebound of settlement, as seen in Berthier's map of the region, and statements such as these are common in the county histories:

most of the inhabitants were living on the lowlands next to the river, while the mountains beyond were covered with the primeval forest dotted with a few log houses. One could travel the entire distance on the main road from Stony Point to Suffern, without finding more than eight or nine human habitations.[40]

The brick industry had a consumptive appetite for local wood and cut into the fine oaks and hickories which grew on the slopes of Hook Mountain and the Tors. The mountains' hardwoods were also useful in various ways for the construction of ships, an activity also important to the economy of both Nyack and Haverstraw. The trees of this once unbroken highland forest, "a tangled and almost impenetrable mass,"[41] were presumably cut and sold by "farmers," although just how much farming was actually practiced on the upland is questionable. As on the Palisades, the story seems to be one of grazing on cutover— unimproved stumpland. The county histories do associate the grazing of Merino sheep, a Hudson Valley farming "craze" in the years 1807–24, with the Hook Mountain region.[42]

The Highlands in the Young Republic

In an ironic way it is once again fortunate that so much of the Revolutionary War revolved about the Hudson Highlands, for descriptive and literary records compiled by Army officers and engineers are plentiful.

Although the highland tract had already been patented, there was, except for squatters, little if any settlement here until after the Revolution. Faden's map of 1777 indicates only the Forts on the Popolopen (Montgomery and Clinton) in the entire area between New Windsor and Haverstraw. The road network was strictly interior and through a "thick wilderness" region that Major Thacher described in 1779: "I rode with Major Meriweather [from Smith's Clove] to West Point, took our route through the woods, over abrupt and rocky mountains, almost impassable for our horses."[43] In the accounts of General Heath, Chastellux, and others the references are repeatedly to "marching into the woods," "a clearing in the woods," "various kinds of forest trees," and "an inaccessible wilderness." Robertson too sketched the highlands as dense with vegetation.[44]

Throughout the highlands much of this "thick and dense" vegetation was secondary growth and underbrush, the successor of a vanished "virgin" growth either converted to charcoal or struck down by fire in early colonial times. Sparks from furnaces or charcoal pits undoubtedly caused extensive forest fires.[45] If much of the valuable timber had been cut from the forest before the Revolution, it is then understandable why Continental troops found it necessary to cut building timbers for the barracks of the Popolopen forts in the Newburgh area, carting them south on the frozen Hudson.[46]

Bernard Romans, the geographically minded botanist turned engineer who laid out the highland forts in 1775, commented upon the quality of the highland forest: "We are in a miserable timber country . . . even fascines are got with more difficulty than stones."[47] Perhaps the most vivid and authoritative record of the highland forest as it appeared at the close of the Revolution is Pierre L'Enfant's watercolor of West Point, a document whose precision of execution and exactness of detail is extraordinary.[48] L'Enfant depicted the encampment of the Continental Army at the "point" in panoramic fashion, showing a rather bleak and barren landscape. Thacher's statement that the encampment was surrounded by vegetation is confirmed, but the forest cover is low, somewhat dense, and bushy in appearance. If a general wooded, overgrown, uninhabited, unfarmed condition is true for the area in question, then by extension the same was likely true of the whole highland precinct from the Northern Gate to the Dunderberg.

The most important aspect of land use in the highlands between the Revolution and 1824, and in this there is a marked similarity with the Palisades and Hook Mountain, is the slow and undramatic pace in which the land was domesticated. Poor glacial soils, rugged terrain, and inadequate transport continued to inhibit the region's growth. Farming was practiced and the land cleared to some extent, since it is known that by 1800 local farmers had carted away much of the original stone used at Fort

Putnam and its outworks. And yet, travelers continued to describe a landscape essentially barren of habitations and wooded throughout. J. W. Eddy's aquatint of "Anthony's Nose on the North River," done around 1795, presents a deeply and impenetrably wooded scene. Maude and Lambert, two English observers independently traveling the river in the early 1800s, refer to the heart of the highlands around West Point as a "desert," "a lofty desert."[49] This does not deny the idea of a wooded highland, for what was being described was the cutover plain around West Point itself and its terrace of low, stunted, "barren" vegetation. It is furthermore possible that farmers had contributed to the elimination of some of the forest given Baron Klinkowstrom's description of the West Point region in 1820 as "surrounded on three sides by rather high hills which are *partly covered* by forests."[50]

A slow and sparse development of the highlands is confirmed by the delayed rise of hamlets and villages. Scattered sawmills and dwellings dotted the area, but their presence is not recorded on the period maps. Colonial stage roads did cut across the highlands (the Continental Road and the Old West Point Road), stopping at isolated farms and hotel-taverns along the route.

Settlement nuclei containing three or four houses and perhaps a tavern were found at Doodletown, around the ruins of the Popolopen forts (the village of Fort Montgomery), and at Caldwell's Landing, or "Gibraltar," a ferry dock at the foot of the Dunderberg. The origin of these hamlets derives from their function as shipment points for the products of the hinterland and as termini on such newly constructed toll pikes as the Dunderberg & Clove Turnpike (1809), connecting Joshua Caldwell's ferry with Doodletown and the interior, and the Fort Montgomery Pike (1814), connecting this Hudson River landing with the Forest of Dean iron mine.

The progress of settlement and turnpike construction is related to the highland iron industry, an activity that both peaked and all but vanished in this same period. The theme of iron manufacturing as a molder of the cultural and physical landscape is an important one.[51] However, such mining identifies largely with areas where iron manufacturing bore directly upon the location of settlements, roads, and the utilization of local hardwoods (for charcoal), and water power. The highlands of northern New Jersey and the Ramapos are examples of this but, in contrast, the Hudson highlands were never very greatly affected by the iron industry.

As in colonial times, the only manufactories were the Queensborough and Forest of Dean furnaces (fig. 10) with the Popolopen Creek area serving as a tree cutting plantation.[52] Elsewhere in the highlands, the ironmakers cleared large tracts of land (e.g., along the Moodna Creek) for the manufacture of charcoal, and sometimes imported farmers to grow food for the iron workers and their families. A pattern of forge, furnace, mine, farm, and connective roadways developed in the highlands. But again, the scope and duration of this development, a "transitory industry" at best, was not nearly as extensive as in the Ramapos, or even the Taconics.[53]

The Forest of Dean works, important in its time for supplying ball to the troops on the Popolopen and the links for the great river chains strung across the Hudson, was never again fully operative after the fall of Fort Montgomery. The Queensborough furnace manufactured its last pig iron in 1812.[54] With the demise of the highland iron industry, farming did not reappear as it did in areas more favored by soils and transport. What followed instead was a general depopulation and reversion to forest: "When the forests were destroyed, and no more charcoal could be made, the fires went out, the miners removed, and nature kindly clothed the scene of desolation with verdure."[55] The highlands, in short, regenerated very quickly to a landscape of overlapping scrub and tree-covered mountain, as depicted in the views of Storm King, Sugar Loaf, Anthony's Nose, and Breakneck Hill done by William Guy Wall in 1820.[56]

To the east of the Hudson, the pattern was much the same. The highland precincts of Putnam County remained virtually devoid of settlement, whereas the lower plains and more accessible shorelines of Westchester and Dutchess were cultivated.[57] Early in the century the Kent and Putnam Valleys were raked over for charcoal production to supply the West Point foundry at Cold Spring. Some iron was mined on a small scale at Canopus Hill in 1820 but, with the exception of the Cold Spring–Nelsonville settlement and the ship landing at Garrison, there appears to have been no other settlement in the highlands east of the Hudson before 1830.[58] If anything, these highlands may have been even more retarded in terms of early settlement and development than the uplands of Rockland and Orange.

The islands in the highland passage (Iona, Constitution, and Bannerman's) exhibit a reasonably uneventful history before 1824. Iona (Salisbury Island on period maps), devoid of any activity in the Eddy drawing, was explored by Maude and was found to consist of only rock, marsh, and scrubwood.[59] Both Constitution and Bannerman's Islands (known respectively as Martelaers Rock and Polopel Island during the war) played a role in the fighting, because of their strategic locations in the narrow highland passage. Fortifications and *chevaux de frise* were constructed. However, as Romans observed in 1775, these island rocks had no value as farmland or habitation and so remained virtually unused after the war.[60]

As to the surroundings, Cornwall, on the northern flank of the highlands and the closest landing to the Northern Gate, dates to around 1800, although initial settlement probably occurred at the time of the Revolution. As "the place of doing foreign business on the river," Cornwall, with its docks, fruit nurseries, and "shipyard" also profited from being near the outlet of Moodna Creek (variously called Murderer's and Martelaer's Creek). An assortment of mills and houses is shown on period maps along the creek and at the landing. E. L. Henry's "The *Clermont* making a landing at Cornwall on the Hudson" is a vivid picture of riverfront activity in 1800; it is drawn with much attention to detail: the waiting carriages, hotels, shore structures and boat docks give evidence of lively commercial activity.[61]

To the north, Newburgh had by its incorporation in 1800

superseded New Windsor as the center of commercial interest on the Newburgh Plain. In this area turnpike construction was rapid between 1800 and 1815 (Newburgh was in keen competition with Kingston for the "western" trade) and the undulating countryside was reportedly heavily farmed and dotted with mills and lime kilns.[62]

In the central and western parts of Rockland and Orange Counties the rugged highland towns remained relatively undeveloped while areas with more level topography or drained by streams affording water power prospered. The Cadwallader Colden estate at Coldenham was still considered to be in an isolated "wooded country" as late as 1796,[63] but on the fertile land in and around Smith's Clove agriculture had become a very "profitable employment" by 1779.[64] The western portion of Rockland had become quite industrial by 1820; the Ramapo iron works, gray and red sandstone quarries at New City and Blauvelt, cotton cloth and twine mills at Sloatsburg, and an assortment of nail manufactories and flour and sawmills elsewhere all attested to a diversified economic base.

What James Percival said of the nation's growth in this postwar era applies directly to the Hudson Valley: "we are to no longer remain plain and simple republics of farmers. . . . we are fast becoming a great nation, with great commerce, manufactories, population, wealth, luxuries."[65]

The regional landscape had rebounded from the war and the scars upon the woodlands would soon be healed and shrouded in what was almost immediately regarded as a rich and profound "Revolutionary heritage." Population in most cases still shunned the "untillable" highlands and uplands of Rockland and Bergen, but below the cliffs and on the lower flanks of the hills competition developed over the use of land. An embryonic recreational pattern was less important in this period than the agricultural-industrial orientation of the river lowlands. Great commerce and its resulting wealth and luxury (soon to be evidenced in estate properties and a class of monied American vacationers) were about to blossom with the completion of the Erie Canal.

Thus, although the river that greeted Lafayette's eyes in

1824 was not radically different from that which he campaigned over in the 1770s, great changes were nevertheless in the making. Quarrying had already tightened its profitable but aesthetically destructive grasp upon the Hudson's western shore.

Chapter 6
The Emerging Scenic
and Economic Landscape
Ambivalence Gives Way to Aesthetics

But we are still too young a nation to have among us . . .
lovers of natural history.
Crèvecoeur, *Voyage dans . . . l'état de New-York . . . ,*
1801.

AFTER THE REVOLUTIONARY War, ideas of art, philosophy, and science, imported from Europe, as well as home-grown nationalism, began to affect images of the New World's landscape held by both foreign travelers and native-born observers. An orderly progression of concepts culminating in an eventual aesthetic landscape is too smooth a scenario. The period is conditioned rather by the co-existence of different tendencies. At least three distinct and inherently contrary approaches were taken to the interpretation of landscape. Many painters thought of, and depicted, landscape with an objective topographic accuracy that denied any aesthetic subjectivity. Some Americans had come under the spell of European landscape concepts but, clinging to older and negative ideas of "mountain gloom," displayed an ambivalence in attitude. And finally, there were the European travelers, many of whom, in the scientist-artist tradition of Alexander von Humboldt, brought the "geography of the aesthetic" to the Hudson's shores.

The Objective Rendition of Topography

Both during and after the Revolution, writers and artists often recorded aspects of landscape in a rather dry, mechanical fashion. Observers were content to document the spread of an agricultural landscape faithfully and unemotionally, noting population increases and diverse industrial activities. These attitudes stemmed from the still-lingering pioneer ethos, which viewed progress and the conquest of nature as something good.

Most Americans, in short, made no attempt to conceive of landscape in aesthetic terms,[1] nor did they have the intellectual hardware to do so. Whether in word or picture, or both, the cooly logical and rationalistic age of Newton, Bacon, and Halley—in effect, "popular utilitarian morality"—still held sway in America. Society related to lithographic scenes of wilderness being subjugated in the name of "pioneer progress."[2]

One senses in many wartime landscapes and regional descriptions feelings of emotional noncommitment. Dominic Serres' "Forcing of the Hudson River Passage" (fig. 12) and other such scenes were done in a militarily precise topographic tradition. While great events are admittedly the subject matter, large segments of landscape (for example, the Palisades) were drawn expertly, but were unexciting in composition.[3] Similarly "placid" landscapes showing military events in the Hudson Valley were drawn by Lord Rawdon and Thomas Davies. While many of the written accounts of the war focus on people and events and make no pretense at describing landscape (e.g. the *Memoires* of Major General Heath and Colonel Tallmedge), others do consider the terrain in detail. The British officers John Simcoe and Frederick MacKenzie both saw action in the Palisades and highland regions, but gave no indication of being at all affected by scenic wonderment or natural beauty.[4]

Figure 12. "The Forcing of the Hudson River Passage" October 9, 1776, by D. Serres
New Jersey Historical Society Iconography

The attitudes of most were probably on a level with the great "amusement" Colonel Putnam's troops had precipitating landslides and bowling over trees on Sugarloaf Mountain by rolling huge boulders down the slopes.[5]

The postwar period in America witnessed a growth of interest in landscape art but, as with the first aquatints and watercolors of Australian scenes, the views were lackluster topographical sketches done by English itinerant artists. As the art historian E. P. Richardson says of this period, "interest in scenery was still . . . closely linked to an interest in topographic views of cities, or of famous 'sites.' "[6]

Huge topographical panoramas executed with an exactitude equal to L'Enfant's View of the highlands[7] also appeared in the New York area in 1795. These painted rolls of canvas, substituting perhaps for the enjoyment of actual travel, offered explicit topographic information in the guise of entertainment. In the first decades of the nineteenth century, one finds views of the

Hudson which may well be accurate as to vegetation and settlement, but which reveal a decided lack of interest in aesthetics.[8]

That works of geographic description based on nonaesthetic objectivity flourished and found a ready market in America in the postwar period is attested to by the popularity of the last great pre-Romantic observer, Jedidiah Morse. A New England Congregational minister and compiler of gazeteers, his publications span the years from 1784 (*Geography Made Easy*) to 1824 (*The Traveller's Guide*). Morse wrote in an era in which the common city dweller and the farmer began to procure much of their world and environmental knowledge from almanacs and gazeteers.[9] Morse's compilations, likely to be found in every schoolhouse and parlor in the republic, were to this era what the "guidebooks" would be to the age of Romanticism. In a sense, Morse's geographies filled a gap between an age of scientism and an age of romanticism that could not have been successfully filled by other forms of writing. He is in fact quite representative of those traditionalists who purveyed the objective topographic description of landscape in early America.[10]

The very popular Morse was probably indicative in his thinking of a population at large not yet acquainted with, or influenced by, general or specific concepts of aesthetics or scenic appreciation. He, as well as other "compilers" such as Elijah Parish and the Reverend David McClure, did describe and enumerate the changes occurring in the actual geographic development of the Hudson Valley. However, given their religious, social, and political prejudices, they (like their artistic contemporaries) were incapable of promoting an aesthetic appreciation of landscape or environment.[11] The potential to develop an aesthetic appreciation was there. The romantic view of nature and man's relationship to it was in fact seized upon by a few Americans, but Morse sought to condemn and vilify "things" European because of the xenophobic excesses of a few biased writers like deWarville and Count Buffon.[12] In an age when others were beginning to feel no guilt in rhapsodizing over the beauties of the Connecticut, St. Lawrence, and Hudson Valleys,

Morse remained the compiler of gazeteer facts, much as the geographers Hakluyt and Cluverius had been two centuries before.[13]

The American Ambivalence

Fortunately for the evolution of aesthetic concept, not everyone reacted in a dispassionately objective manner when confronted with the portrayal of riverscapes and mountain vistas. "With the growing spell of the Romantic movement in the last decade of the [eighteenth] century both foreign visitors and native Americans celebrated with new fervor the esthetic beauties of the American landscape and noted its unique character."[14] Some Americans with what Shepard calls "the subtle orientation," i.e. an awareness and acceptance of the new European modes of environmental thought, were puzzled by a sense of contrary feeling toward the horrors and splendors of nature.[15]

It was the ambivalence that Europeans had felt toward mountain landscape a century before surfacing again in places like the Hudson Valley; if mountains were to be condemned theologically as the work of an anti-God, the satanical "Ruins of a broken world," why were such landscapes beginning to exert an emotional appeal through their vastness and grandeur?[16]

Pre-Romantic concepts of mountain gloom, Old World superstitions of the forest, and puritanically mundane views of nature were dissipated more slowly in the colonies; consequently, there is a time lag apparent between the formulation of landscape theories of the sublime and picturesque and the adaptation of these ideas in America. In *Wilderness and the American Mind* Roderick Nash says that this "double-mindedness" was characteristic of the "ocean of uncertainty" experienced by the more thoughtful Americans:

Romantic enthusiasm for wilderness never seriously challenged the aversion of the pioneer mind. Appreciation, rather, resulted from a momentary relaxation of the dominant antipathy . . . the rhetoric of

appreciation and repulsion [was employed] with equal facility. . . .
Opinion was in a state of transition. While appreciation of wild country
existed, it was seldom unqualified. Romanticism had cleared away
enough of the old assumptions to permit a favorable attitude toward
wilderness without entirely eliminating the instinctive fear and hostility
a wilderness condition had produced.[17]

This ambivalence produced uncertainty as to how one
should respond to landscape. Archibald Robertson, Lieutenant-
General of the Royal Engineers, was the English embodiment of
such ambivalence. The diary and sketches of this "soldier, artist,
and gentle soul" reveal a topographic engineer's approach to detailed geographic accuracy, combined with a budding romanticism. While his diary entries for the "Bergen shore" and the
"Highlands" convey little that could be interpreted as aesthetic
awareness, Robertson, as seen in his sketch pads and canvases,
received instruction in the Italian school of landscape:

His hills and valleys, passes and peaks sweep over the sheet with a vigor
and directness and precision that come from the eye of the engineer.
They are [also] expressed with a charm that tells of an artist joined to
the technical man in unusual and most delightful fusion.[18]

This "most delightful fusion" however had resulted in topogra-
phic-military sketches of the Palisades, Brooklyn Heights, and
the Dunderberg improbably peopled with reclining, idling, pastoralists in flowing gowns and feathered bonnets.[19]

Even in the rather improbable arena of wartime conflict, a
few American military men also found time to pay homage to
the Hudson's finer aspects. Lieutenant-Colonel Tench Tilghman,
a plantation aristocrat's son who served as secretary and aide to
Washington, recorded in his diary the "romantic prospect" of the
relatively unsettled Palisade shore. In the militarily strategic
highlands, he found that "sailing thro' these mountains by
moonlight was a most beautiful sight."[20] General Parsons, com-
mander of the First Connecticut Brigade, stated the dual attraction of the region:

to a contemplative mind which delighted in a lonely retreat from the world where it could rest upon the magnificence of nature, this spot, with its inaccessible mountains covered with deep piles of snow, was "as beautiful as Sharon;" but to one who loved the society of the world, the place presented a prospect nearly allied to the shades of death.[21]

Others equated an essentially dreadful and hideous nature with romantic notions of scenery in a way that would not become popular until the days of Cole and Willis. To nineteenth-century romanticists, it was a perfectly logical association, but to Americans in this period it must have seemed strange indeed to find themselves ambivalently juxtaposing scenic beauty with landscape horror. Charles Carroll found the craggy and cutover highlands to be not unpleasant: "The country . . . has a wild and romantic appearance; the hills are almost perpendicularly steep, and covered with rocks. . . . These highlands present a number of romantic views."[22]

On two occasions at least Army surgeon James Thacher related the sublime and terrifying aspects of the Hudson's landscape; in the highlands opposite West Point (in June 1778) he observed "hideous mountains and dreary forests, not a house in view. . . . Having reached the summit, we contemplated with amazement the sublime scene which opened to our view. . . . huge mountains, rocky cliffs, and venerable forests, in one confused mass."[23]

Thacher's continued confusion and amazement took him through "singular and romantic landscapes" in other parts of the valley, always aware that savages, beasts, and Tories lurked among the wild and prodigious mountains. The vocabulary is pre-Romantic, and yet, almost impulsively, aesthetically pleasing. Only in a fusion such as this could the picturesque qualities of the valley have been actually enriched by the "fire and smoke" and the "roar and thunder" of war.[24]

Before Tilghman and Thacher very few Americans were in a position to accept the Hudson Valley for its scenic merit, and it is all the more remarkable that the two writers did so in time of war. As might be expected, their ambiguous feelings were

Figure 13. West Point in the Highlands
TOP. "The Plain at West Point at the Moment of Exercise"
Jacques Gerard Milbert, *Picturesque Itinerary of the Hudson River and Travels in North America,* Paris, 1828–29.
BOTTOM. "View of West Point," Anon. 1830.
Garbisch Collection.

beginning to be echoed by others. Artists now depicted scenes of
the Potomac and Passaic Falls, of the river cliffs around Quebec
City, and views along the Susquehanna; all were executed with
dramatic atmospheric effects and were populated with romanticized Indians and Old World shepherds.

Henry Livingston's "The Steep Rocks on the West Side of
Hudson's River" (1791) shows the Palisades with both topographic precision and a picturesque quality (e.g. birds soaring
overhead and sloops gracefully plying the river).[25] As an accompanying text explains, such scenery "excites admiration in the
most superficial stranger" and is "not beheld without emotion."
The same interplay between rather barren, angular, and exaggerated landforms toned down by the presence of softly drawn Indian canoeists (no longer forest heathens, but symbols of the
New Romanticism) and well-dressed provincial idlers appears as
well in other works.[26]

No American who had closely observed the Hudson Valley
appears to convey so fine a sense of ambivalence toward the
region's landscape as the Connecticut theologian, poet, and
clergyman Timothy Dwight. As chaplain in Parson's Brigade,
Dwight campaigned in the highlands and was stationed at West
Point. As president of Yale from 1795 to his death in 1815, he
traveled extensively during the summers, eventually publishing a
2000-page, four-volume work entitled *Travels in New England
and New York*. A collaborator and friend of Morse in his geographies, Dwight wrote with much the same purpose in mind as
Morse—i.e., to right "the misrepresentations, which foreigners,
either through error or design, had published of my native country." [27]

But more importantly, Dwight, unlike Morse, appears to
have possessed the intellectual and emotional attitudes necessary
for an aesthetic awareness. His "ability to hold on to old-
fashioned Orthodoxy with one hand while [keeping] the other
one on the pulse of the new age" facilitated a blending of the iron
dictates of basically anti-aesthetic Puritanism with emotions
unthought of by his New England contemporaries.[28]

Dwight worked out his ambivalencies in the Hudson Valley;

he admitted that he expected to find the highlands frightening and revolting upon his first visit to the valley: "I had been taught to expect a hideous passage over these mountains. To the inhabitants of the city of New York, who had conversed with me on the subject, it had appeared very formidable. We found it otherwise." [29]

He chided others for being so destitute of "that taste for the beauties of nature which is one of the principal sources of enjoyment in the present world," and yet seemed unsure at times that "wild and awful" mountains were all that pleasant. While he lauded the Palisade "green stones" for their unrivaled magnificence, his most extraordinarily emotive passages were reserved for the highlands; an emotional duality plagued his mind when atop Sugarloaf Mountain in 1778:

From the summit we were presented with an extensive and interesting prospect. . . . The point of view was remarkably happy, the mountain being so situated as to bring within our reach the greatest number of objects in the surrounding region. . . . there was not a cheerful object within our horizon. Everything which we beheld was majestic, solemn, wild, and melancholy. [30]

The Scientist-Artist Tradition

It is prerequisite to an understanding of the contribution made by European travelers to the growth of an aesthetic landscape in the Hudson Valley to realize that the period 1785–1824 was America's inaugural epoch of that renaissance-type observer, the "scientist-artist."

Only in the late-eighteenth century did beliefs about the world based upon fearful and superstitious attitudes "dissipate through scientific inquiry." [31] It was this line of inquiry into the condition of the natural world and the causes of natural phenomena that led scientists toward both a greater understanding and appreciation of the environment. The great eighteenth-century scientific revolution, as Leo Marx (*Machine in the Garden*) has ob-

served, lent itself well to those natural philosophers and historians with an inclination toward artistic or poetic emotions. The
expanded involvement of geologists, botanists, surveyors, as-
tronomers, and traveling collectors and compilers of specimens
and facts, led to a more familiar perspective from which to view
nature, a perspective from which "the sinister motifs generally
associated with wild country became increasingly untenable." [32]

Bernard Smith says of reaction to reports of explorations
from Oceania that the European public in the period from 1760
to 1830 demanded and expected scientific documentation to be
well illustrated with artwork: Tahitian dancing girls and exotic
scenery for the public back home, and accurate botanical sketches
for the Royal Society.[33] The European imagination was thus
nourished, great strides were made in the natural sciences, and a
marriage of empirical observation and measurement with picturesque and sublime landscapes was created.

The person best exemplifying the naturalist-traveler with a
"picturesqueness of treatment" in this period, and one who
would in later decades have a profound effect upon the romantic
portrayal of the Hudson Valley, was Alexander Von Humboldt.
The manner in which he presented the encyclopedic results of his
travels, "not only a graphic description, but an imaginative conception of the physical world," [34] was already influencing others.
By 1810, largely on the basis of *Voyage aux regions equinoxiales du
Nouveau Continent, fait en 1799–1804,* he was perhaps the most
famous man in Europe save for Napoleon.[35] Humboldt's *Ansich-
ten der Natur* (1808) is a perfect example of the author's (and the
generation's) attempt to integrate the trends of "Scientificism"
and the Enlightenment with those of Romanticism, "the emotions of the mind and the phenomena of the external world." [36]

The tradition of the scientist-artist and the work of Von
Humboldt have a great relevance to the attitudes and works of
American scientist-writers, who were coming into closer contact
with the wilder and more remote regions of the Hudson Highlands, the Catskills, and the mountains of New England. A type
of individual was evolving who would later be personified by
such "naturalists" as John Muir, J. J. Audubon, and John Bur-

roughs. The "artist-naturalist" came to represent the close proximity between landscape appreciation and science.[37]

Probably no American better symbolizes the strength that
this generation found through an accommodation of art and
science than Charles Willson Peale. His Philadelphia museum of
the natural sciences opened in 1786 as an adjunct to his portrait
gallery, and although he himself never partook of a strong romantic taste, the "interactions and harmonious correspondances"
between art and nature portrayed in his museum, along with his
"willingness to explore the relationships between art and
science" in a Hudson River genre scene such as *Exhuming the First
American Mastodon* (1806–8),[38] serve as a bridge from the age of
reason to that of romanticism.

Many English and French travelers to the Hudson Valley reported in this tradition of science complemented by art; this
manner of writing gave credence to a new stimulation found in
the relationship between landscape and pure aesthetics. While this
approach had been only recently established "out in the colonies"
such as America and Australia, it was by post-Revolutionary
times a normal part of the intellectual baggage carried about by
knowledgeable Europeans. The growth of scenic conception and
the application of specific aesthetic concepts in the Hudson Valley owes much to this tradition.

The Hudson Through the Eyes of the European

The value of analyzing travel literature, and especially literature from this period which often relates aesthetic insights to the
"epochs" and "harmonies" of the natural sciences, has been
stated by Clarence Glacken and others.[39] There is an almost
overwhelming availability of such literature as it pertains to the
lower Hudson Valley because New York City—and less
frequently Philadelphia or Boston—was the main port of arrival
and jump-off point for the "grand tour," an itinerary which took
the traveler by sloop and later steamboat up the Hudson to the
canal projects in the Champlain and Mohawk Valleys. After sat-

isfying their curiosity as to the falls at Cohoes and the springs at Saratoga, the voyagers would journey either west through the lavishly advertised Genesee Country and to the falls at Niagara, or proceed north through the Lake George–Lake Champlain region, arriving at Montreal and Quebec City (the Citadel, Montmorency Falls, etc.). In either case, an "exciting" jaunt over the rapids of the St. Lawrence would afford the travelers the advantage of seeing both the Niagara frontier and the cities of the St. Lawrence before arriving back at New York via the Hudson Valley and, after 1823, a stayover perhaps at the Catskill Mountain House.[40]

Consequently, the lengthy inventories of English and French (and occasionally Dutch, German, and Italian) travel accounts compiled by Frank Monaghan, Allan Nevins, and J. L. Mesick are immense repositories of Hudson River materials.[41] The Hudson drew many English tourists before 1824, but unfortunately their accounts, reflecting social and political moods of the day, are more noteworthy for their nationalistic excesses.[42] Others, such as Peter Stryker ("Journal of a Trip from New York to Saratoga and Return, 1788"), were given to landscape description, but he regrettably slept through the Hudson's passage as far as Poughkeepsie and apparently came back through the highlands at night, precluding any scenic response to the mountains.[43]

In what may be taken as representative of the Englishmen who did have the opportunity and background to remark upon the river's beauties, Joseph Lancaster found the Hudson: "a very impressive specimen of the extended scale on which Nature rears her majestic head." Lancaster also stated that his soul was much struck with the grandeur of highland scenery and the "basaltic colonnade" of the Palisades.[44] John Maude, a young commoner whom Van Zandt claims to have been devoid of the common English prejudices, found the highland passage "highly romantic and beautiful." [45] In the case of John Lambert's travels through the region in 1807, there is the impression that he had absorbed well the standard expressions and phrases of aesthetic theory:

the scenes that presented themselves along the shores of the Hudson were in some places of that grand and romantic description, and in others so beautifully picturesque, that they could not fail to interest the spectator at any season of the year. The river affords some of the noblest landscapes and scenery that are to be found in any part of North America. Nature and art have both contributed to render its shores at once sublime and beautiful.[46]

The French travelers too had European social biases, along with a mundane preoccupation with such things as the deplorable conditions of linens and sleeping accommodations in hotels and way stations. But in contrast with the British, the French colored their writings with an often excessive bias in favor of Americans and things American. This bias was probably in part an apologetic reaction to the harsh treatment accorded America in the period before the Revolution by Count Buffon and others, and in part a vibrant curiosity about the "New Democracy" which they felt they had had a hand in creating. More than a few "travellers" had a decidedly positive reaction to the American scene. As political exiles or forced emigrés from the Caribbean, America was the only alternative to the guillotine.

Despite the diverse backgrounds, academic training, and purposes of these French writers,[47] they exhibit a common train of thought and a distinctively similar manner of presentation. Among the scores of "vues et souvenirs de l'Amerique du Nord" and "Voyages Pittoresques dans l'Amerique septentrionale" there is incredible repetition and what must be judged outright plagiarism.[48] Many of the writers were aristocrats who had personal contacts with each other, and therefore learned in advance what was worth seeing, and what regions should be visited in America.

Generally, these travel essays also have in common that remarkably effective synthesizing ability to relate matters of philosophy, history, natural history, geology, and landscape art. It is again that combination of scientist and artist that renders the work of men like Milbert, Crèvecoeur, and Volney so valuable.[49]

Hector St. Jean de Crèvecoeur and Jacques Gerard Milbert, both of whom developed an intimate knowledge of the Hudson Valley, are no doubt the best French sources for insight into the evolving concern for aesthetics and conservation. Crèvecoeur, best known for the sociopolitical essay *Letters from an American Farmer,* had been Montcalm's cartographer during the French and Indian War and later worked as a professional surveyor in parts of New York State and Vermont. In the 1790s he became a naturalized citizen, settling down to the life of a gentleman farmer in Orange County near the highlands. He published his most provocative *Voyage dans la Haute Pennsylvanie et dans l'état de New-York* in 1801. In this "insiders" work, Crèvecoeur made some very practical observations on the nature of the soil's fertility, the directional growth of the New York frontier, and the relationship between land values and road and rail construction. Most compelling is his concern for the disruption of natural "harmonies" and the application of romantic concept to the Hudson Valley.[50] To him, the Palisades, the Tors, and the highlands were "the magic spots" of the Hudson, and these features were already threatened by "man's industry." His beautiful description of the Palisade shoreline is tempered by the presence of houses along the base. Throughout the region he deplored the extinction of wildlife and especially "the distressing habit of sometimes treating trees as enemies." [51]

A regard for woodland conservation on the farmlands of Orange County was largely economic: "The second generation shall regret bitterly that their fathers destroyed so much. This has already been proven in several regions of New Jersey and Connecticut where for lack of wood, the value of land has diminished considerably." But his anxiety over the destruction of the highland forest was aesthetically motivated as well: "If posterity conserves these beautiful woods, it may well enjoy centuries of precious advantages. . . . this may well happen, since for a long time, the whole claim has been the property of several individuals extremely interested in conservation of these forests." [52] He did not specify who these individuals were, but it appears he was referring to the wealthy landowners, individuals who, much to the prophetic wisdom of Crèvecoeur, did contribute to the preservation of the highland forest a hundred years later.

Jacques Milbert had been professor of drawing at the Ecole des Mines, geographer on Baudin's southern hemispheric expedition in 1800, and official "government traveler" to the Pyrenees and Alps; he was a naturalist, a portrait and landscape painter, and was well versed in geology and botany (a "correspondant" of the King's Garden). With this considerable background, he traveled through the eastern United States between 1815 and 1823, recording his impressions in the three-volume *Itineraire Pittoresque du Fleuve Hudson* (Paris, 1828–29). He probably did more to popularize the landscape of the Hudson Valley than any other individual before William Guy Wall (*Hudson River Portfolio*, 1820–25), an artist who, significantly, placed a heavy reliance on the 54 lithographs contained in Milbert's volume, several of which he himself had in fact done.

As had Crèvecoeur and others, Milbert brought to a nation still dominated by the pioneer ethos (he watched the frontier being advanced "with axes, fire and even explosives") [53] a European concern for endangered or misused features of the landscape. Examples of some of the environmental conditions he deplored include excessive and uncontrolled forest clearing by settlers in the Hudson Valley and Adirondacks, sawmill and slaughterhouse wastes polluting both the upper and lower Hudson, overkill of the passenger pigeon and other species. And he cited the need for government intervention to protect the remaining forests from "ignorant and selfish settlers." He was indeed "a conservationist far ahead of his times." [54]

Such a man as this brought his insights and aesthetic proclivities to bear upon the landscape features of the Hudson Valley. In a manner of observation reflective of Von Humboldt, whose influences he acknowledged, Milbert analyzed the geology, botany, and animal life of the Palisades' "Iron Shoreline," and then surrendered to romantic reverie: "when the sun drops behind it [Palisades ridge], the river banks and surrounding landscape don a sombre hue. For a time the crowns of the great trees atop are still golden, but soon night tones prevail everywhere." [55]

Milbert traveled through the region of Haverstraw Bay, sketching Hook Mountain and the Tors. In the highlands, where the steamboat captain slowed down to allow the passengers a greater enjoyment of the sublimities, he picturesquely wrote of

the storm clouds gathering about the Dunderberg while "dol-
phins" and sturgeons churned the waters below, and an eagle
soared through the water gap. Deep into the highlands above
Anthony's Nose, the scenic landscape and man's ignoble designs
clashed head-on: "I should have thought that such a spot, the
very picture of chaos, was inaccessible, but a telescope showed a
woodcutter, armed with his destructive axe, who was attacking
the base of one of these vigorous trees, children of far-distant
centuries." [56] Milbert could hardly ignore the reduction of the
forest and attempts to cultivate the highlands, but what was
progress to others was even at this early date a desecration upon
"these now-benign and now awe-inspiring mountains," so majestically cut by "the Hudson, King of Rivers." [57]

The Hudson's Emerging Romantic Landscape

As has been seen, those who looked at and recorded their
impressions of the Hudson Valley and its highland landforms in
the years after the Revolution did so under the influence of either
American nationalism or European-derived romanticism, or
both. For many, this caused uncertainties in attitudes toward the
regional landscape. The Age of Reason was giving way to the
more subjective feelings of the not-yet-flowering Age of Romanticism. As Charles Sanford said (*Quest for America, 1810–1824*),
national feelings "tended" toward the romantic, but it was "a
restrained, controlled Romanticism," unlike the deeply emotional brand of the decades to come.[58]

Overall, there are several key constituents involved in this
transition which are illustrated better than anywhere by changing
environmental evaluations of the Hudson Valley. Elements of
thought were established at this time which became the corner-
stone of the nineteenth-century interpretation of American landscape. These ideas would eventually lead to the preservation and
park movement both in the valley and nationally.

The major constituents incorporated into the concept of the
emerging landscape aesthetic were the use of nationalism, the

"Doctrine" of historical association, a popular interest in geologic "curiosities" and concepts, and carefully formulated European aesthetic tenets of the "sublime" and "picturesque." These factors began to react with economically exploitative and destructive land-use patterns, sniping and harassing at first and at last emerging triumphant.

Nationalism

Expressions of nationalist feeling took many forms in the young Republic: protectionist tariffs and the related rise of native industry; alternately friendly or cool attitudes toward the British and French, the spatial coalescence of the nation through internal improvements such as turnpikes and canals, the election of 1820 and the "Era of Good Feeling," and the evolution of a distinctively American iconography in the arts and literature. The work of Jedidiah Morse, 80 percent of which was regional description of the states, cannot be disassociated from the flow of nationalism.[59]

Others chose to associate pride in nation with the quality of the landscape itself. The grandeur of the mountains and river valleys, and unmatchable natural abnormalities such as Niagara and Virginia's Natural Bridge led to favorable comparisons with tamer, more "restrained" European landscape features. The nation, through its newspapers, the growing number of "scenery albums," and its own writers and artists, was not only becoming defensive and sensitive about its own scenery, but was growing increasingly proud of it in a decidedly nationalistic manner.[60]

Along the Hudson, canal construction, the rise of port cities such as New York, Newburgh, and Kingston, and increased river commerce and shoreline industry such as the quarries and brickyards were stirring and visible evidences of the way in which the riverscape could be altered by the forces of an economy fired by nationalism. Agricultural domestication and experimentation were seen as further aspects of the nation's and the valley's achievements.

Statements by De Witt Clinton and others associating pride in Hudson River landscapes with nationalism are legion. Washington Irving, although an imitator of and admirer of the European mode, took offense at how his lordly Hudson, with its "fairy mountains" was subjected to the "illiberal spirit of ridicule" so common among English travelers. But he had much faith in the material and spiritual potentialities of a region like the Hudson, and saw no real injury resulting from ill-directed prejudices and jealousies: "The tissues of misrepresentations attempted to be woven around us are like cobwebs woven around the limbs of an infant giant." [61]

When travellers such as Montulé and Milbert rode the Hudson River steamboats, the paddlewheel boxes of which were decorated with patriotic motifs, they were amazed at the "national enthusiasm for these magnificent [river] scenes" that magnetized American passengers at the boat railings; citizens of the republic, each viewing their personal struggles and achievements as a part of the national historical drama, were fortified in their love of country by the Hudson's scenery, and their conversation "had always for its subject the excellence of their country. . . . Although this national spirit, which is nurtured by the newspapers, is a near relative of conceit, it is very beneficial for a people. . . . the Romans, too, had this pride." [62]

Associations with History

The "Doctrine of Association," or the idea that landscape was only scenic when associated with and complemented by the evidences of man, had become an important element of aesthetic concept throughout eighteenth-century Europe. Thus, traveling through Syria and Egypt in 1811 was an aesthetic experience for the Frenchman Volney because of that region's antiquity: "The history of times past strongly present[ed] itself to my thoughts." [63] But with this doctrine came the tendency to deny absolute or intrinsic beauty in the landscape; this had serious repercussions when applied to America: "There were many other charges that could be brought against American scenery . . . [but] none was quite so unanswerable as this single charge of a general historical deficiency."[64] There was in essence, as Lowenthal observed, "a virtual absence of man's artifacts" which "appalled viewers."[65]

This presented areas like the Hudson Valley and the vast and empty Great Plains with a seemingly insurmountable conceptual problem.[66] How could landscape features such as Hook and Storm King Mountains compete with similar features in Europe, where so many centuries had imprinted the land itself with an accumulated wealth of historical drama from which sympathies and feelings would spring? Because this was the New World, and because the Hudson Valley had been developed late and highland areas not at all, the region lacked the vital ingredient of historical association. There were in short no ancient ruins, no "sombre dungeons and dilapidated castles" of another time.[67]

In the mountainous regions of the Hudson Valley, where not even the evidences of an agricultural landscape were present, the dilemma was overcome in several ways. The concept of the noble savage as a form of primitivism (the greater the contact with nature, the better you become; the savage, the wild man of nature, thus exudes nobility, strength and hardiness) became somewhat popular and allowed the landscape to be peopled in word and print with gallant neoclassical later-day Roman warriors of the forest. It gave a sense of history to the region, but obviously did not sit that well with a population so recently conditioned by the pioneer spirit. The romanticization of the primitive appealed largely to gentlemen of class such as Chateaubriand, Freneau, and Cooper and would enjoy greater, more universal acceptance in later years.[68]

Irving on the other hand (along with the artist John Quidor) chose to endow historically deficient landscapes with imaginary characters. It was a perfectly legitimate alteration of the doctrine to contrive people and events for places that had none. In Irving's case, the legends of Sleepy Hollow, the Dunderberg, and the Catskills were taken so seriously that they became a part of almost every historical account thereafter; his fantasizing of the valley has become so embedded in the American consciousness that to this day fictionalized portrayal "seems as real as the facts."[69]

However, the most commonly employed stratagem in the creation of a historical-romantic landscape was not to reincarnate or glorify Indians and Dutchmen, but to play upon the sympathies and feelings associated with places and events in the most recent and traumatic of common experiences—the Revolutionary War.

Throughout this period there was a constant striving to perpetuate "the sense of the Revolution." Local historiographic writing, the canonization of wartime heroes, and the commotion occasioned by Lafayette's return to the Hudson Valley in 1824, were powerful iconographic forces that served to nourish a young nationalism. The portraits of American generals in Peale's museum and Trumbull's historical series (Bunker Hill, Trenton, Princeton, etc.) executed in the late-eighteenth century did much the same in the field of art. Moreover, these same strivings encouraged the sanctification of places such as West Point, Stony Point, Fort Lee, Fort Washington, the Popolopen Forts and Bloody Pond, and Constitution Island. Such holy grounds as these fulfilled the romantic need for historical association.

The "sense of an interesting transaction," especially when associated with the Revolution, was found by Timothy Dwight to lend an air of emotional involvement to the landscape. This quickly led to the romanticization of that landscape. The speed at which this mental transformation occurred in the Hudson Valley was remarkable. Chastellux, for example, viewed the ravages of war and the ruined highland iron furnaces as romantic expressions of landscape even while the fighting was still in progress. Dwight surveyed the "melancholy picture of destruction" at Fort Clinton only one year after its fall to Sir Henry Clinton.[70] By 1800 every British traveler indulged a few tears for "poor Major André" at places along the river's course associated with his capture and execution. And it wasn't long before the ruined battlements of Fort Putnam became the centerpiece of a "sublime and magnificant" landscape; this part of the highlands was not, as a matter of conceptual importance, cutover or burnt-over semi-agricultural land, but "historic ground" "that had been trodden by Washington [and] was his favorite spot."[71]

Interest in Geologic Curiosities and Concepts

The great popular concern shown in geological "curiosities" and geological theorization also stimulated a romantic awareness. In Europe "the layman and the poet in the eighteenth-century were geology conscious"—and followed learned debates on the relationship between the creation of landforms and the role of God. Romantic tours of caverns were immensely popular ("The Grand Tour of the Subterranean World"), artificial caves and grottos were planted on the estates of the gentry, and scientists wrote poetic tributes to the geological irregularities of the landscape.[72]

In America, achievements in the sciences prompted a widespread interest in earthquakes, mountain building, and the unearthing of fossil remains such as Peale's mastodon. Jefferson attempted to classify mastodon bones, Lesueur and McClure completed cross-sections of Appalachian sedimentary beds, and Beltrami pondered the origin of oxbow lakes (earthquakes, he concluded). The milieu engendered by this kind of research enabled travelers and scientists to examine geological events in such a way that God and nature were placed in a closer aesthetic proximity than Puritanical thinking had ever allowed.

In the Hudson Valley, the geological nature of the Palisades formation drew the attention of Milbert and others, while Charles Carroll speculated as to whether Anthony's Nose "had experienced some violent convulsion from subterranean fire."[73] The question posed most often involved the sublime aspect of the highland gorge. To what tumultuous forces of creation did it owe its existence? The generally accepted conclusion, subscribed to by both Dwight and Chastellux, was that this "most magnificant picture" was formed by a body of water that lay to the north of this mountain chain, forcing a rupture through the highland passage in some former age.[74]

Theories of the Sublime and Picturesque

Of all the descriptive terms used in quoted materials in this study and of all the terms used by writers and travelers to describe their reaction to the Hudson Valley none are more repeated and significant than "sublime" and "picturesque." The two terms had "a formal meaning that is far removed from the popular usage of today. In the nineteenth-century the words were governed by the academic doctrines of an established school of philosophy [the so-called 'Scotch school of psychological aesthetics'], and were two of the most important concepts in the universal philosophy of romanticism."[75]

Popularized and perfected by William Gilpin (*Remarks on Forest Scenery* etc.), Uvedale Price (*Essays on the Picturesque*), and essayists such as Joseph Addison (*Pleasures of the Imagination*), the idea that all natural phenomena were either sublime or picturesque (or beautiful) derives of earlier writings by Edmund Burke.[76]

The concept of sublimity, "the chief aesthetic concern of the age," was "one of the most popular catchwords, and it was used on every occasion as a touchstone for aesthetic evaluation."[77] Sublimity was said to be present when a landscape reflected the more vehement or violent aspects of nature. Storms, thunderous cataracts, rushing white water, great winds, mysterious caves, and a jumbled confusion of natural objects, vast and expansive panoramas of "cosmic" sky, ocean, or plain—any combination of these could generate sublimity. They had the power to overwhelm the senses with sheer terror and excite a vision of the Divine Creation.

The picturesque, in contrast, was keyed to a lower emotional threshold. The picturesque required that a landscape be irregular in detail, rough, coarse in surface texture, variegated in color and shading, or perhaps complex and intricate in pattern. "The picturesque will be found always to depend upon the opposite conditions of matter—irregularity, and a partial want of proportion and symmetry." Picturesqueness could also include things which were simply exotic or distant, but in no sense would it summon up "what is formal, geometrical, anticipated, too evidently planified or directed."[78]

These were the hoped-for and admirable qualities of scenery that European travelers looked for. As the use of the terms sublime and picturesque became common in Europe, so too were they applied to the American landscape. The acceptance of this body of landscape theory (and design) in the late eighteenth and early nineteenth centuries marks new beginnings in American social thought. Slowly, picturesque designs for country estates, pleasure gardens, riding paths, and "ornamental" farms emerged from the literary and philosophical sourcebooks of aesthetic theory.

While the transformation from theory to practice—the actual creation of a cultured picturesque landscape within a sublimely endowed environment—reached a much greater degree of expression in the 1840s and 1850s with Downing and Willis, the evocation of "a wild and awful sublimity" in the highlands and beneath the Palisades had already become fashionable with writers like Dwight, Crèvecoeur, and Milbert.[79] It was important for Americans that landscapes like those along the Hudson were interpreted not as picturesque but as sublime. Accuracy of detail and picturesqueness were acceptable in man's creations, but had to be reinforced by the power of natural, though man-interpreted, sublimity. The tamer and more sentimentalized qualities of the picturesque were equated with "the supposedly effete, artificial European nations," whereas wild and tempestuous landscapes in America were testimonials of New World superiority.[80]

By the 1820s, volumes of aquatints depicting merely picturesque scenery did not sit well with Americans. For the same reason, Trumbull's picturesque "View of Niagara" (1807) met with little success: "To a public that viewed the American landscape as untamed, as an unknown quantity, Trumbull presented a carefully balanced painting that reinforced the eighteenth century ideas of benevolent order in the universe."[81] The towering mountains and the craggy precipices of the highlands, better in this sense not to have been greatly altered by the presence of a cultural landscape, were thereafter imprinted with the sublime.

In these specific ways, then, the emergence of a scenically conceived landscape was underway—along with the development of land for economic purposes. The era of simple objective topographic description had waned. Exhorted by the example of visiting European scientist-artists, the conceptual ambivalences of Americans were rapidly colored by elements not so much of the Old World picturesque, but of the raw and mighty sublimely romanticized landscape. Along the Hudson, hallowed ground of war and corridor to the New World, this aesthetic chemistry worked best.

Part 4

Portents of Future Conflict

Romanticism and Economics
Before the Civil War

BY THE CIVIL War the mountain regions of the lower Hudson Valley, never very significant agriculturally, witnessed rural abandonment and the subsequent reversion of many acres to brush, or to a close approximation of the original vegetation. This transition corresponds in some areas to the coming of resorts and estates. The elaboration of the mountain house tradition, and the siting of villas on cliffs and hilltops, associated the Hudson with all that was conceptualized as being romantic and aesthetic in the American environment. Simultaneously, the characterization of New York City as evil led to a further infatuation with the life of rural simplicity and virtue supposedly found beyond the outer fringe of the urban landscape. The sorry, shoddy, immorally wicked ways of city life were popularized in such works as *The Belle of the Bowery* (1846) and *The B'Hoys of New York* (1849).

The increasingly serious effects of commerce, industry,

railroads, and steamboats—consumptive use of the wood supply, the reduction of rural isolation, the subjugation of man to machine—induced undercurrents of pessimism in an otherwise optimistic age. The more sentient individuals could not ignore the manifestations of what the society regarded as progress: the mills and brickyards, the deserted farmscape, and the substitution of the educated traveler by hordes of "tourists." The skepticism of Cole, Willis, and Bryant among others led to an awareness of the limits and fragilities of the land.

Popular sentiment toward landscape had not progressed much beyond the juvenile awe occasioned by the boulder-rolling antics of Putnam's troops. A similar callous interest seems apparent in the 1860s from the popularity of views depicting the ironclad monitor *Passaic* "Trying her Guns at the Palisades" (fig.14).

Figure 14. The Passaic *Trying Her Large Gun at the Palisades.*
Harper's Weekly, Nov. 29, 1862. Courtesy of the New-York Historical Society, New York City.

Meanwhile, romanticism had become the catchword of the era for the socially knowledgeable; they viewed mountain landscape with a European conception, reinterpreted with an American slant. Stunning highland scenery was closely associated with pride in nation. The populace was urged by artists and newspaper editors to dwell upon the richness and uniqueness of the Hudson and such rivers as the Connecticut and Mississippi. Not only was the Hudson chauvinistically regarded as at least the equivalent of anything Europe could offer, but it also contained geological curiosities that, when speculated upon, drew the traveler into a closer union with the cosmos and the infinity of time. Furthermore, the landscape served as a catalyst for a continually renewed spirit of reverence for people and events that shaped the nation's history.

An interesting subsidiary element to romantic concept was the fascination for ruins, and for what they added to a heightened sense of aesthetic awareness. In ink and paint, formulas for expressing the complex emotions of the sublime and picturesque were constructed and vigorously applied. A sense of urgency marked this expression, for many despondently realized that urbanization and technology were obliterating both the wildly sublime, and the picturesquely bucolic.

Chapter 7
The Tentacles of the City Reach North
Steam, Rail, Quarries, and Suburbia Transform the Valley

Transportation is the key to the development of the political, social, and economic history of New York in the years between 1825 and 1860. . . . . Every town—indeed every farmer—felt the impact of the changes brought about by the extension of canals, railroads, and highways.
David Ellis, *Landlords and Farmers*, p. 244.

BETWEEN THE MID 1820s and the Civil War, American culture felt the full impact of nationalism, secessionism, and romanticism; these "isms" profoundly affected the thoughts and conceptions that Americans (and Europeans) harbored about the land and their relationship to it. In the more practical terms of industrial and leisure-oriented activities, these same political and social thought patterns contributed to the reshaping of the landscape itself. Nationalism especially, and its "American System" of internal improvements—with its vision of a vigorous and rising West—stimulated canal and turnpike fever and massive investment in steamboat navigation. Regional rivalries and the profit motive were no doubt equally important in applying the lessons of the industrial revolution, but the result was the same: an era in which environmental patterns were "very closely associated with radical improvements in transportation."[1]

By the 1830s, as a result of transportation innovations and improvements, the Hudson Valley had become one of the "busiest thoroughfare[s] in America. . . . a burgeoning region of country estates and summer resorts."[2] The opening of the Erie Canal in 1825, construction of which had begun in 1818, advanced the growth of New York City at the expense of Montreal and played havoc with established economic patterns; it also directly altered the prosperity and mode of Hudson Valley agriculture. Period lithographs and watercolors invariably depict a lower valley jammed with sloops and steamboats. Commerce was brisk, most river towns flourished, and the lower valley was brought within the industrial and commercial sphere of New York City. First the steamboat, and then the railroad shrank distance and time, and the valley was made more accessible to the pursuits of leisure. Residences, resorts, and recreation consequently became more important. Washington Irving and others of a romantic turn of mind resented the subjugation of the valley to industrial civilization, but the rail lines and telegraph wires were an integral and irrevocable part of the landscape by the 1850s.

Those activities most characteristic of the lower valley, and those influenced by the changes induced upon time and distance by technology, were farming, steamboat navigation, and railroad construction, and the establishment of estates and resorts. Each of these activities influenced, and were in turn influenced by, the process of landscape conceptualization.

Farming

The Erie Canal substantially altered patterns of agriculture in the Hudson Valley. Parallel situations were created in parts of

Long Island and New England, where the canal destroyed agricultural prosperity and caused land to be abandoned.[3] The most immediate effect along the Hudson and in adjacent regions was a westward migration of the wheat belt to the upstate area between Lakes Onondaga and Erie. The Genesee Country replaced the Hudson as "the nation's granary," as wheat reached eastern markets through the canal. The Genesee Valley "yielded more than twice as much wheat per acre as the worn out . . . fields in the Hudson and Mohawk Valleys."[4] Hudson Valley agriculture, especially wheat production, had been in trouble before the advent of the canal, because of soil exhaustion and insect infestation. Perhaps the 1820s should be regarded as the culmination of what would have eventually led to the elimination of wheat anyway. The historian David Ellis speculates upon a modest prosperity tempered by "uncertainty in the Valley," a time during which the land was being worked toward exhaustion with little regard for the loss of soil fertility and little understanding of crop rotation and drainage requirements. Ulysses Hedrick in his *History of Agriculture* agrees that there was widespread agrarian negligence and ignorance: "very little attention was paid to enriching the land. Manure was neglected. . . . there were no commercial fertilizers. . . . When land became too poor for profitable cultivation, it was [simply] abandoned."[5] These difficulties were compounded by periodic blights of rust, mildew, smut, grasshoppers, Canadian thistle, and most severely by the Hessian fly, an insect pest that appeared in the Long Island wheat fields during the Revolution and slowly worked its way up the Hudson Valley.[6]

These same uncertain agricultural conditions of human failure and land exhaustion carry through to the middle of the century. "Rural decline, as evidenced by worn-out fields, abandoned farms, and population decline, was in evidence in much of the [hillier portions of the region] by the time of the Civil War." Grist mills decayed and "Michigan fever" gripped many in the valley. Others succumbed to the pull of urbanization and drifted into the cities, while those left behind continued in their "soil-depleting and slovenly" ways.[7] The Hudson Valley farmscape was compared by foreign travelers with the untidy pigsties of medieval Britain. Even American-born N. P. Willis decried the unattractiveness of the unkempt fencing and animal carcasses that littered the roads and shores of Orange County.[8]

Measures were taken to improve agricultural conditions,[9] and some Hudson Valley farmers were successful in finding alternatives to wheat. Wheat production, however, declined rather than disappeared; Rockland County still had 31 operative grist mills in 1830.[10] But the repeated incursions of insect pests forced local adjustments, and many farmers along the Hudson turned to butter and cheese production. Samuel Eager, an Orange County historian writing in 1846, advised local farmers to shift to grasses ("as common sense dictates") and pasture livestock.[11] Orange County had already achieved a reputation for its specialization in butter and cheeses and was celebrated for the excellence of its dairy products in the DeWitt-Burr *Atlas of the State of New York* issued in 1829.

By 1840, the region was turning more and more to fluid milk. At Cornwall Landing "tubs of butter, forests of hoop-poles, cows, calves, sheep, and lambs" were all loaded on the night boat—along with the passengers—and sent down river to New York.[12] Orange and Rockland (and Dutchess east of the Hudson) were soon incorporated into the New York City milkshed, a move greatly facilitated by the arrival of the railroads. By the Civil War the Borden Milk Company had even expanded its operations northward into Putnam County.[13]

Simultaneously, other specializations evolved as a more generally diversified agriculture became characteristic of the region. Rockland, Orange, and parts of north Bergen specialized in fruit production (apples, peaches, melons and grapes), market gardening of vegetables (especially potatoes), poultry raising, and floriculture. On the hills above the Nyack lowland viticulture was introduced. A penchant for apple orchards, on converted wheat land, was noticeable throughout the Hudson-Mohawk corridor. Raspberries and strawberries were grown at Cornwall and stock breeding at Blooming Grove also developed.[14]

Steam and Rail

The pre–Civil War revolution in transportation was a highly dynamic element in the creation of a "landscape of progress and achievement"[15] in the Hudson Valley. The Hudson, especially, with the breaking of the steamboat monopoly by the Supreme Court in 1824 (Gibbons v. Ogden), became the laboratory for this new technology. Although the Hudson River sloop remained in use commercially well into the late nineteenth century, the "floating palaces" which succeeded the *Clermont* and symbolized the new commercial spirit of the nation began to appear in large numbers by the 1820s. After 1825, highly competitive steamboat companies such as the Hudson River Steamboat Association and the Peoples Line were organized to make the New York–Albany run in increasingly shorter time.[16]

Rockland County's river landings—Piermont, Nyack, and Haverstraw—constructed their own steamboats and carried on a fierce rivalry for passengers and cargo. "In the 1840's Hudson River steamboating was at its peak as far as the number of steamers in the New York-Albany service were concerned . . . Steam boats were everywhere—a common but glorious sight."[17] The year 1840 approximates the high-point of the steamboat's presence and prestige on the Hudson.[18] The novelty soon wore thin and the period 1840–60 revealed to the public the more sordid and tragic aspects of steamboating such as the persistence of blatantly illegal monopolies, price-fixing, and the infamous river races which often resulted in explosions, fires, and disastrous wrecks. Furthermore, by the autumn of 1851 the Hudson River Railroad was opened for business and the river ships, a seasonal operation at best, were no longer the sole—or even the dominant—means of carrying passengers and cargo.

During their brief but active reign, the Hudson River steamboats greatly affected local land use and ecology. They stimulated tourism and recreation by making the upriver region accessible to greater numbers of people. Apart from facilitating weekend and holiday outings and Fourth of July picnics, the sternwheelers and sidewheelers became the commercial link between the river landings and New York City. Boat and boiler construction received an impetus at towns like Nyack where the number of employees in the shipyards was mirrored in the number of craft upon the river.

But probably the most visible impact of steamboating (and later railroading) was the ecological effect of unabated wood-cutting atop the Palisades and in the highlands. It is said that in 1825, when there were but thirteen steamboats in operation, 100,000 cords of wood were cut for fuel in the lower valley and conveyed to the riverbank by the wood slides depicted in the various guidebooks of the era. "The end result was that much of the Valley was clear-cut every thirty or forty years."[19]

Of infinitely greater environmental impact was the railroad, experimented with and developed at an early date in New York State. Despite the engineering difficulties presented by the Hudson's sometimes precipitous shores, there was a substantial rail network along the valley by the Civil War.[20] The Hudson's first line (now Conrail's Harlem Division) came up through Westchester in 1844, reaching the Dutchess County line in 1849. By 1848 the Hudson East Shore line had tunneled and blasted its way to Cold Spring, reaching Poughkeepsie in 1849, and Albany a short time later.

Land use on the western shore had been greatly changed by the appearance of two railroads before the Civil War: the New York-Erie Railroad and the Northern Railroad of New Jersey. By 1851, the Erie connected New York City with Dunkirk on Lake Erie via Piermont and the Sparkill Valley. The period prosperity of the latter settlement, the unique railroad pier and ferry, the engine house, and the maintenance and repair shops can be seen on the O'Connor map of 1854 (fig. 15). Twice the size of Nyack at this time, Piermont was very much a company town, with a large foreign-born population, mainly Irish, who worked the railroad. Although the terminal was eventually shifted to Jersey City and Piermont declined, for several years the town was the focal point of much traffic and commercial activity. The nearby Rockland County Cemetery was laid out on the south side of Mount Nebo in 1847 in anticipation of an exclusive burial

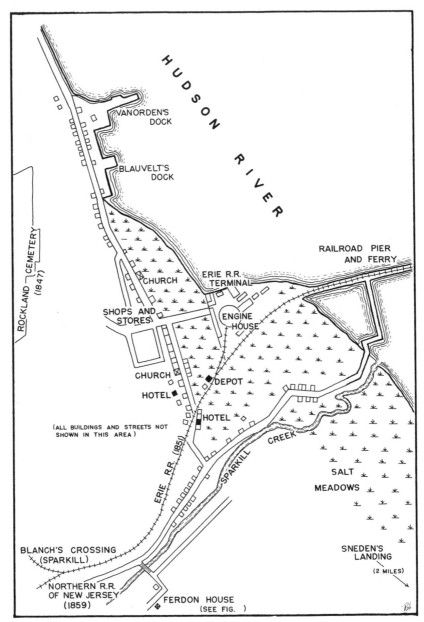

Figure 15. Piermont in the 1850s

Compiled from O'Connor's map "Rockland County, New York" (1854) and Seymour and Tower's "Map of the Northern Railroad of New Jersey" (1859)

(Scale: 1″ ≈ 650′)

trade with New York via the projected rail connection at Pier-mont.[21] By contrast, Sneden's Landing (on the Palisades two miles to the south) was overshadowed by the coming of the Erie; with river and rail commerce being diverted away, the dock decayed and the town declined.

Chartered in 1854 and completed to a junction with the Erie Railroad at Piermont in 1859, the Northern Railroad of New Jer-sey went "roaring up the [Overpeck] Valley like an uncaged lion. It was to be the last of the [local peoples'] isolation from the world."[22] The growth of hamlets on the back slope of the Pali-sades owes its awakening in this period to the Northern Railroad and the station villages it inspired. Schraalenburgh, Tenafly Sta-tion, and Closter are three such settlements which owe their growth to the skyrocketing land values and rampant speculation of 1859. With all roads converging upon the centrally located railroad station, villages grew up where the railroad chose: "When the [rail]road was completed a station was made at Clos-ter. . . . 'Closter City' " It resembled the establishment of some western mining towns during the gold fever "as houses sprung up on all sides."[23] The spatial arrangement of stations, and the grouping of hotels, stores, and houses along the railroad line be-tween Fort Lee and Closter is shown on the map of the Northern Railroad (fig.16). It should be remembered that growth patterns along the railroad route were achieved at the expense of the stag-nating river landings (e.g. Sneden's, Huyler's, and Closter Dock).

Like the steamboats, the railroads too had their environ-mental impacts. They were voracious consumers of wood—for ties, fuel, and housing constructed in the villages they created. In 1858 railroad ties were hewn from the Palisade forest and brought to sawmills built near Englewood.[24] Operating along the shore from Grandview to Nyack, the Rockland County traprock industry expanded due to the demand for rock in sea-wall construction along the East Shore Railroad line in Westches-ter and Putnam Counties.[25]

Although the rail lines had not invaded the highlands to the west of the Hudson, the panorama of steam and rail was an al-most ubiquitous sight in the valley by 1861. To some it por-

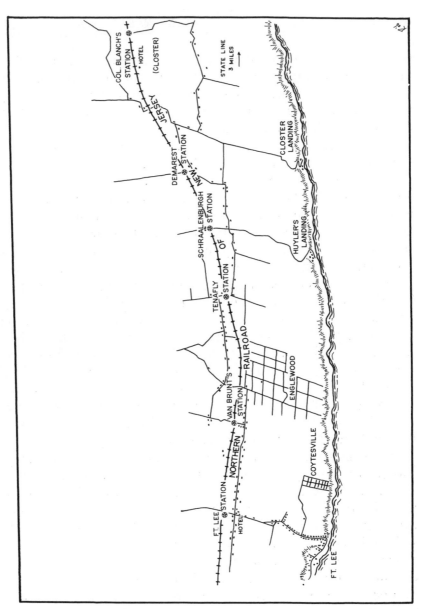

Figure 16. Route of the Northern Railroad of New Jersey in 1859 from Fort Lee to Closter

Compiled from: Seymour and Tower's map, "Route of the Northern Railroad of New Jersey," and G. Cory, "Map of the Counties of Bergen and Passaic" (1861)

(Scale: 1' ≈ .7 miles)

tended evil. Indeed an ecologically bad effect upon the woodland and the encouragement of quarrying were already noticeable. To others, the railroad cars and steamboats, with their crowds of handkerchief-waving passengers, were small intrusions upon the landscape, "like toys for children" [26]—but toys nonetheless capable of massive environmental transformations.

The Resort and Estate Boom

The explosion in resort and estate building was in large part expedited by the transportation revolution, which drew the valley within the day-trip and vacation orbit of New Yorkers. The origins of a resort-recreational pattern adjacent to, and serving the needs of, New York City's population would have been quite impossible without the emergence of a new mobile social stratum, especially an "urban–intellectual civilization." [27] The Catskill Mountain House, opened in 1823, was patronized by those free to partake of sightseeing and vacationing and whose wealth and leisure derived largely from the profits and successes of commerce. These were the *nouveaux riches* who eventually ranged into the Adirondacks and White Mountains in search of the primitive and sublime in nature.

To the cultured traveler of this period the older recreational facilities of the lower valley, such as the Elysian Fields, the carriage roads and picnic groves of upper Manhattan, and the Jersey City-Hoboken area, had become the haunt of low-class city riff-raff, the "vulgarians," or as N. P. Willis called them, "the people." [28] G. T. Strong, the disdainfully bitter, class-conscious diarist, described his weekend "rambles" about the New Jersey shore:

[August 1, 1837] Hoboken! Where all sorts of cits and cockneys and pert nurses and perter misses and dirty loafers . . . do "go-a-pleasuring."

[May 28, 1844] Started after dinner . . . for a walk to Weehawken. . . . pity it's haunted by such a gang as frequents it; its groves are sacred to Venus and I saw scarce anyone there but snobs and their strumpets. Walked on in momentary expectation of stumbling on some couple engaged in . . . "the commission of gross vulgarity."[29]

Strong's need to disassociate himself from such detestable and distracting social elements led him to seek more pleasurable walks and drives along the winding roads and wooded ravines in the Fort Lee area; when time permitted, he would patronize Cozzens' Hotel in the highlands, a resort suitably distant from the crasser city elements. If Strong's feelings are at all representative of the leisured class,[30] the social distastes of recreation with the pleasure-seeking immigrant hordes was in itself conducive to the appearance of weekend hotels and summer colonies both in the highlands and Catskills. Complementary to this motivation, of course, was "the mountain house tradition . . . [as] an integral part of the nineteenth-century effort to absorb the benefits of grand scenery."[31]

Though others would be built at a later date, the three best known highland resorts at this time were the Tappan Zee House on the hills overlooking Nyack (considered a delightful place for "good society"); Monk's Hotel at Lake Mahopac in the Putnam County Highlands; and Cozzens' Hotel, first at West Point and later relocated at Buttermilk Falls (Highland Falls).[32]

Cozzens was the forerunner and would be the standard of those which followed; its attractions and ground plan are shown in fig. 34. The earlier hotel on the academy grounds, while "spacious and splendid," apparently interfered with the discipline of the cadets (although Lossing states that it was simply destroyed by fire)[33] and so was relocated in the late 1840s on a clifftop along the western shore about one mile south of West Point. This is the Cozzens most often painted (see the frontispiece, "Approaching Cozzens") and referred to in travelogues. "It was a place of fashionable resort from June to October," and frequented by such notables as the Prince of Wales, General Winfield Scott, and the artist Emanuel Leutze. The hotel accommodated up to 550 people who found respite in the extensive "pleasure grounds" of walks, drives, and overlooks. The beauty of the nearby waterfalls was enhanced by the presence of ruined mill-works:

Rude paths and bridges were so constructed that visitors may view the great fall and the Cascade above from many points. The latter have a grand and wild aspect when the stream is brimful, after heavy rains and the melting of snows.[34]

It was a well-known nineteenth-century practice to locate landscaped villas or country residences at picturesque vantage points throughout the Valley of the Hudson:

The convenient location and exceptional beauty of the Hudson . . . encouraged wealthy New Yorkers to build summer homes along its commanding heights, and the lower Valley became the scene of America's first vacationland. Even in the early years of the nineteenth century the area south of the Highlands acquired a suburban aspect unknown to the rest of America until long after the advent of the railroad age.[35]

This was the "velvet edged" river valley to which N. P. Willis referred when describing the urban fringe transition from farm fields to lawns and shaded villas. The valley as a retreat for the wealthy, as the guarded preserve of a landed gentry (a condition that characterizes the highlands even today) thus dates to the early nineteenth century. The homes of the wealthy were for the most part situated so that scenic cross valley vistas could be contemplated through the light of leaded, stained glass windows. It was from the verandas and dining rooms of such "summer cottages" that highland and palisade scenery was meant to be viewed. Consequently, an examination of William Wade's incredibly detailed panorama of the river banks in 1846 (figs. 17 and 18) shows a succession of turreted and porticoed cliff-top estates on the New Jersey shore north to the old redoubt at Fort Lee. Patten's travel guide confirms that by 1853 the New Jersey villas, with a view toward the mildly scenic shores of Washington Heights, still extended only to Fort Lee.[36]

Opposite the Palisades, the east side of the Hudson was also occupied by a nearly unbroken expanse of suburban estates,

Figure 17. The Lower and Upper Ends of the Palisades

TOP. The Fort Lee Area

BOTTOM. State Line—Sneden's Landing

William Wade, *Panorama of the Hudson River from New York to Albany*. New York and Philadelphia: J. Disturnell, 1846.

Figure 18. The Palisades in the 1840s
TOP. William Wade, *Panorama of the Hudson River from New York to Albany*. New York and Philadelphia: J. Disturnell, 1846.
BOTTOM. W. H. Bartlett, *American Scenery*, London: Geo. Virtue, 1840. "Palisades —Hudson River," Vol. 1, Plate 7.

"some of them quite palatial in extent," crowning the heights and scattered along the slopes above the shore. "There was almost a mania for buying tracts of land" in places with names suggesting "altitude and outlook"—Highbridgeville, Fordham Heights, Morris Heights, University Heights, Kingsbridge Heights, Mount Hope. Wade again locates this line of hilltop mansions from Haarlem Cove (the Holloway at 125th Street) through Washington Heights to Tetards Hill.[37]

With its fine vistas of the northern Palisades and the Hook Mountain region, "millionaires row" worked its way northward:

the east bank of the Hudson from Riverdale to Greenbush became the favorite retreat of famous writers, generals, inventors, statesmen; a new class of bewilderingly wealthy entrepreneurs—the Astors and Vanderbilts, the Rockefellers, Goulds and Morgans—created great landed estates and transformed the banks of the Hudson into one of the most highly-groomed landscapes in all America.[38]

The variety of taste displayed in these country seats was commented upon by Sears and Milbert and the estates of P. R. Paulding, Messrs. Cruger, Dyckman, Richmond, and others were identified by Wade.[39]

It is evident from the Wade panorama and from the Hudson River Valley Commission's inventory of historic sites in Putnam County (1969) that the highlands east of the river received their share of crenellated Gothic towers and Italianate Downingesque cottages. The shoreline near Garrison and Foundry Cove—with views toward Buttermilk Falls and the West Point plain—was (and still is) dotted with such structures.[40] However, the critical point is that the more rugged slopes of Orange and Rockland appear conspicuously devoid of substantial, estate-type habitations in the Wade panorama. Those pre–Civil War estates referred to in the histories are situated strictly on shoreline promontories: e.g. Philip Verplanck's "beautiful and picturesque" mansion at Plum Point near the mouth of the Moodna and the New York lawyer William Smith's "Rosa Villa" at the tip of Grassy Point. At Cornwall, N. P. Willis, E. P. Roe, and their neighbors were busy relating their simple "republican homes" to their landscaped gardens in accordance with Downing's precepts of union between house and surroundings.[41] But the highlands proper repelled the advances of refined architectural taste.

Much the same is true of the Palisades. Apparently the only "improvements" made by wealthy New York families before the Civil War were the wood slides used to bring firewood to their Fifth Avenue townhouses. Not a single residence of *any* size or pretension was built upon the crest before 1861. At that time William Dana, a New York publisher, built what is said to be the first cliff-top estate—Greycliff, an impressive structure of Palisade traprock and pink Jersey sandstone.[42] Dana no doubt chose to locate his estate here because of the accessibility provided for by the coming of the Northern Railroad, a venture in which Dana, not surprisingly, was part owner.

Changes in the Palisade Landscape

With the exception of changes brought to the Palisades by the railroads, land use along the Palisade cliff and shoreline areas continued, sometimes with elaboration, the patterns established before. Anchored on the south by the village of Fort Lee (with about thirty dwellings, "irregularly grouped in a nook at the foot of the Palisades"),[43] the undercliff zone served principally as the domain of quarrymen, woodhaulers, and fishermen. Their cottages and sheds were perched in crevices, at the landings, and on "a little yellow strand" of sand just wide enough for their purposes.[44] Wade's panorama shows at least two dozen structures along the shore north to the state line; the artist probably eliminated some detail for the sake of scale, since J. J. Greco in *The Story of Englewood Cliffs* claims that in 1849 the Undercliff settlement alone (north of the Englewood Basin) housed 800 persons.[45] A sizable population increase *may* have occurred in these decades, since about four dozen structures are indicated on a "Survey Map of Lands Under the Water of the Hudson etc." compiled for the State Legislature of New Jersey in 1860. The quarry business did expand with the demand for "Belgian" (traprock) paving blocks in New York, and there was increased quarrying around Carpenter's Beach and Allison Point. It was probably near here that Milbert saw "the small sloops which lie along under the shore, loading with building stone from its base."[46]

Whatever the exact number of persons and structures located along the Palisades shore—and this is all but impossible to determine because of conflicting evidences—the curious location of the fishing huts on the narrow beaches and the other habitations were universally commented upon by travelers. The stone or frame dwellings and the boatyards and wharves appeared as diminished as Liliputian "dog-kennels" from the river. The English traveler James Buckingham summed it up quite nicely with this 1838 description of the northern Palisades shore:

Here and there . . . a break in the cliffs would show a little bit of lawn sloping down to the [river], and a pretty little cottage peeping out from the wood in which it was embosomed; and sometimes at the foot of a narrow ravine, would be seen a humble shed, either of a river-fisherman, a quarry [man], or some other labourer.[47]

The extent of forest atop the Palisades, or at least that part of it visible from the river, is a matter of much conjecture. Conflicting descriptions run the gamut from a "bare ridge" to a "ridge crowned by a dense forest." J. G. Chapman, for example, in an 1835 canvas showing a *Hudson River Scene,* depicted a nearly treeless summit, as did J. Hamilton in a similar view twelve years later. But in 1829 William Cammeyer annotated on his "New Map of the Hudson River etc." with respect to the Palisades: "cliff, the summit covered with timber." Later in the same period the author of the *Hudson River Illustrated with Pen and Pencil* spoke of "these majestic ridges . . . surmounted by an extended fringe of forest trees as far as the eye can reach."[48]

The true nature of this forest zone was probably somewhere between the two extremes; the ridge was "selectively logged" for purposes already discussed, but "there appears to be no records of clear cutting of the forests for charcoalings as was done farther north" in the highlands.[49] This agrees with what Wade shows of the forest, i.e. a generally dense and extensive underbrush (secondary growth on neglected farmland and other revegetated areas?), punctuated with solitary, surviving evergreens. This pattern is further corroborated by Buckingham's mention of "brushwood" atop the ridge and by Cole's *The Palisades, New Jersey* (1835) in which the cliff-top is shown to be partially bare and partially vegetated.[50] Gaylord Watson probably came closest in *The Traveller's Steamboat and Railroad Guide:* "These Palisades are sometimes covered with brushwood, sometimes capped with stunted trees, and sometimes perfectly bare.[51]

As was stated above, that part of Bergen County atop the Palisades and inland to the valleys of the Overpeck and Tenakill Creeks (one and one half to two miles west) was subjected to a real estate boom on the eve of the Civil War; here the railroad had transformed a neglected rural backwater into a suburban tract of villages, estates, and hotels;

It is difficult to realize . . . the barrenness and loneliness of the site of Englewood in 1859. The fields were neglected, the one road through it was narrow and sandy, and the brush and undergrowth tall and scraggy. There was at that time not a single house in what now constitutes the village of Englewood. [1882][52]

Nominally, the area was farmed, but in actuality—with the exception of a few melon gardens at the base of the western slope—much of the land (west of the 400-foot contour in fig. 19) was utilized as pasture[53] or uncultivated meadow land reverting, rather quickly it would seem, to brush and scrub. The area was not, as the hyperbolically heroic language of railroad propaganda claimed, "a solitary waste . . . an unknown wilderness . . . a labyrinth of tangled underbrush." It consisted mostly of undeveloped or abandoned properties with a sprinkling of farms and country seats.[54] The county historian W. Woodford Clayton recalled in graphic detail personal observations made across this ridge top in 1859:

Belts of shrubs and small trees, sometimes thirty or forty feet in width, had grown up along the division fences and stone walls on the western

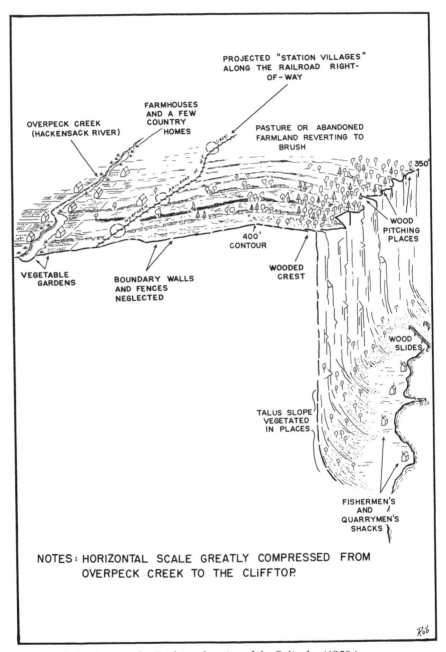

PROJECTED "STATION VILLAGES" ALONG THE RAILROAD RIGHT-OF-WAY

FARMHOUSES AND A FEW COUNTRY HOMES

OVERPECK CREEK (HACKENSACK RIVER)

PASTURE OR ABANDONED FARMLAND REVERTING TO BRUSH

350'

WOOD PITCHING PLACES

400' CONTOUR

VEGETABLE GARDENS

BOUNDARY WALLS AND FENCES NEGLECTED

WOODED CREST

WOOD SLIDES

TALUS SLOPE VEGETATED IN PLACES

FISHERMEN'S AND QUARRYMEN'S SHACKS

NOTES: HORIZONTAL SCALE GREATLY COMPRESSED FROM OVERPECK CREEK TO THE CLIFFTOP.

Figure 19. Land use in the Englewood section of the Palisades (1850s).
An original sketch based upon the written and cartographic sources

slopes where the forests had been cut down. Weeds and bushes were scattered over the fields, and an air of neglect pervaded the whole plot. In traversing these fields going [east] toward the river it was no unusual thing to strike into a tangle of underbrush, vines, and brambles so thick as to absolutely force a return and a change of direction. On reaching the forest line [the 400-foot contour] all fences and division lines disappeared. . . . It was one dense forest of magnificent trees, containing the finest specimens of oak and hickory to be found in the country.[55]

The overall pattern of human activity atop the ridge, as deduced from the written sources, is sketched in fig. 19, while the ownership of property appears in fig. 29. The "farms" were longlot-like strips varying in size and running at an angle to the cliff-face. In fact, some of the surviving stone walls marking these divisions are still seen along the shoulder of the Palisades Parkway near Englewood Cliffs. Ownership extended from the marshes near the creek across the ridge-top to the highwater mark on the Hudson, giving each owner access to meadowland, farmland, woodland, and cordwood "pitching places." When the surveyors and engineers arrived to lay out home sites and town lots in the 1860s, it became apparent to the landholders that the true value of this, "the grandest section of the Hudson River,"[56] lay not in farming but in real estate speculation.

Industrious Nyack and Haverstraw

Thomas Gordon's 1828 map of Rockland (fig. 20) reveals a dense and irregular road grid throughout the county's interior and along the river shore. The many interconnected roads in the vicinity of Kakiat, New City, and Clarkstown suggest a well-established cash-intensive agriculture, a type of farming described at the beginning of this chapter. Industry, with few exceptions (one was the Ramapo Iron Works), concentrated on streams such as the Sparkill, Minisceongo, and upper Hackensack in the eastern part of the county. Many of the roads converged upon Nyack and Haverstraw which, along with Piermont, served as the principal river landings in the county. Nyack especially, with

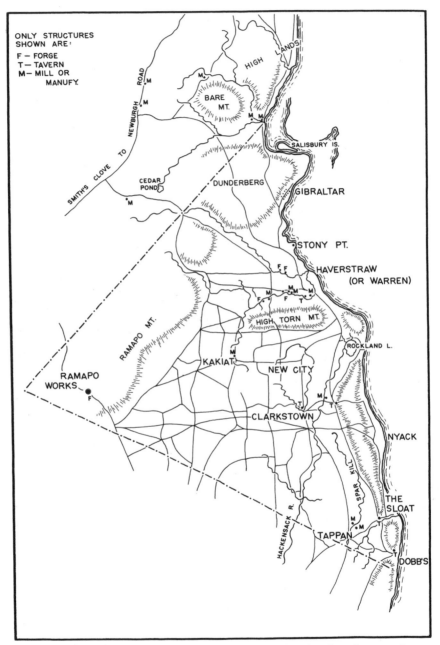

Figure 20. Road patterns and economic activities in Rockland and southeastern Orange Counties, 1828.

From: Thomas Gordon, "Map of New Jersey and Adjoining Areas"

(Scale: 1″ = 1.75 miles)

Figure 21. Hook Mountain—Rockland Lake Landing (1840s)

Top. Steamboat *Iron Witch* about 1846 by J. V. Cornell. The New York Historical Society

Bottom. William Wade, *Panorama of the Hudson River from New York to Albany.* New York and Philadelphia: J. Disturnell, 1846.

the completion of the Nyack Turnpike to Ramapo (across the Blauvelt or Greenbush swamps), experienced a great commercial surge and captured much of Haverstraw's hinterland after 1825.[57]

Apart from their function as transshipment points, the villages in this period continued to prosper, along with the brick and quarry industries. Nyack, with a population of 300 in 1830, relied heavily upon the building stone trade throughout the 1820s and 1830s. Red and gray sandstone as well as traprock were quarried at 31 individual sites along the shore from Grandview to Upper Nyack. Many docks projected into the river, and a dozen vessels a day left with loads of stone. William Cammayer's map of 1829 labels this entire shoreline: "QUARRIES."[58] The industry, however, peaked in the late 1830s and—largely because of competition from quarries in New Jersey—gradually declined in the 1840s and 1850s; it completely collapsed after the Civil War.[59] With its demise, Nyack industry was forced to diversify. Early arrivals were such light industries as shoe, straw hat, and match factories; later, companies that manufactured carriages, pianos, ships, boilers, and smokestacks were established.

By contrast, the Haverstraw lowland probably remained less diversified in its industrial pursuits; the brick and quarry (Tomkins Cove) businesses flourished throughout the nineteenth century. O'Connor's 1854 map shows the riverbank from Grassy Point to the Dunderberg replete with brickyards, landing docks, and lime kilns. The bluffs of sand and clay at Grassy Point became smaller and smaller, "their substance molded into millions and millions of bricks for building up the metropolis" at New York.[60] The classic picture of the "remarkably fine harbor" at Haverstraw, painted by both Bartlett and Milbert, shows the brickworks and their smoke-plumed chimneys, and the ships and their wharves, in the shadows below the crest of High Tor.[61] Two miles north the riverface of Hog Hill, a 150 foot high cliff of blue, variegated limestone, was worked by the Tomkins Cove Lime Company. Here 100 men were permanently employed in the production of limestone, lime (for manuring the fields of New Jersey), and pulverized lime for use as gravel. Lossing observed the workers blasting and pulverizing Hog Hill to the amount of one million bushels of stone per year: "I saw them on the brow of a wooded cliff, loosening huge masses and sending them below, while others were engaged in blasting . . . and near the water the houses of the workmen form a pleasant little village." [62]

Hook Mountain and Rockland Lake: Like the Palisades with Ice

The palisaded highland of Hook Mountain and the Tors was no doubt extensively lumbered over by the 1820s. The local woodland was drawn upon for shipbuilding, for use in the brick-yards, the sawmills, and charcoal furnaces. Permanent settlement, however, seems to have lagged from the sheer emptiness seen in the Verdrietige Hook area on the DeWitt-Burr map of 1829. [63] But by mid-century the western slopes of the mountains and the basin of Rockland Lake formed "a high and well-cultivated valley," [64] with farmhouses scattered about, hamlets sited at Cedar Grove Corners and Hook Corner, and the land divided up into narrow strips as on the Palisade slope. In fact, the ridge top and what lay to the rear closely approximates the Bergen Palisades in appearance and function.

From the river below, Lossing saw "a bold mountain shore, having a few cultivated slopes and pleasant villages." He might have added that the uplands themselves were covered with much secondary growth as depicted by Wade and others. [65] Rockland Lake Village (formerly Slaughter's Landing), as "the most extensive ice-station on the river," [66] was a collection of wharves and ice-houses at the base of a steep declivity. Beginning in 1826 ice blocks were sawed on "the pond" (Rockland Lake) and slid down the declivity to the landing, where they were barged to storage cellars in Greenwich Village. In the 1830s a chute or sluiceway was constructed through the declivity and, when the Knickerbocker Ice Company was incorporated in the 1850s, a gravity-incline railway was built from the lake to the landing. [67] Ice was an important article of commerce on the Hudson (the

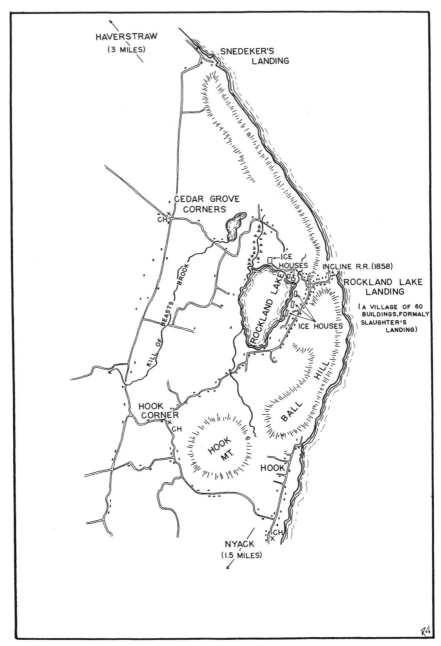

Figure 22. The Rockland Lake and Hook Mountain area in the 1850s
From: O'Connor, "Map of Orange County" (1854)
(Scale: 1″ = .8 miles)

Knickerbocker Ice Company ran a fleet of thirteen steamboats and eighty barges) and also an invaluable additive to the local economy. The numerous ice-houses on the Rockland Lake shore (fig.21) lessened the tax burden on the farmers. Furthermore, "The labor of gathering ice is done in the winter season, when other fields of labor are scarce. The number of men [farmers] thus employed ranges from 2400 to 3000 men, at this place alone.[68]

Beating off competition from the Rondout Creek and Croton River regions, the Knickerbocker Ice Company eventually turned to the railroad for shipment to the city. As in the Adirondacks in the later part of the century, the ice industry on Hook Mountain was certainly both colorful and economically beneficial.

The Patchwork, Forested Highlands

The Hudson Highlands remained relatively isolated and closeted in terms of most human activities. The road pattern was somewhat piecemeal and many sections were not linked to an overall grid. A common theme was expressed by the traveler Harriet Martineau, who plaintively remarked: "how few are the habitations of man."[69] The county historian Samuel Eager explained the slow pace of local development in terms of negative topographic controls and somewhat shortsightedly observed that, "the Highlands bar out any approach to the river, and exclude the possibility of locating a village with any prospect of success."[70]

But by the 1830s there was a sprinkling of small communities, the existence of which depended on exploitation of local resources. Iron mining operations were still carried on in the interior (Forest of Dean), exploratory shafts were sunk, and several small furnaces continued to operate through the Civil War. The Fort Montgomery furnace on Popolopen Creek is shown on period maps, while the Parrott Brothers' Foundry in Cold Spring employed iron ore from Rockland and Orange Counties.[71] Hy-

Figure 23. Dunderberg Mountain, the "Southern Gate"

TOP. "Lighthouse, Caldwell's," W. H. Bartlett, *American Scenery*, London: Geo. Virtue, 1840. Vol. 1, Plate 31.

BOTTOM. William Wade, *Panorama of the Hudson River from New York to Albany*. New York and Philadelphia: J. Disturnell, 1846.

draulic power was another mainstay for semi–industrial communities like Fort Montgomery and Highland Falls. At the latter, a
"beautiful little cascade" powered several flour mills (e.g. Lydig's
Mill) by utilizing the nearby 100-foot drop. Grist, saw, and cider
mills were a rather common occurrence: "Practically every
stream entering the Hudson [north] to Fort Montgomery turned
millstones." [72] A few communities like Doodletown (at the junction of the Albany Road and the Caldwell Pike) and Caldwell's
(at the Peekskill Ferry) owed their origin and staying power to
their closeness to road connections and ferry landings.

Ideally, a village might have arisen along Doodletown Bight
or on Hessian Lake where, as at Rockland Lake, ice cutting
began in the 1830s. An ice house was built at the lake (sometimes
referred to as Sinnipink or Highland Lake) and the blocks slid
down to the Knickerbocker Ice Company's boat dock on Doodletown Bight. [73] Ice harvesting, although one of the highland industries, failed to stimulate settlement in the region.

The resort and recreation functions also became important
to the highlands. Nowhere were hotel facilities and pleasure
grounds as well developed as at Cozzens, but by the Civil War
other such mountain resorts were established at Caldwell's (on
the Dunderberg slopes) and at old Fort Clinton (the Clinton
House). In Cornwall, the northernmost stop on the daily steamboat runs, boarding houses and hotels began to flourish.

Apart from highland scenery, the Revolutionary War heritage was the principal enticement for tourists to this region, and
West Point itself was the ultimate destination of most. "The
Point" and its highly popular attractions and vistas (Kosciusko's
Garden, the North Battery, the parade ground, and old Fort Putnam) were endlessly painted, sketched, written about, and commented upon. Picnics, parasols, and top hats were daily fare at
this, "Gibraltar of America" [74] (fig.24).

Throughout, the highlands presented a patchwork of farm
lots, woodland, and a mixed vegetative carpet of underbrush and
nearly bare rocky ground. Despite the seemingly impractical nature of highland farming, the lower slopes of the mountains were
cultivated before the Civil War. In 1835 Harriet Martineau ob-

Figure 24. Highland Scene: 1840s "Ice-Boat Race on the Hudson."
Currier & Ives, 1840s

served "patches of cultivation on the mountainsides, and slopes of cleared land." Willis, hiking on Storm King in 1853, noticed countless small farms hidden among the rocks and crevices; many of them, however, had reverted to forest.[75] A degree of agricultural domestication is also apparent in the highland paintings by Chambers and others, who show farmhouses, fences, and clearings interspersed among the stylized ruins and country residences.[76] In the 1860s, the Hudson River artists Johnson and Kensett, known respectively for their "intensive realism" and "patience in detail," depicted green and earth-colored field patterns on the lower slopes of Crows Nest and pasture (or newly abandoned pasture) in the vicinity of Buttermilk Falls.[77]

But the dominant element in the highland landscape was of course the forest cover; and here, as in the Palisades section, one is confronted with what initially appears to be conflicting evidence. Mount Beacon, for example, is consistently remarked upon for its bare summit and slopes. "The Bald Summit" of

Storm King (fig. 25) was mentioned by Lossing, who described the highlands in general as being "scantily clothed with stunted trees." Wade, whether by omission or design, depicts large bare patches on Storm King's sides.[78] On the other hand, the highlands in these same years were seen as having "wood-crowned heights," and "a beautiful forest of oak, beech, chestnut, and walnut."[79] Bartlett's view of the southern entrance to the highlands (fig. 23) is topographically precise and annotated with reference to the mountains: "broken rocks—fire-wood . . . wood and rocks . . . woody mountains."[80] The northern entrance at Storm King and Crows Nest was also painted (by W. J. Bennett) as an essentially wooded region. There is furthermore the local story, as related by Eager, of a skeleton found atop Storm King, the remains of a man lost in the mountains years before and not found within the *heavily wooded* upland until 1846.[81]

Hugh Raup, in writing on "Some Problems in Ecological Theory and Their Relation to Conservation," has several explanations for these seemingly inconsistent descriptions.[82] First, the highland region throughout the nineteenth century had undergone repeated fires. Large sections of slope and summit were burnt over every few decades. It is possible that Mount Beacon, for example—which everybody seems to agree was decidedly bare—may have been without the forest cover of the neighboring mountains. Secondly, there was variation from decade to decade in the appearance of the same slope, because of clear cutting at intervals of 30 to 40 years that occurred prior to the Civil War. Therefore, cutting (mostly for charcoal) in the late 1820s would have left a mountainside bare for several decades, only to reappear in the 1860s with a cover of young (and, at least in appearance, "stunted") forest trees. There is, moreover—as Raup again explains—the fact that the highland forest has always been distinguished from its less elevated surroundings by skimpily covered slopes ("barrens" or "balds" to the travelers), stunted or "tufted" trees, and xerophytism. "Beautiful forests" were limited to the well-watered lower slopes, while the crests, where 150-year-old trees attain only a couple of inches in thickness, remained essen-

Figure 25. Storm King Mountain

TOP. William Wade, *Panorama of the Hudson River from New York to Albany.* New York and Philadelphia: J. Disturnell, 1846.

BOTTOM. Wallace Bruce, *Panorama of the Hudson River Showing both sides of the Hudson River from New York to Poughkeepsie,* Bryant Literary Union, 1901 (1906 edition) tially bare. To some, this may have implied man-made clearings, while it was seen more positively by others in terms of a dense or "tangled" woodland, "all . . . clothed with underbrush" from base to summit—scrub oaks and bushes, but nonetheless woodland.[83]

Two interpretations of the same landscape evolved. The forested highlands simply elicited divergent reactions from those who encountered it. It was a rare individual who could interpret the true nature of the woodland, but G. T. Strong, who had received geographic instruction at Columbia University and had socialized with Arnold Guyot and George Perkins Marsh, came as close as any when he walked across the summit of Crows Nest in 1851:

The rugged plateau at the top, with its thick underbrush, its stunted oak spreading their low distorted branches here and there among the rocks, its black, peaty moss stretching far back to the west . . . is a very fascinating place to me.[84]

The Newburgh Plain to the north and the islands in the highland passage showed no sharp deviations from land use activities established in the previous period. While the city of Newburgh itself, like Haverstraw, had attracted brickworks in the 1830s, the surrounding farmlands were viewed favorably by most. The meadows and grain fields at New Windsor, Marlboro, and New Hope were rated among the continent's most fertile regions.[85]

Constitution and Polopel's (Bannerman's) Islands changed but little. Constitution Island provided a pleasant summer retreat for the family of Brooklyn lawyer Henry Warner, who had apparently hoped to create rice paddies in the marshier sections, a fantasy that would be attempted again in these same areas of the valley. Polopel's, with "the solitary house of a fisherman upon it,"[86] underwent only the uneventful transferral of ownership deeds. Before the Civil War, Iona Island (fig. 26) a budding summer resort and popular excursion playground, was known for its

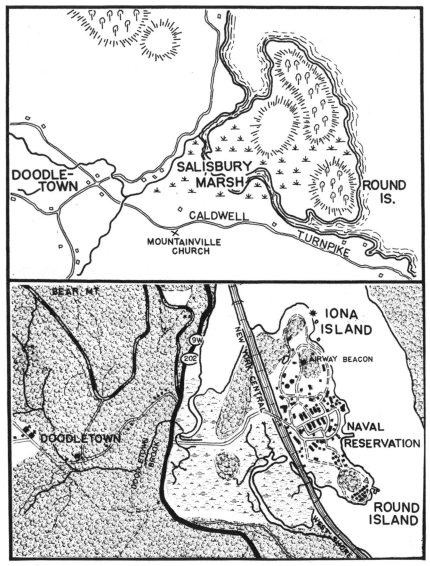

Figure 26. Iona Island in the Nineteenth Century and Today
TOP: Detail from O'Connor's map "Rockland County, New York" 1854
BOTTOM: Detail from U.S.G.S. Peekskill topographic sheet, 1947
(Scale: 1″ ≈ 2000′

"Picnicking on Iona Island." William Cullen Bryant, *Picturesque America,* New York: D. Appleton & Co., 1874.

grape vines and seed-propagation houses. The 20-acre vineyard and the pear tree orchards were the work of a Doctor Grant who is said to have abandoned his viticultural and horticultural experiments around 1864.[87]

Chapter 8
Steam and Iron versus the Romantic and Pastoral

*The "Mountain Gloom" was gone. . . . Mountains had
ceased to be monstrosities and had become an integral part of
varied and diversified Nature.*
M. H. Nicolson, *Mountain Gloom
and Mountain Glory*, p. 345.

*These elevated heights [Hudson Highlands] of dreary aspect,
these hills overhung and darkened with vines and forest trees
. . . should be associated in the minds of our children's children, with all that is pastoral, pleasing, and heroic.*
S. Eager, *Outline History
of Orange County*, p. 521.

THE YEAR 1825 HAS been referred to as a "turning point in
American taste," a time when an awareness of the aesthetic value
of natural landscape had bloomed, marking "a revolution in the
American sensitivity to habitat."[1] This new "iconography of
landscape"[2] was reflected in the rising popularity of travel and
the development of mountain resorts and estates in scenically attractive areas in the Eastern United States.

These innovations in taste, concept, and life style fostered a period of New World romanticism that took as its foremost aesthetic stimuli the cliffs and misty mountain ranges of the lower Hudson Valley. To paraphrase the words of one foreign traveler in 1847, it was the Hudson that had become the focal point not only of national historical and commercial pride, but of poetic and literary achievement as well.[3]

The changes in the conceptions of landscape aesthetics from 1825 to the Civil War are at least as important as the changes in land use. The Hudson was the laboratory where the various elements which made up the romantic landscape were assembled and tested successfully. It became the symbolic spiritual center of the age and "the scene where Americans were first awakened to aesthetic enjoyment of the native landscape."[4]

By the 1820s the overwhelming number of good landscape artists had loosely coalesced into the "Hudson River School" of painting, while New York City flourished as the art capital of the nation.[5] The lower valley was interpreted to society by the likes of Downing, Durand, Church, Cole, and Willis. These valley residents in the fields of architecture, painting, and literature drew the rest of the nation under the spell of the Hudson and popularized the romantic formula: nationalism through art appreciation, the doctrine of historical association, geological phenomena as scenic curiosities, theories of the sublime and picturesque. This valley had become the "ideal" of those who sought to evoke a sense of the primitively and sublimely wild, and to a lesser extent the more subdued picturesque and pastoral, in the landscape.

In this era, the enjoyment of landscape as scenery was opened to the middle class and even "the common people," but it was still very much the domain of the moneyed class.[6] This educated, Eastern-based "aristocracy of taste" (largely the publishers, painters, and their patrons) worked to create images of romantic landscape in the Hudson Valley—images that were disseminated throughout the world. While there was no doubt an element of snobbishness among the sophisticated and genteel patrician society in their sponsorship of artists, libraries, galleries, and books with scenic reproductions, historians agree that the prevailing period attitude regarding landscape concept owes much to the financial backing of this social elite and their strivings for cultural nationalism and an air of intellectual cosmopolitanism.[7]

The art of travel and the science of viewing scenery had become available to all ranks of society through the publication of guidebooks and cheap lithographic reprints of famous landscapes. Although the leisurely pursuit of nature was still associated with high society, and nature to the common traveler was whatever the refinements of patronized taste said it was, "the unlearned had at least entered the outer portal."[8] The cultured traveler who frequented the mountain houses and the estate owner segregated themselves spatially and socially from the teeming masses at the riverfront picnic grounds, but both shared in what the river could offer.

To better understand the manner in which aesthetic concept was so favorably fused with Hudson Valley landscapes, it is essential to establish the social atmosphere in which these developments took place. The period from 1825 to the Civil War was an age of progress and national aggrandizement in which the dominant mood was one of "exuberant optimism" based on the unbridled image of a future "American Empire."[9] Material progress was evident in territorial annexation, the invention and proliferation of the steamboat, and the rapid growth of cityscapes and related social amenities. It was an era in which a firm belief in progress and prosperity was the national credo. The lingering uncertainties of previous eras about the individual's place in society, and the position of America in the world society, evaporated and were replaced with a personal and collective "vision of limitless possibilities, with faith in a boundless future."[10]

The "Course of Empire" and Undercurrents of Doubt

However, just beneath the official surface optimism lay an "elaborately masked" and "concertedly disguised" set of fearful anxieties and apprehensions of doom. Perry Miller believes that this dissenting pessimism and disaffection with the then-current belief in progress was a vital but subterranean apprehension of the whole society. But only the more perceptive individuals like Cole, Cooper, Thoreau and Emerson could vocalize this dismay with materialistic and progressive tendencies: "it is there, at the heart—at what might be called the secret heart—of the best thought and expression the country could produce."[11]

This undercurrent of pessimism had a marked effect upon the evolution of the concept of scenic landscape. Thomas Cole, for example, who did more than anyone to implant a spirit of aesthetics and a sense of pride in the landform features of the Hudson Valley, and whose mission it was to articulate an aesthetic and moral foundation for subsequent landscape painting, believed that the material progress of the valley simply indicated that "we have fallen on evil days. . . . our stream of life, in this leveling age, flows over a great extent, and, fretting and rippling over its gravelly shallows, is too often evaporated in the arid atmosphere of the great world."[12]

The Hudson Valley routeway and the newly constructed Erie Canal were all part of the perpetually westward (and upward) moving "course of empire" expounded upon by William Gilpin and Walt Whitman.[13] To Cole, this was the ghost of other empires that had succumbed to the inevitable historical cycle: a brief moment of glory, followed by downfall and ruin. The cities, especially, were seen as decaying through vice, and it was these same cities—then extending their corrupting tentacles into the Hudson Valley—that he hoped would be overtaken again and again by the forests. Thus, Cole's allegories (e.g. "The Course of Empire"), depicting the rise and fall of a nation before the "juggernaut of progress," provide a striking contrast with the typical romantic evocation of the time: for example, "Hudson River Scenery"—the illustrated title page of an 1831 edition of *Views of New York and its Environs.*[14] The latter shows a landscape in which an equestrian country gentleman and his lady prance blithely beneath a background of highland scenery, all enveloped in a fantasy of billowing cloud. Because the public failed to penetrate the transparency of dramatically romanticized scenes such as these, Cole's allegories—and their sobering message that all was not well in this New World Eden—failed to win an audience.[15]

Ideal from Afar, but Far from Pretty

The evolution of landscape concept in the Hudson Valley, a region so expressive of the national ebullience, is closely related to the dominant ethos of optimism, romantic idealization, and the reaction these feelings evoked in people like the artist Thomas Cole. The creation of a sublime or picturesque landscape, with all its positive and uplifting connotations, rested very much upon the depiction of certain cross valley regions in an idealized and desirable state. The traveler, for example, because of what he read in magazines or saw in lithographs, viewed scenery according to carefully prescribed formulas at certain hours of the day, and only from certain vantage points. He was expected more or less to view mountainscapes and rivershores with elation, and with the distractions and the ugliness mentally screened out.[16]

In the case of the Hudson Valley, where the realities of urban, suburban, and industrial progress clashed with the aesthetic ideal, there was much that had to be screened out. Few who journeyed there ever became aquainted with the more sordid aspects of the townscapes, because the river landings were seen only perfunctorily during the brief and frantic stopovers at the docks. The rivershores were seen from the suitably removed distance of the boat decks; the valleyscape seemed pretty from afar, but in reality was far from pretty. It is interesting as well to note that in some of the highland paintings the farmscape appears to be screened from the view of river travelers by a rather solid vegetative wall.[17] Was agrarian squalor purposely being kept from the eyes of tourists to avoid disillusionment? Abandoned fields, rusting machinery, or worse were hardly pleasing to the romantic eye.[18]

Most travelers' accounts conform to the scenically pleasurable and morally uplifting dictates of the period and reveal little of the hardships of travel and the seediness of the farmscape. Rarely did an individual commit his innermost thoughts and dissatisfactions to paper, but a great many must have been peeved with the mosquitoes, the heat on the boiler room deck of the steamboat, the spilled food and shoving, the poor accommodations, the crowds, and everything else tourists complained about then—and now. For most, the landscape, whether viewed from the deck of the *Mary Powell* in the nineteenth century or from the Dayliner in the 1980s, quickly became boring and lost out to such diversions as sleeping, newspaper reading, and card playing. G. T. Strong was given to grumbling about the dirty and loathsome crowds wherever he went and confided his dis-, pleasure with Hudson River travel to his diary in the summer of 1841: the lost baggage, the oppressive heat, the poor food.[19] Strong, an educated man who could mouth the standard aesthetic phrases when moved to do so, also expressed grave misgivings with his era because of the financial difficulties he was having in the economically depressed 1840s, the friends he had lost in steamboat disasters, and the influx of rowdyish immigrant hordes to the once-fine summer resorts in the New York area. Others no doubt shared Strong's reservations about the optimism of the day and the glories of seeing and traveling this "Classic stream of the United States."[20]

The Melancholy March of Civilization

The development of landscape aesthetics in this period is best seen through the filters of romanticism and social optimism. The Hudson Valley was blanketed with a fluffy layer of idealized imagery which diverted attention from the annoying and trivial aspects of travel and sightseeing—aspects that might have reminded the traveler of the age's subsurface pessimism.[21] Accordingly, environmental realities were sugar-coated to conceal what did not conform to buoyant popular imagery.[22]

While the romantic "Hudsonian" ideal was crucially important to the overall development of aesthetic associations, it was the darker subterranean skepticism, recalling to mind the realities and fragilities of the land, that also produced a concern to preserve and conserve.

Those with artistic sensitivities quenched the public thirst for grandiose and exotic landscapes in this age of optimism; but they too first realized that the advancements in material progress engendered by that optimism would eventually destroy what was romantic and grand in nature. It was entirely predictable that an artist (George Catlin) should have proposed the preservation of the Yellowstone in 1832 to check the "unholy appetites" of man,[23] and that Cole should color his romantic enthusiasm for the Hudson Valley with a melancholy cynicism—a foreboding of the march of civilization through the valley. It was Cole's dissent from and reaction to the "traditional American ethos" of optimism that inspired elements of "memory, history, conservation, and nostalgia" in his artwork.[24] While romanticization of the landscape undeniably contributed to its eventual scenic designation and preservation, the perceptivity of those who saw the hard reality beneath the romantic ideal is equally significant. This "minority opinion" must also be considered as part of the dichotomy that furthered landscape aesthetics before the Civil War.

Analyzing the Elements of Romantic Landscape

Although it defies easy definition,[25] Romanticism is in the least "a complex pattern of ideas and feelings" involving learned dogmas, personal emotions, and even perhaps "the very stuff of dreams."[26] Based in large part upon European concepts, and owing much to the native celebration of wilderness, an American brand of romanticism became the stock-in-trade of literary "annuals" and period guidebooks. By the Civil War it had come to rest firmly upon a sublimity evoked by particular landforms, cross valley mountain and river cliffs especially. To achieve this romantic, aesthetic effect, scenic views, whether paintings or photographs, were often contrived. Such visually pleasing embellishments included a northward-setting sun in the frontispiece view and the wind-whipped flag and bow mast seen in the Hudson River Dayline photograph in fig. 43.

What is more, this romanticism had become part of a carefully regulated formula when used in the literature, and most particularly in illustrations. Such sublime landscape was characterized by a certain spatial perspective and the employment of certain artistic elements that were common to all the lithographs and canvases produced in the romantic era. In analyzing the package of elements that were necessarily present and applying them to the Hudson Valley, we can discover the way mountain scenery was sanctified.

Viewers, whether river travelers or gallery-goers, were commonly impressed with the importance of foreground. In landscapes, the foreground—although not always available to steamboat passengers—was the means by which the observer entered the scene (e.g. a path, a stream or falls, a river road, a railroad track, a cleft in the rocks). And while the middle ground contained the subject matter or object (mountain, river, or townscape), a distant background was also imperative to create a hazy, far-away panoramic effect (one that had its parallel in the contemporary fashion for huge panoramas).

These planes of reference were vital to a properly observed landscape and were accomplished through the use of a standard set of romantic elements. Most lithographs and sketches of cross valley landform regions use identical scenic elements, which were often contrived to exaggerate the natural sublimity. Bartlett's 120 steel engravings of *American Scenery* (25 percent Hudson River views), published in the 1840s, were very similar to those of Milbert, and were copied closely in volumes of scenic views published in the 1850s.[27] Bartlett's views of *The Hudson Highlands from Bull Hill* and *Centre Harbour—Lake Winnipisseogee* are representative of the group and employ the usual compositional formula. An original sketch analysis of these views and of the often depicted *Tomb of Kosciusko, West Point* which was copied from Bartlett by Sears, is found in figs. 27 and 28.

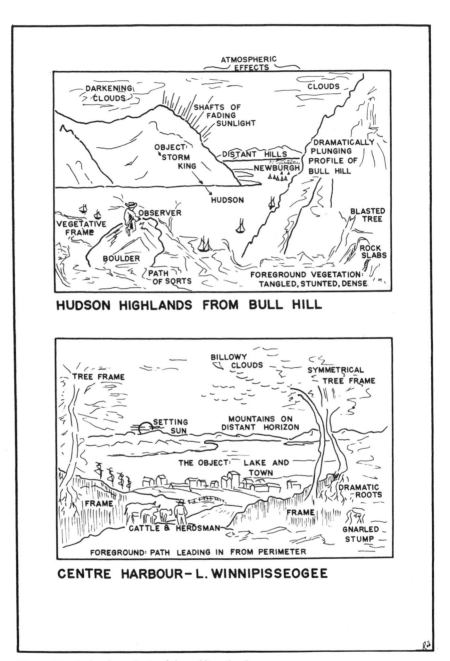

Figure 27. *A sketch analysis of the sublime landscape*
Based upon views contained in W. H. Bartlett, *American Scenery,* 1840

Figure 28. Sketch Analysis: The Tomb of Kosciusko.

TOP. "The Tomb of Kosciusko," Robert Sears, ed., *A New and Popular Pictorial Description of the United States,* New York: Robert Sears, 1848. p. 142.
BOTTOM. Original Interpretive Sketch

The sketchwork analysis of these views reveals how a very precise aura of romantic sublimity was lavishly purveyed via a lithographic formula. Here, sublimity is universally enhanced by diminutive human figures depicted as shepherds, farmers, Indians, city types, or other "idlers." Invariably, they have their backs turned to the foreground, a technique that leads the viewer to identify with the figures and imparts a quality of isolation and spaciousness to the landscape in which people—dwarfed by nature—appear dominated by a powerfully compelling (perhaps frightening) environment.[28]

The illustrations are constructed within a mental frame, or *coulisse,* of either blasted trees, barren cliffs, brooding, shadow-casting heights, rock ledges, upturned rocks, or tree stumps. The purpose of the *coulisse* is both to focus attention to the middle ground and to fortify the landscape with wild, angular, dreary, time-affected items of geological and botanical curiosity. Dramatic atmospheric effects appear (sunrises and sunsets, stars in twilight, storm clouds and heat lightning, and the interplay of light and dark), signifying the beautiful but also tempestuous and frightening aspects of nature.[29]

The Bartlett and Sears engravings are the quintessential representations of romantic imagery at work to achieve a Hudson Valley aesthetic. In the *Hudson Highlands from Bull Hill* the great bulk of Storm King casts its shadowy reflection upon the river. Shafts of fading light radiate beyond the mountain crest, while darkening clouds ride overhead. The Newburgh Plain and distant line of the Ulster County hills shut in the horizon. The almost "barren" or "blasted" vegetation ironically provides a made-to-order sense of ruin.[30] There is majesty, there is fear, there are the conflicting elements of melancholy gloom (time, death, cosmic space) and optimism. The *Tomb of Kosciusko* provides within a single visual expression elements of nationalism and history (through an appeal to the Revolutionary War heritage), geological interest and a sense of "rhapsodic admiration" for God's handiworks (the surrounding mountains and cliffs that compose the cross valley passage), sentiments of melancholy (evoked by the tomb and the theme of death), arcadian or pastoral interest (in the guise of idling figures, and sometimes cows), and lastly, elements of primitive sublimity (blasted trees and dark, mysterious vegetation). Everything in fact conspires to render the landscape sublime in the exact sense prescribed by romantic doctrine, and in accordance with contemporary ideas of what was sublime. Better graphic definitions of prevailing Hudson Valley romanticism would be hard to find. It is this visual formula then, and its literary accompaniment, that serves as the documentary evidence to the birth of a river aesthetic, an aesthetic that is carried into the twentieth century and is vigorously applied to this and every other river valley in which preservation of natural and historical features is a concern.

Above All Else, a Sublime Landscape

Although the adjectives sublime, picturesque, and beautiful were used so profusely and indiscriminately throughout these decades that their meaning sometimes became blurred, enough contrast was retained to indicate varying degrees of romanticism in landscape. The refined softness and seeming orderliness of the estate gardens and lawns in the lower Hudson Valley appealed to the fastidious connoisseur of the beautiful, while the scattering of hamlets and villages at the base of mountains, in coves, and in amphitheatres struck travelers as being picturesquely situated. Lighthouses, churches, hillside cottages, and loftily situated mountain houses were landscape features that were regarded as picturesque but not overbearing. Since picnicking and walking in rural areas had become popular by the 1850s, parks and cemeteries designed by architects like Olmsted (Central Park) and Downing (Rockland County Cemetery) strove to satisfy a preference for the picturesque by emphasizing winding paths and unexpected vistas—a planned irregularity that didn't overwhelm but rather conformed to a human scale.[31]

However, sublime landscape—whether painted or written— was the most sought-after phenomenon; through its varied appeals to patriotism, a sense of fear and melancholy, and emotional and moral involvement, it became the preferred manner in which mountain and highland landforms were viewed. At the Delaware Water Gap and on the Connecticut River at Mounts Tom and Holyoke, as well as at the cloves, stream valleys, and waterfalls of the Catskills, uncultivated clifflike slopes and the panoramic views of nature's titanic upheavals were all admired as sublime scenery. In Quebec, the rock-walled cliffs and capes of the Saguenay were sublime, the broad clay plain of the St. Lawrence merely picturesque.

The Palisades, Hook Mountain, the Tors, and the Hudson Highlands evoked feelings of sublimity where they impinged upon or cut across the river. In each of these locations, painters, poets, and travelers, through their "most rapturous description" of the sublime, sparked a sentiment for mountainscapes "that was to lead in one of its branches to the conservation movement."[32]

While the Palisades and Hook Mountain were, as late as the 1830s, still portrayed in a dull and quite unimposing manner, the general reaction was to endorse their sublime quality. These "dark barrier[s]" towered above the intervals of "flat [and] insipid scenery" elsewhere along the watercourse, and were painted with a fine romantic aspect. No less a purveyor of the Hudson River as sublime than Thomas Cole climbed atop the Palisades to sketch the declivities and columnated face—with the prescribed chiaroscuro and blasted trees.[33]

Storm King, which had been recently christened as such by N. P. Willis because "Butter Hill" did not convey the proper romantic connotation,[34] brooded majestically over the scene with its peak above the tempests; Crows Nest brought to mind the poetic fantasies of Rodman Drake ("The Culprit Fay"); and the Dunderberg presented a romantic "spectacle." This abode of Irving's dream-like spectres presided above the turbulent waters at the southern gate. West Point was regarded as one of the most romantic spots along the river because the surrounding summits, "shutting in the world," produced a "grand and Wild sublimity."[35] The interplay of light and shadow, geologic mystery, and the presence of powerful natural forces, produced this startlingly romantic landscape effect. Fanny Kemble probably said it all when visiting the highlands in 1832: "I was filled with awe. The beauty and wild sublimity of what I beheld almost seemed to crush my facilities. . . . I felt as though I had been carried into the immediate presence of God."[36]

Sublimity above all else, whether seen in the learned yet spontaneous utterings of river travelers or in the carefully formulated landscapes etched in scenery albums, had become the trademark of the romantic Hudson; this durable and enduring characteristic of simple yet profound beauty was firmly established in the national psyche by the Civil War, and would be drawn upon by future generations, who would undertake the task of preservation.

The Landscape of Nationalism

On the Fourth of July 1826, the fiftieth anniversary of American Independence, both John Adams and Thomas Jefferson died. This remarkable event was called the "grand coincidence"—a sign that the nation was invested with a special destiny. It helped perpetuate a sense of potential greatness, Empire in the making, Manifest Destiny.

By this time genre painting had assumed the function of idealizing the national "folk," and many a patriotic breast no doubt swelled with contentment upon seeing George Harvey's volume on *American Scenery:* vignettes of the forest being decimated for building material, and steamboats funneling clouds of smoke skyward, with the nation's capitol bathed in allegorical rays of sunlight in the background. And in the clouds above, progress was symbolized by "union and industry" clasping hands—all, in the artist's words, "an epitome of the historic progression of the United States."[37]

In this nationalistic context, a strong sense of national identity took its cue from pride in monumental, stunning, and sublime scenery. The landscape itself was consciously used to induce emotion and sentiment for national political and cultural esteem.

Merle Curti cites as examples of this the huge panoramas of the Mississippi and Hudson Valleys and the more than 7000 Currier & Ives lithographs that sentimentalized iceboating on the Hudson, picnicking in the highlands, steamboat racing, sleigh riding, trout fishing, hunting, harvesting, sugaring-off, and general enjoyment of a patriotic life.[38]

While George Caleb Bingham was painting inspiring symbols of pioneer freedom marching through the Cumberland Gap, Hudson Valley artists were commissioned by businessmen and collectors who felt a need to develop and promote a sense of Americanism through landscape painting. And Cole, although he would have preferred to paint in a more European fashion, concentrated upon Hudson River landscapes because of the period's and the public's insistence upon American nature. His merchant patrons, "imbued with the nationalism of the time," demanded realistic and detailed Hudson Valley scenes.[39]

Along the Hudson especially, landscape was most observably welded to aspects of nationalism. Even one so critical as G. T. Strong admitted that an American must "feel the prouder of his native land" as he sails up this river. Chauvinistic appeals were made to see the valley in order to obtain "useful instruction" in moral dignity and patriotic duty.[40] Citizens were urged to forego foreign travel in favor of the Hudson's western shore. Bryant's exhortation to Cole before leaving for Europe, the quote used by Thomas Flexner to preface his study of art in this period, is very much a watchword for the era:

> Thine eyes shall see the light of distant skies:
> Fair scenes shall greet thee where thou goest—
> Fair but different—every where the trace of men . . .
> Gaze on them, till the tears shall dim thy sight,
> But keep that earlier, wilder image bright.[41]

Evidences of industry and wealth in the form of highland estates and flotillas of cargo-laden boats plying the waters of the Tappan Zee were thought to provide "interesting and salutary lessons" in American handiwork and enterprise to European visitors. The mountain houses as well were seen as "symbol[s] of a young nation's wealth, leisure and cultural attainments."[42] And

A. J. Downing, a Newburgh landscape architect, associated patriotism with the improvement of one's habitation. For several decades before the Civil War he set forth the viewpoint that the Hudson Valley be covered with both estates and common "republican homes," for which he supplied the blueprints. He felt (*The Architecture of Country Houses,* 1850) that in an age of Jacksonian interest in the common man, it was fitting that plans for unostentatious but proper dwellings be available for those of less-than-gentlemanly wealth who chose to work their mark upon the valley's landscape.[43] The detached country cottages he suggested for the working class, and which have subsequently become an integral part of the valley's landscape, borrowed in detail from European models, but in essence Downing claimed these designs to be uniquely American.

That one attribute of the Hudson Valley that was praised as untarnished nationalistic virtue was its "wilderness." Highland areas of the Orange and Rockland shore still exhibited few signs of civilization's advance and this, although not as prime an example as the Catskills and Adirondacks, was interpreted as a wilderness condition. Abandoned agricultural land was also seen as reverting to wilderness. At least to those who viewed it from the distant city, the Hudson Valley was still very much wilderness. As Nash has said, "wilderness was the nationalist's trump." It gave the American landscape a unique, pristine quality lacking in the Old World:

Seizing on this distinction and adding to it deistic and Romantic assumptions about wild country, nationalists argued that far from being a liability, wilderness was actually an American asset. . . . by the middle decades of the nineteenth century wilderness was recognized as a cultural and moral resource and a basis for national self-esteem.[44]

The Historically Inspired Landscape

Attempts had long been made to impart a romantically necessary set of historical associations to the scenic landforms of the lower Hudson Valley. Beautiful landscapes became sublime when bestowed with Irving's creations, "noble savages," and

Revolutionary War personalities. These efforts were largely successful—most especially in the latter case—and by 1825 the valley's historical and literary inspirations were nearly the rivals of Europe's.

The continued, and even increased, interest in viewing landscape, aesthetically fortified by historical sentiments, was reflected in the period's penchant for Fourth-of-July oratory, the erection of armies of monuments (as at West Point), the founding of town and village historical societies, and the publication of the first county histories (e.g. Eagers, *Orange County,* 1846–47). Such local histories were exercises in sandwiching together Revolutionary War trivia with expressions of delight in local scenery.

In more abstract ways, the compulsion to explore a landscape layered with history and tradition took on shades of escapism. Longfellow evoked the distant, romantic days of Hiawatha; Cooper retreated into the idealized realms of the eighteenth-century landed aristocracy; and Paulding, as had Irving, shifted to the shadowy illusions of olden times along the banks of the Hudson.

Thomas Cole, enamored of Italian landscape, also favored Indian legend and considered Lake George, for example, worthy of the canvas in part because of its associations with the Revolution and the writings of Cooper. Since the Hudson was in most places devoid of truly ancient historical associations, Cole furthermore visualized the highlands as an amphitheatre built by "Titans" in some forgotten age. Whether approached in practical or idealized fashion, the result was the same: the American landscape, already sublimely wild, was doubly favored because it was hallowed ground no longer wanting for the artifacts and lore of man, or man's mental creations. As Willis said of the highlands, the area had become a "neighborhood" enriched with meaning and sentiment, "a spot of earth with a soul."[45]

Along the Hudson's shores the valiant but forlorn defense of Forts Washington and Lee, Cornwallis's heroic ascent of the Palisades at Alpine, the mauling of Wayne's troops near Tappan, André's rendezvous at the Long Clove, the despair of Bloody Pond, the signal fires atop Bear Mountain and Beacon added a human dimension to the grandeur of highland scenery. "Almost the name of every place" reminded one traveler of "that glorious struggle for independence."[46] Apart from its beauty, Frances Trollope found the region romantic because of these same historical associations, as did Almira Read of Massachusetts: "When viewing West Point, the thousand interesting things that transpired here in the American Revolution immediately rush into the mind."[47]

Freeman Hunt's *Letters About the Hudson and its Vicinity* (1835–37) are heavily loaded with romantic descriptions of the river's "diversified scenery, rendered interesting by revolutionary reminiscences."[48] The guidebooks too, echoing the travelers' enthusiasms, were saturated with references to the Hudson's historical ground. Patten's *Glimpses of the United States* (1852) and Knapp's *Picturesque Beauties of the Hudson River* (1835) glow with mention of "grand revolutionary struggles" and "the great Spirits of the War of Independence." Bartlett's *Picturesque America* (1840) was perhaps the best-known and most copied-from guidebook; any wartime episode which gave "a story to the spot" was included in this adoration to landscape in which the Hudson's "venerated garb of antiquity" was described: "It is not easy to pass and repass the now peaceful and beautiful waters of this part of the Hudson [the highlands], without recalling to mind scenes and actors in the great drama of the revolution."[49]

By this time, a very important spatial corollary had been added to the doctrine of historical association. The neoclassical enthusiasm for ruins had carried over into the romantic period and in the literature, in the arts, and even in landscape gardening, "we stumble upon ruins on every side—Ruins of Art, Ruins of Time, Ruins of Nature." European travelers had become addicted to ruined abbeys and the remains of castles, poeticized by Tennyson.[50] The imagination had become haunted with the interrelationships between "the dim memories of indefinite time" and the decay of both man-made and natural objects in the landscape. Again it was the shadowy and remote aspects of historical time that conveyed a sublimity to the landscape. By carrying home pieces of Roman columns and mental images of Stonehenge, a contact was achieved with people and places from distant times that provoked a strange and romantic shiver.

Because there were no ancient historical landscapes in America, "ruins" tended to be either artificial or newly ruined. The popularity of ornamenting estate grounds and gardens with crumbling and decapitated classical columns dates from this period, as do the Gothic and Classical revivals in architecture. By the 1840s a desire to live in a sham medieval environment, a "Scottish baronial" manor, or a "Norman Castle" was as natural as reading Walter Scott.[51] But true ruins could not be comfortably lived in, and America had none anyway. Since "the frame house was a poor ruin. . . . decay[ing] too rapidly, failing to signify the slow ravagement of time," imitation castles were built on the Hudson's banks. River travelers, with the works of Scott on their laps, could see ruined arches and columns placed at conspicuous points along the shore and feel themselves transported backward in time.[52]

Cole and other artists of the Hudson River School painted these ancient and classical fantasies, but because the New World lacked the golden glow of true antiquity the models (ruined aqueducts, towers, battlements, etc.) were largely European, specifically Italian.[53] However, by the 1840s it had become acceptable to draw upon the colonial and Revolutionary heritage as a source of ruins. On the Hudson, the prime example of the period's fascination with ruins were the dismantled stone fortifications of highland Fort Putnam ("silence and decay now mark the spot [of these] moldering ruins"). It was a must for every tourist to do "the complete round of the ruins" at "Old Fort Put," and they were the foreground, or the subject matter, of most highland landscapes.[54]

Sublimity Enhanced Through Geologic Curiosities and Concepts

The Hudson's mountainous landforms were also romantically appealing because of their geologic nature. As people delved into the scientific reasons for the structure and appearance of such "curiosities" as Niagara and Trenton Falls, the Delaware Water Gap, the "Notch" and the "Flume" in the White Mountains, and the Ontario Lake Plain's "Alluvial Way,"[55] the highlands and the palisaded landforms to the south became all the more alluring.

The traprock cliffs in Bergen and Rockland, "this curious wall," "this accident of nature," were acknowledged for their "incredible grandeur," but were also described as to lineal fissures, debris slopes, and structural similarities with other such features on this continent and in Europe.[56] The highland passage was the brunt of much geological speculation, and when an avalanche tore a wide path on the northeastern side of Storm King in 1853, the reasons for this, and the nature of the newly exposed rock, became a matter of great popular interest.[57]

There are discernible explanations for interest in the valley's landforms as geological phenomena. The general public continued to be "geology conscious" in the first half of the century. "The impact of this science was felt by many who had little education" and so a "passionate interest in rocks [became] typical of the 1820's and 1830's . . . reveal[ing] how narrow the gap between science and taste was at this time."[58]

In both Europe and America popular interest kept pace with tremendous strides in research into the geological sciences. Poets and travelers were acquainted with and used Hutton's *Theory of the Earth* (1795), Lyell's *Elements of Geology* (1838), and Hitchcock's *Elementary Geology* (1840). By 1838 the State of New York had surveyed its territory in detail, and had printed hundreds of engravings representing rock strata and other geological features in eleven quarto volumes.[59] Much of this information trickled down to the public through newspapers, the common school, the free library system, and inexpensive magazines. It was an indication of what Curti has called "the popularization of knowledge," a condition which soon led to "long vexatious hours of the tourist's day" being occupied with "much measurement of the 'curiosities' in height and volume."[60] Geology, then, not only furthered the art of tourism, but also, through its quest for explanations as to the origin of landforms, incorporated the idea of God's creation with the passing eons of time. This combination of meditations on the dim past supported by a basic geologic knowledge of geomorphological forms that were considered scenically sublime added much to aesthetic conceptualization.

Landscape artists in this period, especially those of the Hudson River school, were committed to exact realism in the composition of their forms. For Cole and Church an interest in and knowledge of geology was essential to the correct portrayal of rock forms in the Catskills and highlands. Geologic realism in landscape, combined with flourishes of the imagination, is a condition largely attributable to the German (Düsseldorf) School of Landscape and the writings of Von Humboldt. The latter's *Cosmos* appeared in New York in 1850 and is said to have influenced many Hudson River artists. Church, for example, well-versed in topography, meteorology and geology, was directly inspired by the Baron in the compellingly accurate presentation of vegetation, volcanic processes, and climatic elements in his native and South American landscapes.[61]

The contemporary fad for historical ruins also lent itself to the visualization of geologic structures as the "ruins" of the natural world. To see the debris and detritus of geologic processes as ruins, and moreover to "turn rocks into castles and battlements" in the mind's eye, gave the mountain landscapes and cliffs a human association needed to accentuate the romantic even more.[62] Waterfalls and exposed rock strata, caverns, the talus cones beneath the Palisades, the columnar facings of Hook Mountain, and the vast confusion of mountain peaks in the highlands were all identified as "ruins" at various times. In this way (or, alternately, by anthropomorphizing these landforms into profiles or hands), the romantic landscape was amplified through an artificial sense of man-made antiquity and time elapsed.[63]

The Pastoral Image in This Valley of Hurry

The evolution of an aesthetic landscape before the Civil War was, finally, conditioned by the concept of pastoralism. While developed in America by Jefferson, Crèvecoeur, et al. before the 1820s,[64] pastoral imagery was perfected in the arts and literature and in travel reports in this period. The imagery of what is generally termed the "pastoral design"[65] takes as its sociospatial ideal a vaguely defined "middle ground" between the oppressions of civilization and the fears and hardships of wilderness. This is what Leo Marx called a "landscape of reconciliation," a bucolic agrarian asylum or retreat, a "mental suburbia" or semi-primitive garden of rural comfort that became a literary convention of the nineteenth century.[66]

The concept of rural order and virtue, positioned between wild animal nature and urban rational ideals, had been applied to European landscape for many decades, but with enclosure and the encroachment of mills and factories the countryside was fenced and blackened. The imagery faded in Europe, to be resurrected in those colonies where bucolic peace and happiness had not yet been spoiled. The South Sea Islands, Australia, New Zealand, and Tasmania were hopefully regarded as "pastoral arcadias," "rural gardens of tropical delight."[67]

However it was in America that the ideal of a contented, agrarian-based citizenry dwelling in the gentle lyricism of a pastoral setting found its greatest hope, corrupted neither by the oppression and anxieties of mills and cities nor by the primitive, atavistic instincts of the wilderness:

Beginning in Jefferson's time, the cardinal image of American aspirations was a rural landscape, a well-ordered green garden magnified to continental size. Although it probably shows a farmhouse or a neat white village, the scene usually is dominated by natural objects: in the foreground a pasture, a twisting brook with cattle grazing nearby, then a clump of elms on the rise in the middle distance and beyond that, way off on the western horizon, a line of dark hills. This is the countryside of the old republic, a chaste, uncomplicated land of rural virtue. . . . On the whole Americans were unsentimental about unmodified nature. . . . the wilderness was precious to most Americans chiefly for what could be made of it—a terrain of rural peace and happiness.[68]

Although this was the ideal, serious flaws quickly developed in the pastoral imagery. The romantic, mellow image of agrarian bliss did not sit well with the agricultural realities of the day. More and more, the ground between the city and the forest was becoming a despoiled and littered landscape; farming was unrewarding, back-breaking toil subject to the vagaries of nature, urban landlords and markets. Moreover, it was probably apparent to all but the staunchest romantic idealists that America was not to be "a garden, a permanently rural republic." [69]

Many regions of America were conceived of as being representative of the elusive pastoral geography (John Allen has explored the application of the pastoral theme to the Northwest Territories), [70] but again, the Hudson Valley emerges as the finest example of the conflicts and contradictions of this conceptual imagery.

For the New York literary world of William Cullen Bryant, N. P. Willis, and the "Knickerbocker" poets and essayists, the ideal was a rural, gentlemanly retreat on the banks of the Hudson. Willis, for example, a very popular magazine and newspaper essayist and member of the New York social elite, toured the Hudson many times and spoke with Irving, J. Addison Richards, and Downing on matters of landscape modification and appreciation. Willis wrote the text for Bartlett's *American Scenery* in 1840 and his "Idlewild Papers," a series of letters written from his country retreat at Cornwall in 1853–54 for the *Home Journal,* document the contemporary thought of Hudson Valley "gentlemen" concerning the concept of landscape. Though lacking the artistic imagination of Cole and the intellectual calibre of Thoreau, Willis was nonetheless both a creator and reflector of environmental taste. [71] For Willis and those men of "genteel tastes" who were busy carpeting the valley with a "velvet edge" of villa properties, a form of aristocratic English-derived pastoralism was evoked by rearranging the shrubbery and dotting the lawns that sloped down to the river with urns, columns, and cows. In paintings of river estates that strongest artistic symbol of the pastoral, the contented cow, appears regularly. The cow also grazed contentedly about the ruins of Fort Putnam, upon the wooded slopes of Crows Nest, and below the palisaded bluffs in Bergen and Rockland. [72]

In the siting both of country cottages and of the more elaborate estates, a consideration of the pastoral design was involved. The site had to be conveniently removed from, and yet proximate to, "the City." And it had to be short of the admirably wild but inhospitable mountains of the Adirondacks and Catskills, for pastoral rhetoricians were not transcendentalists prone to a hermitic existence in the wildwood.[73] They realized the pleasures of art and society, but preferred the pursual of such pleasures in semi-cultivated or exurban realms atop the Palisades, in country villages such as Nyack, Haverstraw, and Cornwall, and on the mountainous flanks of the Tors and Storm King. Willis's Idlewild was such a "middle location" where civilization could be observed with a degree of detachment: "Busy life was very near. Wild fastnesses of rock were very close behind." It was from this secure and temporarily unspoiled perch that Willis watched "the featureless come-at-ableness of the rest of the Valley of hurry."[74]

The pastoral design was continually subjected to the onslaught of an urban-technological counterforce. "Things are in the saddle and ride mankind" Thoreau had said.[75] With the rapid growth of cities through rural attrition and immigration, the "City Evil" emerged in the guise of slums, poor working conditions, and a host of other urban-related ills (capitalism and materialism), that were condemned by the romanticists. The ugly urbanizing landscape was spreading outward and, with its mechanical tentacles (railroads, telegraphs, steamboats, factories), it was consuming the arcadian countryside. At Cornwall, the human tide disembarking from the New York steamboats made Willis sick for fear of being "lemonaded into insignificance" by the crushing arms of the city. The urbanization, or even suburbanization, of the lower valley foreshadowed "a lessening of personal orbit, a reducing of the individual and prerogative occupancy of the earth's surface."[76]

A pastoral landscape in the Hudson Valley or anywhere else in the Eastern United States was threatened, and probably doomed, by pernicious machines ("instruments of power, speed, noise, fire, iron, smoke"). But railroads and steamboats had captured the public imagination, and "the great majority of Americans welcomed the new technology. . . . welcomed is too weak a verb: they grasped and panted and cried for it." [77] Not everyone, however, was that enraptured by the machine. Romanticists, idealists, transcendentalists, Jeffersonian agrarians, all looked upon industrialism as a direct assault upon the pastoral landscape, and so wrote of and painted the Hudson's scenery each from a different perspective. Indeed, Irving had already criticized his era as "degenerate days of iron and brass" and the intrusion of railroads (and the suburban tracts they made possible) was regarded by Cole and Willis as a shocking and crude encroachment upon the idyllic landscape of the lower valley. By 1844, "the great world was invading the land, transforming the sensory texture of rural life—the way it looks and sounds—and threatening, in fact, to impose a new and more complete dominion over it." [78]

Better than anyone, Willis and Cole expressed the sense of impending loss besetting the pastoral ideal in Rockland and Orange Counties. Willis was forever annoyed that "the rattling monster" on the east shore of the Hudson could bring the city to the highlands in just an hour and a half. "The feel of the city eye" was placed upon his doorstep, and Cornwall "was shoved down to a suburb." He frowned upon the flourishing steamboat landings as purveyors of sin and crime and calculated that some 5000 people, being conveyed to and from the city, "pass[ed] daily under my library window." The same sentiment was echoed in Cole's mournful observation that the railroad and steamboat companies were "cutting down all the trees in the beautiful valley on which I have looked so often with a loving eye." [79] Pastoralism's cracked façade would soon be completely shattered in this romantic valley.

This pastoral dialogue is finally and oddly related to the dilemma and contradiction of the river's technological and industrial sublimity. Befitting an age of ebbing but still potent nationalist optimism, machines were proof of American progress and native inventiveness which made traveling and sightseeing easier. The *New York Daily Times* noted in 1851 that the railroad was regarded as an aid to viewing the beauty of the Hudson's west shore landforms.[80] Perhaps; but even more amenable to the leisurely viewing of scenery was the opportunity afforded by the slower moving steamboats, whose decks served as ideal viewing platforms from which to study and absorb the sublimities of the riverline. In a sense, the steamboat was the perfect invention at the perfect time, a symbiosis of technology and romantic concept.

Still, the subordination of the Hudson Valley to steam and rail presented romantic conceptualizers with a dilemma. They greeted the "iron horses" and "fire-Titans" of the river "as both a national blessing and national tragedy."[81] As with the romantic ambivalence in the previous period, and as reflective of a society challenged by the two-faced God of optimism and pessimism, the more thoughtful writers and travelers were repelled by the mechanical invasion of the landscape, and yet were strangely fascinated by it. Mills, quarries, and brick factories became worthy objects for picturesque lithographs and the thunder of steampipes and the grating of steel rails bespoke an emerging industrial aesthetic. Waterfalls, while picturesque or sublime in themselves, might be made more so with mills.[82] The scenery of the Palisades, Hook Mountain, and the highlands need not be diminished by the presence of quarries, ice houses, wood slides, and sawmills. The river's innate sublimity was, in short, added to by man's technological and industrial sublimity.

As it somewhat betrayed and confused the pastoral design, the concept of industrial sublimity was most assuredly not subscribed to by those who were the prime movers of romantic taste. Willis saw slaughterhouses and brickyards as economic necessities, but felt that the former (in no sense sublime) might be restricted to the less spectacular areas of scenery such as around New Windsor and Newburgh. The brickyards too were indispensable, but should be contained within the localities of Haverstraw and Cornwall, and not be allowed to become

eye-sore[s], in the scenery of the Highlands. . . . For the present—say a forty year hegira of bricks—the traveller is expected to be blind to our "lower story" of landscape . . . to see the unrestorable and beautiful trees hewn ruthlessly down and the green slopes torn open for clay-pits.[83]

New roads were being cut across the highlands in the 1850s, and while they might be desirable in the economic sense, there was something terrible in what they did to the "vast cathedral" of the mountains. Remarking upon the construction of a market road being blasted across Storm King Mountain by the military engineers to connect West Point with Newburgh, Willis regarded this "refinement" as an unthinking acceptance of nature altered technologically:

The Storm King's granite-wall blocks up the way, at present—his mountain precipice rising bare from the deep water of the Hudson—but this can be soon shelved around with money and powder. . . . [it] will be one of the most picturesque drives in the world. A part of it will be blown out from the face of the rock.[84]

Bingham, painting the western waterways in the 1840s, re-fused to include steamboats in his paintings. Cole, never addicted to the pastoral landscape and with visions fixed firmly on the wilderness beyond, probably never came to terms with semi-civilized "middle landscapes." His best retort was to exclude all manner of industry and similar blasphemies from his paintings and concentrate on capturing the disappearing wilds.[85] Cooper and Thoreau, recognizing that wilderness and civilization were both needed for a proper balance in man, swayed between both polarities, but finally opted for a geographical equilibrium, a "middle ground." Willis, as had the Hudson River gentry, sub-scribed to the ideas of romantic pastoralism and attempted to mold a bucolically romantic landscape in and around the high-lands of the lower Hudson Valley. This landscape of the mind, translated into reality as much as possible by landscape architects and their patrons, would be a fleeting and transient setting at best. It seldom coincided with, and was often used to conceal, the harsh material realities of technological and urban fringe tran-sitions, but it was the most suitable accommodation available to the romantically inclined generation between the age of Andrew Jackson and the Civil War.

Part 5
The Valley of Hurry and Spoil

The Romantic Ideal Moves West

DURING THE 1870s the types of land use which affected the valley's visual makeup expanded. Agriculture had become "fancy farming," an exercise in the art of "rural adornment." Productive fields continued to be phased out and specializations geared to local topographic conditions became more common. Farmland was converted to recreational, resort, and residential usage, a transition in part occasioned by the concept of the "therapeutic landscape" as applied to the Palisades, Hook Mountain, and the highlands. Manufacturing and extractive industries, as pursued both in the river towns and on the adjacent uplands, progressively despoiled the landscape.

While certain ideas that were once useful to the visualization of a romantically aesthetic environment lost their vitality, others continued to be used. Sublime and historical associations could add little that was new to a landscape burdened with an almost mechanically predictable romantic phraseology that was no longer inspiring or exciting. Romanticism had gone flat, and technology had attacked the land, if not subjugating it. The Hudson endured nevertheless—with an unperturbed majesty. The "geography of the ideal" had perhaps moved West, but eastern mountainscapes such as that of the lower Hudson Valley possessed a more elusive, but nonetheless time-honored and proven aesthetic.

Chapter 9
Incompatibilities: The Stone Crushers and an Expanding Suburbia

*No man sows, yet many men reap
a harvest from the Hudson.*
John Burroughs, "Our River," 1880.

FOLLOWING THE CIVIL War, changes in land use occurred in the lower Hudson Valley that were both reflective of conditions brought on by the war itself and indicators of future events. Agriculture, for example, although still important in some localities, either continued to decline or become even more specialized and localized. While industries such as steamboat construction and highland iron mining had passed their zeniths, others became more elaborate. On the Nyack and Haverstraw lowlands and in the Fort Lee area light industries diversified. With the coming of dynamite, the techniques of the ever-present and always-industrious quarrymen brought unprecedented destruction to the river's scenery. Residential and outdoor recreational pastimes assumed increasing importance. The valley was also quickly approaching a point in time at which future land use would become a matter of legislative action.

The Art of "Fancy Farming" and "Rural Adornment"

During the 1870s and 1880s, when many of the county histories were written, the authors at times bubbled over with pride in the local agricultural prowess. It was stated that "Clarkstown [in Rockland] was emphatically an agricultural town," and that Harrington Township, on the north Bergen shore, was a large and fertile producer and processor of farm commodities. As late as 1884 Rockland's acreage was two-thirds devoted to agriculture and the Englewood-Alpine area was referred to as "farm country."[1]

But this is somewhat misleading. Local variations and long-range transitions had greatly changed the nature of agriculture in the lower valley. Generally, in the interior parts of the counties immediately to the west, or in some cases on the western slope of the higher ground, the municipalities were still, as they had been since colonial days, primarily farming towns. However, farming had been reduced to a state of minimal importance in the industrially and residentially developed lowlands along the river. Farm buildings were being abandoned or renovated for other uses; for example the Piermont orphan asylum was located in converted farm structures in 1884.

Yet on the fertile slopes of Hook Mountain, the Tors, Crows Nest, and Storm King, people apparently remained unconvinced of the impracticality of agriculture; at Upper Nyack, in the shadow of Low Tor, a changeover from family farm to estate and summer residence occurred in the 1860s and 1870s, while the slopeland adjacent to Hook Mountain and High Tor continued to be operated as "farm properties."[2] It is not clear how intensive or successful these operations were. A sobering but probably unheeded observation was made of similar farms in the highlands by Ruttenber and Clark in 1881:

The agricultural products of this town can never assume much prominence. There is a small amount only of arable land. This is mostly on the plateau above the high, rocky banks of the river, and in the narrow valleys of the streams. A large portion of the town must always be left to its native wilderness, much of the mountain region being too rocky even to constitute grazing lands even if they were cleared.[3]

The agricultural industry itself went through changes in this period, changes induced by a greater accessibility to metropolitan New York and the increased presence of a class of "gentlemen farmers" or rural nonfarmers:

On account of its nearness to New York City, with its four or five railroads, the final result of farming in [Rockland] County must be fancy farming, that is, the lands will naturally fall into the hands of those who have the means and love the pursuit of farming, not so much for the return in money, as the return in health and pleasure.[4]

So that the prominent gentlemen of the county might pursue their interests in "rural adornment," the Rockland County Historical and Forestry Society was created in the 1870s. In other more tangible ways, emphasis was placed upon the conversion of field and pasture to orchard and vegetable garden, entities scaled to the energies and talents of country gentlemen addicted to horticultural experimentation and to the convenience of a large urban market.

Apple orchards, vineyards, and cabbage patches were consequently sprinkled along the Palisade tableland, in the Sparkill Valley from Piermont to Tappan, in the Rockland Lake area, and in the Moodna Valley from Cornwall to Washingtonville on the highlands' northern flank. Finally, throughout the three-county hinterland, the dairy industry underwent internal shifts. The nature of the operation became more and more machine- and factory-oriented ("the new method took the form of cheese factories, creameries, and condenseries"), while the end product shifted to fluid milk: "Though cheese and butter continued to increase for most of this period, more and more areas were turning to the supply of fluid milk for urban consumers."[5]

Recreation, Resorts, and Estates

While commerce and industry were for the most part confined to the interior and river lowlands, and while agrarian activities became less and less detectable in the landscape, the expansion of recreation, resorts, and estates became the most essential
and potentially powerful ingredient of the region's makeup. The
seemingly total subordination of the area to such activities is
clearly seen in a detail of the Fort Lee area in the *Bergen County
Atlas* of 1876, depicting the grounds of the Pavilion Hotel, the
cliff-top estates of the Annett and Wight families, the summer
boarding houses, the Peoples Line ferry dock, and the picnic
grounds at Bluff Grove.[6] Kindred recreational services here were
ideally suited to accommodate the creation of the Palisades
Amusement Park by the late 1880s.

John Krout and Clifford Lord have researched in much detail the meteoric rise of popular interest in outdoor sports and
recreation in this country.[7] The lower Hudson, as a nearby
recreational outlet, served the metropolitan populace in new,
spatially pleasing ways; vacations, day outings, yacht club and
rowing regattas, race tracks, bicycling, fishing, camping, bathing, and hiking. The growth of the "out-of-door" movement
was important in realigning the social landscape of the valley.
This movement was brought on in part by increased leisure time
and money as well as a general shift in attitude away from the
strict observance of the sabbath and blue laws.

In describing the recreational assets of the highlands in 1882,
the author of one guidebook referred to the West Point–Crows
Nest area as "the Central Park of the Hudson."[8] This is in many
ways an apt designation. The minds and the hands of Olmsted,
Vaux, and Downing profoundly affected the shape of the cultural
landscape throughout the lower valley, and in their lifetime the
riverscape and its highland features became a scenically contrived
Central Park, a "democratic pleasure ground" for the urban
masses in desperate need of "the gentle beauty of English pastoral scenery."[9] It was of course not so much "English" scenery
that was desired, but a pastoral landscape that, through its play

upon a green, open, leisurely, and supposedly soothing visual composition, relieved the stresses of urban man.

While the resorts and estates were built for and patronized by the wealthy, it was obvious that the valley also had to serve as a recreational resource for those unable to afford a country home, or a season (even a weekend) at a mountain house. In response to this need, a chain of picnic grounds and public beaches developed on the western bank of the Hudson with names like "Occidental Grove" and "Excelsior Grove." The guidebooks and newspapers encouraged the one-day excursionist to revel in the surrounding scenic grandeur, especially by hiking or touring the mountains and woods along the newly constructed scenic walkways and drives. There were "strikingly lovely" geologic features such as waterfalls, natural pools, and rock formations observable only to those curious and energetic enough to trek away from the riverine pleasure grounds over splendidly laid out pathways, such as those atop the Palisades, in the vicinity of Buttermilk Falls, and most notably along the West Point to Cornwall road. Willis found the latter "quite as smooth and enjoyable as the Catskill Mountain Road."[10]

Apparently very few of the "uncultured urban hordes" ever did more than drown themselves in liquid refreshments at the pleasure grounds, after which they would vomit at the railing and pass out on the deck floor of the steamboats returning to Manhattan. The "rabble" were described as being "deposited" at Iona's picnic grounds in "barges." From the information available, it would appear that a Sunday outing at the bathing beaches along the base of the Palisades or the picnic grounds at Alpine ("more noisy than nice"), Rockland Lake, or Picnic Rock in the shadow of Storm King, was anything but an aesthetic or educational experience.[11] Panoramas of leaping sturgeon and billowy masses of sail had little appeal for a vacationer being shoved about the overcrowded steamboat or vainly searching for a quiet patch of grass at the overcrowded picnic spot. Drake's poetic fantasies of the Hudson were not for the average daytripper.

Much more significant both in terms of an extensive landscape impact, and the evolution of the preservation concept, is the creation of the more proper resorts and estates for the wealthy. The singular importance of the Catskill Mountain House in its relation to American social history and landscape has been dealt with superbly by Van Zandt.[12] In much the same way, the phenomenon of the mountain house resort was engraved upon the face of the lower Hudson Valley.

There were many such resorts, multi-storied and built of wood, mansarded and flag-topped, usually on a promontory overlooking the Hudson. The operation and appearance of Cozzens' West Point Hotel has been discussed as the prototype of its genre. Cozzens ("The Hotel on the Bluff") changed hands after the Civil War and became Henry Cranston's New York Hotel, or simply Cranston's. The new owner, in a fashion soon to be repeated by other hotel operators, published his own brochures that lavishly depicted and enumerated the splendors of the highlands and its river—and especially of his establishment. In the course of 32 pages the hotel grounds, the accommodations and facilities, the "continual feast" of surrounding mountain scenery, are so enthusiastically portrayed as to mimic the sights and scents of Milton's "true Hesperian Paradise." All this only two hours and fifteen minutes from Manhattan via excursion boat; timetables and other details courtesy of Mr. Cranston.[13]

Such vigorously pursued advertising is probably excusable in view of the competition born of the 1870s and 1880s. Numerous equally self-aggrandizing "houses" were built nearby. The Parry House was situated less than one mile from Cranston's, while comparable if somewhat less successful hotels sprung up throughout the highlands. The old Grant mansion on Iona Island was, for example, converted into a hotel. Caldwell's Hotel took advantage of its location at the southern gateway to the highlands (and also of rumors and abortive plans for the Dunderberg Scenic Railroad). Orr's Mills in the Moodna Valley was a popular resort, with almost a dozen boarding houses in the vicinity. And the Storm King Mountain House south of Cornwall ("twelve-hundred feet above tide-water in the heart of pine woods, where the visitors found health as well as recreation"), was alternately a sanitarium, resort, and private club.[14]

The shoreline from Englewood Cliffs to Haverstraw, generally unlike that in Westchester and Putnam Counties, was also conspicuously dotted with river resorts with names like the Fort Lee Park Hotel, McKelvin's Summer Hotel (Piermont), and Ackerson's Rockland Lake Hotel on the river landing. The village of Nyack, doubling its population in the summer months and developing catering and entertainment services based upon the resort hotel and boarding house trade, became "a very popular summer resort. Every year brings a larger throng of guests. . . . Prices have gone up to balance Saratoga rates."[15] The views from the Nyack hills, the rustic atmosphere, and the carriage roads and bathing facilities at the Palmer House, Smithsonian, and Clarendon Hotels provided visitors with "that indescribable sense of peace and forgetfulness which characterizes this enchanting region."[16] Probably the largest and best publicized of the Nyack resorts was the Tappan Zee House, a four-story structure on the riverbank used in the winter months as the "Rockland Female Institute." The building is often depicted in the county atlases and histories, complete with carriageways and guests playing croquet and strolling about the extensive landscaped grounds.[17]

In Bergen County too there were well known hotels designed to accommodate the coterie of summer patrons. Several were developed along the route of the Northern Railroad such as the Highwood House at Tenafly and the Murray Hill Home at Demarest. The latter was known for its artificial lake, Alpine scenery, and "eight acres of lawn laid out in terraces." Access was by an elaborately designed railroad station house built of Palisade stone.[18]

If, as Van Zandt says, basic environmental harmonies are often understood in terms of the social and economic life of landmarks such as resort hotels, then the cultural transformation of the Palisades in this period is best seen in the context of the Palisade Mountain House. This 300-room monstrosity atop Allison Point, "one of the highest and most prominent projections of the Palisades,"[19] embodies in its history much of what the Palisade region had become.

The Mountain House (fig. 29), a landmark familiar to river travelers, was built for Cornelius and Garrett Lydecker and William Dana in 1869. The hotel seems to have been an immediate success, and added more rooms, as befitted one of "the finest hotels in the country."[20] As with the Catskill Mountain House, the Palisade Mountain House was situated at the cliff edge and fronted with a broad columnated porch affording fine views of the valley. A mansard roof and a collection of Victorian-style towers loomed above the cream-colored walls. Apart from its pleasure grounds and winding driveways, the realm of the mountain house extended north along the cliff-top to Palisade Avenue, where a specially built zigzag road descended the rocky slope to the talus zone. Here a wharf was constructed by the Englewood Dock and Turnpike Company (a group of shareholders interested in the hotel) for use as a steamboat landing. Two boats a day landed at the dock and "business was so good that there was a plan [never realized] to build a steam elevator to lift passengers up to the hotel from the waterfront."[21] The mountain house, already accessible to the railroad, was then made approachable from the river. (With respect to accessibility, it might be added that the owners of the mountain house were the first to advocate spanning the Hudson in the present vicinity of the George Washington Bridge.)

The advantages enjoyed by the guests were dwelt upon by the *New York Times* in an 1881 article entitled "Features of Summer Life at the Mountain House." Mentioned were the excellent rail and river connections; the proximity (only nine miles) to New York; bracing and salubrious mountain air; rural and/or wooded surroundings; and of course the unsurpassed vistas. For largely these reasons, the hotel served as a summer retreat for prominent New Yorkers, was used for political gatherings, and was frequented by businessmen, lawyers, and bankers.[22]

After serving its guests for fifteen years, the resort at last shared the fate of many period hotels in the valley; it was destroyed by fire in 1884 and for many years thereafter its skeletal ruins stood along the Palisade crest.

By the Civil War the eastern side of the Valley from Man-

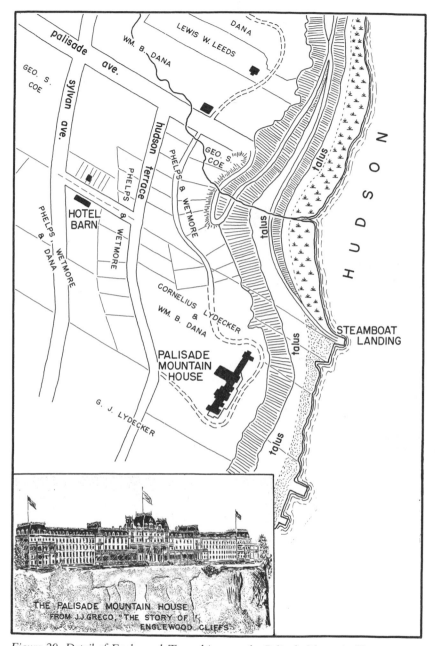

Figure 29. Detail of Englewood Township near the Palisade Mountain House
From: Walker, *Atlas of Bergen County, New Jersey*, 1876. (Scale: 1″ = 260′)
INSERT: The Palisade Mountain House. From: J. J. Greco, *The Story of Englewood Cliffs*

hattan to Poughkeepsie presented "a constant succession of comfortable, elegant, and sometimes ostentatious country houses." At town sites such as Hastings, Yonkers, and Ossining, "society was defined by the height (elevation) of the land."[23] Immigrant laborers, blacks, and the lower echelons of society lived among the coalyards, railroad shacks, and the boat docks while country seats and summer villas were built along Broadway with its fine panoramic views of the western shore. This residential pattern, and specifically the boom in rural estates, was not found in the more remote highland precincts or the more centrally located parts of Westchester and Putnam Counties until greater accessibility was provided by an expanded road and rail network. Land speculation companies and wealthy New York families, in most cases directly or indirectly involved with the railroad, acquired highland and mountaintop properties.[24]

Likewise, road and rail construction through parts of the valley that were relatively isolated before the 1860s resulted in a surge of estate building. Transport lines which brought summer excursionists to the mountain houses opened these same areas to estate building. In Englewood Township, influential landowners with railroad affiliations were the men associated with the Palisade Mountain House and also with the plan to develop a "velvet ribbon" of elegant residences along the Palisade cliff-top.[25] William O. Allison in fact built his own mansion on the grounds of the burnt-out mountain house—an illustration of land-use succession in the area: the transition from undeveloped farmland to resort and residential, and then finally to institutional and recreational use.

As the *New York Times* reported in 1871, "It is well known that a large number of New Yorkers are obliged, through the expense of living in the city, to take up their abode in the river counties. They go in and out at all hours, and form a steady and remunerative passenger traffic."[26] Summer houses and seasonal excursions were giving way to permanent abodes and daily commutation.

From the Hook Mountain region north through the highlands, the villa style summer residence still predominated; the

Cornwall Basin in the 1880s (where a crisp business was done in the building of "portable cottages" for summer use) was regarded as ideally situated for seasonal villas. Highland roads such as the one from West Point through Highland Falls and south to the village of Fort Montgomery sported some of the most delightfully constructed "villa-residences" in the valley.[27] But from Nyack south lay the area within easy reach of the various rail lines and within easy commutation distance of New York.[28] There, the establishment of year-round estates had begun. With the completion of the railroad to Nyack in the 1870s, a suburbanite class began to coalesce in the town. On the rugged eminences of Grandview and overlooking Sparkill Creek, an area served by the Nyack & Northern and Erie Railroads (with connections to the Northern Railroad of New Jersey), ornately frilled houses were built with greenhouses, lawn pavilions, and landscaped grounds. One such residence, known as "the castle," was built by the president of the Erie Railroad. The layout of estate holdings in the area, and the convenience of rail connections in the northern Palisades are seen in fig. 30.

Bergen County, along the line of the Northern Railroad and the Palisade ridge, was called "the real country" by a real estate promoter. An eleven-page pamphlet, entitled "The Home Sites at Undercliff, New Jersey," extolled the commanding landscape of "incomparable loveliness," the panoramic surroundings where: "One is quick to realize that here is the exceedingly rare opportunity of being able to locate an easily accessible home having at its threshold a landscape by which it is forever redeemed from the Common-place."[29] And all one hour by rail from New York.

The railroad and entrepreneurial individuals were both responsible for real estate development in north Bergen. It was primarily through the publicity of the Northern Railroad that Manhattan businessmen were lured to homesites at places like Englewood, Tenafly, Creskill, Demarest, Closter, and Norwood. These station villages were created by the railroad, which simultaneously gobbled up adjacent farms on the Palisade tableland for residential subdivisions. The railroad was depicted as

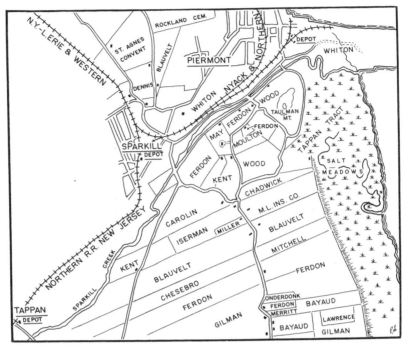

Figure 30. Estate properties and railroad connections in the northern Palisades, 1891
From: *Atlas of the Hudson Valley*
(Scale, 1″ = 1200′)

having wrought "magic change," in its conversion of "inaccessible jungles" of gloomy woods and inaugurating an air of rural ease and "unmistakable business prosperity."[30]

While bank managers and newspaper editors settled down to the pleasure of a pastoral existence in the railroad villages, the bank presidents and the newspaper publishers (along with the railroad magnates) took up residence in even more imposing suburban opulence atop the Palisade ridge.

It was thought that yet another rail line might be built along the crest of the Palisades to further accommodate these well-to-do few. Country estates were already in evidence along the brow of the cliff at Fort Lee by the early 1860s, but it was the next two decades which saw the full "redeeming from forests"[31] of the eight-mile corridor from Englewood to the state line. The cliff-top estates took the same form as the longlot-like farm holdings already established here: narrow bands of park and villa land (seldom more than 800 feet wide) angling toward the cliff edge, below which the property in most cases was sold to others, the traprock companies included. In Harrington Township, a listing of those who owned the Palisade top could no doubt have served as a page of the 1875 New York Social Register.[32]

Quaint but Fading Ways of Life on the Palisades

Atop the Palisades, then, both resorts and estates were being developed—facilitated by the expansion of the railroad and the initiative of real estate developers. Farm houses, fruit orchards, and relict mills still dotted the landscape, and an atmosphere of seclusion was often evoked.[33] At the same time, the deeply wooded nature of the tableland impressed others.[34] In fact, a rather dense recreational and residential pattern was in the process of being formed. By the 1880s, the village of Fort Lee contained almost 1500 people, and was pressing up the Palisade slope and northward toward Englewood Township, which at the same time was "densely occupied with habitations and adjoining buildings." Here the crest of the Palisades was dotted with "the big wooden boxes . . . [that are] stalls for city people in the summer."[35] Inland, the railroads had brought churches, schools, and stores to the station villages. Northward, Harrington Township "ha [d] assumed already the appearance of one long country village."[36]

Little of this, of course, could be seen from steamboats or the opposite shore; the attention of travelers and artists was most often drawn to the activities that took place at the base of the Palisades. A series of quarries and stone slides, bone factories, and other buildings of uncertain function appear along the riverbank of Palisades and Harrington Townships in Walker's 1876 *Atlas of Bergen County* and on Lloyd's 1864 topographical map.[37] Some of the structures indicated may have been the abandoned powderhouses of the quarrymen, recycled for other uses. There were

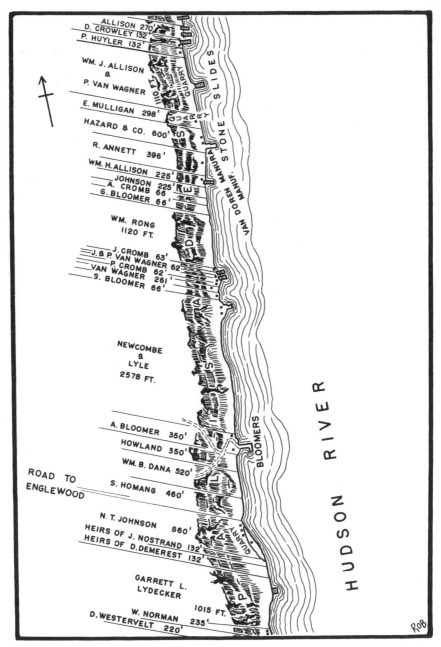

Figure 31. Ownership of property along the Palisades in the nineteenth century. Englewood cliffs area

From: R. C. Bacot, Supt. of Survey, 1865.

saloons, boat docks, and houses at Huylers and Alpine Landings. At the Undercliff settlement ("Fisherman's Village"), "the houses were so near the water's edge a man could toss a pebble from his steps into the Hudson."[38] It was the fishermen and their families who were the object of most observers. The artist Jasper Cropsey documented their activities in 1874 in his study of shad fishermen in the shadow of the Palisades. Other artists interested themselves in the fishermen's wives hanging wash in the front yard of ramshackle huts. The *Times* suggested that New Yorkers might find great pleasure in a Sunday jaunt along the base of the Palisades, where, between the picnic groves and dancing pavilions, fishermen picturesquely dried their nets on the little strips of beach shaded with cedar and elm.[39]

Little time was left, however, for the Palisades shad fishermen. There was a "gradual exodus" of these families throughout the latter part of this period; most migrated westward to the Hackensack Valley.[40] And as reported by the *New York Times,* the Hudson River shad catch was itself declining—as it cyclically or periodically does.[41] Of even greater immediacy were the progressively worsening ear- and earth-shattering practices of the quarrymen and stone crushers. No longer content to chip away at the loose rock and remove the accumulated talus, they were now systematically engaged in dynamiting the cliff-face.

In the Reaches of the Tappan Zee and Haverstraw Bay

Nyack and its environs had undergone a withdrawal from commercial agriculture and primary industry and, with a population of 4000 by 1884, geared itself to a variety of light manufacturing industries. Labor in the multi-storied shoe factories (between five and eight such shops could be found at any given time in these dacades) was the primary source of male employment after the Civil War. Economic slack resulting from the demise of quarrying—the industry here was for all practical purposes dead by 1883—was quickly picked up by service industries related especially to tourism and resort development. A Nyack "business boom" in the 1870s and 1880s is said to have resulted from the upgrading of county roads and the arrival of the railroad.[42] Although it perhaps attracted fewer tourists than Tarrytown, there were "those—and their number is increasing every year— who have discovered that Nyack is one of the most delightful and healthful of all the places of resort upon the river. . . . The west bank of the Hudson will soon dispute the palm with Minnesota as a retreat for invalids."[43]

In contrast, Haverstraw and the Stony Point–Tomkins Cove area continued to emit a strong industrial atmosphere. The illustrations of John Derbyshire's brickyards at Haverstraw and the operations of the Tomkins Cove Lime Company remind one of period lithographs of the smoking and belching industries of the grimy English midlands. In all, there were 42 brickyards operating along the shore of Haverstraw Bay in the 1880s, with a heavy concentration at Grassy Point. Here, on a narrow peninsula of clay and sand that separated the Hudson from Minisceongo Creek, the historian Cole recorded his impressions in 1884:

The person who now stands at the "Narrow Passage" sees to the north a confused scene of brickyards and tenement houses, and perched upon the top of a high sand bank, which is being rapidly dug away, the foundations of a house of former days. . . . the houses of laborers are scattered around, without the slightest attempt at ornamentation.[44]

The Haverstraw waterfront bustled with barges laden with brick. The environment deteriorated visually, because brickmaking was an ugly, earth-scarring operation, and labor problems shook the town when the brickmakers struck and the owners imported French Canadian strike breakers. The heavy social and economic preoccupation with brickmaking was, however, coming to an end; by the late 1880s the clay and sand deposits were almost exhausted.

Manufacturing (especially of brickmaking machinery), shipbuilding, and iron fabrication were also established at Haverstraw; but again, it was the quarrying and processing of stone that was of greater importance. Quarries of red sandstone were located to the west of the village, while the limestone cliff backing the shore at Tomkins Cove was pulverized for the masonry trade and road macadamization.[45] Lime kilns built of Haverstraw brick dotted the shore while the higher wooded ground at Stony Point and inland from the cove housed the laborers and the proprietors, the latter in stately Victorian elegance.

In this period, the railroad was finally extended north to Haverstraw. The New York and Northern Railroad of New Jersey skirted to the west of the Tors, and was opened to Haverstraw in 1874 and to Stony Point one year later. The West Shore Railroad, whose route was much closer to the Hudson, passed within one mile of Rockland Lake and cut through the clove between High Tor and Hook Mountain, reaching Haverstraw and Tomkins Cove in 1883.[46] Trains of the New York–Ontario & Western Railroad used the West Shore Railroad tracks (later bought by the New York Central) as far north as Cornwall, where the line branched off. While it is likely that some residences and summer homes were located here in direct response to services provided by the railroad, the primary appeal of the Haverstraw lowland was undeniably industrial.

Very little was recorded by anyone of the upland between Nyack and Haverstraw in the 1870s and 1880s. Maps and even landscape paintings offer no great detail.[47] There were orchards, vegetable gardens, and a few old farmhouses in an area still considered "impracticable" as far as through roads were concerned. These were the very same essentials that had characterized the area earlier in the century. The mountains appeared to remain "covered with a low growth of wood," young trees, and scrub brush cut periodically for use in the brickyards.[48] Much of the property to the east of Rockland Lake was owned by the Knickerbocker Ice Company, whose ice houses and railroad sidings constituted what there was of an economic landscape. Agricultural decline or neglect was widespread, as seen in the wooded and overgrown fields, much as on the Palisades and elsewhere in the lower valley. A sprinkling of small service centers, not substantially larger than those of the 1840s–1850s, was found across

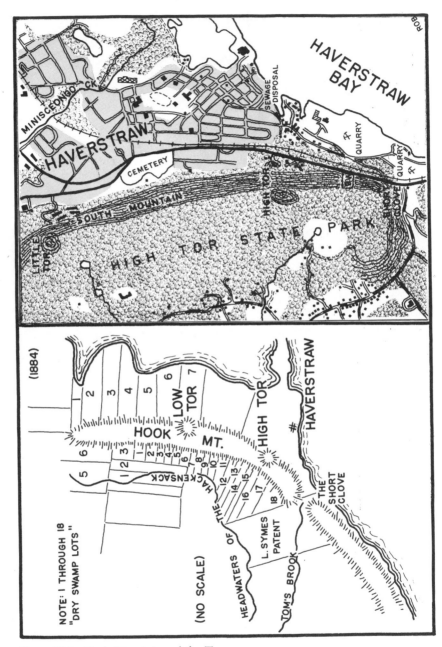

Figure 32A. Hook Mountain and the Tors
TOP: Lot divisions in 1884
From: D. Cole, *History of Rockland County*
BOTTOM: Detail of the area today
From: U.S.G.S. Haverstraw topographic sheet, 1967
(Scale: 1″ = 24,000′)

Figure 32B. Hook Mountain and Haverstraw Bay
"The Port of Haverstraw," Jacques Gerard Milbert, *Picturesque Itinerary of the Hudson River and Travels in North America,* Paris, 1828–29.

the upland, the most notable being the village of Rockland Lake. As evidence that the realm of recreation had penetrated here too, the basic village services included four hotels by 1884.[49]

A Reforested, Primitive Highlands

An illustration accompanying the Hudson River Dayline's Guidebook of 1878 shows a view looking west from Iona Island toward the northern flank of the Dunderberg, West Mountain, and Bear Mountain; the highlands are shown in a perfectly wild, Canadian-like setting with an almost complete absence of settlement and industry. The mountains continued to impress river travelers with their empty and "gloomy majesty," for patterns of human activity were largely hidden from view in a region "clothed with luxuriant foliage" from base to summit.[50]

The charcoal iron industry was moribund by the late 1870s (although iron continued to be mined for shipment to Pennsylvania) and the once so prevalent clear-cutting of the mountainsides for charcoal production had stopped. The forest at last had a chance to grow without the repeated cutting attendant upon charcoal technology, and much of the twentieth-century vegetation dates to this period.[51] A dense forest with undergrowth is mentioned repeatedly by writers in this, an era no longer characterized by rapacious pioneer industries.[52] Forest use of course continued; cordwood was cut. Caldwell, for one, "lumbered" on the Dunderberg near his hotel; there were lumber yards at Cornwall; and hotel and railroad construction no doubt drew upon the local forest. But clear-cutting practices had by the 1880s migrated with the lumber companies to the north woods of Minnesota and Michigan.

Caldwell's (formerly "Gibraltar"), Highland Falls, and Cornwall were the only settlements of any importance in the highlands west of the river. Caldwell's, nestled beneath the shoulder of the Dunderberg, boasted brickyards, tile works, and gravel pits. Highland Falls, "so rarely noted by the river tourist, that few dream of a census report for it of three thousand inhabitants,"[53] serviced the ever-popular West Point area (fig. 33). And Cornwall revealed a more diversified economy of dry goods and shoe shops, coal, lumber, and brick yards, as well as dock, warehousing, and other waterfront facilities.[54] All three towns benefited from the influx of summer guests and also from the construction of the West Shore Railroad along this part of the Hudson in the 1880s.

Futher informative references to the highland precincts are rare. Throughout these decades there are but two references to the highlands in the *New York Times:* one refers to plans for bridging the river between Bear Mountain and Anthony's Nose to connect rail lines on either side of the river; the second entry relates news of the ice harvest in January 1880.[55] Ice harvesting, a means of providing bread for the tables of many river families, was one of the more visible highland industries. In his travel chronicles, Damseaux remarked upon the "great number of

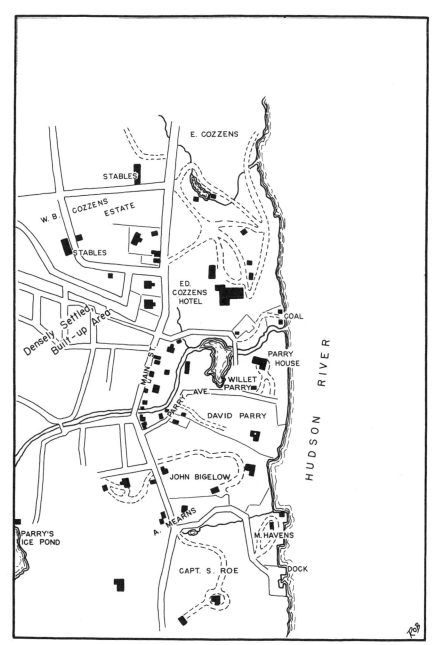

Figure 33. Highland Falls and Cozzens Hotel
From: *Orange County Atlas,* 1878, p. 129.
(Scale: 1″ = 400′)

Figure 34. Cozzens Hotel and Buttermilk Falls.

ABOVE. "Below Cozzens," William Cullen Bryant, *Picturesque America,* New York: D. Appleton & Co., 1874.

TOP RIGHT. Buttermilk Falls: From Wallace Bruce, *Panorama of the Hudson River Showing both sides of the Hudson River from New York to Poughkeepsie,* Bryant Literary Union, 1901 (1906 edition)

BUTTERMILK FALLS

monolithic ice houses" along the middle and upper course of the river, while the naturalist John Burroughs, residing at Highland Falls, composed beautifully descriptive passages on ice harvesting and the river's winterscape.[56]

Only a few firsthand descriptions of the highlands are available—in part because as late as 1880 there was but one road (the Continental Road) across Crows Nest and Storm King. Most roads either stopped at the mountain base or were deflected far to the west; there was only one through road from Caldwell's to West Point. The road grid from steamboat dock and railroad station to estate, farm and hotel, was densest in the vicinity of Highland Falls. Elsewhere, throughout the highlands, as seen on Kirby's detailed and contoured "Map of the Highlands of the Hudson" in 1880,[57] the great bulk of real estate consisted of undeveloped private holdings. The Federal Government had acquired more land in Washington Valley and on the side of Crows Nest, but as seen with the ownership of land around Storm King in fig. 35 undeveloped private properties with few buildings (although field investigation reveals numerous cellar holes) were the rule.

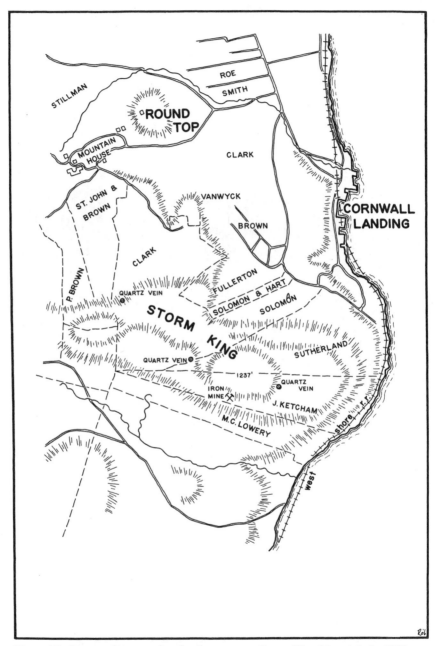

Figure 35. Property lines, road and rail pattern on Storm King Mountain in 1880
From: James Kirby, "Map of the Highlands of the Hudson"
(Scale: 1″ = 1000′)

Recreational facilities catering to the masses were less developed here than in those parts of the valley with greater proximity to New York. Although the poet Willis had an almost neurotic fear of teeming city hordes invading "his" highlands, as he himself admitted, daintily shod city gentlemen and their ladies seldom wandered far from the security of the riverbank.[58] Far more popular than climbing Storm King or Mount Beacon was riding the ferris wheel and carousel on Iona Island. Here amid some 200 acres of woods and marshes was the most frequented summer picnic area and playground in the highlands.[59]

Chapter 10
More Powerful Than the Quarrymen's Dynamite
A Worn Romanticism and Fresh Concerns for Preservation

*The romantic movement and the lust for improvement . . .
caused men to turn away from the no-longer arcadian East
and toward an area where distance and a strange nature held
hope for a rediscovery of the ideal.*
James Vance, *California and the Ideal,* p. 195

IT IS HIGHLY symbolic that in 1865 landscape artists of the Hudson River School should join a government tour of inspection of the Rocky Mountain region. In the 1860s and 1870s geological survey expeditions to the western states and territories often employed the services of painters and photographers. In fact, it was in the West that artists first began to make use of photography for their preliminary studies.[1] Now American landscape painters were being drawn more and more to the undocumented and unspoiled West. Popular interest in scenery, as expressed in Bryant's *Picturesque America* of 1874, prominently included the Plains and the Sierras, the Rockies, and the canyons of the Colorado and the Southwest.

The Westward Shift

This westward shift in artistic horizons is reflective of national and local transitions in aesthetic interest and scenic appraisal which occurred in the decades following the Civil War. As James Vance has said in *California and the Ideal,* because of the detrimental effect of the railroad, and later the automobile, upon the concepts of landscape space and of the contraction of travel distance in the Eastern United States, this region no longer conformed to the arcadian or pastoral ideal.[2] For those in search of romantic landscapes and areas not yet contaminated by the factories and railroads of industrialized, suburbanizing society, the "Great West" now beckoned. Much as the Hudson Valley and the highlands had played a crucial role in the actualization of nationalistic forces in pre-Civil War times, the river valleys of California and the Pacific coast ranges became strongly entwined with the purpose and style of Manifest Destiny. The East of the 1880s was left "beyond the limits of a geography of the ideal."[3]

Yet, while the West might be vicariously appreciated through the work of artists, travel to the Yosemite or Yellowstone was beyond the reach of all but a few. The nation's population centers were still situated on the Atlantic Seaboard and, for those who could afford it, summer vacations and travel were largely directed toward the accessible but more distant—and somewhat "wild"—resort regions of the East. Those localities favored by tourism are vividly depicted in the genre landscapes of Winslow Homer: Long Branch, New Jersey; Newport, Rhode Island; and Gloucester, Massachusetts. And then there were the mountains—the Berkshires, White Mountains, and Adirondacks.[4] Homer's "Adirondack Guide" and other such works evoked a strong sense of the primitive still characteristic of the Great North Woods. The search for the primitive led the gentry of this generation to construct rustic cabins with great stone fireplaces where they could sit and listen to the call of the loon in these eastern backwaters.

A Desecrated Suburban Valley

In the even less remote and more accessible Hudson Valley, the ideal was more elusive. While these same decades brought prosperity to the Catskills and its mountain houses, the lower Hudson had been reduced to a suburban fringe, subject to all the desecrations of "democratized travel." The departure of the Hudson River artists and the lowered status of the Hudson River School say much of what had happened to landscape esteem in this "Gilded Age." The year 1875 is used as an approximate date for the end of the Hudson River School by art historians.[5] Though the realistic depiction of the region was still a popular landscape subject, and although the works of such artists as Cropsey, Johnson, and Gifford were still generally admired, grand Hudson River landscapes in the manner of Cole and Durand were no longer in vogue.[6]

Those landscapists who left the eastern states were likely to be influenced by new ideas expressed by Bierstadt and his so-called "Rocky Mountain School" of painting. Those who continued to paint in the East, and along the Hudson, came under the spell of some combination of luminism, expressionism, or the mannerism of the French Barbizon School. Less topographic detail, less emphasis on the actual subject matter, and more concern with the "emotional exploitation of shapes and colors" is for example apparent in Cropsey's view of the Tappan Zee and Hook Mountain in the 1880s.[7]

The demise of the older Hudson River style of majestic panoramic landscape is indicative of a disillusionment with the American visual milieu in what Lewis Mumford called the "Brown Decades." "The Nation not merely worked differently after the Civil War: the country looked different—darker, sadder, sober."[8] Artists, serving perhaps as sensitive barometers of national feeling, were, as Cole had been, cynical of the crass materialism, the uncouth world of robber barons, and the accelerated pace at which resources were exploited. Suburban valleys such as that of the Hudson were overtaken by mechanization and urbanization. The pre-war buoyancy and (at least surface) confidence in man's ability to relate harmoniously to fellow man and to nature was gone, "the old idealism [having] been consumed in the passions of war."[9]

America as extended genesis, and the Hudson as the pinnacle of the New World arcadian Eden, were broken dreams. Romantically sublime landscapes and transcendental communion with nature were out of place in a world now dominated by land speculation, the chaotic reality of industrialization of the countryside, urban riots, strikes, brutalities, and exploitation.[10] Postwar artists could, and did, react to these conditions in any of four ways: expatriation to Europe; retreat to the more remote and wild areas of the American continent; emotional and psychical retreat inward to landscapes of the mind; or, as Eastman Johnson, J. Alden Weir, and Winslow Homer had done, sentimentalization of the vanishing rural world through painted elegies to barns, country lanes, stone walls, and childhood on the farm. This "contemporary regretful nostalgia for an earlier less-complex America" permeated much of the genre painting in this period and, through its longing for past and supposedly more virtuous landscapes and times, was possibly an element associated with a popular concern to preserve.[11]

In the context of these socio-artistic developments, awareness of the Hudson Valley's landscape continued in the mold cast by previous generations of romanticists, but took on expanded implication as well. Within what has been called a vulgar and cultureless business-dominated society,[12] the once-inspirational scenic landforms of Bergen and Rockland's shores did not become the object of new or intensified modes of landscape interpretation. The aesthetic trappings born of art and literature, and applied with vigor by armies of travelers, continued in use. Various of the romantic elements were de-emphasized, but essentially nothing new was added. While the ethics of materialism and exploitation left little regard for the sanctity or beauty of sublime landscape, romantic scenery did not disappear but rather degenerated into rote, all-too-familiar, and jaded pronouncements.

Simultaneously, landscape concept took on a new slant. The estate and resort building boom, and the placing of more railroad lines and suburban stations, was directly inspired by a view of landscape that was prevalent throughout the nation in the nineteenth century, but that reached its greatest heights in these decades: i.e., the idea that certain climatically gifted regions were beneficial to health, and the prevention and care of disease, particularly malaria. As a reaction against the abuses of industrial society and the moneyed class and their ubiquitous estates, the concept developed of the "therapeutic landscape"—a healing, health-giving earth itself threatened by quarries, brickyards, and factories. This helped re-ignite a dormant but powerful romanticism and, encouraged by events elsewhere, a sense of grandeur about to be lost took on a growing and lasting importance in the Hudson Valley. The bedrock scenic awe that had inspired another era may have become shallow, but this was still the Hudson, the therapeutic valley so near at hand, a familiar ribbon of landscape now seen increasingly menaced by a nation in the throes of its industrial "takeoff."

A Warmed-Over Romanticism

Roland Van Zandt, in documenting the heyday of the Catskill Mountain House and its region, concluded that although prosperity had arrived in the form of the railroad and the building of additional wings to accommodate more guests, something was missing. The writers and artists of the romantic generation were gone, and the driving force behind the popularization of the region had become the entrepreneur, the business tycoon, and the railroad magnate.[13] In this changeover, an element of sophistication, of class, of intellectualism had been lost. The "art" of travel and mountain sojourns had become excuses for socializing, for getting away from the familiar. Traveling to mountains with the intention of going back to nature, to perceive the landscape's beauty, and apply the concepts of romantic doctrine, were—for most—no longer valid.

Because the purpose and style of travel had changed, those who journeyed through the scenic regions of the lower Hudson Valley in this period contributed relatively little to the aesthetics of landscape. The essence of travel had become not to study or contemplate the aesthetic elements of landform, but to observe the manners and habits of different classes of people, modes of transportation, and accommodations. The circumstances of travel had in fact become of greater interest than the landscapes being traveled through.[14]

The rise of recreation among the masses and weekend outings also detracted from appreciation of the scenery. The steamboat traveler of the 1870s, as Mark Twain derisively noted, knew that particular regions possessed majestic and panoramic landscapes only because the guidebooks said so.[15] The so-called "democratization of travel" and the attendant diminishment of true concern for aesthetics must have been especially blatant along the Hudson. Here immigrants—addicted, unlike their Puritanical forebears, to Sunday amusements—created a "hellish bedlam" on board the steamboats, and deprived others of a contemplative mood:

This crowd of excursionists does not belong to the elite of the population: there are petty merchants and their families; working-men and women. . . . all shouting, running, jostling, the men spitting in all directions at once, covering the decks, the carpets, the salons with a sea of tobacco juice. . . . husbands, long-since lost in drunkedness, are stretched out full length on the carpet. . . . whole groups of men, women, and children, unable to find seats, lie pell-mell on the carpet floor; elsewhere one sees drunkards lying crosswise on the decks.[16]

When the Palisades or the highlands are spoken of in the 1870s as being innately aesthetic or romantically inspirational, it is through the phraseology learned from the pre-war generation. The *New York Times* reporters who were sent up the Hudson to compose travel pieces ("Walk Along the Hudson," "Up the

Hudson by Night") wrote of landscape beauties in a mechanical fashion that in the 1840s would have passed for a genuine affection for nature. The *Bergen County Atlas* of 1876 is prefaced by a "Scenic Vignette" of a traveler lost amid the picturesque confusion of the Palisades that might have been drawn 30 years before. Bryant's *Picturesque America,* the last of the impressively oversized picture books (1874), recounts the scenery of the Hudson by using almost the same combination of elements (sublimity, a "blend of history and nature," pastoral imagery) formulated as early as the 1820s.[17] While many aspects of romanticism survived in the literature of the postwar era, the underlying sense of nationalistic fervor and philosophical conviction was absent. The romantic groundwork was well established and still useful, but the warmed-over mouthings of an age now passed were heaped upon it.

Nationalism, as sometimes conducive to a romantic feeling, had died in fratricidal battles along with the innocent high spirits of patriotism so characteristic of the young republic. Newspapers and magazines might still encourage Americans to see the Hudson and the Mississippi before groveling in adoration of things European, but the Civil War had broken the forces of chauvinism and isolationism. Replacing them was an order of wealth and leisure in which the stress was on a "new internationalism and eclectic culture."[18] (This, for example, is seen mostly directly in the Continental influences upon American art in the 1870s and 1880s).

Industrialization and suburbanization had almost completely toppled the pastoral design. The genteel "middle ground" between city and wilderness existed only in a highly artificial state. There is an air of unbelievability in Lossing's sketch of cows lying about the railroad depot at Rockland Lake and in Cranston's description of his Highland Falls hotel: a mix of rough and gentle, not wilderness, not city, but rustic grounds and boulevards "modified by [landscape] art to form a pastoral hideaway."[19] Bucolic imagery was most explicitly evoked to compare the Hudson Valley with the supposedly rustic world atop and behind the Palisades,[20] but the simple farmlands of Bergen (in Palisades and Harrington Townships) had of course fallen prey to development on the eve of the Civil War; the overgrown fields, being either subdivided or held for speculation, conveyed little of "pastoral tranquility." Ironically, it was the publicity of the Northern Railroad of New Jersey that said it best: "The quiet of the ancient hills was broken . . . by the shriek of a commonplace locomotive—a grimy, belching, hissing, thundering locomotive, ever synonymous, in the rustic mind, with the destruction of all that characterizes rural joy and peace."[21]

Pastoral rhetoric, drawing directly upon images used by Willis, Irving, and Thoreau was still purveyed, but with less intensity than before. The sincere yearning of the past for a pastoral world devolved into a popular nostalgia expressed in the continuing appeal of Currier & Ives prints and the debut of *Tom Sawyer* (1876) and *Life on the Mississippi* (1883).

The arousal of romantic emotion through geological curiosities continued to play a role. It would seem that from a story in the *New York Times* entitled "A Sunday on the Hudson" (1878) the rate of disintegration of the Palisade rock, along with other geological topics, were fairly common items of conversation on deck and in the pilot house.[22]

The landscapes of the Hudson, and of the Catskills and Adirondacks, were now aesthetically outclassed by the more stupendous and evocative Western landscapes. Whether it was artists accompanying the survey parties, or journalists, preachers, and speculators from the East, all viewed the volcanic mesas and multicolored sedimentary escarpments as the ruins of forts, pyramids, French cathedrals, Rhineland castles, great cities, and anything else reminiscent of human occupation.[23] The brunt of speculation and study, as well as the concept of the romantic-geologic ruin, still lingered on in the East, but had in these decades found more fertile and fresh ground in the West.

A Most Durable Sublimity and the Benchmarks of History

Those romantic elements of the landscape that proved most durable in their application to the Hudson Valley were the "doctrines" of the sublime and picturesque, and of historical association. In the 1882 *Hudson River by Daylight* several "divisions" of the Hudson are proposed, based upon "something more substantial than sentiment or fancy"—i.e., the aesthetic nature of the land itself.[24] While the Catskills, the hillsides around Poughkeepsie, and the river lowlands around the Tappan Zee were regarded as reposeful, picturesque, and beautiful, the Palisades formation and the highlands still claimed elements of grandeur and sublimity.

Writers, probably largely from tradition, felt the need to pay tribute to mountainous scenic nobility, and continued to write of the "dark and frowning" Palisades. A grand and imposingly sublime view was had either of or from these wild and rugged cliffs which "in calms and storms, in lights and shades, keep watch along the river." The "rare grandeur and beauty" of Hook Mountain and the Tors was highlighted as well through the interplay of lights and shades, "this arc of hills lost in purple mist beneath the summer sky."[25]

The highlands however remained both the topographic and aesthetic highpoint. "While . . . nations fade and grow around the granite ledges," the eye beholds a "continual feast" of sky effects, romantic dells and ravines, and threatening cliffs, all perpetually changing in the colors and shades of morning, evening and night.[26] The "grand" Dunderberg sat amid the thunder and storm clouds of the coming tempest while the evening star rose above the summit of Crow's Nest: "Old Cro' Nest, like a Monarch, stands, Crowned with a single star."[27] The grimly majestic Storm King, "with sides all scarred and torn by storms and lightning," filled the lover of scenery with exquisite pleasure by the way it ruled and protected the valley from the effects of the thunderclouds.[28] All along the western shore the vertical columns and granite masses were bathed in sublimity through the effects of shadow and sunshine. Although not the Rockies, nature here was tempestuous and threatening still.[29]

The mental association of great historical events and personalities with specific places within the valley remained perhaps the most effective means by which a quality of romanticism was imparted to the landscape. Colt's guidebook (1871) put it to poetic verse: "Historical association and old romantic traditions linger along the banks where 'Hudson's wave o'er silvery sands, winds thro' the hills afar.' "[30] Railroad companies, hotel owners, county historians, and even real estate propagandists all seized upon the Hudson's rich historical tableau for their individual purposes. The Northern Railroad, for example, described the stops along its route in terms of the Revolutionary War heritage, while another company issued publicity with pictures of the Palisades region complete with lurking Indians along the shore and a cloud-filled sky occupied by the wispy ghosts of Dutch burghers, pioneers, and continental soldiers.[31] Cranston meanwhile found it profitable to advertise his hotel by stressing the historical associations of its vicinity (the first seventeen pages of his 1883 *The Hudson Highlands* are in fact Revolutionary history).

All manner of fanciful and factual associations were constructed to provide a sense of human involvement with the landscape. Fairies, gnomes and ghosts were the poetic mainstays in celebrating the highland peaks, while Indian and Spanish legend, and especially the recent memory of N. P. Willis, were used to evoke sentiment for the Cornwall area.[32] Much speculation developed at this time about buried treasure and "lost" highland mines. That Captain Kidd had concealed vast treasures somewhere in the neighborhood of Storm King or the Dunderberg was taken to be more than folklore. An English-financed salvage company was organized to excavate the waters below the Dunderberg (Kidd's Point); a coffer dam was erected, a steam operated pumping apparatus installed, and 40 men were kept employed there for four years at a cost in excess of $80,000.[33] Pieces of coin and cannon were apparently found (Lossing however claims that they were from a British warship), but the enterprise was abandoned for want of money. Nevertheless, the venture supplied the highland passage with yet another picturesque and romantic ruin: the decaying coffer dam and pumping apparatus.

While other parts of the nation had almost immediately begun to glorify places associated with the Civil War, the Hudson Valley continued to draw vitality from the Revolutionary period: "It is not easy to pass and repass the now peaceful and beautiful waters of this part of the Hudson without recalling to mind the scenes and actors in the great drama of the Revolution."[34] The county histories published in these years devoted fifty or more pages to the role of the county in the war, and the guidebooks are replete with lengthy passages relating incidents of that "glorious struggle" (e.g., Taintor Brothers, 1887).

Memories were reinforced by Centennial celebrations in 1876, when every landform and town in the lower valley was associated with a seemingly endless series of battles, skirmishes, secret rendezvous, and assorted acts of heroism. The riverline was dotted with reference points at which scenery and history were inseparably blended.[35] Where the Army encamped, where Washington slept (of course), where André walked, and where Kosciusko meditated.

The River's Therapeutic Image

Recent studies into the relationship between environmental and medical literature have investigated the role played by malaria in the 1870s and 1880s; interesting land use patterns often resulted from misinformation about the disease. Kenneth Thompson has studied the effects of these erroneous notions on California's horticulture. It was supposed that the Australian eucalyptus had a capacity to prevent malaria by absorbing or neutralizing the noxious gases that presumably caused the disease. The tree was, as a consequence, eagerly introduced into the state's landscape.[36] James Vance has analyzed the "medical climatology" of California's regions as a major factor in that state's nineteenth-century growth at the expense of areas beset by malaria, and with supposedly less restorative and healthful environments.[37]

Van Zandt, in *The Catskill Mountain House,* dealt with the self-proclaimed clinical or health-giving properties of a malaria-free mountain region that published medical propaganda to promote tourism and recreation.

Through such studies of the beliefs about the causes and nature of malaria (and of cholera and yellow fever), the fascinating interrelationships between medical conceptions—or misconceptions—and patterns of population growth and recreational development are unfolding. The Hudson Valley, when looked at in this way, is seen to have healthful qualities. Even before the Civil War, and continuing until the discovery of a mosquito as the agent of malarial fever in the 1890s, the pattern of land use in the highlands and clifftop areas in Bergen and Rockland Counties directly reflected popular medical misconception,[38] which also served to fortify the wobbly romantic image.

"The etiological view of malaria until the end of the nineteenth century was based on the miasmatic theory of disease. In essence, the theory stated that organic materials, decomposing under moist conditions and mild temperatures, produced some kind of toxic gas or miasma." As malaria ("bad air" in Italian) and other summer scourges wreaked havoc in the Atlantic and Gulf coastal cities, the population was beset with much uncertainty as to the cause of the disease; some even blamed it on the moon or government policy.[39] It was however widely accepted that swampy or poorly drained areas in the tropics and at low elevations in the mid-latitudes was conducive to this "American plague," a suspicion European travelers repeatedly confirmed.[40]

Coastal or estuarine marshes in or near cities were regarded as nonhygienic locales, thus furthering anti-urban sentiments. Also, the railroad—desirous of property fronting on the river—made profitable use of the concept by propagandizing the idea that the rivershore was a malarial swamp ridden with fever and ague; the properties were consequently "dumped" on the railroad company at very low cost, only to be resold after an immediate "sanitary improvement" at a grossly inflated price.[41]

Writing in the *Transactions of the American Climatological Association* in the 1880s, Charles LeRoux advised invalids and those seeking to avoid malaria to ask themselves a series of "test questions" about the atmospheric and sanitary conditions of the resort at which they planned to stay. He felt that it was very important that there be no swamps, that the vicinity be well-drained, and that the atmosphere be free of "miasmata." Certain locations on the Gulf Coast—places also having rail connections to nearby cities and frequented by "good" society— were considered ideal.[42] LeRoux also noted the great advantage of air saturated with the essence of pine balsam. It was to such coniferous mountain air that many an eastern city-dweller escaped. The flight from an environment supposedly conducive to malaria had a profound impact upon the development of mountain resorts in the Catskills and Adirondacks after the Civil War. The hygienic importance of altitude and the absence of "the fever" in a mountain environment was well publicized in the brochures distributed by the railroad and mountain house developers.[43]

In the lower Hudson as well, much of the recreational, resort, and even residential pattern is explained by this miasmatic conception of disease. In a landform region already possessed of a romantically aesthetic allure, references were made to the clinical or health-giving properties of these same areas. The region of the Palisades, the Tors, and the highlands became the "Romantic-Climatic countryside." The higher elevations in the three-county area were proclaimed for their "hygienic virtues." The air was said to be "laden with health-giving properties," an atmospheric purity which enabled N. P. Willis, for one, to live fifteen years longer than he should have.[44] It was furthermore theorized that a "Death Line" occurred on the Hudson around the Tappan Zee which demarcated the malaria-free inland regions to the north from the malaria-prone shore and coastal areas to the south (the top of the Palisades excluded, of course). At this line, where insects die and their bodies accumulate in the "Infunorial Cemetery of the Sea," a change in atmospheric quality was said to be apparent.[45]

These concepts contributed significantly to the institution of the summer vacation, and the blossoming of a resort and recreational landscape in the valley. Physicians often sent patients suffering from assorted physical ailments to the highlands, "where the invalid may court and win smiling health."[46] The malarial and choleric conditions characteristic of urban summers also sent those like G. T. Strong packing to the mosquito-free confines of the highland hotels; he summarized quite nicely the medical thinking of his day, and graphically portrayed what drove him north:

The stinks of Centre Street lift up their voices. Malarious aromata rampage invisible through every street, and in the second-rate regions of the city, such as Cherry Street, poor old Greenwich Street, and so on, atmospheric poison and pungent foetor and gaseous filth cry aloud and spare not, and the wayfaring man inhales at every breath a pair of lungs full of vaporized decomposing gutter mud and rottenness.[47]

Tens of thousands who could afford to, and those who thought as Strong did, partook of "mountain air" along the Bergen and Rockland shore. The towns of Closter and Palisades became known for their "notably healthy" malaria-free air, while the Palisade Mountain House advertised the healthful qualities of its surroundings: "the air is exceedingly clear and salubrious, and has proved extremely beneficial to invalids and children of delicate constitutions."[48] Other resort houses in the Nyack–Rockland Lake area stressed the blend of scenery, history, good society, and a healthful summer climate. At places like Piermont and Grandview health seekers could relax in a wholesome physical setting with the additional benefit of the hydropathic cure— restorative mineral springs and waters. Nyack's Tappan Zee House boasted "entire freedom from malaria and mosquitos" and the absence of swamps on the borders of Rockland Lake ensured that the seasonal resident would not be subject to the fevers.[49] The highlands naturally had an established reputation for "New York Mountain Air." Mosquitoes and other biotic evils were infrequently found there. The summer hotels at Highland Falls and at West Point catered especially to city families seeking recourse from malaria.[50]

Real estate developers and estate-owners too understood the importance of highlands and cliff-tops. The county historian Cole specifically stated that wealthy citizens had sought out country seats along the banks of the Hudson, where the danger of disease might be avoided in the summer months. Bergen County developers offered home sites along the Palisades crest with "No Mosquitos, No Malaria, No Salt Air," and contrasted these conditions with the immense malaria-inducing marshes in the less favorable Hoboken and Jersey City areas.[51]

Ironically, the opening of suburban tracts in Bergen and the landscaping of estates in Rockland and Westchester Counties seemingly encouraged "miasmatic" conditions. In 1878 the *Times* reported an increase of malaria in the Hudson Valley and attributed it to three activities: the damming of streams and inlets by the suburban railroads, thus impeding drainage and leaving pond vegetation to rot in the sun; the overturning and exposure of large new bodies of moist ground for housing, leaving the ground exposed to the fermenting influence of air and sun; and lastly, the planting of ornamental groves and forests on estates, thus covering miles of relatively open ground along the river and excluding the great disinfectants—sun and air.[52]

The picturesque landscaping of villa grounds, the explosion of recreational activity, the image of the diseased and dirty city, the ideal of the healthful and restorative countryside were all the results of the concept of the therapeutic landscape. A sagging romanticism was thus shored up once again.

A Growing Sense of Lost Grandeur and Threatened Beauty

By the 1860s concern for wilderness began to be associated with the idea of preservation. The philosophical and the nostalgic, as cultivated in the romantic era by essayists and artists, became the practical. Landscape appreciation became more and more synonymous with the quest for protection. And socially conscious "easterners of artistic and literary bents"[53] were inspired especially by the incomprehensible scale of western landscapes: the Mariposa Big Trees, the Yosemite, the High Sierras, the Yellowstone. Artists and photographers who "recorded the grandeurs of our wilderness . . . strongly influenced public opinion toward their preservation in national parks."[54]

In 1864 Congress granted the Yosemite Valley to California

for "public use, resort and recreation, and shall be held inalienable for all times."[55] Olmsted, who had been commissioned to manage the park, realized "the enjoyment of the emotions caused by natural scenery" and outlined principles for the proper maintenance of such landscapes. In 1872 Yellowstone, the first of the national parks, was created by Congress ostensibly from admiration for spectacular scenery and a moral concern for nature. Shepard, however, underscores the not-so-idealistic motivations of party politics, and describes the National Park Act as "an act of faith without apparent theology."[56]

Parkman's *Oregon Trail* was re-issued in 1873 and this too was regarded as a contribution to the conservation movement; the book expressed concern for the landscape of the Rockies—defiled by hordes of polygamous Mormons, gambling houses, and screeching locomotives. Other indications of the growing resort to federal policy to regulate the use of the land and its resources were Carl Schurz's annual report as Secretary of the Interior for 1877 (the germ of the National Forest idea), and John Wesley Powell's *Report on the Lands of the Arid Region of the United States* (1878).[57]

In the East, where the maturing of extractive industries (milling, tanning, quarrying) openly conflicted with the so-called "harmonies of nature," the preservation impulse was greatly stimulated by G. P. Marsh's *Man and Nature* (1864).[58] In Marsh's view, man was ensnaring himself in an environmental crisis by subverting the balance of nature. If society and government did not soon assume a responsibility for the land, the nation would—as Cole and other romantic pessimists had feared—join the ranks of ruined empires. The superabundance of natural resources was, in short, a myth. Marsh's influence was most directly felt in the Adirondacks, where the ecological integrity of the mountains was secured by the creation of a State Forest Preserve in 1885, an accomplishment attributable both to Marsh's pioneering insights and to the fact that the Adirondacks had become "the playpen, the sandbox of the rich."[59]

These national and regional anxieties over the preservation of landscape shook the consciences of many who wrote about the

Hudson Valley. For the first time, a body of literature characterized by what might be called an awareness of impairments inflicted upon the mountain and highland environment by "civi-
lized greed" became apparent.

"Artificial appliances" such as dams and mills were seen as
detracting from the once-picturesque rivers and streams of
Bergen, and although such features might have an industrially
aesthetic appeal for some, it was not so for all.[60] Others grew
disturbed because the crest of the Palisades was losing its rural air
of seclusion to the railroad and its commuter towns. Railroads
were deplored because they trampled and obliterated scenes of
historical importance which added to a landscape's aesthetic appeal ("We are a nation of anti-archaeologists").[61] While the top
of the Palisades was stripped of its once-forbidding, primitive
aspect, the abruptness and grandeur of the cliff-face was diminished because of the offensive collection of rubbish and debris ac-
cumulating in some places. In the spring of 1878 a reporter for
the *New York Times* found the Bergen shore north of Fort Lee
covered with: "dogs, geese, goats, greasy gamins, and great
odors. In fact, high tide is the only time to visit . . . if you have
a nose in the party."[62]

It is apparent that artists blotted out much of the seediness in
their romantic portrayals of the Palisade cliffs in the 1870s. Likewise, Gifford's view of Hook Mountain from Haverstraw Bay
failed to acknowledge the considerable presence of industrial
blight in that area. Factories on the Haverstraw lowland and the
dynamiting of the flanks of Hook Mountain were frowned upon
by many, and the loss of historical burying grounds, houses, and
roadways as well as natural landmarks (the shoreline particularly)
was bitterly lamented. The high river bank, once lined with
beautiful estates, had been sacrificed to the brickyards, and this
picturesque setting "had passed away forever."[63] The Valley of
the Minisceongo, beneath the Tors, had also been defiled: "a
once romantic dale swept by a dark wild stream, the roar of
whose water is now mingled with the thousand wheels of extractive factories."[64]

Conflicts between industry and scenery, which would

plague the future history of the highlands, began to emerge in the 1870s and 1880s. To be sure, most people found no fault with West Point artillery crews' using the slopes of Crow's Nest for target practice ("these shells in bursting threw up enormous masses of earth and the impressions made were visible for years after" in the form of wet areas where runwater was caught and moss thrived),[65] or gunboats "testing" their weapons on the face of the Palisades (fig. 14); but some things did rile the lover of patriotically inspiring scenery: for instance, the local residents who carried off the stone remains of Fort Putnam piece by piece.[66] The foremost culprits in the desecration of highland scenery, however, were three: the railroads, the quarries, and the billboards.

As Willis had feared, "paleotechnic disorder" wrought changes upon the isolation and appearance of the mountains. Colt's guidebook of 1871 leveled the accusing finger at the railroads for disregarding the contours of the land in cutting rights-of-way: "its career of mangling life and limb is inaugurated by a whole sale mangling of the beauties of nature."[67] Quarries, too—blasted open and enlarged by more efficient techniques—drew the fire of those who enjoyed viewing the curious rock formations and the sublime grandeur of the mountains. Kirby's map of 1880 shows a quarry near Fort Putnam while others were said to be operative on the sides of Anthony's Nose and Breakneck. The blasting away of "the Turk's Head,"[68] a well-known natural rock formation on Breakneck, was especially regretted; the only consolation the guidebooks could offer the disappointed traveler was that the man who operated the dynamite plunger was himself blown up.[69]

Perhaps the most interesting incursion upon highland scenery, and one which provoked much criticism, was the use of the rock faces as advertising billboards:

We refer to the occupation of smooth rocks by great staring letters, announcing the fact that one shopkeeper in New York has "Old London Dock Gin" for sale, and that another sells "Paphian Lotion for beautifying the Hair." We protest in the name of every person of taste who travels upon the river and the road, against any disfiguring of the picturesque scenery of the Hudson Highlands, by making the out-cropping rocks of the grand old hills play the part of those itinerants who walk the streets of New York with enormous placards on their backs.[70]

Foreign travelers, such as Damseaux, were especially critical of employing scenic landforms to recommend gargling oil, tobacco, and toothpaste to the notice of the multitude. Whether this crass form of advertising grafitti was a product of American genius, or if it was indeed imported from Europe, along with the more desirable concepts of landscape appreciation, is an intriguing question.

By the late 1880s, at least, a pattern of dissent had been achieved with respect to the grosser abuses evident in the misuse of scenic landforms in the valley. A foundation of romanticism, actively applied to America's western landscapes, but inherently present in the established, accumulated imagery of eastern landscapes, was primarily responsible for the sentiment of preservation. John Burroughs of Highland Falls, very much in tune with the river's ecology, composed his poetic works in the 1880s through the cumulative descriptions and concepts learned from the preceding generations.[71] Although a well-grounded aesthetic tradition had evolved and was buffeted by a respect for the land's therapeutic value, the actual social and political campaign to halt the assaults upon the valley's beauty had not yet begun. That would be the task of the next generation.

Part 6

The Convergence and the Clash

Something To Be Saved and Protected Forever

A WELL-DEVELOPED aesthetic background was enlisted in the fight to preserve these mountainforms in the late nineteenth century. By the 1890s the contest between industry, blight, the progress of man, and preservation entered a critical phase. Quarrying reached what some regarded as criminal proportions, and the ire of various citizens groups prompted remedial action by the governments of New York and New Jersey. Study commissions which investigated the ravages of quarrying in the lower Hudson Valley were no doubt influenced by the logic and achievements of a snowballing national conservation movement. Apart from the practical concerns of recreation, natural history education, and perhaps even defense, the idealistic values of sublimity and the perpetuation of historical remembrances played a fundamental role in the establishment of an interstate administrative body and the condemnation and gradual extinction of the quarries. The popular acceptance of the park, and the subsequent step-by-step extension of its jurisdiction to include areas upriver, was immeasurably facilitated by the simultaneous and interrelated rise of the historical preservation movement. The idea of landscape as an aesthetic and historical resource, which for over a century had paralleled the forms of land use that were growing increasingly more objectionable, was ultimately effective in preserving that land.

The application of aesthetic concept clashed with discordant forms of land usage. Although it had peaked in the decade before the Civil War, the tradition of sublimity had been so firmly implanted in the Hudson Valley that the century-long foundation of aesthetics proved stronger than the economic-industrial dictates of the century. The evolving scenic-recreational landscape with its administrative body was the product of culture and concept; worn but tough images of a spatial ideal had in the end transformed and reshaped the reality itself.

Chapter 11
The Emerging Recreational Landscape and the Birth of the Palisades Interstate Park

The hand of the spoiler has been laid upon both the crest and the face of this mountain range.
J. J. Croes, New York State member
of the Palisades Study Commission, 1895

OF ALL THE decisions made regarding utilization of the land in the lower Hudson Valley since colonial times, and of all the spatial adjustments to changing economic and social conditions, none were more significant in their long-range consequences than those related to quarrying. The preservation impulse, nurtured for several decades by a strong sense of mountain aesthetics, quickened in the 1890s as a direct reaction to the quarrymen's depredations of cliff and highland scenery. This concern caused the creation of the Palisades Interstate Park Commission and the eventual designation of much of the western shore solely for purposes of recreation.

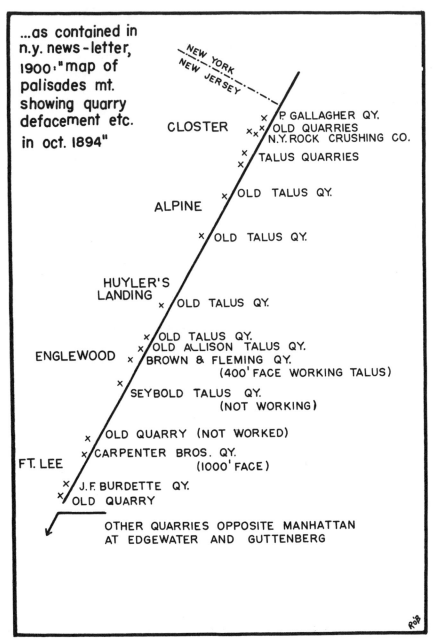

...as contained in
n.y. news-letter,
1900: "map of
palisades mt.
showing quarry
defacement etc.
in oct. 1894"

NEW YORK
NEW JERSEY

P. GALLAGHER QY.
CLOSTER   OLD QUARRIES
                 N.Y. ROCK CRUSHING CO.

TALUS QUARRIES

OLD TALUS QY.

ALPINE

OLD TALUS QY.

HUYLER'S
LANDING   OLD TALUS QY.

            OLD TALUS QY.
            OLD ALLISON TALUS QY.
ENGLEWOOD   BROWN & FLEMING QY.
                (400' FACE WORKING TALUS)

            SEYBOLD TALUS QY.
                (NOT WORKING)

            OLD QUARRY (NOT WORKED)
            CARPENTER BROS. QY.
FT. LEE   (1000' FACE)

            J.F. BURDETTE QY.
            OLD QUARRY

            OTHER QUARRIES OPPOSITE MANHATTAN
            AT EDGEWATER AND GUTTENBERG

Figure 36. Diagram of the Palisades quarries in 1894
(No scale)

Quarrying and the Reaction to It

The quarrying of traprock, limestone, sandstone, and even granite had been going on in the lower valley long before the Civil War. But with the introduction of dynamite and more powerful earth-moving and steam-crushing equipment, the columnar cliffs of the Palisades and Hook Mountain and the slopes of several highland peaks began to be undermined. Throughout the 1870s and 1880s the valley "reverberated with explosions far more devastating than heard in the Revolutionary War, as dynamiters did a mercilessly efficient job of reducing slopes to traprock." [1] Huge columns of basalt were broken into a fine gray aggregate for macadamizing the streets of New York and constructing bulkheads along the waterfront. By the 1890s, when the quarries appeared as hideous, unsightly blots from Edgewater to Englewood and Hook Mountain, there was an even greater demand for crushed stone in concrete for building construction in Manhattan. Quarry defacement along the Palisades as of 1894 was plotted by the Geological Survey of New Jersey and is shown diagramatically in figs. 36–37.

Even greater defacement was underway on the river face of Hook Mountain below Rockland Lake ("the story of the Palisades over again? Yes and worse."). [2] Blasting of the similar traprock cliff-face at a series of three pits each more than 500 feet wide was heard across the river in Tarrytown. Here the quarrymen again created a scene of increasing desolation. "Acres of bare rock and broken soil scar the cliff and make it an offense to the eye. The explanation for this vandalism is given in one word—gravel." [3]

The highlands presented the stone crushers and builders with a variety of unconsolidated gravels in narrow glacial depressions, and with an almost inexhaustible supply of granites. The ugly scars on the mountain walls, the marred riverbanks, and the unsightly company shacks were mentioned in the Hudson River guidebooks. [4] The traveler's attention was drawn especially to the disfigured and blasted side of Breakneck Mountain, once a river

Figure 37. Quarrying on the Palisades
ABOVE: "Scene of Blasting Operations, Two Miles Above New York City"
RIGHT. "At This Point, For the Past Ten Years, Trap-Rock Has Been Blasted for Road-Making"
From: *Truth* magazine, 18, no. 4 (April 1899): 107.

landmark because of its perfect likeness to a human face ("the Turk's Head").

At first, most criticism of the "menace" of quarrying stemmed less from the defacement of the landscape than from the massive, window-rattling explosions heard for a radius of 20 miles.[5] A survey of articles, editorials, and letters to the editor in the *New York Times* reveals that objections to quarrying itself appear only after 1893. In the following decade the newspaper columns are replete with news of the latest dynamitings—and of efforts to preserve the landscape—as well as opinionated comments by foreigners and wealthy Americans, about how to "save the Palisades."[6]

"Public opinion" never seems to have been firmly opposed to quarrying, despite the claim by some that an "aroused" concern on the part of the general public was evident as early as 1890. As a visitor from Britain observed in 1894: "I am astonished to find that the very scenery Americans talk so much about . . . is being defaced, desecrated, and destroyed, and I cannot find any American who seems to care much about it."[7]

Editorializing several years later on public indifference while "the noblest feature of the metropolitan landscape" was becoming "a ragged horror" at the hands of the Palisades quarry companies, the *New York Times* condescendingly concluded that popular sentiment—"the sentiment of the money grubber"—may even have sided with the spoilers:

Probably the average cis-Hudson Philistine who surveys the ruin wonders how much the destroyers will make out of the job and whether the rock is to be used for curbstone or underpinning. . . . The work would have been stopped long ago if the community as a whole had been capable of being moved either by the love of landscape beauty or the horror of landscape ugliness.[8]

The stimulus and direction given the preservation movement derived largely from relatively well-off, well-educated, politically active civic groups. In the forefront of the battle throughout the 1890s were such organizations as the Federation of New Jersey Women's Clubs, the Federation of Churches, the Palisades Protection Association (composed of influential men with homes on the heights of Spuyten Duyvil, Riverdale, and Kingsbridge), and the somewhat amorphous association of estate owners with properties atop the Palisades.

By 1894 a "healthy agitation" for preservation existed largely through the efforts of these groups.[9] As with all such issues, however, differences arose over how objectives should best be met. For obvious personal reasons, and perhaps for more altruistic ones as well, estate owners from Englewood to Alpine believed that their properties should not be disturbed by plans for park or forest preservation. John Stoddart, a resident of Alpine, reminded the public that the owners of landscaped estates on the Palisades ridge were "lovers of natural scenery," who had done nothing to mar the beauty of the area. To the contrary, it was they who often opened their park-like kingdoms to hikers and campers and who had supported state laws prohibiting advertising signs on the cliff edge. Therefore, they felt that preservation could best be achieved by focusing on the blasting operations on the narrow strip of beach between cliff base and river. The state should condemn *this* property, acquire it, and then create a park and scenic river drive.[10]

On the other hand, owners of property in Manhattan and other interested New Yorkers, who "saw the foreground of their western view falling into ruin before their eyes,"[11] appealed to the Federal Government to acquire and protect the whole Palisade cliff from top to bottom for use as either a military reservation or a national park. The idea of preservation for military reasons apparently stirred more of a response on the part of the public, and in 1894 the state legislatures of New York and New Jersey appointed investigatory commissions. The Governor of New Jersey and the state senators from Bergen and Rockland Counties reportedly supported the commissions' studies, and hoped that their recommendation for some form of condemnation act would result in the beach lands' purchase by the states.[12]

These commissions, after doing their fieldwork, and photographing and gathering all information pertaining to the Palisades, reacted favorably to the prospect of a military reservation. In accordance with their recommendations, both state legislatures passed bills ceding the face and base of the Palisades to the Federal Government. It was said that the New York metropolitan area ought to have a military command post high atop the Bergen cliffs "as a defense against foreign and domestic foes." The installation of barracks, ammunition dumps, and parade grounds was thus, with somewhat convoluted logic, believed to be the path toward protection of the picturesque cliffs. The *New York Times* seriously doubted the strategic utility of the Palisades (unless of course an enemy attacked New York City from Boston via Albany!).[13] Fortunately for posterity, the measure was rejected by the Congress in 1895, and again when the matter came up in 1898 as part of the Spanish-American War paranoia.

Meanwhile, as New Jersey tried for injunctions against several of the companies, the "vandalism" continued unabated. One company made a half-hearted effort to restore the landscape by reseeding worked-out quarries,[14] but others such as the Carpenter Brothers demolished more and more landmarks. Washington Head and Indian Head, profile-like columns to the north of Fort

Lee, were dramatically and ceremoniously dispatched by the Carpenters in 1897 and 1898. It was calculated that if Indian Head were rendered to rubble, it would yield 2.5 million cubic yards of traprock and keep the crushers busy for one year; accordingly in March 1898, a contest was held to choose a young girl to be awarded the honor of plunging the stately cliff into oblivion: "7000 pounds of dynamite [were] set off by Miss Alice Haggerty of Coytesville, N.J., a pretty slip of an Irish girl, who giggled as she did it. . . . The body of Italians who had done the preparation work cheered enthusiastically when the destruction had been accomplished." [15] The little drama seemed slightly perverse to some; reflecting upon the loss, and the use for which the traprock was destined, the Secretary of the Federation of Women's Clubs could only comment: "The glorious heritage of the people of the state [of New Jersey] is being trampled under the foot of man and beasts in the streets of Gotham." [16]

The quarry conflict was at last resolved at the turn of the century, primarily through the initiative of the Federation of Women's Clubs of New Jersey. This group secured passage of a bill through the New Jersey legislature in 1899 empowering the Governor to appoint a five-member commission to study the condition of the Palisades and suggest remedies for their preservation. Simultaneously, conservation forces in New York State (most notably "The Society for the Preservation of Scenic and Historical Places and Objects"), with the solid backing of Governor Theodore Roosevelt, influenced the passage of a similar bill by the foot-dragging New York legislature. The New York commission of five was to act in conjunction with the New Jersey state commission, but their findings and recommendations were expected to have very tough going, especially in the New Jersey legislature. Although three successive New Jersey Governors openly favored Palisades preservation (Governors Werts, Griggs, and Voorhees), the indifference and occasional hostility of legislators representing downstate or south Jersey interests was a consistent stumbling block. Despite the nagging suspicion that preservation would largely benefit those who enjoyed the view from the New York side of the Hudson, the legislators from

Hudson, Bergen, Essex, Passaic, and Union Counties rallied to the preservation cause, while "south of Elizabeth and west of Plainfield, there [was] no sentiment for the preservation of the Palisades." [17]

Finally, in March 1900, the study commissions' recommendations for a permanent interstate park commission, with power to acquire land along the Palisades for recreational purposes, passed the New York legislature and was signed into law by Governor Roosevelt. With one last great effort, preservation advocates in New Jersey overcame opposition from legislators and quarrying company lobbyists, and saw Governor Voorhees sign the bill into law in that state.

Knowing that the newly formed Palisades Interstate Park Commission would soon be acquiring land, the quarrymen worked feverishly throughout the summer and fall of 1900. They removed more than 12,000 cubic yards of rock per day from the Fort Lee-Englewood area, inflicting some of the worst damage that had ever been done. Functioning with a limited, $15,000 budget, the Palisades Commission nevertheless conducted extensive surveys of the area, and with financial aid from J. Pierpont Morgan, bought out the Carpenter Brothers for $132,500. Blasting stopped forever on Christmas Eve 1900 so that "the conservation of the Palisades and the extension of the Interstate Park in the following thirty years began as a Christmas gift to the people of the two states." [18]

Land Acquisition by the Palisades Interstate Park Commission

After its creation in 1900, the two most significant steps taken by the Palisades Interstate Park Commission were the consolidation of park land at the Palisades, and the extension of its jurisdiction to the north. The basis for these objectives was largely achieved by the Hudson-Fulton Tricentennial celebration in 1909, at which time the park was formally dedicated.

Originally, the commission had agreed to include within the park only the lands from the top of the cliff face to the riverline—the area that had been subject to "the misdirected energy" of the stone cutters. But later, as the estate owners probably suspected all along, policy was changed to incorporate those lands atop the cliffs as well.[19] With additional funds provided by the states and money from philanthropic families, acquisition proceeded as quickly as the title and ownership claims of some 112 owners holding 147 parcels of land could be resolved. The clifftop properties, which averaged seven acres, were in some cases donated to the commission. The Lydia Lawrence estate ("Cliffside") at Sneden's Landing, with its cascading falls, grottoes, pools, and fountains, was one of the most impressive gifts made to the commission in these years.[20] By 1905 75 percent of the land from Fort Lee to the state line had been purchased; negotiations were continuing for the remainder.

Very soon the "commission had as raw material thirteen and a half miles of cliffs and talus slope and shore front, badly scarred in some places, but on the whole retaining so much of their original wild and inaccessible character that one writer at the time called them 'The Unknown Palisades.' "[21] In September of 1909 when the park was dedicated in a ceremony held at the old Cornwallis headquarters below the cliffs, the final property deeds had been transferred to the commission.

Decisions affecting land use came almost simultaneously with the acquisition proceedings. It was the job of park personnel to "civilize the park enough to make it usable by city people." In the summer of 1905 camping within the park was condoned by the commission and the *New York Times* reported that "life under the Palisades is starting in on a new era."[22] The salt marsh below Englewood Cliffs was filled in to create a recreation area, and linked to upper Manhattan via ferry. Bathing beaches, hiking trails, camping facilities, and numerous concession buildings were all established beneath a stabilized slope and along a straightened shoreline. Surveys for a river roadway were made at this time, although the Henry Hudson Drive was not opened until 1921. By 1909 the commission had proposed a scenic drive along the top of the Palisades, the Palisades Interstate Parkway, not started until 1947.[23]

Except for the Tallman Mountain section at the north end of the Palisades in New York State, which would be snapped from the jaws of the Standard Trap Rock Corporation of Sparkill in 1928, quarrying had been halted, and the Palisades protected as far north as Piermont. By 1906 it became apparent to many preservationists that there was a manifest need to extend the jurisdiction of the commission northward through Rockland County, where "Hook Mountain, one of the most impressive promontories upon the west bank of the Hudson [was reported] to be in imminent danger of disfigurement."[24] In fact, the contour of Hook Mountain had already been much assaulted by several traprock companies, but it was not until this date—with a knowledge that a victory could be won as at the Palisades—that attention was focused on areas farther north.

Postcards depicting the defacement of Hook Mountain were issued by the American Scenic and Historical Preservation Society. The Rockefellers and Morgans publicly supported a bill to extend the commission's protective jurisdiction northward.[25] The quarrymen's "outrageous actions" resulted in the "Extension of 1906" (fig. 38), whereby the commission was authorized to acquire land as far north as Stony Point, already under Federal protection. This area would eventually encompass the Blauvelt, Rockland Lake, Hook Mountain, and High Tor State Parks. At Hook Mountain itself, through acquisition and condemnation in the years between 1911 and 1915, the worst aspects of quarrying came to an end.[26] However, the Tors, eyed hungrily by the quarrymen, were not acquired until 1943—and then only in part.

By 1909 the highlands west of the Hudson were also brought within the realm of the commission for several very pressing reasons. Park facilities in the Palisades area proved so popular that recreational overuse forced a search for additional space. The highlands were looked to because "This region, protected like the Palisades by its ruggedness, had likewise remained in an undeveloped state. . . . The region was going back into wilderness and the time was ripe for it to be conserved for human recreation."[27] What eventually triggered the extension of the commission's jurisdiction was a move on the part of the New

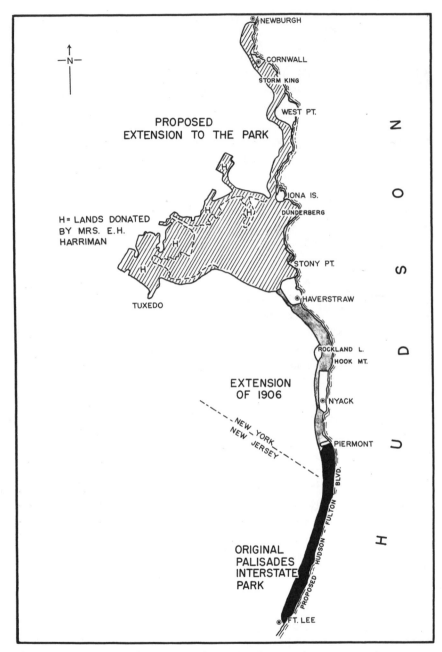

Figure 38. Palisades Park in 1909 with actual and proposed extensions
From: C. W. Leavitt Jr.'s map accompanying message of Governor Charles E. Hughes, December 1909
(Scale: 1″ = 3.3 miles)

York State Prison Commission to develop facilities near Bear Mountain. That a scenic region with vast recreation potential should be utilized for such an inappropriate purpose produced a public outcry. Fortunately, these events coincided with the Harriman gift of 10,000 highland acres to the state under condition that work on the prison facility be discontinued, and that the area between the Hudson and the Harriman property (fig. 38) be secured for park land by the state. In 1910 Governor Charles Evans Hughes ordered an abandonment of the prison project, appointed the commission as administrator of the Harriman estate, and extended the commission's jurisdiction north to Newburgh and west to the Ramapos.

A remarkably wide leeway was granted the commission. "It was given the power to select and locate such mountain lands along the west bank of the Hudson River . . . as in its opinion might be proper and necessary for the purpose of preserving the scenic beauty." [28] A state bond issue of $2.5 million in 1910, along with substantial and repeated gifts of money in the following decades, allowed further acquisitions. "Successive land ownership maps for the years between 1911 and 1929 show the Harriman and Bear Mountain Parks growing from scattered blocks, to a solid area, from Bear Mountain . . . nearly to Tuxedo and Sloatsburg in the Ramapo Valley." [29]

When 300 years of exploration and progress on the river were celebrated in 1909, the groundwork had thus been laid for the establishment of one of the greatest recreational attractions ever to be situated on the doorstep of a metropolis the size of New York. Battles and decisions affecting the utilization and management of the landforms had at last culminated in a form of land usage worthy of the "titanic majesty" of the landscape itself.

Land Use at the Palisades

By 1900 a rather abrupt transition in land use had emerged at Fort Lee; it appears as sharp today as it did on Wallace Bruce's photographic panorama of the Hudson's shores in 1906 in fig.

39. South from Fort Lee to Guttenberg in Hudson County was a ribbon of coal sheds, rail facilities and ferry landings, the Lorillard tobacco works, and assorted manufacturing plants. Edgewater, "an industrial and commercial community," housed thousands of workers in shabby quarters both below and above the cliffs.[30] South of the flag-topped boat dock and hotel at Fort Lee, the "model suburb" of Palisade, New Jersey, was being developed on 1000 cliff-top acres. But while industry hummed and real estate developers pieced together thousands of building lots below the old redoubt at Fort Lee, the area to the north was being secured by the Palisades Interstate Park Commission.

Activities not conducive to recreational usage were gradually phased out of the park area. Simultaneous with the cessation of quarrying was the tearing down of residential structures. Oddly, some still believed that the crest of the Palisades might "some day abound in castles and luxuriant homes," making it one of the finest residential boulevards in the world.[31] Such of course was not to be, and the development of estate properties with actual buildings never amounted to more than a handful even at its highpoint. The Victorian and Gothic boxes with their pergolas and settees projecting out onto the rock buttresses were few and inconspicuous in prints and photographs through the 1890s. The era of estate building came later to the Palisades than elsewhere in the valley, and its inroads were aborted in the 1890s and 1900s.

Perhaps it was just as well, for as the *New York Times* observed, a summer home or an estate in the Hudson Valley was no longer fashionable or even financially manageable. Apart from being a tremendous tax burden to its owners, the possession of estate property—in the highlands, on the eastern shore, and on the Palisades too—paled in social prestige when the "American gentry" turned to Long Island, Newport, and Europe for their amusements.[32] The desertion of the valley by the Fremonts, Aspinalls, Warrings, and Kingslands was, however, compensated for by the conversion of estate property, and sometimes the buildings as well, to institutional use. The only case of this occurring on the Palisades, and the only nonconforming use allowed within the park area, was the construction of St. Michael's

Figure 39. The Palisades Opposite Yonkers

TOP. From Wallace Bruce, *Panorama of the Hudson River Showing Both Sides of the Hudson River from New York to Poughkeepsie,* Bryant Literary Union, 1906.
BOTTOM. Today

Villa for the Sisters of St. Joseph of Newark. (Originally conceived of as a place for the teaching and training of young women for domestic services, the Italianate buildings became, and still are, a conspicuous landmark on the old Allison property.)

Below the Palisades, where recreational facilities were being created, the fishermen's houses, so evident in earlier photographs, were being bought by the Palisades Interstate Park Commission. Anticipating a vacate order from the commission, many of the families had left in the late 1890s, but there were apparently some who remained as long as 1908–9. The abandoned houses and mills were demolished by the park agency; the Cornwallis house at Alpine, because of its historical interest, was preserved. As the shad had disappeared from the increasingly "sludge infested waters,"[33] now it was the fishermen's turn.

What of the landscape inherited by the commission? Was it a region as wild as the Catskills or the Colorado Rockies, as described by the *New York Times?* Apart from those areas scarred by the quarries, the tomato gardens and woodlots maintained by the undercliff dwellers, and the areas of parkland associated with the cliff-top estates, the Palisades region remained heavily wooded. From the river, the cliffs and their summits appeared half hidden in trees and vines, a jungle of underbrush allowed to proliferate with the demise of farming. An inspection of photographs taken of the areas around Sneden's Landing and Palisades, New York, in 1903 reveals an open woodland with little underbrush at the former, while the latter, probably representative of the area at large, is thoroughly wooded.[34] Collins claims that the Palisade forest at this time was a nearly unbroken tract (12,000 acres) primarily of oak and chestnut, and this is substantiated by official reports. East from the suburban railroad zone, the study commissions reported in 1896 a "plateau of rock, covered with thin soil, strewn with boulders, and, excepting unimportant clearings, still chiefly clothed with unbroken forests."[35]

In the same report the State Geologist of New Jersey is quoted to the effect that the entire area for a width of 1.5 miles back from the river is 90 percent covered with oak, chestnut, and cedar 40 to 80 feet in height and 30 to 50 years in age. It might be added that the talus slope, too, "a vital part of the beauty of the Palisades," presented a mixed deciduous growth (a "shelving woodland") far denser than at the time of the Civil War.[36] It was the thinning out of this forest and the cutting of underbrush that occupied an army of Palisades Park employees, some of whom were former shad fishermen, for a number of years.

On Hook Mountain and in Surrounding Lowlands

Nyack and Haverstraw were no longer directly involved with any land use decisions. Policy had come to be determined by the Palisades Park Commission, and with decreased travel time from the metropolis, it was mostly an "outside" population that derived the greatest recreational pleasure from commission properties.

By the 1890s Nyack's population had grown to more than 6000, but growth rapidly came to a halt and would not again climb noticeably until the popularization of the automobile. The village furthermore suffered heavily as a result of the depression of 1893: the shoe shops closed, the local hotels lost their appeal, and boat-building became geared to pleasure craft only. Both Haverstraw village and township, reeling under the effects of a brickyard disaster in 1906 and the continual draining of population from rural areas, actually lost population.[37] The village, subsisting basically on the manufacture of brick and cement until the 1940s, would not grow markedly until the suburban explosion following World War II.

Hook Mountain and the Tors had been, and would continue to be, distinguished from the surrounding industrial and residential lowlands at Nyack and Haverstraw by their recreational and scenic merit. Land use before and after 1906 very closely approximates that of the Palisades. As in previous periods, there is again a shared history: limited estate usage, spotty garden farming, the arrival and departure of the quarry companies and the struggle for preservation, and—in the end—incorporation within the Pali-

sades Interstate Park. It should suffice to say that the region survived as a woody, "rough and uninhabited"[38] upland, vividly
portrayed by Bruce in fig. 40.

In the Hudson Highlands

Writing about the future of the highlands in 1908, Headley
in his *History of Orange County* wondered what would become of
the old estate properties and farmlots which were being abandoned. Stillman reports that scratch farming was practiced in
some places into the early 1900s, but that much abandonment
was occasioned by the thin soil.[39] Birch, as the pioneer vegetative species in this region, was overtaking the fields on the lower
slopes while higher up a forest of pine and mixed hardwoods was
rebounding from the charcoal iron industry and cordwood cutting. In fact, to most who saw the highlands around the turn of
the century, this area must have appeared as a "jungle wilderness," a primitive tract of unbroken and wildly wooded forest,
seemingly unimproved and undisturbed since the days of the
Revolutionary War.[40] To the observer perhaps casually acquainted with the area's history, the dark and thickly foliaged
hillsides seemed as they should: "Although we hear much about
the evils of deforestation, the Hudson shows little evidence of its
ravages. In many places it must be much as it was when Hen-
drick Hudson himself viewed it." Indeed, Hugh Raup, reporting
on his "Botanical Studies in the Black Rock Forest," found the
twentieth-century tree cover to contain the same species, heights,
and relationships as the pre-occupation forest; in summation he
wrote: "There is considerable evidence that the local arrangement
and composition of the types have persisted with little modification since pre-colonial times."[41]

Surveys of the woodland conducted by the Palisades Park
Commission provided a more authoritative evaluation of the
vegetative cover in 1910. Far from being an "unbroken forest
tract," the highlands were found to be "ragged in many places,
from overcutting, fires, and the effects of the chestnut blight."[42]

Figure 40. Hook Mountain

Top. From Wallace Bruce, *Panorama of the Hudson River Showing Both Sides of the Hudson River from New York to Poughkeepsie,* Bryant Literary Union, 1906.
Bottom. Today

Patches of abandoned pasture and open woodland were also much in evidence. The job of the commission was to prepare this sparsely populated "primeval" region of lakes and woods for recreational usage. This involved replanting certain areas with evergreens, and thinning out the underbrush, as was done below the Palisades.

Those few villages in and on the margin of the highlands that had managed to survive past the 1890s met with varying fates. Caldwell's, with a hotel and ferry landing of former importance, lost all semblance of settlement despite efforts to create a summer colony and scenic mountain railway.[43] Later, when the Dunderberg Road was built (as a part of U.S. route 9W) and the nearby mountain was acquired by the Park Commission, the settlement—referred to as Jones Point on the topographic sheets— was only a small grouping of frame houses. Highland Falls, with 2400 people by 1910, remained an attractive summer community and functioned as the service center for the "Point." Land-use changes were nonetheless apparent here too: many of the older "country style residences" and resort hotels had succumbed, being replaced by buildings of an institutional nature. Various churches assembled properties in the area, and the site of Cranston's Hotel was occupied by the Ladycliff Academy.

The Storm King Mountain area, where engineering work had started on the New York City aqueduct in 1908, still had Cornwall as its economic focal point. As a river landing for coal and as a shipment point for fruit and garden vegetables bound for the city market, the town of 1900 people (in 1900) functioned as a "business place without any pretense of beauty." Some industries and residences had migrated westward and uphill away from the landing to form the nucleus of what is today Cornwall Village. Mill industries still dotted the hinterland around Orr's Mill and West Cornwall, but the inducement of further industry to Cornwall itself (still something of a summer resort) was looked upon unfavorably by some of the wealthier neighbors who objected to "the class such work would bring among them."[44] And up on the high, rugged mountain of granite that sends its shadow over the village, the Interstate Park arrived (in

1922) with a gift of several hundred acres in Storm King Mountain's Black Rock Forest.

On the islands in the Hudson and in the highlands of Putnam County, land use changes approximated those of the western shore. In many cases, land that was once occupied by resorts or estates was now government property. Constitution Island was deeded to the Federal Government as a part of the West Point reservation in 1909. Iona Island, a vineyard, pleasure resort, and picnic ground of former times, was barred to the public and used as a supply depot by the Navy.[45] At the northern gate, Pollepel Island became "Bannerman's Island" after it was purchased by David Bannerman in 1900 for use as a safe storage place for both Civil War and Spanish-American War surplus. Alongside their residence, the owners built an arsenal in the form of a European castle and landscaped the rocky grounds with trees, shrubs, and gardens.[46]

In the highlands east of the river, farming had become an all-but-vanished way of life. Private camps and summer recreation centers were opened, and religious organizations began to acquire large tracts of land for monasteries, schools, and summer retreats.[47] Although the highland peaks in Putnam and Dutchess Counties (Anthony's Nose, Taurus, Breakneck, and Sugarloaf) did not play an active role in the preservation movement before 1909, their subsequent history was a direct reflection of what happened at the Palisades, at Hook Mountain, and in the western highlands before that date: the blasting out of the mountainside for granite at Taurus in the 1930s, vigorous and successful action by conservation groups to end the quarrying, and in the 1970s, the creation of a 2500-acre state park on lands in part donated by the Rockefellers.

Chapter 12
The River, the Park, and the Mountain

If the aesthetic base is asserted by a community, it will be recognized by law. Let people understand that landscape is a public possession, that beauty in nature, the curve of hill and colour of foliage, is educational, and that the loss of these things is a serious one to them and to their children.
Edgar Mayhew Bacon, *The Hudson River from Ocean to Source,* 1902

BY THE LATE nineteenth century time was ripe for landscape preservation. If concern for environment does indeed "comprise a great submerged interest in our culture, of the order of a great batholith, out of sight but always there, made evident by scattered outcrops of concern,"[1] then the late 1800s was one such outcrop. Now a change in national consciousness, resulting from and in the conservation movement, had occurred and "a national mood or temper existed that had been absent, with a few exceptions, a generation before."[2] Between the creation of the Adirondack Park and the Sierra Club in 1892 and the Theodore Roosevelt-initiated gathering of one hundred national leaders at the White House Conference on Conservation in 1908, a period of great activity transpired which has been called the "first wave" or Classical Period of the American Conservation-Preservation movement. Locally, this time period climaxed very appropriately in the first decade of the new century, with the creation and enlargement of the Palisades Interstate Park system and the Hudson-Fulton celebrations.

Conservation and Its Effect Upon Hudson Valley Preservation

There are various complex reasons why conservation made such remarkable strides around the turn of the century, and why the reaction to quarrying, for example, coalesced into an active concern to save what was environmentally aesthetic. The rise of Progressivism was compatible with the ideals of the "Conservation Crusade": foresters and wealthy landowners were revolted by the indiscriminate lumbering of the Eastern woodlands; people became aware that resources were limited; and the dynamic personality of Theodore Roosevelt as Governor of New York (1898–1900) and later as President (1901–8) did much to aid efforts at conservation. And then there was the ever-present popular sentiment for the past, the primitive, the wild, and even the rural.[3] These reasons and sentiments were prominent too in the increased public awareness of the spectacular rate of animal slaughter and "market hunting." Endangerment and preservation of wildlife again involved Roosevelt (ironically a hunter) and his efforts to organize wildlife conferences in the 1880s culminated in the opening of the New York Zoological Park in the Bronx in 1899.

The closing of the frontier brought a wider acceptance of conservation,[4] while the census of 1890, and Turner's subsequent insights into its implications made clear that the continent's resource base was finite, and that a new frontier was needed, a new outlet for the energies and anxieties of the nation. With the frontier gone and the wilderness far removed, conservation itself became that new frontier, a means by which to express and perhaps reduce the uneasiness over population growth (brought about especially by immigration), urbanization, and industrialization. "For a civilization that had begun to notice its first gray hairs, conservation was welcome tonic for the land as well as for the minds of its inhabitants."[5]

While the brunt of conservation in these decades was in the economic and political areas of landscape management (forest utilization, dry-lands reclamation), purely aesthetic motivations were woven into the movement as well. Though party politics played a role in securing the preservation of the Yosemite and the Yellowstone (and to a lesser extent, the Adirondacks), a feeling of respect for the wonder and awe of nature's sublime works was present.[6] A combination of practical politics and economic dictates *and* aesthetic values led to national and state parks and preserves.[7] Gifford Pinchot, as chief of the Forestry Division and author of *The Fight for Conservation* (1910), propounded doctrines of management and resource utilization not only designed for social practicality ("Conservation means the greatest good to the greatest number for the longest time"), but for aesthetic awareness too. Pinchot was patronized by Olmsted and influenced by the philosophical ideals of Marsh (who in turn was influenced by the Romantics and Transcendentalists).[8]

Huth, in *Nature and the American,* states emphatically that conservation philosophy at this time consisted of both utilitarian and idealistic viewpoints, and that a recognition of the need to include spiritual and aesthetic values in making decisions about managing resources did exist.[9] In New York State an aesthetic groundwork that had taken almost a century to construct obviously existed. The preservation of the scenery at Niagara, Watkins Glen, and Letchworth Park was not without aesthetic incentives, nor was that of the Hudson.

The preservation of the Palisades and the subsequent decision to extend the interstate commission's protective jurisdiction northward to include Hook Mountain and the Hudson Highlands was primarily a reaction against quarrying. However, competition for land use and resources had developed. Whereas the traprock companies saw talus and basaltic columns as dollars, others thought that pleasant highland and cliff-top locations could best be utilized for residences or resorts. The New York State Commission for the study of the Palisades, regarded the practical value of the Palisades as a potentially productive forest (with recreation for the millions) as very worthwhile, while the military valued the region for its assumed strategic importance. Everyone, it appears, had alternate suggestions for best employing this stretch of riverfront. As today, the river was seen as a public convenience to be used for one's personal purposes.

The general public, chastised by the press for its lack of concern, evidently wavered. Nash feels that the East Coast man-in-the-street knew in a very superficial way what conservation was by 1909, but had only a vague appreciation of the movement's objectives.[10] "T.R." knew what was best for the country, so conservation must be all right. This attitude is confirmed by newspaper accounts of public (dis)interest in the formal dedication of the Palisades Interstate Park, and the Hudson-Fulton celebrations. The momentous significance of these events, in terms of historical achievement and regional preservation, was lost on a citizenry more infatuated with balloons and fireworks (fig. 41).[11]

The conservation movement remained primarily an upper-class phenomenon. It attracted the well off and the well educated, as well as those who had social contacts with experts in the environmental area. The continuing strength of the aesthetic concept is no less associated with the valley's social and economic elite today. As documented by William Tucker in "Environmentalism and the Leisure Class," the delaying actions taken against the Storm King project by a small but determined group of wealthy people—"tweedy people living at the end of country roads"—marked "the birth of the environmental movement" in the United States, much as it did the birth of the conservation movement some eighty or ninety years ago.[12]

Whatever the strengths that such an elite brought to the environmental movement, and whatever the shortcomings of a popular aesthetic awareness, then and now, it was universally accepted that the Hudson's western shore had scenic value, and should be preserved for purposes of aesthetics and recreation. It was a landscape that was, no matter what, still spoken of as

Hudson-Fulton
CELEBRATION

Figure 41. Hudson-Fulton Celebration Souvenir Program Cover. New York: New-comb Pub. Co., 1909.

sublime, exquisitely charming, and magnificent in its composition. While the praise might be less frequent, and perhaps made with less conviction than in the past, Bruce's 1906 panorama of the Hudson was a successful and popular work which still portrayed the lower valley in terms of grandeur, sublimity, and picturesqueness. In addition, John D. Rockefeller thought so highly of Palisade scenery that he purchased land on Washington Heights from which to view his properties on the Bergen cliffs. And while the Hudson River artists were either dead or painting elsewhere, a few still elucidated the river's beauties. One of these was Van Perrine, "the painter of the Palisades." He lived and worked on the Palisades, painting the cliffs on bright May mornings and in December storms, with a love of and sympathy for nature.[13]

Apart from those who might periodically lapse into fascination with the industrially picturesque,[14] the shared opinion of the more informed citizens was that industry, specifically traprock quarrying, was unsightly and destructive of visual beauty. The greatest indignation over quarrying, as expressed in innumerable newspaper editorials and reports from the 1890s to 1909,[15] was over its destruction of scenery. Competition for land was not, as elsewhere, the main issue. The "defacement," the reduction of aesthetically pleasing mountain forms to scarred cliffs and heaps of overhead rubble, angered and motivated those who eventually led the successful preservation campaign.[16]

Vacuous Appeals to Nationalism and Pastoralism

The role of a romantically inspired concept of landscape was crucial to the preservation of scenic landforms. What was regarded as aesthetic was saved for posterity by an interstate compact. But within that conception, which has been traced back to its inception in the early 1800s, some elements were found to add meaning and strength to the park movement while others, conditioned by the spirit of the times, played a relatively minor role.

Nationalism, as in the post–Civil War period, succumbed to an air of internationalism in business and the arts. This was "the cosmopolitan period of American painting,"[17] a time when European styles and mannerisms assumed a progressively greater acceptance. Expatriation became common among American painters (e.g. Whistler, Cassatt, J. S. Sargent), and interests, in part because of the closing of the frontier and the loss of exploitable horizons, shifted to the Old World.

It is difficult to say how much genuine popular emotion was stirred by the Spanish-American War, but the evocation of patriotic feeling as a tool of landscape appreciation was not an abiding characteristic of the preservation movement in the Hudson Valley. Attempts were made to equate conservation and preservation with love of nation; isolated appeals to patriotism and "national dignity" were even made in the name of aesthetics. Theodore Roosevelt urged Americans to support the work of conservation because a judicious use of resources was a part of "the patriotic duty of insuring the safety and continuance of the nation." The *New York Times,* arguing that the ideals of the nation were being undermined by quarrymen, informed its readers that a love of Hudson River landscape "springs out of the soil into the Patriot's blood."[18]

This kind of appeal was much more effective when made to pride in the historical American landscape. It was a sense of the past deserving of honor and pride which seemed more relevant than the contemporary nation's need for these same qualities of appreciation. This may explain why the historical associations of the Palisades were looked upon favorably, whereas the suggestion of using the cliffs for ammunition dumps and barracks ("The Palisades National Military Park" to defend the nation) was coolly received. By the late 1800's nationalism, patriotism, national pride, or whatever the term used, was a concept of importance in landscape preservation only as a corollary of historical association, and not in and of itself. In the verse of Wallace Bruce:

The Highlands and the Palisades
Mirror their beauty in the tide,

The history of whose forest shades
A nation reads with conscious pride.[19]

The economic landscape and those social ideals which created it also conspired against the use of pastoral imagery as an effective aesthetic element. As the twentieth century dawned, as Leo Marx has said, a mechanical hell symbolized by utility, science, and industrialized production had supplanted that other "kingdom of force" symbolized by beauty and green landscapes.[20] Business values and urban living were felt to be undermining character, taste, and morality. The vast size and highly organized nature of the economy and government posed obstacles to the effectiveness of the individual; "progress" appeared to have brought confusion, corruption, and debilitating overabundance.[21] Headley, in his comments on the Town of Highlands in Orange County, lamented that people too often appraised the area in terms of assessed real estate values and industrial potential: "There was nothing allowed for sentiment or native grandeur in that cold, business estimate."[22]

The calculating stress on investment returns, and the power of corporate man and machine to transform landscape, is clearly seen in the real estate publicity issued by Bergen County developers in 1906. The Hudson River Realty Company, which had been acquiring and assembling properties for subdivisions into 15,000 building lots immediately to the south of Fort Lee, issued a brochure explaining and justifying its "beautification" of the southern Palisades: "The rare forest of virgin timber, out of which [the housing tracts are] being carved suffers to a certain extent from the encroachments of civilization, but the streets, after all, form picturesque ribbons through a vista of green foliage."[23]

This same brochure also included an interesting visual contrast which says much about the commercial attitude of the day. The cover illustration, obviously the preferred condition, showed the Palisades completely settled upon and lined with houses top and bottom, while an electric trolley line snaked its way up the cliff and an obscenely fat little ferry puffed its way across the river. Relegated to the back cover was the "unimproved" landscape, the identical stretch of shoreline enveloped in woods and without so much as a single habitant. "What [better] site could be selected for a home?"[24] The vulgarity of what was being said, and its very subversion of the pastoral design, was not apparently realized.

Real estate developers aside, the railroad was probably still the greatest corrupter of the pastoral. Drawing upon imagery developed by the Romantics, the Hudson's West Shore Railroad was described in Ingersoll's *Illustrated Guide* as "marr[ing] the beauty of the banks."[25] Codman, in his equestrian travels through the highlands, blamed the railroad for tainting rural religious virtues: "the railroad has dealt a heavy blow upon the theology of our fathers." He echoed a universal requiem for the long departed and no-longer-reattainable pastoral landscape: "As we travel over this wide and stone-walled road along the banks of the river, beholding the smoke of factories and hearing the noise of machinery and railroad-engines, let us close our eyes and ears to the surroundings, and go back in our thought to the time when all this was a wilderness."[26]

Greater than the railroads' despoilation of rural landscapes (and morals) was its speed, which made impossible a decent perception of the landscape being traveled through. Railroad passengers thus developed little appreciation of scenery—or of a theoretically pastoral region—between their points of origin and destination. By the 1890s railroads had contrived to change "the whole scale and character of the landscape by the introduction of speed and by disregard for natural configurations . . . spoiling the littorals of rivers and lakes."[27] For Henry James, traveling through the valley by rail in 1907, appreciation of the landforms and contemplation of the pastoral were spoiled; there was simply no time allowed. James regarded the train as a convenient but not very ideal way to study landscape: "to use the train at all was to put one's self, for any proper justice to the scenery, in a false position."[28] The view from the rails represented a new and feverish America. Soon the romantic-pastoral-scenic landscape would be even further desecrated by that "terrible cold and heartless mechanism of destruction"—the automobile.

After 1909, with road reconstruction in progress to accommodate motor cars, aesthetic concept in the Hudson Valley faded deeper into the background as this "fascinating amusement" beguiled a population "content with little more than a perfunctory view of the scenery, which, however, cannot be thoroughly 'taken in' when running at a rate of over twelve miles an hour."[29]

Other circumstances, too, contributed to the demise of pastoral imagery. Of great importance was the continued diversion of the national vision away from areas such as the Hudson Valley and toward the West and the city. Southern California lured Easterners, attracted by what they imagined to be a winterless, health-giving, uncrowded, and as yet unindustrialized garden.[30] The strength of this pastoral image drew over 1.6 million Easterners to California between 1890 and 1909. Significantly, the Fort Lee and the New York City based motion-picture studios, which had used the Palisade region as a backdrop for "western" and "rural" scenery, also began their migration to California.[31]

Meanwhile, artists and architects for the most part had turned away from a no-longer-inspiring pastoral countryside to a romanticization and idolization of things urban:

As art directions changed in the last quarter of the century, American landscape gave way to canvases depicting Americana—genre paintings, representations of life in the almost measureless gray city at the big stream's wide mouth. The river retired into the mists.[32]

The Hudson River School had become an anachronism, as ashcans and tenement houses became fashionable. As cityscapes began to dominate art exhibitions ("The Exhibition of the Eight" in 1908 is a good example), architects turned toward skyscraper construction and the study of new structural techniques in building. In the arts, at least, the country cottage and inspirational scenery were no longer relevant.[33]

But artistic thought does not necessarily reflect the contemporary culture. A social concern for cities and the creation of urban amenities became prevalent only after the artistic vanguard had stimulated interest. The American public in 1900, as at most other times in the nation's history, held firmly to the doctrine of "the city evil."[34] New York City, with over a million inhabitants by 1890, was equated with the moral failure that resulted from material success. Writers continued to milk the theme of how country boys and girls were corrupted by the wickedness and the vices of hedonistic, money-minded urban existence (e.g. Warner's writings on Wall Street in the 1880s and 1890s and Upton Sinclair's *The Money Changers* in 1908).[35] A defense of natural scenery, and an interest in preserving what was aesthetic or pastoral beyond the city's fringe, became a means of protesting the commercial sordidness of cities. New York State between 1900 and 1910, became the focal point of a "back-to-the-farm" campaign, in which the amenities of a pastoral life were contrasted, by publicists and railroad companies, with the "evils" of congested cities.[36]

Guidebooks might still try to convince the river traveler that the people who lived atop the Palisades in the early years of this century did so in "rustic fashion,"[37] but it should have been apparent to most that something had gone wrong with the pastoral ideal in America. All that was bucolic or rustic could not be perpetuated because of the unrelenting spread of industry across the countryside. Pastoralism's fatal weakness, as Leo Marx has said, was its static nature and its inability to cope with inevitable change. In the Hudson Valley and elsewhere in the eastern United States there was nothing in the landscape—no tradition, no standard, no institution—that could refuse acquiescence to machines and stand up against the forces of which the railroad was the vanguard and the symbol. "As the work of Thoreau and Melville and Mark Twain had testified, the pastoral dream was no defense."[38]

Aesthetic Building Blocks of Preservation

Three elements from earlier times endured: an interest in geological composition, in sublime appearance, and in historical associations. As the *New York Times* noted in a Sunday, full-page illustrated article in 1905, the Palisades of the lower Hudson were the most "geologically, scenically, and historically interesting" landform features east of the Mississippi.[39] And, in arguments that would later be applied to Hook Mountain and the highlands, the New York State Commission for the Preservation of the Palisades observed that the rivershore and cliffs must be kept intact because the stunning rock formations were geologically educational; historical sentiment (perpetuation of the Revolutionary War heritage especially) was embedded in these rock layers; and the landform itself was sublimely aesthetic.[40]

Geological Curiosity

Popular curiosity about geological formations, and speculations upon the earth's history can be traced uninterrupted from late colonial times. While somewhat *déja-vu* in the late nineteenth century, the "records of the earth's creation, [so] full of significance and interest" was one of the forces that inspired the interest in preserving those landforms so informative of God's and nature's work:

Beautiful scenery has more than an aesthetic value. . . . If the [scenic] reservation contains boulders or glaciated rock surfaces . . . then the mind of the thinking person is set to working and the thoughts are lifted to the contemplation of the wonderful qualities of nature. Thus the reservations of natural beauty become open-air universities of the people.[41]

Aside from the animals, a prime attraction of the New York (Bronx) Zoological Park when it opened was the geological aspect of its 264 acres; the early guidebooks and newspaper accounts describing the zoo played up such curious and scenic "souvenirs" as the glacier-scraped ridges, glacial striations on the smooth rock boulders in the crocodile pool, trembling peat bogs, and the pink granite "rocking stone."

The "geological wonder" of the Hudson's landforms was discussed in newspaper stories and the Palisades Study Commission, in its 1895 report, gave extensive coverage to tracing the origins of "the primeval rocks" and explaining their nature and formation.[42] Even after 1900 "the great mystery concerning the creation of this region" was celebrated along with the representation of the highlands and Palisades as ruins of civilization, and the perennial comparison of these landforms with similar geologic structures elsewhere. As a further indication of the popular interest in geological phenomena, the New York News-Letter of January–February 1901, presented a lengthy description of the highlands, devoted almost entirely to geological background.[43] It also appears that a running debate was conducted between various guidebooks on the exact elevation of specific highland peaks. Accusations of willful exaggeration and fabrication (Were the heights of highlands peaks purposefully overstated to furnish a greater sublimity?) flourished to the delight of the public, until the United States Geological Survey confirmed the precise elevations.[44]

Landscape Historically Amplified

The historical overtones that were so very effectively used throughout the preceding decades were without doubt most important in the preservation of aesthetic landforms in the Hudson Valley. Scenery continued to be enhanced by history in the minds of many, and for those influential and active in the cause of both scenic and historical preservation, the glorification of the past by the demarcation of historic sites witnessed its greatest strides in the years 1890–1909.

The tradition of amplifying aesthetic and topographic descriptions with historical references was still strong and pervasive. The guidebooks of course reveled in this type of association, and newspapers and magazines "described" places in terms of history, folklore, romance, and myth. The county histories wallowed in the most obvious colonial, revolutionary, and literary associations. The first of several popular river biographies, Bacon's The Hudson River from Ocean to Source, Historical, Legen-

dary, Picturesque (1902), indicates the author's directional bias through the title itself. Travelers loaded their narratives with long and sometimes irrelevant accounts of aboriginal economics, André's character, and Irving's ghostly presences. After all, the very essence of the river and its landforms was, as Henry James had put it, "a shimmer of association" with the dim and mysterious past.[45]

The shoreline from Fort Lee northward was once more bathed in a historical light. The events and times recalled were by now worn images, but they were needed to further verify the depiction of a romantic region besieged by despoilers. Ingersoll's *Illustrated Guide* lingered on the Revolutionary history of the Palisades and Mack's 1909 *The Palisades of the Hudson* plunged unreservedly into anything of historical merit that could be associated with the cliffs.[46] Aesthetically pleasing ruins were plentiful too: the ruins of the mountain house at Englewood, ruined docks and roofless houses below the shadow of the Palisades, a battery of deserted mansions all along the Bergen and Westchester shores. These same romantic Palisades, blessed with so much of historical worth, were being blasted into traprock and this, to anyone with scenic or historical sentiments, was "rather dreadful."[47]

Near the Haverstraw Flats other cliffs and headlands of historical importance were threatened. The preservation of Hook Mountain became a primary objective of the American Scenic and Historical Preservation Society. There was so much grand scenery possessed of pure historical value in this area that Codman admitted he had not the space to chronicle it all.[48]

As ever, the Hudson Highlands, under various forms of commercial and institutional transgressions ranging from proposed prisons to quarries, remained a "kaleidoscope of blended history and beauty."[49] This region had the correct "mathematical formula" to render it aesthetically compelling and therefore worthy of salvation: an overabundance of Revolutionary War episodes, literary associations, and a growing stock of real and artificial ruins—all embedded within an innately sublime landscape.[50]

As the movement to establish the Palisades Interstate Park

neared its climax, the correlation of scenic preservation with historical association was clearly significant. The rise of the conservation movement was complemented by the founding of patriotic and historical associations and societies with interests in the then-contemporary problem of landscape preservation.[51] The most active and persuasive of the groups was the New York State-based American Scenic and Historical Preservation Society (1901). This society's crusade drew its support from the same anxieties bedeviling the conservationists: "the speed with which modern civilization obliterated cherished parts of former environments." The constitutional purpose of the organization was stated by the society's president: "to promote popular appreciation of and protect the scenic beauties of America and respect for the history of the Nation, its honored names and its physical memorials."[52]

Time, decay, and "improvement" had ruthlessly destroyed places and objects in the landscape. The Palisades Commissioners, however, recognized this union of history and aesthetics, and recommended that the government intervene on behalf of the "Revolutionary War Heritage" and preserve the Bergen cliffs. It was therefore fortunate that the Hudson Valley was able to lay claim to so many associations with that war's history. The job and function of "round[ing] out the American Revolution"[53] by safeguarding historic sites, a persistent nineteenth-century desire, was perhaps the second most important factor in the preservation of the scenery.

Sublimity and "The Last Classic Elegance" in America

Above all else, the doctrine of sublime scenery was the underlying ideal called upon to justify preservation. The sublime aesthetic was not expressed with that same mesmerizing fervor that had sent boatloads of romanticists into ecstasy. Society was now more pressed for time, while changes introduced by the railroad caused a transition in perceptual attitudes away from

Figure 42. A Selection of Hudson River Travel Brochures
New York Public Library: Uncatalogued Collection of Pamphlets and Books Pertaining to the Hudson River and Valley.

awareness of the vertical toward what J. B. Jackson has called "the awareness of horizontal space" in landscapes.[54] Still, an appreciation of the mountainous, however repetitive and unoriginal, was perpetuated by the guidebooks, and vigorously drafted by the perservationist groups in their battles.

The Rand McNally *Illustrated Guide* of 1903 is representative in content and literary style of the several guidebooks published in this era (fig. 42). Drawing upon the phraseology and emotion of the nineteenth century, a sense of mystery and reverence was found appropriate to the ever-changing colors and moods of the Palisades, this "sublime escarpment." The "bold grandeur" and "sublime aspects" of Hook Mountain were mirrored by the golden sunshine upon the purple shades of the Tappan Zee. The highlands, while their sublime spectacle might be lessened in the monotonous light of noon, revealed a majestic sublimity "of no mean degree" when seen in twilight, in moonlight, or in storm.

This region of "jutting rocks and swelling hills" was considered, as it had always been, "the culmination of the [river] journey in point of scenery."[55]

Other guidebooks also displayed the expected enthusiasm for the highland passage, an experience said to be equivalent to "going through a picture-gallery filled with masterpieces."[56] The guidebooks of the Hudson River Dayline Company held that this region, even stripped of its historical associations, guaranteed an unrivaled sublimity because here "Nature outdoes art" and the imperfect artifices of man.[57] Henry James delivered what might be considered the capstone of aesthetic tribute, a bow to sublimity all the more significant in that it was written from the window of a speeding Pullman. The misty highlands, draped in the "luminous mystery" of premature spring heat, was seen with an intense romanticism as storm effects played upon the topography like "some great gray water-color brush." The mountain promontories, perhaps "the last classic elegance" in America, had taken their place in "the geography of the ideal, in the long perspective of the poetry of association," as in the days of Irving and Cole and, for James at least, retained it still.[58]

The varied grandeur and sublimity of mountain landforms was cited by the Palisades Commissioners as reason enough for preservation; the New Jersey Women's Federation regarded it as the "practical duty of women to conserve the beauty of Nature."[59] And it was the duty of all Americans, according to the newly formed American Scenic and Historical Preservation Society to rescue what was left of Hook Mountain's once-sublime configurations.[60] Nature made some things so beautiful that it was impiety to deface them by blasting and crushing. During the heat of this preservation campaign it was stressed that all people, whatever their cultural background or lack of intellectual attainments, had the capacity to enjoy sublimity and would be poorer for its loss. Wallace Bruce, for example, related an incident in which a party of Arizona Indians was taken up the Hudson by boat; palatial estates made no impression on them, but in the region of highland scenery "these wild men stood erect, raised their hands high above their heads and uttered a monosyllabic expression of delight, which was more expressive than volumes of words."[61] The message was clear: Reverence of scenery was more than just cultural; it stemmed from something deeper. The grandeur and sublimity of nature could be appreciated to some extent by all because it brought an uplifting sense of joyousness and inner peace. Therefore it must be preserved for all people, for all time.

Sublime nature was seen, moreover, as an elixir for the shot and shattered nerves of urban man, a view advanced in the early 1900s by John Muir.[62] Surely, landform regions that were sublime, whether along the Hudson or in the Yosemite, were worthy of preservation not only for their inherent grandeur, but also for their beneficial effect upon the health of mind and spirit in a period of great change and stress. "Just to be in frequent perceptual contact with the reassuring, enduring earth" provided a permanent frame of reference in the world, "a psychological security factor of considerable importance."[63]

It is a complex but rewarding thing coming to terms with these few square miles of riverscape. To be sure, this fragment in time, this fragment in space has its own history, patterns, and character; but there is absolutely nothing parochial about this river. There is a universality, a great and cyclic chain of philosophy and events that draws a larger meaning from this ribbon of rock that forms the Hudson's vertical shores. From the valley of the Hudson came ideas of scenery and landscape, formulated by romantics and travelers, that became the philosophical charter of the national conservation movement. That the future of the valley's cliff and highland scenery was largely secure by 1900 was facilitated by the acceptance of a preservation ethic nationally, an ethic in human–land relationships in no small part produced by the Hudson's cross valley aesthetics.

The distant skies of the American West had drawn away the talents of Frederick Law Olmsted to manage the Yosemite Park for a time and those of John C. Frémont to explore and survey its vast territories. But in a final symbolism, Frémont's personal search for the "beneficent, ideal" landscape returned him to the

Figure 43. The Highlands from the Steamboat Deck.
ABOVE. From: *Hudson River Day Line* magazine, New York: R. Stillson Co., 1903.
RIGHT. From New York Public Library, A Scrapbook of Postcards and Other Views, New York State—the Hudson River.

East; the circle had closed in again upon the Hudson, where it had begun. In 1900, "the Great Pathfinder," for all his association with the vision of the raw, new West, was buried in the Rockland County Cemetery—a quiet patch of green with graceful, curving lanes reflecting Olmsted's theories of landscape design—laid out on the hills above the Hudson's waters.[64]

The universality of the river and its beauty is more than just spatial, it breathes life and meaning across the decades as well. When Storm King was seen threatened in the 1960s, economic values were thrown into contention with scenic values—values drawing their substance from all that had transpired in the nineteenth century. Writing from a tradition as old and solid as that of N. P. Willis himself, Calvin W. Stillman in "Issues in the Storm King Controversy" cited associations with the literature and artwork of the Romantic period as reasons to preserve "one of the most spectacularly beautiful spots in Eastern North America." Of the river and the mountain he wrote:

It is a moving experience to see the great river slip between its head-lands. . . . It is moving to think of the time it took the river to cut through this block of granite. Such great natural phenomena remind us of the age of the earth, of the forces of nature, and of the punity of man. . . . this meaning is positive, personal, and beyond articulate expression. It is something we treasure, something dear to us; something whose preservation is important to us.[65]

The important elements of romanticism reverberate: time past (both human and geologic) and the aesthetic of continuity.

In its revised version, plans for the Storm King project would probably have minimized scenic damage and not endangered the mountain's appearance at all; but the call to preserve beauty had gone forth, and would not retreat. The devices, strategies, and trappings of the preservation movement aside, at the heart of it all was the simple, gentle presence of beauty.

That same beauty had motivated Charles Evans Hughes in 1909. Amid the hoopla and triviality of popular festivities marking the dedication of the Interstate Park and the Hudson-Fulton celebrations, Hughes, then Governor of New York, grasped the significance of the moment, in terms of its historical and spatial impact. His address at the dedication captured the essence of the preservation movement in the Hudson Valley; it serves as a time-less credo—one that is just as relevant today as it was on that autumn day so long ago:

Of what avail would be the material benefits of gainful occupation, what would be the promise of prosperous communities, with wealth of products and freedom of exchange, were it not for the opportunities to cultivate the love of the beautiful? The preservation of the scenery of the Hudson is the highest duty with respect to this river imposed upon those who are the trustees of its manifold benefits.[66]

Figure 44. Storm King Mountain

Epilogue

"We lost the fight" said Con Edison's chairman in succinctly describing the historic, precedent-setting compromise agreement arrived at by environmental groups, utility comapnies, and government agencies in late 1980. In return for not building at Storm King—which was still apparently felt to be desirable—the electric utility companies in the Valley would not be required to install closed-cycle cooling systems at their nuclear and oil-powered plants along the Hudson. The agreement, containing this trade-off and other provisions that include biological studies of fish populations, restocking of the river, and scheduled shutdowns during the spawning season, climaxed nearly twenty stubborn years of litigation.* In the end fish were important as was economics (in the form of increased construction costs and diminished power needs), but one also senses something stronger in the background—the poetic and aesthetic magic of that very place, that very name Storm King. Perhaps only such a historically confirmed and culturally embellished piece of the American sublime landscape could have fired and re-fired the preservation struggle for all those years. Appropriately, and befitting its crowning location at the highlands' northern gate, the mountain will now generate not power but, like so much of the rivershore to the south, a "psychic income" in the form of recreation and visual enjoyment forever.

*A more detailed account of the proceedings and provisions is given in *The New York Times,* Dec. 20, 1980, p. 1.

Notes

1. "America's River"

1. Robert Boyle, *The Hudson River, A Natural and Unnatural History,* expanded edition (New York: Norton, 1979), p. 59.

2. Roland Van Zandt, *The Catskill Mountain House* (New Brunswick: Rutgers University Press, 1966), pp. 3ff.

3. It is treated as such in Jerome Wyckoff, *Rock Scenery of the Hudson Highlands and Palisades* (Glens Falls, N.Y.: Adirondack Mountain Club, 1971) and R. H. Torrey et al., *New York Walk Book* (New York: The American Geographical Society, 1951).

4. Although parts of the western shore are either privately (Harvard's Black Rock Forest), municipally, or federally owned (West Point Reservation), most areas are now contained within the administrative domain of the Palisades Interstate Park Commission. The Park itself comprises parts of three counties (Bergen, Rockland, and Orange) and consists of 11 mostly disjointed sections that reach north to and beyond the Storm King area, some 40 miles north of the Park's southern end near the George Washington Bridge; 24 of the intervening shoreline miles on the western side of the Valley are Park property (as of 1976), which, including parkland and parkway, totals 77,321 acres.

5. Van Zandt, *The Catskill Mountain House,* pp. 3ff.

6. Jan Broek, "The Concept Landscape in Human Geography," *Comptes Rendus du Congres International de Geographie* 2 (1938): 109.

7. For a detailed listing of such works see the bibliography.

8. This is a type of applied geography that has some precedent in Van Zandt's *The Catskill Mountain House* and in William Verner, "Wilderness and the Adirondacks—An Historical View," *The Living Wilderness* 33 (Winter 1969): 27–46. Verner relates changing concepts of landscape to the legislative struggle to achieve park status.

9. Grant Jobson, "Rock on the Hudson with Caissons Rolling," *The Journal News* (Rockland County), 1974, p. 12A.

10. Another interesting theme developed by Lowenthal, and touched upon throughout the course of this work, is that of "landscape featurism" or the accentuation of separate or individual (visually isolated) topographic forms. This tendency is inherent in the century of concept focused upon here and is, as Matthew Baigell says, one of the most persistent themes in our national culture: "the American vision interprets each object for itself, not as a part of an integrated field" (*American Painting,* p. 193).

Ideas regarding the countryside and sublime wilderness are developed by Lowenthal in "The American Scene," *Geographical Review,* 1968 pp. 78ff. Elsewhere ("English Landscape Tastes," p. 205) Lowenthal and Prince describe this as "Antiquarianism" or the habit of "seeing landscapes through past associations, this valuation of places according to their connections with a presumed or inferred history . . . [it] emerges now as a nostalgic desire to put the clock back to any or every era, now as an urge to commemorate the past by preserving all relics of former times."

Lowenthal's more recent "Past Time, Present Place: Landscape and Memory," *The Geographical Review* 65 (January 1975): 1–36 is also an analysis of nostalgia and its implications for landscape appraisal; it ties together and reiterates ideas expressed in previous articles.

11. Roger Bird, "Yearning for Something Solid," *The Montreal Star,* Oct. 11, 1973, p. 12.

12. *Time,* August 21, 1972, p.42.

13. Link, *The Hudson by Daylight* (New York: Hudson River Day Line, 1878), no page; and Lossing, *The Hudson from the Wilderness to the Sea* (New York: Virtue & Yorston, 1866), p.223.

14. deDamseaux as quoted in Van Zandt, ed. *Chronicles of the Hudson: Three Centuries of Travellers' Accounts* (New Brunswick, N.J.: Rutgers University Press, 1971), p.293.

15. Atwood, "The Mighty Hudson," *National Geographic* (July 1948):1; and *The New York Times,* October 15, 1972, real estate section.

16. Lowenthal, "The American Scene," p.78; Ewen G. Simpson as quoted in William Tucker, "Environmentalism and the Leisure Class," *Harper's,* December 1977, p.75.

17. Nash Castro as quoted in the America the Beautiful Fund's Newsletter, *Better Times,* editorial column, 1978.

18. Lowenthal, "Past Time, Present Place," p.2.

19. Lowenthal, "The American Scene."

20. Frederick Jackson Turner, "The Significance of the Frontier in American History," *Annual Report,* The American Historical Association (1893): 190–227.

21. Evelyn Dinsdale, "Spatial Patterns of Technological Change: The Lumber Industry of Northern New York," *Economic Geography,* 41, no. 3 (July 1965): 252–74.

22. There is observable in all historical description and travel accounts a dichotomy between the west and east sides of the valley. Villas and villages characterized the landscape of the eastern shore while "wilderness" and "empty lands" were to the west. The guidebooks continued to play upon this generalization throughout the 1800s, juxtaposing the "thickly inhabited" regions of the Bronx and Westchester with the "solitary and inaccessible" western shore. See for example: E. Ingersoll, *Illustrated Guide to the Hudson River* (New York: Rand McNally & Co., 1909), p. 37. This distinction, the "east side as history and the west side as geography," is of course a simplification. But enough contrast did exist, and still does, in land use and conception for the western shore to be regarded as "sublime" and the eastern shore as *merely* "picturesque."

23. Russell Headley, ed. *The History of Orange County, New York* (Middletown, N.Y.: Van Deusen & Elms, 1908), p.265.

24. Wallace Bruce, *The Hudson River by Daylight* (New York: American News Company, 1875), p.219.

25. Benson J. Lossing, *The Hudson from the Wilderness to the Sea* (New York: Virtue & Yorston, 1866), pp. 281,287, and 285.

26. World's Fair Souvenir Program (New York: Carey and Sons, 1939): no page.

27. *The New York Times,* January 26, 1932, p.21.

28. *The New York Herald Tribune,* editorial, February 7, 1938.

29. Pete Seeger, "Song of the Clearwater," *Parade,* November, 26, 1978, pp.5–6.

30. Boyle, *The Hudson,* pp.282ff.

31. Alice J. Hall, "The Hudson: That River's Alive," *National Geographic,* 155 (January 1978):62–88; David Bird, "Despite Abuse, Hudson Remains a River of Life," *New York Times,* November 29, 1979, pp.B1–B3.

32. As quoted in the newsletter *New York State Environment,* March 1979, p. 1.

33. Boyle, *The Hudson,* p.282.

34. A good reference on the demise of the Commission is Marshall Stalley, "Before the Axe Fell: Environmental Planning and the Defunct Hudson River Valley Commission," *Landscape Architecture,* 62 (July 1972): 300–327, 348.

35. Henry James, "The American Scene;" as quoted in James Vance, "California and the Search for the Ideal," *Annals of the Assoc. of American Geographers* 65 (June 1972): 195.

36. Donald G. McNeil Jr., "The Hudson is Forever," *New York Times,* January 30, 1980, p.27.

37. James T. Flexner, *That Wilder Image* (New York: Little, Brown, 1962), p.19.

38. Arthur Schlesinger, " 'Progress' and the History of the Hudson," *The New York Times,* October 30, 1971.

2. From the Palisades to the Highlands

1. J. G. Broughton et al., "Geology of New York: A Short Account," Educational Leaflet no.20 (Albany: University of the State of New York, 1966), p.50.

2. E. Ingersoll, *Illustrated Guide to the Hudson River and Catskill Mountains* (New York: Rand McNally & Co., 1909); T. W. Strong, *The Hudson Illustrated with Pen and Pencil* (New York: the author, 1852); Edmund Patten, *A Glimpse of the United States . . .* (London: Effingham Wilson Pub., 1853), p.42.

3. Marie Van Vorst, "The Hudson River," *Harpers* (1905), no page.

4. To denote Fort Lee as the start of the Palisades furthermore conforms to the regional organization of maps and text presented by the American Geographical Society in: R. H. Torrey et al., *New York Walk Book* (New York: AGS, 1951). The lower Palisades (near Weehawken and Guttenberg) "are less interesting and are obstructed with buildings" (p.32). In sharp contrast with the almost two-century-old collection of docks, sheds, industries, and intensive residential usage is the undeveloped parkland atop the cliffs and north of the Revolutionary War remains at Bluff Point and Fort Lee.

5. Ralph S. Tarr, *The Physical Geography of New York State* (New York: The Macmillan Co., 1902), pp. 61–63; A. K. Lobeck, *Panoramic View of the New York Region . . .* , Scenic Folder no.1 (New York: The Geographical Press, 1952); Palisades Interstate Park Commission, *Sixty Years of Park Cooperation: A History 1900–60* (Bear Mountain:

PIPC, 1960). The geological history of the Palisades formation is also presented at length in "The Hudson River, Part I—The Palisades," *New York News-Letter,* 33, no.6 (November–December 1900).

6. Torrey et al., *New York Walk Book,* pp.19 and 21.

7. Jerome Wyckoff, *Rock Scenery of the Hudson Highlands and Palisades* (Glens Falls: Adirondack Mountain Club, 1971), p.21.

8. In the Hackensack Valley the sandstones were quarried for building material by the Dutch at an early date while associated deposits of mudstone, siltstone, and especially clays were utilized in the early manufacture of brick.

9. Palisades Interstate Park Commission, *Sixty Years,* p.22.

10. A more detailed account of the glacial history is contained in: R. Salisbury, *The Glacial Geology of New Jersey,* vol.5 of *Geological Survey of New Jersey,* 1902. See especially pp. 535–40.

11. J. Wyckoff, *Rock Scenery,* p. 13. The author estimates the age at about 190 million years.

12. Ralph Tarr, in *The Physical Geography of New York State,* notes that "The typical feature is that of a ridge or a series of ridges, of tilted trap rock, either lava flows or intrusions, etched into relief as are the ridges of harder rock in other mountains" (p.63). Other comparisons are often made with North Mountain in Nova Scotia and the "Giant's Causeway" in Northern Ireland.

13. Wyckoff, *Rock Scenery,* p.21. He compares the Palisades columns to the "Devil's Postpile" in California and the landforms of the Columbia River gorge in Washington State. A comparison might also be made to the palisaded northern shoreline of Lake Superior in Ontario.

14. Palisades Interstate Park Commission, *Sixty Years,* pp.21–22.

15. Wyckoff, *Rock Scenery,* p.63.

16. These locations are found on the detailed pictorial maps in the *New York Walk Book,* pp.27–29.

17. James Buckingham, excerpt from his travels in 1838 contained in Roland Van Zandt, ed. *Chronicles of the Hudson* (New Brunswick: Rutgers University Press, 1971), p.223.

18. E. Ingersoll, *Illustrated Guide,* p.36.

19. The Sparkill Gap and capture of the Hudson theory originated with D. W. Johnson, *Blue Book . . . Geological Field Excursion* (New York: Columbia University Press, 1926). For further details on this see both Broughton et.al., *Geology of New York,* p.35 and Wyckoff, *Rock Scenery,* p.45.

20. Northern Railroad Company of New Jersey, *Summer in the Palisades* (New York: Lange, Little & Co., 1875), p.31.

21. See: David Cole, ed. *History of Rockland County, New York* (New York: J. B. Beers, 1884), pp.17ff.; "The Hudson River, Part I—The Palisades," *New York News-Letter,* p.2; W. Woodford Clayton, *History of Bergen and Passaic Counties* (Philadelphia: Evarts & Peck, 1882), p.15; and American Museum of Natural History, *The Geology, Flora, and Fauna of the Lower Hudson Valley* (Concord, N.H.: The Rumford Press, 1912). It is in fact interesting to note that land developers in this part of Rockland today employ the very desirable and positive sounding phrase "Atop the Palisades" to advertise garden apartments and condominiums situated on the slopes of Low Tor (see for example the *New York Times* Sunday Real Estate section, September 26, 1971).

22. Interview with Ina B. Alterman, Prof. Geology, Lehman College, 1974.

23. Translated as "tedious" by most writers but as "grevious" or "vexatious" point by Benson Lossing, *The Hudson from the Wilderness to the Sea* (New York: Virtue & Yorston, 1866), p.360.

24. *Ibid.*

25. Cole, ed. *History of Rockland County*, pp.17–18.

26. *Ibid.*

27. Referred to variously in the historical literature as the High and Low "Torns" or "Towers" or "Spires."

28. Maxwell Anderson, *High Tor*, in B. Mantle, ed. *Best Plays of 1936–37* (New York: Dodd, Mead), p.3.

29. Wyckoff, *Rock Scenery*, p.79.

30. Buckberg or "Bockberg" Mountain is a small elevation (793 feet) to the southwest of the Dunderberg, which was called Goat Hill by the Dutch. For information on the land-use history of this feature, see Cole, ed. *History of Rockland County*.

31. Stony Point itself is an oval shaped peninsula of rock linked geologically to the east side of the valley. The "point" has been referred to as a "boss of the Fordham gneiss" (American Museum of Natural History, *The Geology . . . of the Lower Hudson Valley*, p.7), but is in fact composed of Ordovician diorites around an exposed core of olivine. These rocks are components of the Cordlandt Mafic series found in the Peekskill area (fig.3).

32. Cole, ed. *History of Rockland County*, p.320; *Geological Survey of New Jersey, 1874,* (New York: Geo. Cook), an annotated map. At the Tomkins Cove quarry the marble is called "Wappinger limestone," but is believed to be the continuation of the Inwood marble (Alterman).

33. The Ramapo fault runs through Mahwah, Suffern, and swings east to Stony Point and has been linked to at least nine "quakes" since 1783. One of the most recent occurred in December 1972 and prompted this explanation from the *New York Times:* "The fault lies where the two kinds of rock i.e. lowland sediments and highland metamorphics meet at the mountain base. There are occasional movements, tremors, rumbles, and sounds that approximate sonic booms because the two types of rock interact against each other. Each year, the red [Triassic] rock is being forced westward, albeit infinitesimally, by the pressure of a geological wedge in the middle of the Atlantic Ocean." ("Two fissures cause Bergen Tremors," March 25, 1973.)

34. Lossing, *The Hudson*, p.249; E. M. Ruttenber and L. H. Clark, *History of Orange County* (Philadelphia: Evarts & Peck, 1881), p.32; Samuel Eager, *An Outline History of Orange County* (Newburgh: S. T. Callahan, 1846–47), p.582.

35. See A. K. Lobeck, *Panoramic View*.

36. Wyckoff, *Rock Scenery*, p.26.

37. Broughton et al., *Geology of New York*, p.18: There remain "obstacles to reconstruction of the geological history of the Hudson Highlands. . . . In essence only a fragment of the original rock record remains. Much of the Highlands region, moreover, has never been mapped in detail.

"The general sequence of Precambrian events in the Highlands was the same as in the Adirondacks. Both were parts of the ancient geosyncline whose accumulated wedge of sedimentary and volcanic rocks was compressed into a high-standing mountain range during the Grenville Orogeny. But in more recent times their histories have diverged significantly. While the Adirondacks remained relatively stable during the Paleozoic, the Hudson Highlands became part of the basement of the Appalachian Geosyncline. As such they were deformed both by the Taconic and Acadian Orogenies and by Triassic faulting."

38. The Ramapo Valley graben was produced by the erosion of fault blocks at different rates (and is now occupied by the New York State Thruway). Drift topography consisting of kames (at Harriman) and sandstone fragments (from Schunemunk) is characteristic of the area. See Wyckoff, *Rock Scenery*, pp.56, 74–75.

39. *Ibid*.

40. "Minerals in this gneiss may include those found in granite, plus other minerals such as chlorite and epidote. During metamorphism these minerals usually segregated into layers or bands, which often became folded or broken." *Ibid.*, p.18.

41. Kurt E. Lowe, "Storm King Granite at Bear Mountain, N.Y.," *Bulletin of the Geological Society of America* 61 (1950): 137–90.

42. Ruttenber and Clark, *History of Orange County*, p.625. Copper was mined for a while (late 1700s) at the Manitou copper mines near Manitou Mountain but had sulfur impurities; it was found in association with iron pyrite. (See also Torrey et al., *New York Walk Book*, pp. 116–17.)

43. Cole, ed. *History of Rockland County*, p.18.

44. Theodore Kury, "Historical Geography of the Iron Industry in the New York–New Jersey Highlands, 1700–1900," Ph.D. dissertation, Baton Rouge: Louisiana State University, 1968, p.17. Although some hematite and limonite occur, the preponderance is of magnetite ore formed by "metamorphism, or replacement of minerals by percolating waters."

45. Wyckoff, *Rock Scenery*, p.67. The author states that the only other true fiord in the eastern United States is at Somes Sound in the state of Maine.

46. Ruttenber and Clark, *History of Orange County*, p.42.

47. Wyckoff, *Rock Scenery*, p.78.

48. Iona Island is also significant in physical geographic terms in that it is often regarded as a "dividing line of temperature"; here the sea breeze gives way to a more continental climate and the vegetation is consequently affected as well. This view is given by Lossing, *The Hudson*, p.269 and in other historical sources.

49. The toponomic designations include: Pollaples, Manahtis, Sieve, Pollipel, Poltlepel, Polypus, and Polopel among others. For more on this aspect see: Charles S. Bannerman, *The Story of Bannerman Island* (Blue Point, N.Y.: Francis Bannerman Sons Inc., 1962), pp.4–6.

50. Timothy Dwight, *Travels in New England and New York*, 4 vols. (New Haven: S. Converse, 1822), p.303.

51. Bannerman, *The Story of Bannerman Island*, pp.7–10.

52. Torrey et al., *New York Walk Book*, p.111.

53. *Ibid.*, p.150.

54. This formation is a 1700-foot high, 8-mile-long ridge of Devonian sandstone and conglomerates. The Schunemunk Mountain formation of the Hamilton group is apparently the oldest of the rock formations that constitute the Catskill delta, laid down in late Devonian times. Further details of the geologic evolution are found in Torrey et al., *New York Walk Book*, ch. 16, "Schunemunk Mountain."

55. For more detail see: "Orange County Soils," Soil Association Leaflet No.2 (Ithaca: Cornell State College of Agriculture, 1954); Eager, *An Outline History of Orange County;* Ruttenber and Clark, *History of Orange County*, p.754. The Newburgh–Beacon Plain is of course much less forested than the highlands and the undulating surface is peri-

odically interrupted by isolated ranges and headlands in Orange (the Marlboro Hills, Illinois Mountain, Danskammer Point). The soils north and west to the Shawangunks and Catskills and east to the Taconics, are developed from glacial till and derived of limestones, slates, and sandstones. Acidic and well-drained, they are eminently suitable for agriculture except in areas where excessive wetness or stoniness interferes with field or orchard crops. Despite their stony terrain, the Town of New Windsor and the Cornwall Basin have historically elicited a strong praise for their well-kept and prosperous farmscapes. Much the same can be said of the Dutchess County countryside from Beacon to Poughkeepsie.

3. The European Landscape in the Valley

1. For example, as Ulysses Hedrick points out in his *History of Agriculture in the State of New York* (New York: Hill and Wang, 1966), the farmscape during the seventeenth century is described only in occasional travelers' reports (p.67). In some cases town records do not start until well into the eighteenth century; New Windsor's records begin in 1763 although the town was settled several decades before (E. M. Ruttenber and L. H. Clark, *History of Orange County*, p.210). The town and county histories, the usual repositories of invaluable local data, are often not so illuminating as one would hope in dealing with the pre-Revolutionary era. Westervelt's otherwise instructive *History of Bergen County* (New York: Lewis Historical Pub. Co., 1923) devotes all of three pages to the period between 1700 and 1775, half of which is one family's genealogy. Thus, particulars are sometimes unavailable and, where possible at all, deductions must be made from general comments which pertain to the entire valley or to places elsewhere in the colony. Collins, in a biogeographic study done of the Palisades ("The Biotic Communities of Greenbrook Sanctuary," Ph.D. dissertation, New Brunswick: Rutgers University, 1956), consulted early deeds and maps to ascertain the seventeenth-century pattern of farms and land holdings, but came to the conclusion that "It is not clear just what was the disposition of the Palisades ridge" (p.53). Tax lists are available for New Jersey only from the 1770s. Martin and Coates's account of the ferry at Sneden's Landing ("The Story of the Ferry, 1698–1898," [Palisades, N.Y.: The Palisades Library, 1903]), conceded that commercial operations probably began as early as 1698 but that, until the Revolutionary War, the record is a blank. In a similar vein Russell Headley's compilation, *The History of Orange County,* (Middletown, N.Y.: Van Deusen & Elms, 1908) found that little was known with regard to land titles and settlement prior to the Revolution in Orange County (see p.262).

2. Frank B. Green, *The History of Rockland County* (New York: A. S. Barnes & Co., 1886), pp.44,45.

3. *Ibid.;* Headley, ed. *The History of Orange County,* p.41.

4. Ruttenber and Clark, *History of Orange County,* p.24.

5. Esopus was a collection of farmhouses behind a fortified palisade created in 1655 through the insistance and personal supervision of Governor Stuyvesant. Despite the Order of 1640 for the scattered farmers to coalesce, despite repeated massacres of the settlements of the New Jersey shore, in Harlem, the Bronx, and up river, the settlers resisted.

6. W. Woodford Clayton, *History of Bergen and Passaic Counties* (Philadelphia: Evarts & Peck, 1882), p.41; Westervelt, ed. *History of Bergen County,* p.81.

7. Westervelt, *Ibid.*, p.97. Two northerly patents were granted in 1669 and 1676: (1) Captain John Berry's plantation from the Hackensack to the Saddle River with his residence in the present vicinity of Hackensack; and (2) David Demarest, a Huguenot, 3000 acres on the east side of the Hackensack from New Bridge to Old Bridge and east as far as the line of the Northern Railroad of New Jersey (see Clayton, *History of Bergen and Passaic Counties*).

8. D. W. Meinig, "The Colonial Period, 1609–1775," in J. H. Thompson, ed. *Geography of New York State* (Syracuse: Syracuse University Press, 1966), p.137.

9. Green, *The History of Rockland County*, notes that in 1640, "Captain De Vries, sailing up the Hudson in search of a location for a colony," arrived at about even with Tappan. Here he found, in the meadows south of the present Piermont, "an extensive valley containing upwards of two or three hundred morgens of clay land, which is three of four feet above the water mark. A creek coming from the highlands runs through it containing good mill sites" (p. 8). This land De Vries purchases from the Indians, gave it the same of Vriesendale, and began "the formation of an establishment for trade with the savages" (p. 3).

10. David M. Ellis, *Landlords and Farmers in the Hudson-Mohawk Region, 1790–1850* (Ithaca: Cornell University Press, 1946), p.10. Dixon Ryan Fox, *Yankees and Yorkers* (New York: New York University Press, 1940) states two reasons for failure: (1) lack of emigration because of good social and religious conditions in seventeenth-century Holland; and (2) lack of interest on the part of the home government in active colonization. This is a theme developed in chapters 2 and 3 (pp. 27–85).

11. E. M. Bacon, *The Hudson River from Ocean to Source* (New York: Putnam, 1902), p.92. Fox, *ibid.*, p.68. The Dutch, throughout northern New Jersey and the Hudson Valley inclined toward a dispersed, non-nucleated pattern, focused on the individual bouwerie. On the west side of the valley individual farms "were scattered over the lowlands and were two and sometimes three miles from the river and entirely without protection." (*Olde Ulster*, 1(1905):130). There was in short no economic or cultural factor tending to induce a concentration of population.

12. Cadwallader Colden, "The Colden Papers." *New York State Historical Society Collections*. Statements to this effect are found throughout volume 7.

13. D. W. Meinig, "The Colonial Period," pp.146–47.

14. W. Woodford Clayton, *History of Bergen and Passaic Counties*, p.41 and F. A. Westervelt, ed. *History of Bergen County*, p.26.

15. Carl Nordstrom, *Frontier Elements in a Hudson River Village* (Port Washington, N.Y.: Kennikat Press, 1973), p.29. A detailed account of this diffusion is found in D.D. Demarest, *The Huguenots of the Hackensack* (New Brunswick, N.J.: The Daily Freedonian Steam Printing House, 1885).

16. Ruttenber and Clark, *History of Orange County*, pp. 787–809, p.213. The patented lands immediately to the north of Cornwall were taken up by Chambers and Sutherland in the 1720s but: "The land had been previously cleared of timber, as appears on a petition from Chambers for an additional tract (June 17, 1720), in which he states: "The petitioner, with great labor and expense, hath, for some years passed, settled, cultivated, and manured a small farm to the northward of Murderer's Creek, up on Hudson's River, but before the land was granted to him (1709), most of the timber that stood thereon was cut down and removed for the use of the crown, so that he hath not a sufficient quantity for farming." Ruttenber also states that migratory companies of Palatine German woodsmen

were employed by the crown for this purpose (p. 755). Settlement in the Blooming Grove area, north and west of the highlands, could have been affected by Queen Anne's Grant of 1720. The western boundary of the village of Cornwall coincides with this line.

17. Peter Kalm, *Travels in North America*, 2 vols. (New York: Dover Pubs., 1964), 1:331. Original English version: 1770.

18. Collins, "The Biotic Communities of Greenbrook Sanctuary," p.47.

19. Cole, ed. *History of Rockland County*, p.197.

20. Westervelt, ed. *History of Bergen County*, pp. 289–90 and W. Woodford Clayton, *History of Bergen and Passaic Counties*, p.41.

21. Arthur Mack, *The Palisades of the Hudson* (Edgewater: The Palisade Press, 1909), p.32.

22. Kalm, *Travels in North America*, 1:327.

23. These lines from Smith are quoted both by Van Zandt, *Chronicles of the Hudson*, p.73 and by Bacon, *The Hudson River From Ocean to Source*. Smith's reference to the Orange County line is the New Jersey–New York boundary, Rockland County being carved out of Orange County at a later date.

24. Governor Pownall's *A View in Hudson River of the Entrance of What is called the Tappan Sea*, is contained in *Iconography of New Jersey*, "Bergen County, the Palisades," Book III, p.8 and in the Eno Collection of New York City Views, New York Public Library.

25. This great frontier migration is colorfully documented by Fox, in *Yankees and Yorkers* and by Meinig, "The Colonial Period," pp.131–34.

26. Green, *The History of Rockland County*, p.51 and Kalm, *Travels in North America*.

27. E. M. Ruttenber and L. H. Clark, *History of Orange County*, present a similar version compiled by Wm. Pelletreau in 1884; this is also contained in Cole's *History of Rockland County*. A sampling of the dated patents includes: Samuel Staats (1712) around Fort Montgomery; G. & W. Ludlow (1730) at Highland Falls; Patrick MacGregorie (1720) on Butter Hill; and Richard Bradley (1712) on Bear Hill (Bear Mountain) and Popolopen Creek.

28. Peter Kalm, *Travels in North America*, pp. 327–28.

29. Richard Smith in Van Zandt, *Chronicles*, p.73. These were probably in Washington Valley and in the Valley of Popolopen Creek.

30. Kury, "Historical Geography of the Iron Industry," p.9.

31. As quoted in Headley, ed. *The History of Orange County*, pp.264, 267; Ruttenber and Clark, *History of Orange County*, p. 811. The Moore House was frequented by Washington himself during the war, as was the Robinson House—the only two houses in the West Point area. The Robinsons were Tories whose house served as Arnold's headquarters during his command at the Point.

32. See the vegetative map in Thompson, *Geography of New York State* and Peter Wacker, *The Musconetcong Valley of New Jersey* (New Brunswick: Rutgers University Press, 1968). This in fact was the "climax" vegetation for the entire length of the Hudson Valley from Glens Falls to Manhattan.

33. This problem of source materials was discussed by J. B. Harley of Exeter University, See papers of the IGU meetings, Montreal, 1972.

34. As regards these aspects of settlement in Putnam County see: Willitt C. Jewell, "Putnam County," in L. Zimm, ed. *Southeastern New York, A History* (New York: Lewis Historical Pub. Co., 1946), 2:977; and Kalm, *Travels in North America*, pp.328ff.

35. Green, *The History of Rockland County,* p.39 and Westervelt, ed. *History of Bergen County,* p.26.

36. See map in Kury, "Historical Geography of the Iron Industry," p.63.

4. Seeds of a Less Hostile View of Nature

1. This is precisely the view of early settlement in Australia taken by Bernard Smith, *European Vision and the South Pacific, 1768–1850: A Study in the History of Art and Ideas* (Oxford: the Clarendon Press, 1960), pp. 136, 176. Explorers, settlers, and later, roadmakers and surveyors, "had no time to admire views" because they were caught up in the act of settlement itself. Hunger, loneliness, and hostile nature were their most immediate dictates.

2. Edward Porter Alexander, "Scenic and Historic Possessions," in Alexander Flick, ed., *History of the State of New York* (New York: Columbia University Press, 1937), 10:255–89.

3. The era of Dutch political control (1609–64) is characterized by a noticeable historiographical research vacuum, because virtually nothing in the way of original research and documentary preservation was attempted in the two centuries after Hudson's voyage. There is a cartographic paucity as well and specific references to, and descriptions of, localities in the highlands or along the "Bergen Heights" are rare.

4. Very few of the sources used in this chapter agree on the literary or educational background of the colonists. Moreover, the positive and negative influences of the patroonship system upon a dispersed settlement pattern have been argued with equal validity. The rudeness and voracity with which Yankees pushed into Dutch lands coexists with a version emphasizing the nonviolent, neighborly, elbow-rubbing nature of this demographic movement.

The power of misconception, particularly with regard to the Dutch in New Netherland, has been potent and durable. For the longest time it was believed that an underground passage connected the Dutch church at Sleepy Hollow with Philipse Castle on the Pocantino (Helen Reynolds, *Dutch Houses in the Hudson Valley before 1776* [New York: Payson and Clarke, 1929]); it was an imaginative piece of fiction that passed for fact. In a slightly different vein, Washington Irving had stated in 1809 that there were salmon in the Hudson; the belief was picked up by fishermen who have for generations now lamented the "fact" that there are no more salmon in the river. Through recent ecological investigations, Boyle (*The Hudson*) has established the fact that the Hudson was never a salmon-run river.

5. Goodwin, *Dutch and English on the Hudson,* pp. 41–42; 110–11, 120–21.

6. Paul Wilstach, *Hudson River Landings* (Indianapolis: Bobbs-Merrill Co., 1933), p. 215; see also Boyle, *The Hudson,* p. 52.

7. Reynolds's *Dutch Houses,* p. 11, was prefaced by a somewhat more reserved version of the relationship: "Passing up and down the river in sailboats, the white men long feared the unknown dangers of the hinterland. The forests were uncut . . . and land travel was full of peril." Clifton Johnson, *The Picturesque Hudson* (New York: Macmillan, 1909), p. 16.

8. Merle Curti, *The Growth of American Thought* (New York: Harper, 1964), p. 34.

9. Carl Carmer, *The Hudson.* The Rivers of America Series (New York: Rinehart, 1939), pp. 285–86.

10. Jan Maas, "Bannerman's Arsenal: Haunted by the Past," *New York Sunday News,* June 30, 1968; Albert Atwood, "The Mighty Hudson," *National Geographic,* July 1948, pp. 1–36.

11. A basic assumption herein accepted is that the "higher" or "elitist" literary and artistic levels of the culture group are reflective of, and at times serve to create, those attitudes characteristic of the whole culture. The recorded thoughts of poets, doctors, scholars, land agents, and government officials, "offers evidence on the nature and spirit of the culture of which it is a product." Rosalie and Murray Wax, "The Vikings and the Rise of Capitalism," *The American Journal of Sociology,* July 1955, p.2. It is implicit in this assumption that "whatever differences in ways of life and whatever conflicts of interest" separated the various social strata within the culture, they all "shared a common Christian conception of human nature, of social relationships, and of the nature of knowledge and of beauty." Curti, *American Thought,* pp. 3–4.

12. Bakeless, *The Eyes of Discovery,* p. 15: "The casual observations of weary men, often in danger of their lives, mostly untrained in observation, almost always so exhausted by the mere effort to stay alive that they had small leisure or energy for the scanty notes and journals that they left behind."

13. H. M. Tomlinson as quoted in Lowenthal, "Geography, Experience and Imagination," p. 256.

14. John Codman, *Winter Sketches,* p. 158; Bacon, *The Hudson River,* p. 6; Johnson, *The Picturesque Hudson,* p. 10.

15. Verrazano as quoted in New York Historical Society, *Collections,* 2nd series, 1:46.

16. Robert Juet as quoted in *ibid.,* pp. 324–30.

17. By 1710 the promotional tact of land agents was so well refined that the farmers on the Rhenish Palatinate migrated en masse under the spell of the English agents' "Golden Picture Book" of the New World. See: Carmer, *The Hudson,* ch. 7; "The Wild Animals of New Netherland," is depicted in E. B. O'Callaghan, ed. *Documentary History of the State of New York,* 4 volumes (Albany: Charles Van Renthuysen, 1851); Kenneth Clark, *Landscape into Art* (Boston: Beacon Press, 1963), p. 9.

18. J. K. Wright, "Terrae Incognitae: The Place of the Imagination in Geography." *Annals of the Association of American Geographers,* 37, no. 11 (March 1947):6.

19. See a review of Van Der Donck's *A Description of the New Netherlands* in *New Jersey History* (by Leiby, 1970): 51.

20. Adrian Van Der Donck as quoted in New York Historical Society Collections, 2nd series, volume 1: 147. Hereafter cited as "Collections."

21. Typical of this type of promotion was the work of the New Amsterdam poet Jacob Steendam (*Noch Vaster, A Memoir of the First Poet in New Netherland,* p. 53). The publicists, hoping to lure in more Dutch migrants and unfavorably disposed to the growing number of Yankee squatters in their midst, recruited Steendam. His twelve-page adulation of nature and the land in New Netherland was sent home in 1661, but was too late to be effective. He praised the abundance of wild fruits and soft breezes that dissipated the fog and mist; the land appeared in different hues of blue and red and held within itself the power to cure those afflicted with melancholy and those who cower: "It is the land where milk and honey flow;/Where plants distilling perfume grow;/Where Aaron's rod with budding, blossoms blow;/A very Eden."

22. *Ibid.,* p. 38; see also Henry C. Murphy, *Anthology of New Netherland or Translations from the Early Dutch Poets* (1865).

23. Wright, "Terrae Incognitae," p. 1.

24. *Olde Ulster*, 3 (1907):34; Van Der Donck in "Collections," 1:138.

25. Bartlett James, ed. *Journal of Jasper Danckaerts, 1679–1680*, p. xviii. Danckaerts was an agent of the Labadist Sect which hoped to establish the first communal settlement in America. He traveled about the New World from Virginia to New England looking for a suitable site for the colony. Choosing Maryland for its religious tolerance, he returned to America in 1683 with the nucleus of a colony which located in northeastern Maryland. *Ibid.*, pp. 198, 201.

26. *Olde Ulster*, 1 (1905):4. Roderick Nash, *Wilderness and the American Mind* (New Haven: Yale University Press, 1967) points out that the association of the wilderness with God was the first step away from "the wilderness as demon" concept and toward an aesthetic awareness. *Ibid.*, p.104.

27. *Ibid.*, pp. 120ff., 536; Irving Elting, *Dutch Village Communities on the Hudson* (Baltimore: Johns Hopkins University Press, 1886), p. 51.

28. Van Der Donck in Boyle, *The Hudson*, p. 37.

29. *Olde Ulster*, 2 (1906):48–49.

30. Much use has been made by geographers of folkloric materials in regional and historical geographic research. See *Dissertation Abstracts* for specific titles and authors.

31. Paul Shepard, *Man in the Landscape*, p. 180.

32. Irving's sources are of much scholarly disagreement, but they seem not to have been Dutch. He probably created more than he recorded (B. Clough, ed. *The American Imagination at Work* [New York: Knopf, 1947], p. 367). His first visit to the Catskills to familiarize himself with old Dutch families and "curious old Dutch places" (*Olde Ulster*, 1 [1905]:10) was in 1832—many years after his *Knickerbocker History* and *The Sketch Book*. Irving's "Dutch" tales of the Tappan Zee, like that of the "unresting oarsman" and the "stormship," were Old World derived, and Carmer states emphatically that Irving's Catskill legends were likely Old World Germanic in derivation, or, in the very least, New World Palatine German (*The Hudson*, p. 77). It is also quite possible that many of the valley's legends came from Negro folklore. The Dutch children were often pictured huddled around an evening fire imbibing tales from the black servants in the household—a picture perhaps itself based on legend, but Irving too had a childhood remembrance of gazing at the headlands from the bow of a Hudson River sloop, being regaled with grotesque and frightening tales by the black deckhands.

33. Clark, *Landscape into Art*, pp. 16ff. Realistic and perceptive landscapes were painted by Van Eyck and Bosch in the fifteenth century; Breughel stands as the "master of naturalistic landscape" in the sixteenth century; the "landscape of fact," which was to influence eighteenth- and nineteenth-century painting, was composed by Rembrandt and Ruysdael in the seventeenth century.

34. Virgil Barker, *American Painting, History and Interpretation* (New York: Macmillan, 1950), p. 53.

35. The sketch has not survived, but must have been one of the first attempts at landscape in America.

36. *Olde Ulster*, 2 (1906):48.

37. Barker, *American Painting*, p. 92.

38. Huth, *Nature and the American*, ch. 1.

39. Nash, ed. *The American Environment, Readings in the History of Conservation* (Reading, Mass.: Addison-Wesley, 1968), p. 3.

40. Marjorie Hope Nicolson, *Mountain Gloom and Mountain Glory: the Development of*

the Aesthetics of the Infinite (Ithaca, N.Y.: Cornell University Press, 1959), pp. 95–96; 62. Nicolson traces European attitudes toward mountain scenery in late Christian times and concludes that until the coming of the Romantics, "ethical order and harmony" were always essential to the concept of beauty in landscape; thus "condemnation of mountains was based upon Christian ideas of pride and humility and classical beliefs in limitation and proportion" (p. 68). Perhaps only a small hill could be pleasing, and that for its "restraint." "Lowness is more worthy than greatness" (p. 69).

41. *Ibid.*, pp. 67, 37.

42. John Josselyn, "An Account of Two Voyages to New England," as quoted in Samuel Green, *American Art, A Historical Survey* (New York: Ronald Press Co., 1966), p. 3.

43. Green, *American Art*, p. 20; Matthew Baigell, *A History of American Painting* (New York: Praeger Pubs., 1971), pp. 30, 22; Green, *ibid.*, p. 102; Barker, *American Painting*, p. 74; E. P. Richardson, *Painting in America* (New York: Crowell, 1965), p. 46.

44. Elizabeth Winslow, ed. *Jonathan Edwards: Basic Writings* (New York: The New American Library, 1966), p. 85. Edwards found God reflected in the beauty of nature as a young man: "God's excellency, his wisdom, his purity and love, seems to appear in everything: in the sun, moon, and stars; in the clouds and blue sky; in the grass, flowers, trees; in the water and all nature."

45. Cadwallader Colden, *Colden Papers*, 4(1920):416ff.; 5(1921):10ff.

46. Smith as quoted in Corning, "Rockland County," p. 456.

47. Barker, *American Painting*, p. 73.

48. Pownall, *Topographic View*, as contained in both the Eno Collection and the Iconography of New Jersey (1768); Howat, *The Hudson and its Painters*, p. 23. The valley's forests in colonial times are often described as unbroken, dark, primeval. "Endless forests, black, untrodden, silent as the grave, covered the land when Europeans first sighted it. . . . a savage might skulk from the Hudson to Lake Erie without once exposing himself to the glare of the sun" (Hedrick, *History of Agriculture*, p. 5).

49. What the Dutch in fact encountered, and what they admired for utility and beauty, were many broad savannas and Indian gardens. See *Olde Ulster*, 1(1905):97.

50. Shepard, *Man in the Landscape*, p. 179; Nash, *Wilderness and the American Mind*, p. 8.

51. Intimations of those old Teutonic fears surfaced recently in an article by Jesse Miller, "Forest Fighting on the Eastern Front in World War II," *Geographical Review*, April, 1972, pp. 186–202. It is herein implied that the German command, in contrast with the Russians, loathed forest fighting and that this condition somehow derived from a deep-seated cultural attitude of avoiding forests. Clark, *Landscape into Art*, p. 37.

52. That fear was the emotion that led the Puritan pioneers to view the environment negatively is also stated by Ian Nairn, *The American Landscape*: "The basis of this, I am sure, was fear—the great forests and rivers of America, perpetual reminders of something stronger than man" had to be destroyed. By so doing "America . . . prove[d] its manhood and virility by stomping on Nature." (p. 14). And he might have added, by blaspheming it and excoriating it in the literature.

53. Washington Irving, *Sketch Book*, p. 211; Clark, *Landscape into Art*, p. 5.

54. Interestingly enough, Curti (*The Growth of American Thought*) states that the New England quakes of 1727 and 1755 were by then accounted for as part of the natural order rather than the supernatural. See also Marcia Kline, *Beyond the Land Itself: Views of Nature in Canada and the United States* (Cambridge: Harvard University Press, 1970).

55. Bakeless, *The Eyes of Discovery*, p. 157.

56. Shepard, *Man in the Landscape*, p. 54.

57. Duffus, "Again the Palisades are Threatened," *New York Times*, July 10, 1928, section 5, pp. 4ff.

5. A Busy Valley, A Young Republic

1. D. W. Meinig, "The Colonial Period," in J. H. Thompson, ed. *Geography of New York State*.

2. *Ibid.*, p.140.

3. *Ibid.*

4. R. Van Zandt, *Chronicles of the Hudson*, p.39. The author estimates that of the total engagements in the Revolutionary War, one-third were fought along the banks of the Hudson.

5. Robert Boyle, *The Hudson River*, ch. 12.

6. From Thomas Janvier's study of Greenwich Village as quoted by Bacon, *The Hudson River from Ocean to Source*, p.62.

7. The Elysian Fields were, in the early 1800s, a fashionable pleasure ground at the lower end of the Palisades. The grounds contained a spring of clear water of great repute known as Sibyl's Cove. It appears that by the 1820s and 1830s the grounds became the haunt of "the common folk" and with a Coney Islandish atmosphere, lost its more polished clientele. Murder and crime became associated with the Elysian Fields, for example through Poe's celebration of the murder of Mary Rogers. The fields are portrayed in Bacon, *ibid.*, pp. 79, 83.

8. Ulysses Hedrick, *A History of Agriculture in the State of New York* (New York: Hill and Wang, 1966), p.266, and David Ellis, *Landlords and Farmers*, p.163.

9. Robert Erskine, Map of the Northern Part of New Jersey, 1777, as contained in Cole, ed. *History of Rockland County;* Robert Erskine, *West of the Hudson*, 1781, in *Magazine of American History*, 5(1880):8; and Simeon DeWitt, *Map of the State of New York*, 1802, New York Public Library.

10. Ellis, *Landlords and Farmers*, p.80.

11. Carl Nordstrom, *Frontier Elements in a Hudson River Village*, pp.40ff; and Ellis, p.166.

12. Thompson, ed. *Geography of New York State*, p.165. The farmers of the region, as in other parts of the Northeast, supplemented their income through the production of pearlash and potash (second only to wheat, and used for fertilizer and soap), collecting bark for the local tanneries, and lumbering and ice harvesting in winter.

13. Sauthier's map of 1777 and Montressor's map of 1775 show only Fort Lee. The Erskine map of 1777 (see note 9) shows Fort Lee and Sneden's. It can be inferred from the county histories (Westervelt and Clayton for example) that Liberty Pole (Englewood) was extant by the Revolution.

14. S. S. Maples, ed. *Closter, the First 285 Years* (Closter: Pub. by the Fiftieth Anniversary Committee, 1954), p.7.

15. A depiction of the landing of Lord Cornwallis's forces in New Jersey done by Lord Rawdon in 1776 is contained in the Stokes Collection, vol. 1(1497–1789), New York Public Library.

16. Dominic Serres, *The Forcing of the Hudson River Passage (October 9, 1776)*,

done for the Captain of the Gunboat Tartar, in the "Iconography of New Jersey," N.J.H.S. and also contained in *New York Historical Society Quarterly,* 36 (October 1952):458. Thomas Davies sketched the attack on Fort Washington showing the Palisades in the background. See "Stokes Collection," vol. 1, N.Y.P.L.

R. Van Zandt, *Chronicles of the Hudson,* p. 81: Charles Carroll of Carrollton, on a mission to Canada on behalf of the Continental Congress in 1776, passed along the Bergen shore and saw that, at least from the river view, the steep and rocky banks were clothed with "pine trees growing amidst the rocks."

17. Archibald Robertson, *His Diaries and Sketches in America, 1762–80* (New York: New York Public Library, 1930), plate 4. John Graves Simcoe, *A Journal of the Operations of the Queen's Rangers* (New York: Printed for the author, 1844), pp. 80ff.

18. F. A. Westervelt, ed. *History of Bergen County,* p. 362 states that "In 1776 there were farms on the hill."

19. S. Eager, *An Outline History of Orange County* (Newburgh: S. T. Callahan, 1846–47), p. 592 and Arthur Mack, *The Palisades of the Hudson,* p. 9. W. W. Clayton, *History of Bergen and Passaic Counties,* p.66 presents this quote: "On Sunday Afternoon [July 22] . . . a party of refugees and Torries . . . landed at Closter Dock, and advanced to the neighborhood called Closter, from which they collected and drove off a considerable number of cattle and horses."

20. F. B. Green, *The History of Rockland County,* p. 28.

21. S. Collins, "The Biotic Communities of Greenbrook Sanctuary," p. 28.

22. *Ibid.,* p.50.

23. *Ibid.,* p.56.

24. Arrowsmith, Aaron and Lewis, *A New and Elegant General Atlas,* 1812 and Amos Lay, *Map of the State of New York with Part of the State of Northeastern New Jersey.* Both contained in New York Public Library.

25. S. Collins, "The Biotic Communities of Greenbrook Sanctuary," p.46.

26. Palisades Interstate Park Commission, *Sixty Years of Park Cooperation,* pp.16–17.

27. James J. Greco, *The Story of Englewood Cliffs* (Englewood Cliffs, N.J. Pub. by the Tercentennary Committee, 1964), p.11.

28. Cole, ed. *History of Rockland County,* p.220. The Sparkill was apparently deep enough to accommodate the larger Hudson River sloops, one of which capsized in the creek with the loss of nine lives. See also Green, *The History of Rockland County.*

29. Nicholas Gesner, "Diary, 1830–50," Original and Handwritten, contained in Palisades Free Library, Palisades N.Y. no page.

30. E.g. Yeager's *Characteristic Scenes of the Hudson River* (1820s), and Henry Livingston's *The Steep Rocks on the West Side of the Hudson's River* (1791). William Guy Wall, *The Palisades,* no. 19 of the *Hudson River Portfolio,* Stokes Collection, vol. 2 (1790–1829). This same view also contained in Darrell Welch, "The Hudson River Portfolio," *New York State Conservationist,* April–May 1972, p.18.

31. Green, *The History of Rockland County,* p.11 and St. Jean de Crèvecoeur, *Voyage dans la Haute Pennsylvanie et dans l'état de New-York . . .* 3 volumes (Paris: Chez Maradan, 1801), pp. 117–18.

32. A. E. Corning, "Rockland County," Louise Zimm, ed. *Southeastern New York, A History,* vol. 3 (New York: Lewis Historical Pub. Co., 1946) states that the quarry was located on the Hudson between Sparkill Creek and Grandview. It was opened as early as 1736. S. Collins, "The Biotic Communities," p.56.

33. Carl Nordstrom, *Frontier Elements,* p.76.

34. Cole, ed. *History of Rockland County*, pp. 146, 147.

35. *Ibid.*, p. 146.

36. *Ibid.*, p. 18. Cole says that one of the first buildings at Queen's College (later Rutgers University) was built in 1809 of sandstone quarried on the shore near Nyack.

37. Jacques Milbert, *Picturesque Itinerary of the Hudson River and Travels in North America*, 2 vols. (Upper Saddle River, N.J.: The Gregg Press, 1969), p.30.

38. Cole, ed. *History of Rockland County*, p.178 and Green, *The History of Rockland County*, p.172.

39. As quoted David Cole, ed. *History of Rockland County*, p.128.

40. *Ibid.*, p.163; Louis-Alexandre Berthier, "Route of the French Army across New Jersey, August 1781," from *New Jersey Road Maps of the Eighteenth Century* (Princeton: Princeton University Press, 1964), p. 3ff.

41. Cole, ed. *History of Rockland County*, p.205.

42. The Merino sheep craze was started when Robert Livingston imported them to his Hudson Valley estate. By 1807, wool prices had skyrocketed and in 1810–11 there were 25,000 Merinos imported from Spain. As Hedrick, *A History of Agriculture*, states: "a mania to stock up with Merinos took possession of the public and lasted until fancy prices dwindled and mismanagement and the neighbor's dogs upset the speculation spree" (p.373).

43. James Thacher, *Military Journal During the American Revolutionary War* (Hartford: Silas Andrus & Sons, 1854), June 14, 1779, p.166.

44. Archibald Robertson, *His Diaries and Sketches in America*, Plate 50 shows the Dunderberg as a heavily vegetated rocky headland projecting into the river. Francois-Jean Chastellux, *Voyage de Newport à Philadelphie, Albany . . .* (Newport: Printed on the Press of the French Fleet, 1781), pp. 88 and 91.

45. T. Kury, "Historical Geography of the Iron Industry," p.67. Kury believes that careless sparks from furnaces and pits caused many fires.

46. Conversations with Calvin Stillman, 1974; S. Eager, "Town of Newburgh," in *An Outline History of Orange County*.

47. As quoted in Eager, *ibid.*, p.572.

48. L'Enfant was an architect, engineer, and draftsman (as well as urban designer). For illustration see John Howat, *The Hudson River and its Painters* (New York: The Viking Press, 1972), pp. 149–50 and plate no. 34.

49. See selections from Maude and Lambert in R. Van Zandt, *Chronicles of the Hudson*.

50. Baron Axel Klinkowstrom, "A Swedish View of West Point in 1820," *New York History*, July 1952, p.315.

51. T. Kury, "Historical Geography of the Iron Industry."

52. *Ibid.*, p.63.

53. See Christopher Rand, *The Changing Landscape, Salisbury, Connecticut* (New York: Oxford University Press, 1968).

54. The Forest of Dean Mine had an overhead bucketline to the river at Dock Hill (Fort Montgomery); it was operative as late as 1936 (Stillman); Ruttenber and Clark, *History of Orange County*, p.801.

55. Cole, ed. *History of Rockland County*, p.330.

56. William Guy Wall, *View near Fort Montgomery*, *Hudson River Portfolio*. This view, and a watercolor of the highlands looking south from Newburgh Bay, are presented in John Howat, *The Hudson River and its Painters*, plates 28 and 53.

57. Francois-Jean Chastellux, *Voyage de Newport à Philadelphie*, p.192. Of Dutchess County, Chastellux observed: "the land seems fertile enough. . . . wheat is mostly grown, oats being reserved for newly cleared land. . . . flax is also grown."

58. Willitt C. Jewell, "Putnam County," pp. 965ff.

59. Maude in Van Zandt, *Chronicles of the Hudson*, p. 132.

60. See H. Crampton Jones, "History of Constitution Island," *New York History*, July 1952, pp. 279–93 and Charles S. Bannerman, *The Story of Bannerman Island*, p. 24.

61. Eager, *An Outline History*, p.597; Russell Headley, ed. *The History of Orange County*, p.178.

62. Thompson, ed. *Geography of New York State*, p.154; C. Carroll in Van Zandt, *Chronicles of the Hudson*, p.82; Lambert in *Ibid.*, p.145. Lambert described the region in 1807: "The country . . . is covered with rich farms, plantations, orchards, and gardens, and studded with neat and handsome dwelling-houses. The cultivated parts are intersected with small woods, copices, and clumps of trees, which add much to the diversity of the scenery. . . . In several places along shore are elegant mansions and country seats. . . . the county appeared to be well inhabited."

63. See Samuel Colden's letter of 1796 as contained in Eager, *An Outline History*, p.245.

64. James Thacher, *Military Journal*, June 10, 1779, p.164.

65. J. G. Percival, "Report of the Proceedings and debates of the Convention of 1821," in Charles Sanford, ed. *Quest for America, 1810–24* (New York: Doubleday, 1964), p. 452.

6. *The Emerging Scenic and Economic Landscape*

1. The ideas of progress and the "conquest of nature" are integral parts of the Australian pioneer ethos as well. See: B. Smith, *European Vision and the South Pacific, 1768–1850: A Study in the History of Art and Ideas* (Oxford: The Clarendon Press, 1960), p.176.

2. Charles Sanford, ed. *Quest for America, 1810–1824* (New York: Doubleday, 1964), p.22.

3. D. Serres, *The Forcing . . .* (October 9, 1776), Iconography of New Jersey and *The Rose and the Phoenix*, Stokes Collection, N.Y.P.L.

4. Lord Rawdon, "Cornwallis' Landing at Alpine," (November 1776), Iconography of New Jersey; Th. Davies, "View of the Attack on Fort Washington, 1776." vol. 1, 1497–1789, Stokes Collection; William Heath, *Memoires of* (Boston: Thomas and Andrews, 1798), p.435; H. P. Johnson, ed. *Memoirs of Colonel Benjamin Tallmedge* (New York: The Gilliss Press, 1904); John Graves Simcoe, *A Journal of the Operations of the Queen's Rangers . . .* (New York: Bartlett & Welford, 1844); Diary of Frederick MacKenzie, two volumes (Cambridge: Harvard University Press, 1930).

The question might be raised as to whether most military men would even write about landscape. Yes, as much as, if not more than, the ordinary traveler. From the aesthetic perspective? Yes, assuming an educated, gentlemanly upbringing.

5. See Thacher, *Military Journal*, p.134: "the happy effect of such industry," as carried out by Putnam's troops, produced a permanent scar; "we viewed the path made by the descent of Putnam's Rock. Col. Rufus Putnam ascended the mountain with forty men, who were, for amusement, employed about two days in precipitating from the

summit a rock of many tons weight. . . . in the passage it cut down trees of a large size. . . . The rock was of such size, that a part of it remained above water, and Col. Putnam, standing on the top, holding in his hand a bottle of spirits, gave to it the name of Putnam's Rock."

6. E. P. Richardson, *Painting in America,* p.127; V. Barker, *American Painting,* p.287. Barker has said of John Hill's collection of "Picturesque Views of American Scenery" (1819): "These aquatints . . . never hint at anything subjective. To be sure, many of the people who first looked at the prints seemed to have read emotion into them, for their appearance on the market was at a time when the associated ideas of the romantic and picturesque were making a considerable stir."

Wm. Groonbridge, *Washington Heights* (1793), and George Beck, *Falls of the Potomac* (1796–97). George Washington, who seems to have appreciated landscapes (Richardson, *Painting in America,* p.127), bought two of Beck's views of the Potomac.

7. Howat, *The Hudson and its Painters,* plate 34 and Barker, *American Painting,* p.289.

8. The works of George Heriot and Joshua Watson done in the years 1815–16, although not strictly topographic, are of this genre. See: George Heriot, *Palisades Rocks,* 1815, Iconography of New Jersey; Joshua Rawley Watson, *Part of the Palisades with the Highlands of the Hudson in the Distance* 1816(?), Iconography of New Jersey. For other works by Watson (e.g., *Looking Down the Hudson from Niock*) see illustrations 8, 10, 11, 12, 13, 14 in the same collection.

9. Merle Curti, *Growth of American Thought,* pp. 60–61.

10. In the forty years from 1784 to 1824 Morse published nine major geographical works, and for this achievement (along with the subsequent 48 U.S. and foreign editions), is often designated "The Father of American Geography." While Brown has analyzed the glaring deficiencies of content in Morse's work (he was often untruthful and in error, inconsistent, contradictory, hasty and careless) and Warntz has very convincingly argued the deleterious effect of the Reverend's writings upon American academic geography, the further point might be made that he did nothing to advance a sense of environmental aesthetics in the nation. His rote and uninspired regional descriptions, including those of the Hudson Valley, may in fact have had a regressive effect upon the acceptance of aesthetic principles in this country.

Morse was familiar with, and indeed made use of, travel accounts published in Europe, and sometimes on French printing presses operating at Newport, New Orleans, and Philadelphia. The London editions, as attested to by the library of President Stiles at Yale, were readily obtainable. Yet while he was exposed to their sources (sources containing romantic concepts of philosophy and the arts), it is evident that he did not avail himself of the conceptual materials. His failure to incorporate them into an American context is due to a lingering Puritanical strain that led him to reject the social and environmental ideas of the Jeffersonian and European "anti-Christs" and to effectively box himself into the dusty vest pocket of eighteenth-century Congregationalism, and also to a strong vein of nationalism (or perhaps more correctly, a New England parochialism) that was instigated by the alleged injustice committed against America in the writing of European travelers. Morse was possessed by a missionary zeal which led him to accuse Europeans of making hostile, uncomplimentary, prejudiced, and unpleasant lies, and fabrications prompted by "sinister motives."

For further reference to Morse and his writings, see: William Warntz, *Geography Now and Then: Some Notes on the Academic History of Geography in the U.S.* (New York: American Geographical Society, 1964) and Ralph Brown, "The American Geographies of Jedidiah Morse," *Annals of the AAG*, September 1941, pp. 145–217.

11. It is interesting to note in this regard that developments in the realm of art paralleled those in geographic writing. At this same time, Connecticut produced a school of portraiture (sometimes called atavistic, primitive, and retrograde) that deviated substantially from the mainstream of American painting. Ralph Earl and other "conservative" Federalist painters clung to another, less polished tradition which was in sharp contrast to the elegant mannerisms imported from Europe. See for example, Green, *American Art*, pp. 157–62.

McClure, a missionary to the Delawares on the Pennsylvania frontier, was an associate of and "informer" of the Rev. Parish. The latter, in conjunction with Morse, published the *Gazetteer of the Eastern and Western Continent* in 1802 and *A New System of Modern Geography* in 1810. On his own he wrote *Sacred Geography—Or a Gazetteer of the Bible* in 1813.

12. Edouard de Montulé, *Travels in America, 1816–17*, p. 31. The thesis that the unfavorable climate of America had caused a wholesale degeneration of animals, plants, and the human species was carried to absurd lengths by Corneile de Pauw in his *Recherches philosophiques sur les Americains*, published in 1768. Fantastic as these claims were, they corrobrated in part the views held by Buffon and deWarville; both Jefferson and Franklin did much to refute these remarks and "researches."

13. Morse was coincidentally much like Hakluyt—an armchair geographer, compiler, and a minister who attempted to glorify the British Empire through the medium of geographic nationalism.

14. Curti, *American Thought*, p. 145. Chateaubriand, in his Middle Eastern travels (1806–7), took with him an inbred denigrating Judeo-Christian interpretation of nature; he was capable nonetheless of finding marvel in nature's beauties. See Norman Thrower and Clarence Glacken, "On Chateaubriand's Journey from Paris to Jerusalem, 1806–7," *The Terraqueous Globe: The History of Geography and Cartography* (Los Angeles: University of California, 1969).

15. Shepard, *Man in the Landscape*, p. 176.

16. Nicolson, *Mountain Gloom and Mountain Glory*, see material on the Sacred Theory of the earth and the Burnet Controversy, pp. 193ff.

17. Nash, *Wilderness and the American Mind*, pp. 65–66.

18. H. M. Lydenberg, ed. *Archibald Robertson, His Diaries* pp. 1, 44.

19. *Ibid.*, plates 49 to 53.

20. Tench Tilghman, *Memoirs of* (Albany: J. Munsell, 1876), August 18, 1775, pp. 79–80.

21. Charles Cunningham, *Timothy Dwight, 1752–1817, A Biography* (New York: Macmillan, 1942), p. 71.

22. Charles Carroll as quoted in Van Zandt, *Chronicles*, p. 81.

23. Thacher, *Military Journal*.

24. *Ibid.*, pp. 166, 134; C. Stedman, *History of the American War*, 1:405–6 as quoted in W. H. Carr and R. J. Koke, *Twin Forts of the Popolopen* (Bear Mountain: Bear Mountain Trailside Museums, 1937), p. 40. In a strangely similar fashion Stedman found that the "magnificent pyramid of fire" created by the scuttling of American vessels after the fall of Fort Clinton produced wonderful reflections upon the mountain walls, the whole scene being "sublimely terminated" by explosions and darkness.

25. Henry Livingston, *The Steep Rocks on the West Side of Hudson's River viewed from the North, The New York Magazine,* June 1791, as contained in the Iconography of New Jersey.

26. See for example: an aquatint by J. W. Edy, *View of St. Anthony's Nose on the North River,* c. 1790–95 and a print published in 1802 by Jukes and Robertson, *Hudson's River from Chambers Creek looking thro' the High Lands,* c. 1795–1800 as contained in the Stokes Collection, vol. 1, 1790–1829. Edy had done a similar view of Quebec City and Jukes and Robertson had published a similar view of the Passaic Falls.

27. Dwight held a similarly high regard for things New Englandish as Morse, and felt disdain for the dirty, ill-repaired houses, the profusion of taverns, and lack of schools found outside the region (i.e. in New York, particularly the Hudson Valley!).

Dwight's publications include: *The Conquest of Canaan,* a poem in eleven parts (Hartford: 1785); *A Statistical Account of the City of New Haven* (New Haven, 1811); *Theology: Explained and Defended,* 5 vols. (Middletown: 1818–19); and *Travels in New England and New York,* 4 vols. (New Haven: 1821–22).

28. Leon Howard, *The Connecticut Wits,* p. 363.

29. Dwight, *Travels,* 3:300.

30. *Ibid.,* pp. 308, 303. Nash, *Wilderness and the American Mind,* presents William Byrd of Virginia as a prime example of an American beset by the same ambivalences as Dwight (pp. 48ff). Byrd, educated among the London gentry, in his *History of the Dividing Line . . .* recorded "the first American commentary on wilderness that reveals a feeling other than hostility" (Nash, p. 51). Byrd confronted the wilderness as one determined to show his aesthetic sophistication and his *au courant* learning, and to blot out any stigma of colonial provincialism. He also wrote from a position of wealth.

31. Merle Curti, *Growth of American Thought,* pp. 116ff., also considers the American Enlightenment and its attendant theme of environmentalism as contributory to a greater union between society and the physical environment. That is, it was reasoned by Jefferson, Crèvecoeur, et al., if laws, customs, and institutions are governed by a nation's physical resources, then a greater familiarity had better be developed with the latter.

32. Nash, *Wilderness and the American Mind,* p. 54.

33. B. Smith, *European Vision and the South Pacific,* pp. 152ff. In practical terms, it meant that Cook's expeditions to the South Seas (1760s through 1780s), Flinder's expedition to the Society Islands (1801), and Baudin's southern hemispheric voyage (1800–4) all carried appointed artists whose job it was to scientifically record the natural habitat as well as the more sublime aspects of landscape: "It was thus possible to adopt two attitudes to new landscapes: they could be documented faithfully after the manner of coastal profilers, or they could be composed picturesquely in the manner of geological curiosities. These two attitudes, revealing two types of interest in Pacific phenomena, persist in the published engravings" (p. 18).

34. *Encyclopedia Britannica,* 11th edition, 1910, 13:875.

35. By Von Humboldt and Aime Bonphard (Paris: 1807); B. Smith, *European Vision and the South Pacific,* p. 152.

36. Von Humboldt, *Aspects of Nature* (1808) as contained in Eric Fischer et al., eds., *A Question of Place, The Development of Geographic Thought* (Arlington, Va.: H. W. Beatty Ltd., 1969), pp. 63–65; Glacken, "Terraqueous Globe," p. 47.

37. The artist-naturalist was to be a nineteenth-century phenomenon representative of the close proximity between landscape appreciation and science. See: William Truettner and R. Bolton-Smith, *National Parks and the American Landscape,* p. 24. So-called natural

history accounts, usually very sympathetic to the natural environment, were produced, for example, by Catsby and by Byrd. Regional descriptions, such as Belknap's three volume *New Hampshire*, appeared, and "natural history circles" were formed by topographers, surveyors, doctors, and artists in Philadelphia (with counterparts in European cities). William and John Bartlett were well versed in the romantic outlook and "out of sheer love of nature" constructed a detailed regional picture of the Piedmont and Atlantic coastal plain. Statesmen-scientists such as Jefferson and Franklin well illustrate the probing, rationalistic mind accommodating itself to the curiosities of nature. Jefferson seems as well to have evolved an appreciation of the sublime (Huth, *Nature and the American*, ch. 2). The world of men such as these would influence the aesthetic outlook of writers and painters in the coming generation (Baigel, *History of American Painting*, p. 75).

American horticulture too, as an expression of the comforts and pleasures to be derived from the organization of landscape, dates from the mid-eighteenth century (e.g. Middleton Gardens, South Carolina). Because of the work of Hosack (Elgin Gardens and Hyde Park) and A. J. Downing Sr. (the Newburgh nurseries), nowhere did this art and science "flourish more luxuriantly than in the Hudson Valley." (Carlton B. Lees, "The Golden Age of Horticulture," *Historic Preservation*, October–December, 1972, pp. 32–37.)

38. See Baigel, *American Painting*, plates 4–19, p. 86; Barker, *American Painting*, plate 42.

39. See Glacken, *Traces* and "The Terraqueous Globe." This body of writing was used extensively by Ralph Brown in *Historical Geography of the U.S.* He employed English, French, and German travel accounts in the reconstruction of geographic conditions on the Atlantic Seaboard in 1800 (*Mirror for Americans*). Among the French "geographical writers" he found useful (p. 546) were Volney, Liancourt, and Michaux. Merrens, in his study of *Colonial North Carolina in the Eighteenth Century* (Chapel Hill: University of North Carolina Press, 1964), found regional travel literature characterized by much environmental-aesthetic content.

Another unstated but obvious advantage of using foreign travel literature is the geographic comparisons which repeatedly spring to European minds and which are not usually had through native American sources. It allows the reader a greater sense of comparison if, as was done, the Hudson in 1810 is seen as evocative of the Rhine and the highlands as reminiscent of their Scottish counterparts. One who made these comparisons was J. B. Dunlop (D. H. Wallace, ed., "From the Windows of a Mail Coach, a Scotsman looks at New York State in 1811," *New York Historical Society Quarterly*, no. 1 [January 1956]: 272.)

40. About this same time, people began to tour the mountains of Australia. B. Smith, *European Vision and the South Pacific*, p. 174.

41. Frank Monaghan, *French Travellers in the U.S., 1765–1932*, a bibliography (New York: the Antiquarian Press, 1961); Allan Nevins, *American Social History as Recorded by British Travellers* (New York: Holt, 1923); Jane Louise Mesick, *The English Traveller in America, 1785–1835* (New York: Columbia University Press, 1922), p. 370.

42. C. Lafayette Todd, "Some Nineteenth-Century European Travellers in New York State," *New York History*, October 1962, pp. 336–70. For a variety of reasons good British travelogues, such as those by Captain Marryat, Basil Hall, John and Reginald Fowler, date from the 1830s and 1840s, an epoch of travel which Nevins refers to as "the period of Tory condescension." It would seem logical that a sense of embarrassment and bitterness might have precluded Englishmen from touring areas so recently and intimately associated with the Revolution and the War of 1812–14. It was obviously a "time when

the usual upper-class English traveller had come to taunt and ridicule" (Van Zandt, *Chronicles*, p. 131.).

43. Peter Stryker, "Journal of a trip from Belleville, New Jersey to Preach in Vacant Congregations Westward and Southwestward, 1815–16." Rutgers Library.

44. Joseph McCadden, "A Britisher Tours the Hudson, An Account of Joseph Lancaster's Trip up the Hudson in 1818," *New York History*, July 1951, pp. 296–315.

45. John Maude, excerpt from his "Visit to the Falls at Niagara in 1800," as contained in Van Zandt, *Chronicles*, p. 132.

46. John Lambert, "Travels through Canada and the United States of North America in the Years 1806, 1807, 1808," as contained in Van Zandt, *Chronicles*, p. 145.

47. Montulé claimed to be interested in observing "the caprecious irregularities of nature" (*Travels in America*, 1816–17, n.p., author's foreword); Volney desired to show how "manners" were influenced by geographical situations (*A View of the Soil and Climate* . . . p. ix); Chastellux intended to "render a service to Americans by making known [to them] through word and picture . . . their natural wonders." (*Travels in North America* . . . n.p. foreword); and Beltrami hoped only to "observe in passing the most striking and interesting objects of nature . . . a superficial glance at what falls in my way." (*A Pilgrimage in Europe and America* . . . , pp. 33, 42).

48. In a field not yet protected by international copyright law, Chastellux plagiarized from Liancourt and both were in turn plagiarized by Morse. This, a more or less universally accepted practice, resulted in confusion as to who coined which phrase or first advanced which idea.

49. Chastellux, *Travels in North America*, p. 94; Montulé, *Travels in America*, pp. 149–50. Chastellux was able to philosophize upon the geological and historical associations of the charming, marvelous, magnificent, curious scenery in the "wild and warlike abode" of West Point. Montulé, although admittedly "lending a romantic complexion" to his writings, was much concerned with the "epochs of nature" and how they might be interpreted through successive stages of vegetative growth. (He unfortunately missed a chance to perceive the variation of Hudson Valley landscapes because of an almost continuous rainstorm.)

50. "Harmonies of nature" is a phrase employed by Crèvecoeur and many other Europeans at this time; it was picked up decades later by G. P. Marsh and Arnold Guyot. Crèvecoeur in *Voyage*, outlined what to him constituted the sublime in a natural setting (p. 258).

51. Crèvecoeur, *Voyage*, pp. 121, 37.

52. *Ibid.*, p. 139.

53. Milbert, *Picturesque Itinerary*, p. xx.

54. *Ibid.* For more on Milbert see: Constance Sherman, "A French Explorer in the Hudson River Valley," *New York Historical Society Quarterly* 45 (1961):255–80.

55. Milbert, *Picturesque Itinerary*, p. 27. Morse, incidentally, recorded nothing of the Palisades, aesthetic or otherwise.

56. *Ibid.*, p. 32.

57. *Ibid.*, p. 34.

58. Sanford, ed., *Quest for America*, p. xii.

59. Brown ("Jedidiah Morse," p. 172) and Warntz (*Geography Now and Then*) both make this point. That Morse's geographies achieved such a fast and wide popularity with Americans is in no small way due to the fact that his *Universal Geography* was heavily weighted to American places.

60. These ideas are paraphrased from Nash, *Wilderness and the American Mind*, ch. 4. Examples to support these statements are given by him.

61. Washington Irving, *The Sketch Book*, "English Writers on America," pp. 56–64, 59.

62. Milbert, *Picturesque Itinerary*, p. 41; Montulé, *Travels in America*, letter 23. This is a trait also observed among the early residents of Ontario and the Maritimes (R. Cole Harris, "Opening Address etc.").

63. See C. Volney, *The Ruin*, p. 8.

64. Van Zandt, *The Catskill Mountain House*, p. 191.

65. Lowenthal, "The American Scene," p. 66.

66. Van Zandt, "The Scotch School of Aesthetic Theory and the Natural Description of the Oregon Trail," *Smithsonian Journal*, no. 4 (Fall 1949):156–72. Van Zandt points out that at a later date Parkman in describing a desolate scene along the Platte found only one means to impart an aesthetic element to the landscape: "Again and again throughout the course of *The Oregon Trail* a scene in nature is saved from a total lack of aesthetic appeal by the presence of the colorful American Indian."

67. This perhaps explains the popularity of a writer like Walter Scott in America between 1813 and 1823. As Curti (*American Thought*, p. 231) suggests, he satisfied an American yearning for the antique and remote.

68. The Theory of Primitivism and the Noble Savage has been written on at length by Nash, *Wilderness and the American Mind*, pp. 50ff. It has a broad application to the Hudson Valley, but is best studied in a national context with reference to European enthusiasms for "The Wild Man as Superman" tradition (Nash) dating to the sixteenth century. B. Smith, *European Vision*, has also developed a lengthy treatise on European reaction to the South Sea Islanders in these same years and discusses the difference between "soft" and "hard" primitivism (p. 25ff).

69. See Lewis Leary, "Washington Irving," Pamphlets on American Writers, no. 25 (St. Paul: University of Minnesota, 1963).

70. Chastellux, *Voyage*, p. 18; Dwight, *Travels*, p. 305.

71. Of course Ticonderoga, Saratoga, and other such "shrines" outside the lower Hudson Valley were accorded similar historical-romantic interest.

72. Nicolson, *Mountain Gloom and Mountain Glory*, has shown the importance of these theological-geological controversies in the seventeenth and eighteenth centuries in the evolution of a "new aesthetic" (pp. 225ff.). Interest in geology became so great and indiscriminate in eighteenth-century England that the slagheaps and shafts of the mining districts, previously looked upon as eyesores, became legitimate themes for poetic description (p. 340).

73. Charles Carroll as quoted in Van Zandt, *Chronicles*, p. 81.

74. Chastellux, *Voyage*, p. 89. See also Dwight, *Travels*, p. 312–13.

75. Van Zandt, "The Scotch School," p. 157.

76. See: Clark, *Landscape into Art*, Chs. 4 and 5; E. Burke, *Philosophical Enquiry into the Origin of Our Ideas of the Sublime and Beautiful*; Nash, *Wilderness and the American Mind*, p. 45. Nash also has a good set of bibliographical references to the evolution of English thinking on the sublime and related concepts in the seventeenth and eighteenth centuries. Burke's sublime is also discussed by E. E. Vessell, ed., *The Life and Works of Thomas Cole* (Cambridge: Harvard University Press, 1964).

A third conceptual category was that of the "beautiful," but it appears a confusing and seldom employed term. Since the romantic found sublimity or picturesqueness in most landscapes, these terms became loosely synonymous with all natural beauty. The term "beautiful," as applied in the late 1700s, did have a specific meaning, however, and is herein defined by Shepard (*Man in the Landscape*): "The beautiful landscape was characterized by symmetry, graceful curves, grazing animals, and a mixture of lawn, water, and trees. In contrast to the sublime, which stimulated feelings of self-preservation, the beautiful was said to affect the 'subconscious' with ideas of procreation."

77. Van Zandt, "The Scotch School," p. 157.

78. A. J. Downing, *The Architecture of Country Houses,* p. 29; Lowenthal and Prince, "English Landscape Tastes," *Geographical Review* 55 (1965):186–222. For a further explanation of the "picturesque," see Shepard, *Man in the Landscape,* pp. 124–25.

79. Dwight, *Travels,* p. 313; Crèvecoeur, *Voyage,* p. 119ff.

80. Sanford, ed., *Quest for America,* pp. 304–5.

81. *Ibid.*

7. The Tentacles of the City Reach North

1. H. Thompson, ed. *Geography of New York State,* p. 140.

2. Roland Van Zandt, *The Catskill Mountain House* (New Brunswick, N.J.: Rutgers University Press, 1966), p. 208. Although the Hudson was a leading commercial artery by the 1830s, the Ohio–Mississippi River system no doubt had a greater volume of traffic.

3. Hugh Raup, "The View from John Sanderson's Farm: A Perspective for the Use of the Land," *Forest History,* April 1966, pp. 2–12. Here the author presents a similar study of agricultural decline in central-western Massachusetts and directly relates this to the rise of a competitive agriculture in the Midwest, made accessible to New England by the Erie Canal.

4. David Ellis, *Landlords and Farmers,* p. 272. The pattern of westward wheat belt migration was of course repeated after the 1850s, when the Genesee Country was supplanted as the nation's granary by Ohio and other midwestern states.

5. *Ibid.,* p. 92; Ulysses Hedrick, *A History of Agriculture,* p. 74.

6. David Ellis, *Landlords and Farmers,* p. 168.

7. *Ibid.,* pp. 277, 275.

8. N. P. Willis, *Outdoors at Idlewild or the Shaping of a Home on the Banks of the Hudson* (New York: Scribner, 1855), p. 115.

9. This pitiful state of agrarian affairs did not go unchallenged, because it was during this same period that positive measures were taken to help the farmers. The New York State Agricultural Society was organized in the 1830s and agricultural publications (e.g. *The Cultivator,* 1833) attempted to persuade the farmers that their land, with proper scientific management, was not inferior to the supposedly richer lands of central and western New York and Ohio. The movement to tidy up the farmscape by ditching, draining and painting; to introduce farmers to the "new" agriculture via county fairs (see: Fred Kniffen) and agricultural courses; to depict farming as a gentlemanly and honorable occupation (via Cincinnatus Societies); and the efforts to stem the rural to urban tide have all been studied in detail by county historians and geographers. See for example: S. Eager, *An Outline History of Orange County,* pp. 524–25; David Cole, ed. *History of Rockland County,* pp. 99ff.; Ulysses Hedrick, *History of Agriculture,* pp. 121–22; and Donald Marti,

"In Praise of Farming: An Aspect of the Movement for Agricultural Improvement in the Northeast, 1815–1840," *New York History*, July 1970, pp. 371–75.

10. A. E. Corning, "Rockland County," p. 645.

11. Eager, *History of Orange County*, p. 19.

12. Russell Headley, ed. *The History of Orange County*, p. 166.

13. See: Willitt C. Jewell, "Putnam County," and Headley, ed. *The History of Orange County*, p. 166. The first consignment of Orange County milk reached the New York City market via the Erie Railroad in 1842; by 1848 the whole region north and west to Port Jervis was tapped as part of the City milkshed.

14. For a more detailed account of these distributions and specializations see the appropriate chapters and pages in: Corning, "Rockland County," Hedrick, *History of Agriculture*, and Eager, *History of Orange County*.

15. R. Cole Harris, Opening Address, Historical Geography Sessions, 22nd International Geographical Congress, Montreal, 1972.

16. Donald Ringwald, *The Hudson River Dayline* (Berkeley: Howell-North Books, 1965), pp. 4ff.

17. *Ibid.*, pp. 7, 11.

18. Hedrick, *History of Agriculture*, p. 237 and R. Van Zandt, *Chronicles of the Hudson*. Van Zandt places the great age of steamboat navigation on the Hudson between 1824 and 1838.

19. Robert Boyle, *The Hudson River*, p. 61.

20. U. Hedrick, *History of Agriculture*, p. 257. The full rail network is shown in Thompson, ed. *Geography of New York State*, p. 164. Rail lines developed first in the Mohawk Valley (1830s), while New Jersey pioneered the first (horse-drawn) rail line between Paterson and Passaic in 1831. Thompson (p. 163) also suggests that the Hudson Valley's somewhat later development was due to New York City's complacency with steamboat and canal service. The city was not threatened commercially by railroads until the 1846 trans-Taconic rail link between Albany and Boston.

21. Cole, ed. *History of Rockland County*, p. 224.

22. D. Ackerman, "Historic Closter," *Proceedings*, Bergen County Historical Society, no. 7 (1910–11):25.

23. *Ibid.*, p. 26. Closter was furthermore fortunate in that Ramapo iron ore was shipped out from this station.

24. J. J. Greco, *The Story of Englewood Cliffs*, p. 18; F. A. Westervelt, ed. *History of Bergen County*, p. 358.

25. When a West Shore Railroad was eventually constructed in the 1880s, much straightening-out and filling-in of the Rockland and Orange shoreline would become necessary, a fact already responsible for the disappearance of numerous points and bays between Tarrytown and Ossining on the eastern shore.

26. B. Lossing, *The Hudson*, p. 215.

27. R. Van Zandt, *The Catskill Mountain House*, p. 8.

28. William Bartlett, *American Scenery*, 2 vols. (London: Geo. Virtue, 1840).

29. George Templeton Strong, *Diaries*, pp. 53—72, 236–37.

30. N. P. Willis echoes similar feelings: "It is to be regretted that the fashion of visiting Haboken [*sic*] and Weehawken has yielded to an impression among the "fashionable" that it is a vulgar resort. This willingness to relinquish an agreeable promenade because it is employed as well by the poorer classes of society, is one of those superfine ideas which

we imitate from our English ancestors. . . . the presence of innumerable "vulgarians" . . . produc[es] all the background effect as necessary to the ensemble. The place would be nothing—would be desolate, without them: yet in England and America it is enough to vulgarize any—the most agreeable resort, to find it frequented by the 'people.' " N. P. Willis in W. Bartlett, *American Scenery*, no page.

31. Paul Shepard, "The Cross Valley Syndrome," *Landscape* vol. 10 (1961):4–8.

32. Lossing, *The Hudson*, p. 435. The Lake Mahopac region, "associated for years with all that is beautiful and romantic in rural scenery," became known to tourists with the construction of Stephen Monk's Hotel and boarding house in 1834. By the Civil War Mahopac enjoyed a resort business said to be a rival to that of Saratoga. In the 1850s "picnic trains" (of the Harlem Division) came up from New York to patronize the growth of Monk's and half a dozen other hotels. See W. C. Jewell, "Putnam County," pp. 960ff.

33. Known as "Roe's West Point Hotel," similarly destroyed by fire. See Lossing, *The Hudson*, p. 253.

34. *Ibid.*, p. 251; 256.

35. Van Zandt, *The Catskill Mountain House*, p. 9.

36. Edmund Patten, *A Glimpse of the United States . . . During the Autumn of 1852* (London: Effingham Wilson, 1853), p. 42; N. P. Willis, *Outdoors at Idlewild*, p. 46.

William Wade's *Panorama of the Hudson River from New York to Albany* is referred to extensively throughout this chapter. "Drawn from Nature" and engraved by Wade himself, the panorama was published simultaneously in New York and Philadelphia by J. Disturnell in 1846. The copy photographed for use in this study is found in the Science and Technology Room of the New York Public Library and consists of 32 pages of copper-engraved, color-tinted strips. The research value of this panorama depends of course on the thoroughness or liberties taken with the landscape depicted by Wade, but little biographical information is available on the panoramist, or his sources or methods of data collection. A records search at the library reveals only that a William Wade, engraver and draftsman, had a business on Broadway at least from 1845 to 1850. Wills and death notices, as reported in the *New York Times* and the *New York Evening Post,* establishes only that there were several William Wades living and working in New York around this time. The panorama itself has recently been reprinted for sale by the Sloop Clearwater Inc.

37. E. M. Bacon, *The Hudson River*, p. 651; Cole, ed. *History of Rockland County*, p. 154; Wallace Bruce, *The Hudson, Three Centuries of History, Romance and Invention* (New York: Bryant Union Co., 1907), p. 56; Lossing, *The Hudson*, p. 364: With a commanding view of the Palisades, Edwin Forest, for example, built a castellated granite residence on Font Hill (Mount St. Vincent) in 1838. Lossing felt that such an "architectural event" would have been more appropriate to the rugged hills of the highlands.

38. R. Van Zandt, *The Catskill Mountain House*, p. 271.

39. Robert Sears, *A New and Popular Pictorial Description of the United States* (New York: author, 1848), p. 144; Jacques Milbert, *Picturesque Itinerary*, p. 25.

40. Among others, there are at least five representative surviving nineteenth-century structures at Garrison: (1) Moore House, stone Gothic residence, 1847. Designed by Richard Upjohn; (2) Glover house, board and batten, c. 1850; (3) Beltcher-Gish house, brick Victorian, c. 1850; (4) Hurst-Pierpont house, brick Gothic, 1836, designed by Towne and Davis; (5) Sloan house, stuccoed, c. 1865.

41. Wade shows a two-story, double chimneyed structure on the shoulder of Bear Mountain labeled "Mrs. A. D. Pell." But there is no reference to this residence in the county histories.

A. J. Downing, *The Architecture of Country Houses* (New York: Dover Pubs., 1969), p. 203.

Smith's elegant country residence, with verandas and bay windows, stood atop the now-leveled high bank of the river: "At that time the whole tract was covered with beautiful groves of oak and chestnut trees, and the place was a perfect picture of natural beauty." Cole, ed., *History of Rockland County*, pp. 153–54. Lossing, *The Hudson*, also locates the "cottage" of a Mr. Lambertson of New York City in the isolated and "wild domain" of Storm King Valley, although it is vague as to how estate-like this summer retreat was (p. 210).

42. J. J. Greco, *The Story of Englewood Cliffs*, p. 20.

43. F. A. Westervelt, ed., *History of Bergen County*, p. 361.

44. Harriet Martineau as quoted in R. Van Zandt, *Chronicles of the Hudson*, p. 209.

45. Greco, *The Story of Englewood Cliffs*, p. 17.

46. Jacques Milbert, *Picturesque Itinerary*, pp. 14–15.

47. For example: J. Fowler, *Journal of a Tour in the State of New York in the Year 1830* (London: Whittaker Treacher & Arnot, 1831), p. 40; T. W. Strong, *The Hudson Illustrated with Pen and Pencil* (New York: the author, 1852), p. 4; Milbert, *Picturesque Itinerary*, pp. 14–15; Buckingham as quoted in Van Zandt, *Chronicles of the Hudson*, p. 225. Shad fishing, eeling, and perhaps oystering (17.5 million bushels of oysters were harvested annually from the Hudson starting in the 1830s) were the mainstays of the Hudson River fishermen.

48. S. Collins, "The Biotic Communities," p. 64; J. G. Chapman, *Hudson River Scene* (1835), "Iconography of New Jersey;" Wm. Cammeyer, "A New Map of the Hudson River, the Post Roads between New York and Albany, the Northern and Western Canals . . ." (1829); Strong, *The Hudson River Illustrated with Pen and Pencil*, p. 4.

49. Collins, "The Biotic Communities," p. 47.

50. Buckingham as quoted in Van Zandt, *Chronicles of the Hudson*, p. 223; Thomas Cole, *The Palisades, New Jersey*, oil on canvas, 1835, "Iconography of New Jersey."

51. *Travellers Steamboat and Railroad Guide to the Hudson River* (New York: Gaylord Watson, 1857).

52. W. W. Clayton, *History of Bergen and Passaic Counties*, p. 275.

53. S. Collins, "The Biotic Communities," confirms the importance of pasturing (horses, cows and sheep) with biogeographic evidences: "Evidence of open pasture consists of stumps of red cedar trees. This species often is common in pastures because it thrives in sunny habitats and is not generally preferred as food by domestic animals.

"Cattle and other animals were allowed to wander freely through the woods, but were fenced out of the small gardens which were sometimes cleared to the ridge" (p. 70).

54. Northern Railroad Company of New Jersey, *Summer in the Palisades* (New York: Lange, Little & Co., 1875), pp. 2, 5; Greco, *The Story of Englewood Cliffs*, p. 14; Adaline Sterling, *The Book of Englewood* (Englewood: Pub. by the Committee on the History of Englewood, 1922), p. 37.

55. Clayton, *History of Bergen and Passaic Counties*, p. 259.

56. Northern Railroad, *Summer in the Palisades*, p. 5.

57. C. Nordstrom, *Frontier Elements*, pp. 78ff.

58. Cammeyer, "A New Map of the Hudson River," 1829.

59. Corning, "Rockland County," Belleville, N.J. is named as the prime source of competition.

60. Cole, ed. *History of Rockland County*, p. 320.

61. For example see: Milbert, *Picturesque Itinerary*, plate no. 6, "Port of Haverstraw."

62. Lossing, *The Hudson*, pp. 278–80.

63. Simeon DeWitt, *An Atlas of the State of New York* (New York: David Burr, 1829).

64. Lossing, *The Hudson*, p. 305.

65. *Ibid.*, p. 317. Wade's panorama shows the ridge of Hook Mountain fairly well covered with vegetation, as does the work of other artists. For example, the same condition is seen in J. V. Connell's rendition of the Steamboat *Iron Witch* passing below the mountain (1846). New York Historical Society Collection.

66. Lossing, *Ibid.*, p. 304.

67. Green, *The History of Rockland County*, see ch. 10. It is the sluiceway that was depicted by Wade and Connell in the 1840s and the railroad by Lossing in the 1860s (p. 305).

68. Cole, ed., *History of Rockland County*, p. 123; Ibid.

69. Harriet Martineau as quoted in Van Zandt, *Chronicles of the Hudson*, p. 209.

70. Eager, *An Outline History*, p. 129.

71. Simeon DeWitt, *Atlas of the State of New York*, 1829.

72. Corning, "Rockland County," p. 645.

73. Cole, ed. *History of Rockland County*, p. 329. The ice depot is sketched in Lossing, *The Hudson*, p. 265.

74. William Cullen Bryant, *The American Landscape* (1830), as quoted in John Howat, *The Hudson River and its Painters*, p.149. A compendium of works on and references to West Point in these decades would indeed be immense. The following few literary and graphic references are as representative as any: "The Grand Duke Bernhard's Visit to West Point (1825)," *New York History*, January 1945, pp. 78–89; N. P. Willis's text about and Bartlett's West Point prints in *American Scenery*, pp. 6–7, 30–32, 38–42; Milbert, *Picturesque Itinerary*, plates 7, 8; B. Lossing, *The Hudson*, pp. 224ff.; paintings such as Samuel Gerry's *West Point, Hudson River*, (1858), Robert Havell's *West Point from Fort Putnam*, (1848) as contained in John Howat, *The Hudson and its Painters*.

75. Harriet Martineau as quoted in Van Zandt, *Chronicles of the Hudson*, p.209; Willis, *Outdoors at Idlewild*, pp.260 and 43.

76. See Howat, *The Hudson and its Painters*, plates 35, 36. Wade also shows what are apparently farm clearings throughout the highland portion of his panorama.

77. Howat, *Ibid.*, pp. 148–49. David Johnson, *West Point from Fort Putnam*, 1867 and John F. Kensett, *View Near Cozzens Hotel from West Point* (1863).

78. Lossing, *The Hudson*, pp. 213, 207; see: Wade's Panorama; Freeman Hunt, *Letters About the Hudson River* (New York: author, 1837), pp. 195–96; George Cooke, *West Point Above Washington Valley*, (1833) vol. 3, Stokes Collection; and an anonymous view printed by A. Weingartner in 1856, vol. 4, Stokes Collection.

79. Eager, *An Outline History*, p. 584 and "The Grand Duke Bernhard's Visit," p. 88.

80. John Howat, *The Hudson and its Painters*, plate no. 30.

81. S. Eager, *An Outline History*, p. 584; W. J. Bennett, *West Point from Phillipstown*, (1830), vol. 3, Stokes Collection.

82. See Hugh Raup, "Some Problems in Ecological Theory," p. 19.

83. F. Kimble (1832) as quoted in Van Zandt, *Chronicles of the Hudson*, p. 199 and Buckingham (1838) in *Ibid.*, p. 225.

84. G. T. Strong, *Diaries*, vol. 2, August 4, 1851, p. 60.

85. F. Kimble as quoted in R. Van Zandt, *Chronicles of the Hudson,* p. 207; John Fowler, *Journal of a Tour in the State of New York.* The British traveler was one who didn't. In contrast to the ripe fields of the Genesee Country he found the Newburgh area barren, half cleared, and stocked with hideous looking pigs and sheep. "For an English farmer . . . anything but desirable"; Lossing, *The Hudson,* p. 214; Eager, *An Outline History,* p. 123; and Buckingham as quoted in Van Zandt, *Chronicles of the Hudson,* p. 228.

86. Lossing, p. 215.

87. Lossing, *The Hudson,* p. 269. Some of the 11 seed propagation houses and other structures are seen in Lossing's print "Iona, from the Railway," p. 271.

8. Steam and Iron versus the Romantic and Pastoral

1. Wolfgang Born as quoted in Van Zandt, *The Catskill Mountain House,* p. 257; Shepard, "The Cross Valley Syndrome," *Landscape,* 10(1961):5.

2. Barbara O'Doherty, "Landscape Painting in America, 1825–75," in *The American Vision, Painting 1825–1875* (N.Y.: The Public Education Association, 1968).

3. Sarmiento, *Travels in the United States in 1847* (Princeton: Princeton University Press, 1970), p.219.

4. Shepard, *Man in the Landscape,* p.179. These same ideas are expressed by Christopher Tunnard and Henry Hope Reed in *American Skyline* (Boston: Houghton Mifflin, 1953), p.85.

5. Van Zandt, *The Catskill Mountain House,* p.171. The term Hudson River School of landscape, which is used repeatedly throughout this chapter, must be qualified at the outset. William Guy Wall's *Hudson River Portfolio* is considered the forerunner of this "school," an entity which most art historians date from Cole's first sale of his landscapes in Manhattan in 1825 (Vessell, ed. *The Life and Works of Thomas Cole,* p.xxvii and Van Zandt, p.257). Kensett, Church, Wittridge, and dozens of other artists came to be included in this "school" by the 1840s and 1850s.

There is, however, disagreement on the use of the term "school." Baigell and Vessell agree that these artists' work "bears the unmistakable stamp of a corporate style" (Baigell, *American Painting,* p. 110) and that they shared a common view of man's relationship with nature, a nature which they attempted to render with accuracy through careful observation (Vessell, p. xxvii). Jones however considers the "school" a more amorphous and disconnected phenomenon: "The Hudson River School was not a school, was only in small part involved with the Hudson River, was not even a group of men living in one area, nor did all its "members" have a single style. The name came from a belittling critic who grouped the nineteenth century landscape painters together for what he considered their provincialism and geographical limitations. It was a good name, picturesque, homelike, and easy to remember; it was picked up quickly and has long been in almost exclusive use by artists, critics, collectors, and the general public." *The Hudson River School* (Geneva, N.Y.: W. F. Humphrey Press, 1968), p. 1. Catalogue of the exhibition gallery of the Fine Arts Center at the State University College of New York at Geneseo.

6. Willis, *Outdoors at Idlewild,* p. 67: "Nature, like love, costs money to appropriate and make the most of."

7. Barker, *American Painting,* pp. 392 and 391; Curti, "The Patricians," in *American Thought,* pp. 220ff.

8. Kenneth LaBuddle, "The Mind of Thomas Cole," Ph.D. Dissertation, University

of Minnesota, 1954, pp. 31–32: "Nature was what the observer was prepared to find after seeing what the artist selected from and improved upon in Nature."

9. *Ibid.,* p. 205.

10. Perry Miller, *Errand into the Wilderness* (Cambridge, Mass.: Belknap Press, 1964), p. 206.

11. *Ibid.,* p. 214.

12. Vessell, ed. *The Life and Works of Thomas Cole by Louis Legrand Noble* (Cambridge: Harvard University Press, 1964), p. 284. From one of Cole's last letters, Catskill, N.Y., February 1, 1848; Truettner and Bolton-Smith, *National Parks,* p. 18.

13. Vessell, ed. *The Life and Works,* p. xxxiv.

14. Baigell, *American Painting,* p. 112 and plate 6–4; published by Peabody of N.Y. in 1831 and contained in Stokes Collection, N.Y.P.L., vol. 3, 1830–47.

15. LaBuddle, "The Mind of Thomas Cole," pp. 198ff.

16. Lowenthal and Prince, "English Landscape Tastes," p. 195. As the authors point out, European travelers had actually become accustomed to using rose-tinted "Claude Glasses" to frame their landscapes.

17. David Johnson, *West Point from Fort Putnam,* (1867) and John Kensett, *View near Cozzen's Hotel from West Point* (1863), plates 33 and 32 in Howat, *The Hudson and its Painters.*

18. The point might be made that as with the English poets Gray ("Elegy in a Country Churchyard") and Goldsmith ("Abandoned Village") a sense of nostalgic melancholia was produced by scenes of rural desolation and decay. But this was not likely an association to be made by Americans in an era of agrarian and industrial positivism.

19. G. T. Strong, *Diaries,* July 13, 1841: "Boat tolerably built, and hot as a locomotive Dutch oven. I never suffered so much from the heat as this day—not a breath of air, and the glassy water reflecting back the sun and putting us between two fires. . . . I hate travelling even when there's some prospect of enjoyment, for I'm sure to get in trouble with my baggage or my breakfast or something else" (p. 162).

20. Curti, *American Thought,* pp. 390ff.; Gaylord Watson, *Travellers Guide,* p. 11.

21. As Shepard observes in "The Nature of Tourism," a "high proportion of the ordinary tourists' time was devoted to securing accommodations, conveniences, and safety. "The most acute reality was composed of rates, schedules, and meals" (p. 30). The great preoccupation with the trivia of travel was expressed by Isabella Bishop, the first woman fellow of the Royal Geographical Society, who described the "very undignified scramble [that] takes place" for the railroad seats with windows overlooking the Hudson's west shore scenery (as quoted in Van Zandt, *Chronicles,* p. 282).

It furthermore seems probable that the Palisades were shortchanged in their aesthetic compliments because of the "manifold embarrassments and troubles" encountered by riverboat passengers attempting to take in scenery during the initial phase of the trip. The guidebook prepared originally in monthly installments by Bartlett and Willis, *American Scenery,* prepared the traveler for the grandeur of the Palisades shoreline, but the landform was in many cases approached too quickly to be properly appreciated: "With most persons, to mention the Palisades is to recall only the confusion of a steamer's deck, just off from the wharf, with a freight of seven or eight hundred souls hoping to 'take tea' in Albany. The scene is one of inextricable confusion, and it is not till the passenger knows whether his wife, child, or baggage, whichever may be his tender care, is not being left behind at the rate of fifteen miles in the hour" (p. 14).

22. Simultaneous with this, the Trans-Appalachian West was romanticized and ide-

alized out of all proportion with the grueling and squalid conditions of frontier existence.

23. George Catlin, as contained in Nash, ed. *American Environment*, p. 8.

24. Kenneth Keniston, *The Uncommitted, Alienated Youth in American Society* (New York: Dell, 1965), p. 180.

25. The term has at least 40 definitions according to Samuel Green, *American Art*, p. 239.

26. Curti, *American Thought*, p. 230; Agnes Jones, in a forward to *The Hudson River School*, has listed the five major characteristics of the Romantic movement in America: (1) love of nature, taking two directions—the peaceful, pastoral, arcadian line of Claude Lorrain and the rigorous, stormy, terrifying wilderness of Salvator Rosa; (2) an acceptance of emotion and sentiment, denied during the 1700s, but leading to nauseating sentimentality by Victorian times; (3) recognition of the dignity of each individual, in part stemming from the reaction against the industrial revolution; (4) an interest in the Gothic and a passion for the Middle Ages; (5) a spirit of wonderment and a passion for questioning (p. 3).

27. B. Cowdrey, "William Henry Bartlett and the American Scene," *New York History*, October 1941, p. 394.

28. Lowenthal regards this "notorious" grandness of scale ("the hero alone in space") as a cardinal quality of all American landscape painting. This is certainly the case with Bartlett's views. See Lowenthal, "The American Scene," pp. 62ff. The way in which a definite organizational scheme was used to view and paint landscapes in the nineteenth century, and especially the use of a "frame," is discussed in Hildegard Binder Johnson, "The Framed Landscape," *Landscape*, 23, no. 2 (1979): 27–32.

29. Thomas Cole's "Oxbow of the Connecticut" is perhaps the classic example of nature's duality as expressed on canvas. The painting contrasts a placid and lush natural landscape bathed in sunlight with storm clouds and rain. See Howard S. Merritt, *Thomas Cole*, Introduction and catalogue for the Memorial Art Gallery at the University of Rochester, February–March, 1969, plate 31.

30. A barren vegetative environment induced a nineteenth-century feeling for "desolate sublimity" as Van Zandt found in his analysis of Parkman's *Oregon Trail*. See Van Zandt, "The Scotch School of Aesthetic Theory and the Natural Description of the Oregon Trail," *The Smithsonian Journal*, no. 4 (Fall 1949): 107.

31. Shepard, *Man in the Landscape*, p. 92 and Green, *American Art*, p. 181: architecturally, a "picturesque eclecticism" as expressed in Italian villas, Egyptian and Moorish buildings, Swiss chalets, and English thatched cottages satisfied a yearning for the romantically exotic or remote.

32. Shepard, *ibid.*, p. 5.

33. See: William Guy Wall's *The Palisades* (1820s), no. 19 of the *Hudson River Portfolio* and David Handley, *The Tappan Zee from Tarrytown*, p. 46 in *Scrapbook Containing About One Hundred and Twenty Water Color Sketches of New York City* etc., (1833–91) Prints Division, N.Y.P.L. Trollope, *Domestic Manners*, p. 366; J. G. Chapman, *Hudson River Scene*, an oil on canvas done in 1835. Iconography of New Jersey (possibly the work of H. Inman). Thomas Cole, *The Palisades, New Jersey*, an oil on canvas which hangs in the New York Historical Society auditorium, Iconography of New Jersey. LaBuddle suggests (p. 43) that Cole's tree stumps were not so much symbolic as actual vegetative examples he encountered in his travels, but a strong suggestion of "Salvatoresque" symbolism seems likely as well.

34. N. P. Willis instigated the toponomic change from Butter Hill to Storm King. In 1832 he explained to his readers in *Outdoors at Idlewild* that "the tallest mountain, with its

feet in the Hudson at the Highland Gap, is officially the Storm-King"(p. 188). The new designation was thought more romantic and euphonious and was confirmed by Willis with legendary association—i.e., that the monarch of the mountain was the foreteller of storms.

35. Kemble as quoted in Van Zandt, *Chronicles,* p. 197 and Patten, *A Glimpse of the U.S.,* p. 47.

36. Kemble, in Van Zandt, p. 199. This is very similar to Cole's description of the sublime; see: Vessell, ed. *The Life and Works,* letter dated October 8, 1826 (p. 42), describing a Catskill peak near Windham.

37. Walter Karp, "The American Land as it Was," *American Heritage,* December, 1969, pp. 16ff. George Harvey (1800–78) bought an estate on the Hudson not far from Irving where he studied the "ever-varying atmospheric effects of the American climate" (Richardson, *American Painting,* p. 171); Bartlett, *American Scenery,* p. 1.

38. Curti, *American Thought,* p. 397.

39. Howat, *The Hudson and its Painters,* p. 28 and Merritt, *Thomas Cole,* p. 12. See also LaBuddle, "The Mind of Thomas Cole," pp. 6–7.

40. See Sears, ed., *A New and Popular Description,* p.6 and Shepard, "The Nature of Tourism," *Landscape,* Summer 1955, p. 30.

41. As quoted in the preface to Thomas Flexner, *That Wilder Image* (New York: Little, Brown & Co., 1962).

42. Sears, ed., *A New and Popular Description,* p. 6; Van Zandt, *The Catskill Mountain House,* p. 27.

43. Downing also worked at revamping the landscaped gardens of American estates along English lines; he, as had his father, took a sharp interest in *Landscape Gardening* (1841) and the aesthetic and practical enjoyments of horticulture. The influence of his ideas can be seen in the *Estate Portraits,* a series of five, sketched by E. Whitefield in June of 1841 (N.Y.P.L., Prints Division). Downing's most influential work was *The Architecture of Country Houses* (1850), a work in which he urged "the union of house with its surrounding scenery" (p. 203). He was governed by the principles of utility and beauty combined and, as such, stands as a forerunner of the School of Functional Architecture. See W. G. Jackson, "First Interpreter of American Beauty: A. J. Downing and the Planned Landscape," *Landscape,* Winter 1952, pp. 11–18.

44. Nash, *Wilderness and the American Mind,* pp. 74, 67.

45. Willis, *Outdoors at Idlewild,* p. 190.

46. John Fowler, *Journal of a Tour of the State of New York in the Year 1830* (London: Whittaker, Treacher & Arnot, 1831), p. 39.

47. F. Trollope, *Domestic Manners of the Americans* (1832), p. 367ff. The British traveler naturally reacted more emotionally to the scenes of Clinton and Cornwallis's victories and to those places which played a role in André's life. Almira H. Read as quoted in Genevieve Darden, ed. "A Visit to Saratoga: 1826," *New York History* 50 (1969): 284.

48. Freeman Hunt, *Letters About the Hudson,* pp. 156–57, 15.

49. Samuel Knapp, *The Picturesque Beauties of the Hudson River and its Vicinity* (New York: 1935), p. 6 and Patten, *A Glimpse of the U.S.,* p. 109; Bartlett, *American Scenery,* pp. 18, 64, 26.

50. Nicolson, *Mountain Gloom and Mountain Glory,* p. 336; Tennyson as quoted in Nicolson, Epilogue.

51. Green, *American Art,* p. 213.

52. Shepard, *Man in the Landscape,* p. 187. Such structures lined the shore near Hyde

Park, and further north John Cruger built ruined arches on an island in the Hudson and scattered Mayan sculpture among them.

53. Cole, particularly, never forgave the American landscape for not having a Colosseum or a Chartres; he wrote, "we feel the want of association such as cling to scenes in the Old World. Simple nature is not quite sufficient. We want human interest, incident and action, to render the effect of landscape complete." As quoted in Shepard, *Man in the Landscape*, p. 183. Much of Cole's alienation toward American life and society in general seems to stem from this and related factors (e.g., the insistence of his patrons that he stay away from European allegories in which ruins appeared). See LaBuddle, "The Mind of Thomas Cole."

54. Sears, ed., *A New and Popular Description*, p. 47; Kemble as quoted in Van Zandt, *Chronicles*, p. 199 and Havell's "West Point from Fort Putnam," plate 49 in Van Zandt. See also Sears, p. 315. The ruins of Ticonderoga appear in The Stokes Collection, vol. 3, 1830–47. Another curious example of the ruin was *The Newport Ruin* as sketched by W. G. Wall: "There are those who feel it had been a fortress . . . but still I can never admit this picturesque ruin has been a mill" (Stokes Collection).

55. "The Alluvial Way" was a 130-foot-high ridge road along the southern shore of Lake Ontario. It was one of the great natural curiosities of the state. This and other local glacial features attracted the comments of Fowler (*Journal of a Tour*, p. 148) and others.

56. Watson, *Travellers Guide*, p. 22; Sarmiento, *Travels*, p. 221; Trollope, *Domestic Manners*, p. 366.

57. The theory of Dr. Mitchell was most often alluded to by Fowler, *Journal of a Tour*, p. 42; according to this theory: "this thick and solid barrier [the highlands] seems, in ancient days, to have raised a lake high enough to cover all the country to Quaker Hill and the Laconic [*sic*] Mountains on the east, and to Shawangunk and Catskill Mountain on the west . . . but by some convulsion of nature, the mountain chain has been broken, and the rushing waters found their way to the New York Bay." The Storm King avalanche swept away farms, mills, dam, and bridge near Cornwall Landing according to Willis, and quickly became one of the river sights for travelers on the East Shore Railroad and the steamboats. Willis, *Outdoors at Idlewild*, pp. 137–38.

58. Shepard, *Man in the Landscape*, p. 243; Smith, *European Vision*, p. 254.

59. Sears, ed., *A New and Popular Description*, pp. 147–48.

60. Curti, *American Thought*, p. 336 and Shepard, "Nature of Tourism," p. 30.

61. Green, *American Art*, p. 256; the influence of the Dusseldorf School is discussed by Green (pp. 254ff.); Von Humboldt's impact upon American landscape is considered by Shepard, *Man in the Landscape*, p. 136; by B. Smith, *European Vision*, pp. 151ff.; and by Truettner and Bolton-Smith, *National Parks*, p. 24.

62. Shepard, *Man in the Landscape*, p. 185 and Smith, *European Vision*, p. 227.

63. Shepard claims that the imagery of the ruin was first applied to the romantic or sublime concept via geological features; later, actual historical ruins were borne along on this same imagery. Shepard also states that the personification of nature by likening objects of the physical world to parts of the human body is attributable to a deep-seated, unconscious primordial "earth-mother" drive ("The Cross Valley Syndrome," p. 7). The image of the ruin could be and was, also applied to vegetative forms such as "the huge trunks of old decaying trees" as described by Buckingham atop the Palisades in 1838 (Van Zandt, *Chronicles*, p. 223). Shepard again suggests that trees were perhaps intentionally fired to create dead, blasted, or twisted ruins. (*Man in the Landscape*, p. 186). Anthropomorphizing of the landscape was a favorite technique of Cole. Ponds were likened to eyes and trees with

enfolding or entwining branches which were seen as human appendages engaged in gestures of affection (LaBuddle, "The Mind of Thomas Cole," p. 43). In works by both Cole and Church an added generative or life-giving force was imparted to nature through a characteristic reddish "living" color.

64. Leo Marx, *The Machine in the Garden,* traces in great detail the importation of the ideal from Europe and its modification to American circumstances from colonial times through the nineteenth century.

65. *Ibid.,* ch. 1.

66. Leo Marx, *Machine in the Garden,* p. 88ff.

67. Smith, *European Vision,* pp. 23 and 198.

68. Marx, *Machine in the Garden,* pp. 141–42.

69. Willis found Hudson Valley farmers particularly "stupid" and a degraded class of people. A far cry from the Jeffersonian vision, but to Willis there was nothing romantic about "rustics" and their untidy farmyards; there was nothing idyllic about animal carcasses on the landscape: "On the Romantic banks of the Hudson we do not bury our cows! Since last August, almost a twelve-month, the carcass of one has lain at water's edge, within stone's throw of the lovely village of Cornwall." *Outdoors at Idlewild,* p. 44. Leo Marx, *Machine in the Garden,* p. 138.

70. John L. Allen, "The Geographical Images of the American Northwest, 1673 to 1806," Ph.D. Dissertation, Worcester, Mass.: Clark University, 1969.

71. Willis's biographers are Cortland Auser, *Nathaniel P. Willis* (New York: Twayne Pub. Inc., 1969) and Henry Beers, *Nathaniel Parker Willis,* (Boston: Houghton, Mifflin, 1885).

72. The symbolic pastoral cow is seen in J. G. Chapman, *View of the Palisades,* a steel plate engraved for the *New York Mirror,* 1838; W. J. Bennett, *West Point from Phillipstown,* 1830, Stokes Collection; and J. F. Weir, *View of the Highlands from West Point,* 1862, in Howat, *The Hudson and its Painters,* plate 40. Shepard (*Man in the Landscape*) examines the "cow theme" and finds that it derives from seventeenth-century England, or perhaps even to Italian renaissance painting depicting the lactating cow as woman as earth symbol. (pp. 110ff.). Lowenthal too has investigated the need for idling or reclining cows ("at least three") as an element of picturesque painting and landscape gardening in seventeenth-century England (see Lowenthal and Prince, "English Landscape Tastes," pp. 193–95).

73. Vance has stated an important distinction between two conceptual reactions to the environment in this period ("California and the Ideal"). He, as does Van Zandt, differentiates between two simultaneously existing manners of thought: The "Hudsonian" and "Concordian" views (p. 189). The "Hudsonian" view was essentially emotional, romantic, and sentimental involvement with nature (landscape). This position was taken by Cole and the Hudson River School, who based their works upon no elaborate aesthetic concept: "It was an art of enthusiasm and delight, of observation and affection, modest, intuitive, undogmatic in spirit" (Richardson, *American Painting,* p.216). Contemporaneous with this was the "Concordian" view held by Thoreau, Emerson, and intellectuals of a transcendental inclination. This is somewhat of an unfair categorization since Cole (an orthodox Episcopalian) might be considered to straddle the line because he found God in nature (not as nature!). Transcendentalism itself, as propounded at Walden in the 1850s, is a rather nebulous doctrine, but might be defined as a form of mystical faith or ethical philosophy expressing a general belief in the individuality and perfectability of man and the idea that all power, wisdom, and authority come from nature. Man could transcend the

conditions of the material world through intuition and imagination and find the source of truth and spiritual values in nature through a union with God through (or in) nature. *This* was "the preservation of the world." A further analysis of Transcendentalism is found in Huth, *Nature and the American*, ch. 4; Nash, *Wilderness and the American Mind*, ch. 5.

74. Willis, *Outdoors at Idlewild*, pp. 190, 120.

75. As quoted in Nash, *Wilderness and the American Mind*, p. 89.

76. Willis, *Outdoors at Idlewild*, p. 184.

77. Leo Marx, *Machine in the Garden*, pp. 191 and 208. Marx elaborates upon the machine mania that captured the American imagination in the 1840s: "Stories about railroad projects, railroad accidents, railroad profits, railroad speed, filled the press; the fascinating subject is taken up in songs, political speeches, and magazine articles. . . . The entire corpus of intoxicated prose seems to rest on the simple but irresistible logic of first things first: all other hopes, for peace, equality, freedom, and happiness, are felt to rest upon technology" (p. 192).

78. Irving, *Knickerbocker History of New York*, p. 176; Leo Marx, *ibid.*, p. 31.

79. Willis, *Outdoors at Idlewild*, pp. 31, 28, 50; Cole as quoted in Tunnard and Reed, *American Skyline*, p. 91.

80. As quoted in Van Zandt, *Chronicles*, p. 274.

81. Sanford, ed., *Quest for America*, p. 98.

82. The mills at Buttermilk Falls were often spoken of as romantic additions to the scenery along this stretch of river. The mill power potential of Glens Falls and at the falls of the Passaic was juxtaposed with the inherent beauty of the natural landscape.

83. Willis, *Outdoors at Idlewild*, pp. 215, 396; 340.

84. Willis, *ibid.*, pp. 347, 320 and similar expressions in *Hurry-Graphs, or Sketches of Scenery . . .* (New York: Scribner, 1851), pp. 132–33. Willis also attempted to smooth over the scenically destructive effects of the railroads and telegraph wires by envisioning the machinery as an endemic and not really disruptive part of the natural harmony. The railroad was seen not as a mechanical intrusion, but "more like a meteor shooting across the face of a cloud." He even suggested using the depressed or elevated engine smoke plume as a barometric indicator of the dampness in the atmosphere. The New York–Albany telegraph line presented Willis with his most difficult effort; to find a saving grace in the wooden posts, which obviously showed a blatant disregard for the scenery they spanned. Surely, here was "a plump conflict between utility and beauty." New York City's electric utility, Consolidated Edison, would have been proud of the way in which Willis resolved the problem: he found pleasure and relaxation in the music of the wind as it whipped through the wires, wires also favored as perches by little birds. Faunal life could not possibly blend in so well with an unnatural element!

85. Nash, *Wilderness and the American Mind*, p. 76ff. Settlement and the trappings of civilization do appear on Cole's canvases, but only when his patrons demanded it (La-Buddle, "The Mind of Thomas Cole," p. 79). For him, it was unfortunately necessary to do business with these "copper-hearted barbarians" and "dollar-godded utilitarians" (Vessell, ed. *The Life and Letters*, p. 141; letter dated March 6, 1836).

9. Incompatibilities

1. D. Cole, ed. *History of Rockland County*, p. 113; W. W. Clayton, *History of Bergen and Passaic*, p. 210; Cole, *Ibid.*, p. 18; and F. A. Westervelt, ed. *History of Bergen County*, p. 349.

2. Upper Nyack Centennial Committee, *History of Upper Nyack,* p. 21; Cole, ed. *History of Rockland County,* p. 113.

3. E. M. Ruttenber and L. H. Clark, *History of Orange County,* p. 820.

4. Cole, ed. *History of Rockland County,* p. 100.

5. Eric Brunger, "A Chapter in the Growth of the New York State Dairy Industry, 1850–1900," *New York History,* 36 (April 1955):136–45.

6. A. H. Walker, *Atlas of Bergen County, New Jersey* (Reading, Pa.: Reading Pub. House, 1876), p. 154.

7. John Krout and Clifford Lord, "Sports and Recreation," *History of New York State* (1876), p. 154.

8. Thursty McQuill, *The Hudson River by Daylight* (New York: author, 1882), p. 37.

9. *New York Times,* magazine section, "Frederick Law Olmsted, Creator of 'The Central Park,' " December 31, 1972, pp. 12ff.

10. McQuill, *The Hudson River by Daylight,* p. 37.

11. A good account of such facilities at Iona Island is contained in Cole, ed. *History of Rockland County.* pp. 328–29. "Picnic Rock" is referred to as being in the neighborhood of Storm King by Ruttenber and Clark, *History of Orange County,* p. 778.

12. R. Van Zandt, *The Catskill Mountain House.*

13. Henry Cranston, *The Hudson Highlands* (New York: The New York Hotel, 1883).

14. Russell Headley, ed. *The History of Orange County,* p. 169. Fire destroyed the Storm King Mountain House in the 1890s when it was owned by James Stillman.

15. Mrs. S. S. Colt, ed. *The Tourist's Guide through the Empire State* (Albany: author, 1871), p. 33.

16. Northern Railroad Company, *Summer in the Palisades,* p. 35.

17. See F. A. Davis, *New Historical Atlas of Rockland County* (New York: Davis and Kochensperger, 1876), p. 17.

18. W. W. Clayton, *History of Bergen and Passaic,* p. 213 and as depicted in Northern Railroad Company, *Summer in the Palisades,* p. 23.

19. Northern Railroad Co., *Summer in the Palisades,* p. 13. Also known as Lydecker's Point, immediately below the "Devil's Elbow," one third of a mile to the south of the Englewood Basin and the junction with Palisades Avenue and Hudson Terrace. The grounds are currently occupied by St. Peter's College of Newark, formerly St. Joseph's Orphanage run by the Sisters of Peace.

20. All were wealthy property owners in the vicinity of Englewood Cliffs. The Lydeckers were involved in New Jersey politics and Dana was a New York publisher.

21. Northern Railroad Co., *Summer in the Palisades,* p. 15; J. J. Greco, *The Story of Englewood Cliffs,* p. 27.

22. *New York Times,* May 8, 1881, p. 5.

23. John Codman, *Winter Sketches from the Saddle by a Septuagenarian* (New York: Putnam, 1888), pp. 77, 88.

24. Willitt C. Jewell, "Putnam County," p. 846; R. H. Turner, *Field Trip Guide to The Land Use Patterns of the Mid-Hudson Valley* (West Point: U.S. Military Academy, 1974). The role of directorships and contractors in the old New York Central Railroad appears to have been intimately related to the pattern of estate holding and mansion construction in Putnam County.

25. Greco, *The Story of Englewood Cliffs,* p. 39.

26. *New York Times,* June 11, 1871, p. 4.

27. Ruttenber and Clark, *History of Orange County*, pp. 780, 754, 814.

28. See: David Ward, *Cities and Immigrants*, ch. 5, "Local Transportation and Suburban Expansion" (New York: Oxford University Press, 1971).

29. H. P. Phelps, *The Home Sites at Undercliff, New Jersey*, pp. 8–10, 7.

30. In 1873 the Jersey City and Albany Railroad was built two miles to the west and parallel with the Northern Railroad as far north as Tappan. Here too station villages sprung up along the route: Schraalenburgh, Frankfort, Randall, et al. Today, this is the West Shore Railroad along Washington Avenue and Schraalenburgh Roads through Bergenfield, Dumont, and Northvale. See: Northern Railroad Co., *Summer in the Palisades*, p. 4.

31. F. A. Westervelt, ed. *History of Bergen County*, p. 167.

32. See: "Harrington Township" in Walker's *Atlas of Bergen County*, p. 97. Mentioned are General Stryker, W. C. Baker, Charles Nordhoff, S. Miles, J. Cleveland Caddy (architect of the Demarest Railroad Station), Calvert Vaux, et al.

33. The sense of a peaceful world atop the Palisades can be gleaned from the writings of John Codman, *Winter Sketches*, p. 161ff, and can be had from such paintings as J. G. Brown, *View of the Palisades*, (1867). This view shows the wooded summit in a "quiet monumentality." John Howat, *The Hudson River and its Painters*, plate 12.

34. Codman, *ibid.*, p. 161: "Today [1888] the crests of the Palisades are densely wooded as they were two hundred and seventy-nine years ago." Clayton, *History of Bergen and Passaic*, p. 13, "largely covered with natural forest trees."

35. Clayton, *History of Bergen and Passaic*, p. 212; "Up the Hudson by Night," *New York Times*, May 15, 1878, p. 8.

36. Clayton, *ibid.*, p. 212.

37. Walker, *Atlas of Bergen County*, pp. 81 and 97; J. T. Lloyd, "Topographical Map of the Hudson River," (1864).

38. From the poet Katherine MacLean, as quoted in J. J. Greco, *The Story of Englewood Cliffs*, p. 12. Undercliff, today a picnic grove maintained by the Palisades Park Commission, is located below a recess in the 380-foot cliff-face just north of Englewood (the Englewood Boat Basin).

39. See: J. Howat, *The Hudson and its Painters*, plate 10; J. Burroughs, *Our River*, sketch by Mary Foote; *New York Times*, May 19, 1878, p. 4.

40. Greco, *The Story of Englewood Cliffs*, p. 15.

41. David O'Reilly, ed. *The Shad Book* (Poughkeepsie: Hudson River Sloop Restoration, 1974), p. 21.

42. A. E. Corning, "Rockland County," p. 21.

43. Mrs. S. S. Colt, *The Tourist's Guide*, p. 32.

44. Cole, ed. *History of Rockland County*, p. 153.

45. *Ibid.*, p. 177; Colt, *Tourist's Guide*, pp. 36–37.

46. See map of Rockland County with rail lines in Cole, ed., *History of Rockland County*, p. 1.

47. J. Howat, *The Hudson and its Painters*, plate 22, Sanford Gifford's *Hook Mountain, Near Nyack, on the Hudson* (1870's).

48. Cole, ed., *History of Rockland County*, p. 320.

49. *Ibid.*, p. 122.

50. T. Nelson, *American Views, Views of the Hudson* (New York: T. Nelson & Sons, 1878 [?]), p. 7.

51. T. Kury, "Historical Geography of the Iron Industry," p. 112.

52. E.g. Bryant's *Picturesque America*, p. 7.

53. Colt, *The Tourist's Guide*, p. 50.

54. Ruttenber and Clark, *History of Orange County*, p. 763.

55. *New York Times*, October 9, 1870 and January 14, 1880.

56. Emile deDamseaux in R. Van Zandt, *Chronicles of the Hudson*, p. 291; J. Burroughs, *Our River*, p. 3.

57. James P. Kirby, "Map of the Highlands of the Hudson, Orange County" (Newburgh N.Y., 1880).

58. N. P. Willis, *Outdoors at Idlewild*, p. 125.

59. Good descriptions of Iona Island at this time are contained in Cole, ed., *History of Rockland County*, p. 328 and Henry Christman, "Iona Island and the Fruit Growers Convention," *New York History*, October 1967, pp. 348–49.

10. *More Powerful Than the Quarrymen's Dynamite*

1. Bierstadt and Moran explored this technique in their renditions of Western landscapes.

2. Vance, "California and the Search for the Ideal."

3. Truettner and Bolton-Smith, *National Parks*, n.p. and Vance, *ibid.*, p. 193.

4. See Lloyd Goodrich, *Winslow Homer* (New York: George Braziller, 1959).

5. Vessell, ed., *Life and Works of Thomas Cole*, p. 26 and Jones, *The Hudson River School*.

6. Green, *American Art*, p. 371; J. Cropsey, *Hudson River near Hastings*, (1876) and *Shad Fishing on the Hudson*, plates 9 and 10 in Howat, *The Hudson and its Painters*; D. Johnson, *West Point from Fort Putnam* (1867) and *Foundry at Cold Spring*, (1870's), plates 33 and 42 in Howat; S. Gifford, "Hook Mountain" (1870s) and *Sunset on the Hudson* (1876), plates 22 and 9 in Howat; L.C. Tiffany, *View of the Palisades* (1870) in Iconography of New Jersey and J. D. Woodward, *The Palisades . . . from below Hastings* and *Pinnacles of the Palisades* in *The Art Journal of America*, August 1874, p. 154; September 1874, p. 174.

7. Green, *American Art*, p. 371. The Hudson River artist George Inness of Newburgh is perhaps best representative of the transition away from the realism of the early school to the mannerisms and styles adopted in the 1870s and 1880s. See references to Inness in Green, *American Art* and Baigell, *American Painting*.

8. Lewis Mumford, *The Brown Decades: A Study of the Arts in America, 1865–1895* (New York: Dover, 1955), p. 6.

9. Green, *American Art*, pp. 318–19.

10. Mumford, *Brown Decades*, p. 49 and Curti, *American Thought*, p. 6.

11. Green, *American Art*, p. 395 and Vance, "California," p. 190: "The close of the Civil War left the United States a very different nation from that which surrounded the romantics and pastoralists of the fifties . . . The prosperity that came from economic takeoff was accompanied by grim costs. Health in cities declined, both from their enlargement and from their attraction of ships and immigrants which brought cholera, Yellow fever, and other epidemic diseases. . . . No wonder there seemed to be a persistant craving that affected city dwellers, which made them long for yet another taste of the countryside they had so recently left."

Lowenthal, "The American Creed of Nature as Virtue," *Landscape* 19 (1959): 25.

12. Green, *American Art*, p. 319 and Curti, *American Thought*, p. 6.

13. Van Zandt, *The Catskill Mountain House*, p. 222.

14. A good example of the almost total disregard of the Hudson's scenery in this period is Jacques Offenbach's trip along the river by rail in 1876; see: Van Zandt, *Chronicles*, pp. 286–88.

15. See Lowenthal, "The American Scene," p. 72.

16. Curti, *American Thought*, pp. 524–25; in Van Zandt, *Chronicles*, pp. 294–97, Emile deDamseaux, 1877.

17. Title page to the 1876 edition of *Atlas of Bergen County, New Jersey* (Reading, Pa.: A. H. Walker).

18. "A Sunday on the Hudson," *New York Times*, June 19, 1882, p. 15; Van Zandt, *The Catskill Mountain House*, p. 221.

19. Lossing, *The Hudson*, p. 265 and Cranston, *The Hudson Highlands*, p. 20ff.

20. Burlingame in Bryant, *Picturesque America* (1874), pp. 21–22: "One sees the stream lying so far below that it seems almost in another world, and looks across into the blue distance in the east as he might look out from a great and magical window that gave a glimpse into an entirely different life. For nothing could present sharper contrasts than do the two regions separated by this natural wall. On its west lies the quietest farming country, with its people leading simple, uneventful, *pastoral* lives. . . . But on the eastern side, in the places along the banks of the river, is every kind of dwelling, from great country-seats to smallest suburban cottage, is found a class utterly different."

21. Northern Railroad, *Summer in the Palisades*, p. 14.

22. "A Sunday on the Hudson," *New York Times*, May 27, 1878, p. 8.

23. Shepard, *Man in the Landscape*, pp. 239 and 258; Lowenthal, "Recreational Habits and Values: Implications for Landscape Quality," *New York State Planning News*, July–August 1969, p. 11.

24. McQuill, *The Hudson River by Daylight*, p. 21.

25. Colt, ed., *The Tourist's Guide*, p. 35 and Lossing, *The Hudson*, p. 300; lines from William O. Stoddard, "The Gates of the Hudson," p. 12 in William Cullen Bryant, ed. *Picturesque America*, 2 vols. (New York: D. Appleton, 1874).

26. Stoddard, *ibid.*, p. 12; Charles Taintor, *The Hudson River Route* (1887), p. 40; Lossing, *The Hudson*, p. 254; Cranston, *The Hudson Highlands*, p. 18.

27. Verse by G. M. Morris of Undercliff, N.J. as quoted in Colt, ed., *The Tourist's Guide*, p. 52.

28. McQuill, *The Hudson River by Daylight*, p. 45; Burlingame in Bryant, *Picturesque America*, p. 7; and Lossing, *The Hudson*, pp. 212–13.

29. A not-too-surprising ancillary concept was the doctrine of sublime topography added to by the works of man. Picturesqueness continued to be associated with the works of man, especially the seemingly more destructive aspects inflicted upon the landscape. The busy foundries at Cold Spring and Poughkeepsie were said to be "the most strangely beautiful and striking feature of the mid-Hudson's scenery, while steamboats—no longer disharmonious invaders like the railroads—added to the picturesque panoply of river scenery (Lossing, *The Hudson*, p. 205). It was symptomatic of these decades to be so totally fascinated by the progress of industry that people were often blind to the environmentally discordant aspects of such progress. The brickyards, lime kilns and rock quarries were sometimes found to be visually pleasing. Lossing presented several woodcuts of the lime kilns at Tomkins Cove and Marlborough; industry is shown amid a snow-covered scene of people ice fishing, skating and sleighing, a scene that would have been more aesthetic according to Lossing if the woodcuts had been larger (pp. 195 and 230). In similar fash-

ion, Davis's *Atlas of Rockland County* (1876) includes a view of the Tomkins Cove Lime Co., set peacefully beneath a tree-covered hillside overlooking a placid stretch of river. There is also an implication of picturesque industry in Nelson's *American Views* (1878) in which "tiny ships loaded with building stone from the [Palisades] above" seem not out of place or inappropriate in an otherwise romantically picturesque scene (p. 2).

30. Colt, ed., *The Tourist's Guide,* p. 12.

31. Northern Railroad, *Summer in the Palisades,* p. 27 and a New York Central publicity blurb, "The Hudson River," no date, p. 3, New York Public Library, NC, 16.

32. See Ruttenber and Clark, *History of Orange County,* pp. 777, 778, 273.

33. Cole, ed., *History of Rockland County,* p. 327; Lossing, *The Hudson,* pp. 217, 273.

34. *Picturesque American Scenery,* p. 31.

35. Treason Hill above Haverstraw was where Arnold arranged the betrayal of West Point; Polopel's and Constitution Islands were the sites of forts, *chevaux-de-frise,* and iron chains; Molly Pitcher hailed from the highlands; beacon fires to "summon the hardy militia to the defense of the Highland forts" would forever glow in the patriot's mind atop Storm King and Beacon. Tappan, Spy Rock, Ramapo Clove, Continental Spring; the King's Ferry, the Alpine defile, Stony Point, Fort Lee, the "Military Highway."

36. See: K. Thompson, "The Australian Fever Tree in California: Eucalyps and Malaria Prophylaxis," *Annals of the AAG,* June 1970, pp. 230–44.

37. See: Van Zandt, *The Catskill Mountain House,* p. 249ff. and Vance, "California."

38. In research published largely in the 1890s, the results of laboratory and field techniques confirmed the anopheline mosquito as the transmitter of the disease, initially caused by a blood parasite. Laveran, a French Army officer, and Ronald Ross, whose observations were made in India, are credited with these research findings. See: Thompson, "The Australian Fever Tree," p. 233 and B. D. Prescott, "Malaria: Malady of the Marshes," *Scientific Monthly,* November 1943, pp. 452–56.

39. Van Zandt, *The Catskill Mountain House,* pp. 253–54. Malaria was more or less a constant presence, but cholera reached epidemic proportions in New York in 1866, 1867, and 1873.

40. *Ibid.,* p. 221. Montulé (*Travels in America*) for example associated marshes with an unhealthy climatic situation: "This was most noticeable at Louisville, which was thought to be unwholesome. A single marsh of very small area gave it this bad reputation, but since work on drying it has been started the climate is observed to be more healthful" (p. 126).

41. Codman, *Winter Sketches,* pp. 21–22. Codman also notes that the draining of the Croton River at mid-century was seen by many as a dangerous move in that the resulting swamps would breed malarial infection (p. 115).

42. LeRoux in Barbara Rosenkrantz and William Koelsch, eds., *American Habitat: A Historical Perspective* (New York: The Free Press, 1973), p. 321. Specifically, Pass Christian, Miss. is mentioned.

43. Van Zandt, *The Catskill Mountain House,* p. 252ff. and *Chronicles,* p. 221.

44. Ruttenber and Clark, *History of Orange County,* p. 42; Cole, ed., *History of Rockland County,* p. 18; and Colt, ed., *The Tourist's Guide,* p. 52. Shepard in "The Nature of Tourism," *Landscape,* Summer 1955, pp. 29–33 has also stated the importance of this concept.

45. Willis, *Outdoors at Idlewild,* pp. 399–400.

46. Hunt, *Letters About the Hudson,* p. 156.

47. G. T. Strong, *Diaries,* June 20, 1854, pp. 177–78.

48. Westervelt, *History of Bergen County*, p. 343; Cole, ed., *History of Rockland County*, p. 224; J. J. Greco, *Englewood Cliffs*, p. 78; Northern Railroad, *Summer in the Palisades*, p. 14.

49. Northern Railroad, *Summer in the Palisades*, p. 57 and Lossing, *The Hudson*, p. 435; Cole, ed., *History of Rockland County*, pp. 17–18. Despite the juxtaposition of the disease and the insect in cases such as these, the cause and effect relationship between the two was not apparently realized.

50. See: Cranston, *The Hudson Highlands*, p. 19; Baron Axel Klinkowstrom, "A Swedish View of West Point in 1820," *New York History*, July 1952, p. 316.

51. The seasonal migration of wealthy families here might favorably be compared to the rise of Atlanta, in the early 1800s; as a reaction to the disease-ridden conditions in southern tidewater cities such as Charleston and Savannah, wealthy plantation families removed—at first seasonally and then permanently—to the higher and therapeutically safer elevations of the Piedmont. Northern Railroad, *Summer in the Palisades*, p. 46; Phelps, *Home Sites*, p. 5.

52. *New York Times*, October 10, 1878, p. 4.

53. Nash, *Wilderness and the American Mind*, p. 96.

54. *The Smithsonian* (August 1972): 34. The photographer W. H. Jackson for example propagandized for the establishment of National Parks in the far West in 1869. The role of the "explorer-photographer" in the idealization of Western landscapes and the creation of Park areas is commented upon by Gene Thornton, "The Idealized Grandeur of Nature," Arts and Leisure Section, *New York Sunday Times*, June 29, 1975, a photography review based on an exhibition at the Metropolitan Museum of Art: "Era of Exploration: The Rise of Landscape Photography in the American West, 1860–1885."

55. Huth, *Nature and the American*, ch. 6 and Olmsted in Nash, ed., *The American Environment*, p. 22. Yosemite was administered by the state which acted as a "trustee" until 1905 when a National Park was created and the Valley ceded back to the Federal Government.

56. Shepard, *Man in the Landscape*, p. 249.

57. Both reports are contained in Nash, ed., *The American Environment*, pp. 24, 28.

58. The full impact of industrial development and its impact and effect upon the man–land relationship was mainly experienced after the Civil War. See: L. Hacker, et al., "The Beginnings of Industrial Enterprise after the Civil War" and "The Maturing of Industry," in Alexander Flick, ed., *History of the State of New York*. George Perkins Marsh, linguist, art collector, congressman from Vermont, historian, lawyer, ambassador, and sometimes "father of American Geography" (now claimed as the "father of American Ecology"), subtitled his work: *Physical Geography as Modified by Human Action* (N.Y.: Scribner, 1864). Extracts from this volume appear in Nash, ed., *The American Environment*, pp. 13–18 and Fisher et al., eds., *A Question of Place*, pp. 370–79. An article dealing with Marsh by Franklin Russell, "The Vermont Prophet," appeared in the Summer 1968 issue of *Horizon* (pp. 17–23). Marsh's biographer is David Lowenthal: *George Perkins Marsh, Versatile Vermonter* (New York: Columbia University Press, 1958).

59. Boyle, *The Hudson*, p. 82. The work of the elite in fencing off their estates, forbidding the hunting of certain animal species within these confines, and the hiring of game wardens to enforce the rules had a positive effect upon Adirondack ecology, no matter what the primary motivation behind the staking out of mountain estates might have been. Stipulations such as these are associated with at least one of the Palisades estates in this period. Sterling writes that the Phelps estate, which stretched from the

Hackensack to the Hudson, was opened to "lovers of nature" for walking and driving, under the condition that no one "interfere with the *superior rights* of birds and small game to this, their home" (pp. 86–87 in *The Book of Englewood*).

60. Clayton, *History of Bergen and Passaic*, p. 14.

61. Taintor, *The Hudson River Route*, (1887), p. 20; CHF, "The Top of the Palisades," *New York Times*, May 19, 1878, p. 4.

62. "The Top of the Palisades," *ibid.*

63. Corning, "Rockland County," p. 726 and Cole, ed., *History of Rockland County*, pp. 151, 153.

64. Cole, *ibid.*, p. 77.

65. During the Civil War the Parrott Brothers cannon manufactured at Cold Spring were so tested as were other weapons in subsequent decades. The implied disregard for mountain scenery reminds one of Colonel Putnam's rocksliding foray during the Revolution.

66. Lossing, *The Hudson*, p. 225. Obviously, the natives did not share the scenic sentiments and penchant for charming ruins indicative of travelers and city people.

67. Colt, ed., *The Tourist's Guide*, p. 104.

68. See: Colt, *ibid.*, p. 52 and Lossing, *The Hudson*, p. 208. Alternately referred to as the "Turk's Face" and placed by Link, *The Hudson by Daylight*, on Mount Taurus.

69. Link, *ibid.*, p. 75.

70. Lossing, *The Hudson*, p. 257. Both Lossing and Bacon, *The Hudson River*, make reference to the outlawing of this disfigurement by an act of the New York State Legislature, but the date of and nature of such a law is difficult to determine from their statements (Bacon, p. 198).

71. Burroughs, "Our River," e.g., pp. 490–91.

11. *The Emerging Recreational Landscape*

1. Laurence Rockefeller, "Palisades Interstate Park," p. 1, a speech delivered in 1957 to the Garden Clubs of New Jersey at the Greenbrook Sanctuary.

2. American Scenic and Historical Preservation Society, "Hook Mountain . . . now being destroyed by Stone Crushing Works," being a souvenir postcard issued in 1905(?). N.Y.P.L. collection of uncatalogued materials on the Hudson Valley.

3. E. M. Bacon, *The Hudson River from Ocean to Source*, p. 222.

4. E. Ingersoll, *Illustrated Guide to the Hudson River*, p. 76.

5. "Explosions of giant powder" and the resulting "clouds of gray dust" are mentioned as to the distance heard and seen in Palisades Interstate Park Commission, *A History*, p. 17 and "The Palisades," *New York News-Letter*, p. 1. Bacon, *The Hudson River*, felt that the blasting of Hook Mountain was a public offense to the ear and the nervous system, p. 222. The *New York Times*, perhaps only somewhat facetiously, noted in a July 23, 1905 article that newspaper editors and reporters in Bergen and Hudson Counties had been jarred out of their beds by the early morning explosions, and proceeded to condemn this practice in print.

6. The period from September to November of 1897 is particularly good for an impression of this genre of material.

7. Laurence Rockefeller, "Palisades Interstate Park," p. 5; Palisades Interstate Park

Commission, *A History*, p. 17; Th. Anderson's letter to the editor, "An Englishman's Plea for the Palisades," *New York Times*, October 18, 1894., p. 4.

8. "The Palisades," an editorial, *New York Times*, November 22, 1897, p. 6.

9. "To Save the Palisades," *New York Times*, November 25, 1894, p. 17.

10. J. Stoddart's letter to the editor, "How to Preserve the Palisades," *New York Times*, October 24, 1894, p. 4.

11. Palisades Interstate Park Commission, *Sixty Years of Park Cooperation: A History, 1900–60*, p. 17.

12. "To Save the Palisades," *New York Times*, November 25, 1894, p. 17. Prior to this, New Jersey had passed several ineffective measures aimed at stopping the defacement. Lofty purpose ("to forever thereafter preserve unbroken the uniformity and continuity of the Palisades") lost out to grim reality on two counts: (1) the laws were not retroactive and therefore did not apply to lands already owned by quarry interests—which in effect was over 90 percent of the shoreline north of Fort Lee; and (2) "the Palisades" was defined narrowly as the vertical cliff face only and not the talus slope, or whatever the quarrymen contended to be the talus zone.

13. J. J. Croes, *The Palisades of the Hudson* (New York: The Palisades Commission for the Acquisition of the Palisades of the Hudson by the U.S., 1895), p. 12 (the Women's Clubs of New Jersey were cool to this proposal, however); "To Save the Palisades from Ruin," *New York Times*, September 29, 1895, p. 20.

14. The Trainor Brothers Company reportedly reseeded and set out bushes, but in the opinion of the *New York Times* actually did little to negate the total environmental damage: "It takes from thirty to forty years to tone down the baldness on one of these spots; and to fully recover one would certainly not take less than a century." September 29, 1895, p. 20.

15. "Indian Head Destroyed," *New York Times*, March 5, 1898, p. 20. For a description of the destruction of Washington Head see: "An Old Cliff Blown Up," *ibid.*, September 27, 1897, p. 10.

16. "Question of the Palisades," *New York Times*, October 29, 1897, p. 4.

17. "Outlook for the Palisades," *New York Times*, January 14, 1900, p. 10.

18. Palisades Interstate Park Commission, *A History*, p.20. G. W. Perkins, President of the Commission, elicited great gifts of money and land from his friend J. P. Morgan and "this relation was of immense value in the later development of the Park" (p. 19). Complete possession of the Carpenter Brothers' holdings was attained in 1901 for an additional $122,500.

19. J. J. Greco, *The Story of Englewood Cliffs*, p. 39.

20. Arthur Mack, *The Palisades of the Hudson* (Edgewater: Palisade Press, 1909), p. 33.

21. Palisades Interstate Park Commission, *A History*, p. 20.

22. "Hudson's Palisades turned over to Campers this Summer," *New York Times*, July 23, 1905, part 3, p. 7.

23. For a detailed account of recreational developments and the extensions of park boundaries in the Palisades section in the decades after 1909 see: Palisades Interstate Park Commission, *A History*, p. 45ff, and S. Collins, "The Biotic Communities," pp. 77–80.

24. "The Palisades," editorial, *New York Times*, February 28, 1906, p. 8.

25. "To Save the Palisades," *New York Times*, January 14, 1906, p. 1.

26. The Tors, the object of quarrymen as well, were not acquired until 1943 and

even then the Appalachian Stone Company proceeded to blast away at the back side of High Tor, on property immediately adjacent to the Park.

27. Palisades Interstate Park Commission, *A History*, pp. 23–24.

28. *Ibid.*, p. 26.

29. *Ibid.*, p. 31.

30. F. A. Westervelt, ed. *History of Bergen County*, p. 353.

31. Wallace Bruce, *The Hudson, Three Centuries of History*, pp. 55–56.

32. The *New York Times* rather blithely accused these millionaire families of never really being "wholly or essentially American." As a consequence of their action many Hudson Valley estates were either put up for sale or left in a state of decay by the late 1800s. This was also economically disastrous for the valley in that the village and tradespeople who provided services for the estates were left unemployed. See: "Ruins along the Hudson, Many Deserted Mansions on Historic Spots," *New York Times*, July 6, 1882, p. 10.

33. Greco, *The Story of Englewood Cliffs*, p. 15; Arthur Mack, *The Palisades of the Hudson*, p. 27; Howat, *The Hudson and its Painters*, p. 125.

34. See the illustrations accompanying: Nicholas Gesner, "Diary, 1830–50," plates 72 and 73.

35. Collins, "The Biotic Communities," p. 74; H. Winton, et al., *Report of the Palisades Commissioners of the State of New Jersey* (Somerville: The Unionist-Gazette Printer, 1896), p. 6.

36. "The Wondrous Palisades," *New York Times*, July 23, 1889, p. 2; J. J. Croes, *The Palisades of the Hudson*, p. 5.

37. Population decrease for the village: *1900*, 5900; *1910*, 5600; for the township: *1900*, 9800; *1910*, 9300; the county too showed a similar decrease in population between 1900 and 1910. The Great Haverstraw Landslide occurred in the winter of 1906. The entire shore embankment collapsed, destroying dozens of houses and killing 29 people. The cause was believed to be the undermining of the embankment for the excavation of brick clay. "Stoves overturned, fires started . . . and only a snow saved half of Haverstraw from destruction." A. E. Corning, *Rockland County*, p. 715.

38. E. Ingersoll, *Illustrated Guide*, p. 60.

39. Russell Headley, ed. *The History of Orange County*, p. 142; Calvin Stillman, "The Issues in the Storm King Controversy," *Black Rock Forest Papers*, no. 27, (1966): 3.

40. "The Hudson Hinterland," *New York Times*, July 23, 1900, p. 7; Headley, *Orange County*, p. 266; *Snapshots on the Hudson*, no publisher, no date, p. 11. (N.Y.P.L.).

41. *Snapshots, ibid*; Hugh Raup, "Botanical Studies in the Black Rock Forest," *The Black Rock Forest Bulletin*, no. 7 (1938): 101.

42. Palisades Interstate Park Commission, *A History*, p. 29.

43. R. H. Torrey, et al., *New York Walk Book*, pp. 85–86; E. Ingersoll, *Illustrated Guide*, p. 78.

44. Headley, *Orange County*, p. 181.

45. The U.S. Navy paid $160,000 for Iona Island in 1899 and proceeded to construct 160 low-lying brick and concrete storage buildings. The structures were linked to the west shore via two causeways over the Salisbury Marsh. See "The Highlands," *New York News-Letter*, p.6. Today, Iona Island, as Palisades Park property, is once again being developed as a recreation area.

46. For details see C. S. Bannerman, *The Story of Bannerman Island*. Barges filled with stone were also sunk to create a "Venetian approach."

47. Details are found in W. C. Jewell, "Putnam County." Instances of estates' being

handed over for religious purposes include Jacob Rupert estate (became St. Basil's [Greek Orthodox] Academy); Stuyvesant Fish estate (became the home of the Capucian Fathers); and the Osborn estate (became the Society of the Atonement's "Graymoor").

12. The River, the Park, and the Mountain

1. The metaphor of the batholith is developed by Calvin W. Stillman in "This Fair Land," a paper prepared for the Conference on Landscape Assessment at the University of Massachusetts at Amherst in November 1973 and published in: Erwin H. Zube, et al., eds., *Landscape Assessment: Values, Perceptions, and Resources* (Stroudsburg, Pa.: Dowden, Hutchinson & Ross, 1975), p. 18.

2. Nash, ed. *The American Environment*, p. 37.

3. For more on the nature of these other causes see: C. Van Hise, "History of the Conservation Movement," in Ian Burton and Robert Kates, eds. *Readings in Resource Management and Conservation* (Chicago: University of Chicago Press, 1960), pp. 189–201.

4. See Nash, ed. *The American Environment*, p. 38; C. Glacken, "The Origins of the Conservation Philosophy," in Burton and Kates, eds. *Resource Management*, p. 155.

5. Nash, ed. *The American Environment*, p. 38.

6. See W. K. Verner, "Wilderness and the Adirondacks—An Historical View," *The Living Wilderness*, Winter 1969, pp. 27–46; Grant McConnell, "The Conservation Movement—Past and Present," in Burton and Kates, eds. *Resource Management*, p. 150.

7. Robert Underwood, "The Neglect of Beauty in the Conservation Movement," in Nash, ed. *The American Environment*, pp. 68–71; Joshua Taylor, p. 14 in the forward to Truettner and Bolton-Smith, *National Parks and the American Landscape.*

8. Nash, ed. *The American Environment*, p. 39ff.

9. Huth, "The Roosevelt Era," in *Nature and the American* and Nash, ed., *The American Environment*, p. 67. Underwood, as editor of *Century* magazine, was quite upset that "beauty as a principle" was given the back seat and was at the time somewhat neglected by conservationists in favor of material and economic motivations. He chided the Federal Government particularly for taking a position that seemed to equate conservation with efficient use and dollar returns. What about great scenery? However, Underwood's criticism (1910) of the movement for a lack of strong aesthetic driving force must be viewed in the context in which it was written: the Ballinger-Pinchot controversy over the illegal acquisition of Federal lands by large corporations, and President Taft's alleged abrogation of conservationist responsibilities. This dual (practical and aesthetic) component of the conservation movement revolves about a critical point concerning the origin and nature of that movement and its evidences in the Hudson Valley. These decades are characterized not only by the material, economic, and politically motivated achievements in landscape and resource management (e.g. the Forest Preserves, the Corps of Forest Rangers, the Reclamation Act of 1902, assorted irrigation projects, and the establishment of distant National Parks), but by scenic appreciation as well. Parks dating from this period include: Mount Rainier, 1899; Crater Lake, 1902; Mesa Verde, 1906; Glacier, 1910; Rocky Mountain, 1915; and Grand Canyon, 1916.

10. Nash, ed., *The American Environment*, p. 67.

11. For details of the Hudson-Fulton Celebrations see daily issues of the *New York Times* starting on December 25, 1909.

12. William Tucker, "Environmentalism and the Leisure Class," *Harper's*, December

1977, p. 52. As to the role of an elite affecting land use and landscape, it has been suggested that the Hudson Valley whaling industry so badly stank up those estate properties downwind from the city of Hudson that the estate owners forced the abandonment of the industry here further negating that city's pretensions toward becoming the state capital.

13. *A Retrospective Collection of Paintings from the Palisades,* an exhibition catalogue of Van Perrine's Palisades paintings held at the Durand-Ruel Galleries, New York, 1904. For more on Perrine see: Claude Bragdon, "Van Deering Perrine, A Painter of Light," *Art and Decoration,* May 1924, pp. 14–15.

14. That strange picturesqueness sometimes evoked by the industrial and mechanical appeared again in various writings. Bruce, despite a powerful concern for environment, saw the Haverstraw brickyards and the "mile-long pier" at Piermont as hardly marring the landscape, and maybe even picturesque. The blasting of the Palisades was not overly bothersome because "as fast as man destroys, nature kindly heals the wound" (*The Hudson* [1907] pp. 61 and 56). Bacon too thought that the Palisades could manage to hide their scars with foliage, and J. J. Croes, a member of the Palisades study commission, seriously believed the quarries capable of *adding* to the picturesqueness of the shore (Bacon, *The Hudson,* p. 222). The *New York Times,* however, faulted a public in awe of the quarrymen and their machines. (November 27, 1897, p.6) This same preoccupation is seen in a number of Currier & Ives prints depicting locomotives, steamboats, and fire engines.

15. For example see: the *New York Times Index* listings for these years under "Palisades," "Hudson River," and "Hudson Highlands."

16. Geological Survey of New Jersey, "Map of Palisades Mountain showing Quarry Defacement . . ." 1894 and presented in the *New York News-Letter,* November–December, 1900; Ingersoll, *Illustrated Guide,* p. 76.

17. Barker, *American Painting,* p. 549.

18. Theodore Roosevelt, Opening Address, at a Conference of Governors in the White House, 1908 as contained in Nash, ed., *The American Environment,* p. 52; The *New York Times,* "To Save the Palisades," September 23, 1897, p. 5 and "Save the Palisades from Ruin," September 29, 1895, p. 20.

19. J. J. Croes, *The Palisades of the Hudson,* p. 8; Bruce, *The Hudson* (1907), p. 79.

20. Leo Marx, *Machine in the Garden,* p. 347.

21. Nash, "Conservation as Anxiety," in Nash, ed., *The American Environment,* pp. 85–93.

22. Headley, *History of Orange County,* p. 261.

23. Hudson River Realty Company, *Palisade—A Story of One Thousand Acres of Beautifully Wooded Land transformed into a Model Suburb* (New York, 1906[?]), p. 17. Although the housing tracts were developed in the area of Palisade, New Jersey (to the south of Fort Lee and linked directly to Manhattan via the 125th Street ferry), the propaganda is probably similar to that of other such developers working throughout northeast Bergen, and later Rockland and Orange Counties.

24. *Ibid.,* p. 9.

25. Ingersoll, *Illustrated Guide,* p. 106.

26. Codman, *Winter Sketches,* p. 66.

27. Green, *History of Rockland County,* p. 317.

28. Henry James, "New York and the Hudson: A Spring Impression," *North American Review* 181 (1905):826. Note: scenic stops for pictures were later incorporated into railroad excursion trips.

29. H. B. Brown, "The Status of the Automobile." *Yale Law Journal* February 1908 (reprinted in the *New York Times,* "The Horseless Carriage Means Trouble," May 25, 1973.

30. See: Vance, "California and the Search for the Ideal," p. 195ff. A more purely social or intellectual factor which also obstructed the perpetuation of pastoralism in the Eastern United States was what Curti (*American Thought,* p. 632) calls the cult of the self-made man. As a form of late-nineteenth-century romanticism, the cult popularized the idea of getting ahead on one's own efforts. Material progress and riches were within the reach of every Horatio Alger hero, who read magazines like *Pluck and Luck* and *Work and Win.* There is an indirect relationship here with pastoralism in that the cult subscribed to a belief in the great benevolence of capitalism and industry. Through the work ethic, through the factory and the machine, one rose above the environment (incidentally destroying what was scenic or rustic along the way).

31. These companies included Biograph, Solax, and The Edison Company of New Jersey. See "Museum to Recall State's Film Role," *New York Times,* News of Northern New Jersey Section, January 19, 1975, p. 24.

32. C. Carmer, in Howat, *The Hudson and its Painters,* p. 24.

33. *Ibid.,* p. 5. Those artists such as Homer and Ryder who continued to dwell on nature and landscape as subject matter departed dramatically from the Hudson River tradition. Homer's later works of the Maine Coast are almost abstract and emotionally expressionistic statements of man's struggle with the environment. Ryder, in a vaguely similar fashion, explored the symbolism and mystery of the sea.

34. Arden, "The Evil City . . . ," *New York History* 35 1954, p. 262.

35. *Ibid.*

36. William Hoglund, "Abandoned Farms and the 'New Agriculture' in New York State at the Beginning of the Twentieth Century." *New York History* 34 (1953): 185–201; J. Leonard Bates, "Fulfilling American Democracy: The Conservation Movement, 1907–1921," in Nash, ed. *The American Environment,* pp. 79–82. Bates states that part of the conservation impulse stems from the revulsion of materialism and urban moneyed interests. The attempt to revive the image of virtuous pastoralism and lure former farmers and European immigrants away from the city, was designed primarily to counter the state's decline in rural population between 1880 and 1920 (see Hoglund). The movement was, however, a failure largely because of economic realities and perhaps too because of the moribund nature of the pastoral image, an image which reflected the actual subjugation of the countryside (rural and suburban areas and all that was scenic within their confines) to the economic and social geographic pressures of the city.

37. Ingersoll, *Illustrated Guide,* p. 32.

38. Leo Marx, *Machine in the Garden,* pp. 112ff.; 353.

39. "Hudson's Palisades Turned over to Campers this Summer," *New York Times,* July 23, 1905, part 3, p. 7.

40. Croes, *The Palisades of the Hudson,* pp. 10–16. Also cited as reasons for preservation were the recreational and military advantages of the area.

41. Mack, *The Palisades of the Hudson,* p. 2; President Kunz of the American Scenic and Historical Preservation Society as quoted in Nash, ed., *The American Environment,* p. 78.

42. "The Wondrous Palisades . . . ," *New York Times,* July 23, 1889, p. 2; Croes, *The Palisades of the Hudson,* pp. 1–2.

43. Headley, ed., *The History of Orange County,* p. 265; Hudson River Dayline Com-

pany, *The Most Charming Inland Water Route on the American Continent* (New York: L. Stillson Company, 1903), p. 16; *New York News-Letter*, "The Highlands," January–February 1901, pp. 1–23.

44. Bruce, *The Hudson*, p. 83: "Strangely enough," he notes, "the altitude of the mountains at the southern portal of the Highlands has been greatly overrated." Bruce speculated upon the reasons for such exaggeration, explaining that the true height of the Dunderberg (865 feet) had always been given as 1098 feet. Anthony's Nose too was boasted of as 1228 feet by all the river guidebooks, but was stated to be 900 feet by the Geological Survey.

45. Henry James, "New York and the Hudson," p. 831.

46. Ingersoll, *Illustrated Guide*, pp. 30ff. and Mack, *The Palisades of the Hudson*, pp. 9ff.

47. Bacon, *The Hudson River*, p. 201. Estates atop the Palisades were being vacated in anticipation of the establishment of the park and, as the *New York Times* reported on July 6, 1882, many estates between Yonkers and Dobb's Ferry were up for sale, American millionaires having gone to Europe, leaving their Hudson Valley mansions to decay and rot.

48. Codman, *Winter Sketches*, p. 182.

49. Bruce, *The Hudson*, (1907), p. 91.

50. Apart from the "ruins" at Fort Putnam and on Constitution Island, the abandoned iron mines and furnaces, old hotels and summer resorts, the salvage apparatus at Kidd's Point, and the abandoned estates on the Putnam shore were all regarded as true "ruins."

51. E.g. Sons of the American Revolution (1889); Colonial Dames of America (1890); and the New York State Historical Association (1899). Many other ethnic- or religious-based historical societies also evolved in the 1890s, and thereafter, reflecting a popular interest in history and the work of historical preservation. There is evidence as well of a burst of activity in historical preservation; a state historian was appointed in 1895). See Alexander Potter, "Scenic and Historic Possessions," in Flick, ed., *History of the State of New York*, pp. 255–89.

52. Nash, ed., *The American Environment*, p. 75.

53. Croes, *Palisades of the Hudson*, p. 12 and W. J. McGee, "The Conservation of Natural Resources," in Nash, *ibid.*, p. 46.

54. J. B. Jackson, "A New Kind of Space," *Landscape*, Winter 1969, pp. 33–35.

55. Ingersoll, *Illustrated Guide*, pp. 36, 47, 76–77.

56. *New York News-Letter*, "The Highlands," January–February 1901, p. 6.

57. Hudson River Dayline Company, *Most Charming Inland Water Route*, pp. 26–31.

58. Henry James, "New York and the Hudson," pp. 827–28.

59. Mack, *Palisades of the Hudson*, p. 2; "To Save the Palisades," *New York Times*, September 23, 1897, p. 5.

60. "Souvenir Postcard" issued by the American Scenic and Historical Preservation Society c. 1905, N.Y.P.L. Collections.

61. Bruce, *The Hudson*, p. 98.

62. John Muir, "Our National Parks," (1901) as quoted in Nash, ed., *The American Environment*, pp. 71–74. The value of scenery as a health-producing amenity for body and mind—the need for green, open space—of course became one of the integral arguments of all conservation theory in the twentieth century.

63. Edward Stainbrook, "Human Needs and the Natural Environment," Bureau of

Sport Fisheries and Wildlife, Department of the Interior, *Man and Nature in the City* (Washington, D.C.: U.S. Government Printing Office, 1969).

64. See: Albert Finn, *Frederick Law Olmsted and the American Environmental Tradition* (New York: George Braziller, 1972).

65. Calvin Stillman, "The Issues in the Storm King Controversy," p. 3.

66. As quoted in Nash, ed., *The American Environment,* p. 70.

Selected Bibliography

Major Conceptual Works

Curti, Merle. *The Growth of American Thought,* 3rd ed. New York: Harper & Row, 1964.

Dodge, Richard. "The Aesthetic in Geography." *The Journal of Geography,* 38, no. 7 (October 1939): 257–59.

Fischer, Eric; Robert Campbell and Eldon Miller. *A Question of Place: The Development of Geographic Thought.* Arlington, Va.: Beatty, 1969, p. 446.

Huth, Hans. *Nature and the American.* Berkeley: University of California Press, 1957.

Lowenthal, David. "American Attitudes Toward the Conquest of Nature." *Annals of the AAG* (Association of American Geographers), 48 (1953): 278.

—— "The American Creed of Nature as Virtue." *Landscape,* 19 (1959): 24–25.

—— "Geography, Experience and Imagination." *Annals of the AAG,* 51 (September 1961): 241–60.

—— "Not Every Prospect Pleases: What is Our Criterion for Scenic Beauty?" *Landscape,* Winter (1962): 19–23.

—— "America as Scenery." *Geographical Review,* 56 (1966): 115–18.

—— "The American Scene." *Geographical Review,* 58 (January 1968): 61–88.

—— "Recreational Habits and Values: Implications for Landscape Quality." *New York State Planning News,* July–August 1969, pp. 1–12.

—— "Past Time, Present Place: Landscape and Memory." *Geographical Review,* 65 (January 1975): 1–36.

Lowenthal, David and Hugh Prince. "English Landscape Tastes." *Geographical Review,* 55 (1965): 186–222.

Marx, Leo. *The Machine in the Garden: Technology and the Pastoral Ideal in America.* New York: Oxford University Press, 1964, p.392.

——— "Open Space as Literary Metaphor." *Proceedings,* 23rd Annual University of Massachusetts Landscape Architects Association Conference, November 1968.

Miller, Perry. *Errand into the Wilderness.* Cambridge, Mass.: Belknap Press, 1964.

Nairn, Ian. *The American Landscape: A Critical View.* New York: Random House Co., 1965, p.152.

Nash, Roderick. *Wilderness and the American Mind.* New Haven: Yale University Press, 1967, p. 256.

Nash, Roderick, ed. *The American Environment: Readings in the History of Conservation.* Reading, Mass.: Addison-Wesley Publishers, 1968, p.236.

Nicolson, Marjorie Hope. *Mountain Gloom and Mountain Glory: The Development of the Aesthetics of the Infinite.* Ithaca, N.Y.: Cornell University Press, 1959, p.403.

Novak, Barbara. "American Landscape: The Nationalist Garden and the Holy Book." *Art in America,* January–February 1972, pp. 46–57.

Raup, Hugh M. "Botanical Studies in the Black Rock Forest." *Black Rock Forest Papers,* Bulletin no. 7 (1938) Cornwall, New York.

——— "Some Problems in Ecological Theory and their Relation to Conservation." *British Ecological Society Jubilee Symposium,* March 1964, pp. 19–28.

——— "The View from John Sanderson's Farm: A Perspective for the Use of the Land." *Forest History,* April 1966, pp. 2–12.

Shepard, Paul. "They Painted What They Saw." *Landscape,* 3 (Summer 1953): 6–11.

——— "The Nature of Tourism." *Landscape,* 5 (Summer 1955): 29–33.

——— "The Cross Valley Syndrome." *Landscape,* 10 (1961): 4–8.

——— *Man in the Landscape: A Historic View of the Esthetics of Nature.* New York: Alfred Knopf, 1967, p.290.

Smith, Bernard. *European Vision and the South Pacific, 1768–1850: A Study in the History of Art and Ideas.* Oxford: the Clarendon Press, 1960, p.275.

Smith, Henry Nash. *Virgin Land: The American West as Symbol and Myth.* New York: Vintage Books, 1950, p.305.

Vance, James. "California and the Search for the Ideal." *Annals of the AAG,* 65 (June 1972): 185–210.

Van Zandt, Roland. "The Scotch School of Aesthetic Theory and the Natural Description of the Oregon Trail." *Smithsonian Journal,* no.4 (Fall 1949): 156–72.

——— *The Catskill Mountain House.* New Brunswick, N.J.: Rutgers University Press, 1966, p.416.

General Works

American Museum of Natural History. *The Geology, Flora, and Fauna of the Lower Hudson Valley*. Concord, N.H.: The Rumford Press, 1912, p.11.

Bakeless, John. *The Eyes of Discovery, America as Seen by the First Explorers*. New York: Dover Publications, 1961, p.439.

Bergen County Historical Society. *Proceedings*. Englewood: Press of the *Evening Record*, various volumes between 1902–11.

Beukema, Herman. "The Role of Geology in the History of the Hudson Highlands." *New York History*, July 1952, pp. 268–78.

Brooks, V. W. "The Highlands of the Hudson as a Playground for the People." *World's Work*, September 1909, pp. 12001–9.

Broughton, J. G., et al. *Geology of New York: A Short Account*. Albany: University of the State of New York, Educational Leaflet no.20, 1966, p.50.

Brown, Ralph. "The American Geographies of Jedidiah Morse." *Annals of the AAG*, September 1941, pp. 145–217.

—— *Historical Geography of the United States*. New York: Harcourt, 1948, p.596.

Bryant, William Cullen, ed. *Picturesque America*. 2 vols. New York: D. Appleton & Co., 1874.

Burroughs, John. "Our River." *Scribner's Monthly*, 20, no.4 (1880): 481–93.

Croes, J. J. *The Palisades of the Hudson*. New York: The Palisades Commission for the Acquistion of the Palisades of the Hudson by the United States, 1895, p.16.

Cunningham, Charles. *Timothy Dwight, 1752–1817, A Biography*. New York: Macmillan, 1942.

Dickinson, Robert. *Palisades Interstate Park*. New York: American Geographical Society, 1921, p.44.

Downing, A. J. *The Architecture of Country Houses*. New York: Dover, 1969, p.484. (Originally: D. Appleton & Co., 1850).

Ellis, David M. "Land Tenure and Tenancy in the Hudson Valley, 1790–1860." *American History*, April 1944, pp. 75–82.

—— *Landlords and Farmers in the Hudson-Mohawk Region, 1790–1850*. Ithaca: Cornell University Press, 1946, p.347.

—— Frost, H. et al. *A Short History of New York State*. Ithaca: Cornell University Press, 1957, p.705.

Elting, Irving. *Dutch Village Communities on the Hudson River*. Baltimore: Johns Hopkins Press, 1886.

Flick, Alexander, ed. *History of the State of New York*. 10 vols., New York: Columbia University Press, 1937.

Fox, Dixon Ryan. *Yankees and Yorkers*. New York: New York University Press, 1940.

Hall, Alice J. "The Hudson: That River's Alive," *National Geographic*, January 1978, pp.62–88.

Hall, Edward. *The Palisades of the Hudson River, The Story of their Origin, Attempted Destruction and Rescue.* Albany: American Scenic and Historical Preservation Society, Annual Report, 1906, pp. 143–71.

Hedrick, Ulysses P. *A History of Agriculture in the State of New York.* New York: Hill and Wang, 1966, p.465.

Hoglund, William A. "Abandoned Farms and the 'New Agriculture' In New York State at the Beginning of the Twentieth Century." *New York History,* 34 (1953): 185–201.

Hopkins, Franklin. "The Preservation of the Palisades." *Scenic and Historic America,* 2 (December 1930): 19–27.

Howell, William T. *The Hudson Highlands.* 2 vols. New York: Lenz & Riecker Inc., 1933–34.

Johnson, John. "Geological and Economic History of the Hudson River." *Hudson River Ecology,* Hudson River Valley Commission: Papers of a symposium held on October 4–5, 1966 at the Onchiota Conference Center, Sterling Forest, Tuxedo, N.Y.

Kline, Marsha. *Beyond the Land Itself: Views of Nature in Canada and the United States.* Essays in History and Literature, Cambridge: Harvard University Press, 1970, p.75.

Krout, John A., and Clifford L. Lord. "Sports and Recreation." In Alexander Flick, ed. *History of the State of New York,* 10:215–54. 10 vols. New York: Columbia University Press, 1937.

Lees, Carlton. "The Golden Age of Horticulture." *Historic Preservation,* October–December 1972, pp. 32–37.

Lowe, Kurt E. "Storm King Granite at Bear Mountain, N.Y." *Bulletin of the Geological Society of America,* 61 (1950):137–90.

Mack, Arthur C. *The Palisades of the Hudson.* Edgewater: Palisade Press, 1909, p.58.

Marti, Donald. "In Praise of Farming: An Aspect of the Movement for Agricultural Improvement in the Northeast, 1815–1840." *New York History,* July 1970, pp. 351–75.

Martin, Paul and Ella Coates. "The Story of the Ferry, 1698–1898." Palisades, N.Y.: The Palisades Library, 1903.

Nordstrom, Carl. *A Finding List of Bibliographical Materials Relating to Rockland County, N.Y.* Orangeburg: Tappan Zee Historical Society, 1959.

—— *Frontier Elements in a Hudson River Village.* Port Washington, N.Y.: Kennikat Press, 1973.

O'Callaghan, E. B., ed. *The Documentary History of the State of New York.* 4 vols. Albany: Charles Van Benthuysen, Public Printer, 1851.

Palisades Interstate Park Commission. *Sixty Years of Park Cooperation: A History, 1900–60.* Bear Mountain, N.Y.: Palisades Interstate Park Commission, 1960.

—— *Composite Annual Report, New York-New Jersey: 1976.* Bear Mountain, N.Y.: Palisades Interstate Park Commission, 1976, p. 48.

—— *Artists in Residence, 1975-76-77, Palisades Interstate Park.* Bear Mountain, N.Y.: Palisades Interstate Park Commission, 1977.

Phelps, H. P. *The Home Sites at Undercliff, New Jersey.* New York: author, 18—, N.D. but 19th century.

Ransom, J. M. *Bergen County: A Bibliography of Historical Books, Pamphlets, and Maps and Certain Other items Pertaining Thereto.* Bergen County Historical Society, 1960.

Ringwald, Donald. *The Hudson River Day Line.* Berkeley: Howell-North Books, 1965.

Rosenkrantz, Barbara and William Koelsch, eds. *American Habitat: A Historical Perspective.* New York: The Free Press, 1973.

Sanford, Charles, ed. *Quest for America, 1810–1824.* New York: Doubleday, 1964.

Schlesinger, Arthur. " 'Progress' and the History of the Hudson," *New York Times,* October 30, 1971.

Seeger, Pete. "Song of the Clearwater," *Parade,* Nov. 26, 1978, pp. 5–7.

Silloway, Persey. *The Palisades Interstate Park: A Study in Recreational Forestry.* Syracuse: Syracuse University Press, College of Forestry, Bulletin no. 10. 1920, p.79.

Stanford, Peter. " 'A Peculiar Note of Romance,' The Heritage of the Hudson River Steamer." *Sea History,* Spring 1978, pp.7–13.

Stillman, Calvin W. "The Issues in the Storm King Controversy." *Black Rock Forest Papers,* Harvard Black Rock Forest, Cornwall, N.Y.: 1966.

—— "This Fair Land," in Erwin H. Zube, et al., eds. *Landscape Assessment: Values, Perceptions, and Resources.* Stroudsburg, Pa.: Dowden, Hutchinson & Ross, 1975.

Tarr, Ralph S. *The Physical Geography of New York State.* New York: Macmillan, 1902.

Thompson, John H., ed. *Geography of New York State.* Syracuse: Syracuse University Press, 1966.

Thrower, Norman and Clarence Glacken. *The Terraqueous Globe: The History of Geography and Cartography.* Papers read at a Clark Library Seminar, April 27, 1968. Los Angeles, University of California, 1969.

Torrey, R. H., et al. *New York Walk Book.* New York: The American Geographical Society, 1951.

Truettner, William and R. Bolton-Smith. *National Parks and the American Landscape.* Washington, D.C.: Smithsonian Institution Press, 1972.

Tucker, William. "Environmentalism and the Leisure Class," *Harper's,* December 1977, pp.49–80.

Turner, R. H. *Field Trip Guide to the Land Use Patterns of the Mid-Hudson Valley.* West Point: U. S. Military Academy, 1974.

Warntz, William. *Geography Now and Then. (Some Notes on the Academic History of Geography in the U.S.).* New York: American Geographical Society Research Series, no.25, 1964.

Winton, H., E. Meany, and C.B. Thurston. *Report of the Palisades Commissioners of the State of New Jersey*. Somerville: The Unionist-Gazette Print., 1896.

Wyckoff, Jerome. *Rock Scenery of the Hudson Highlands and Palisades*. Glen Falls: Adirondack Mountain Club, 1971.

Art History Interpretations

Baigell, Matthew. *A History of American Painting*. New York: Praeger, 1971.

Barker, Virgil. *American Painting, History and Interpretation*. New York: MacMillan, 1950.

Clark, Kenneth. *Landscape into Art*. Boston: Beacon Press, 1963.

Cowdrey, Bartlett. "William Henry Bartlett and the American Scene." *New York History*, October 1941, pp.388–400.

Flexner, James T. *A Pocket History of American Painting*. New York: Washington Square Press, 1950.

—— *The Light of Distant Skies: American Painting, 1760–1835*. New York: Harcourt, 1954; rpt. Dover, 1969.

—— *That Wilder Image: The Painting of America's Native School from Thomas Cole to Winslow Homer*. New York: Little, Brown, 1962.

Green, Samuel. *American Art, A Historical Survey*. New York: Ronald Press, 1966.

Howat, John. *The Hudson River and its Painters*. New York: The Viking Press, 1972. (Published for the Scenic Hudson Preservation Conference).

Howat, John, et al. *Nineteenth Century America, Painting and Sculptures*. New York: New York Graphic Society Ltd., Exhibition Catalogue for the Metropolitan Museum of Art, April–September 1970.

Jones, Agnes H. *The Hudson River School*. Geneva, N.Y.: W. F. Humphrey Press, 1968. Catalogue for the Exhibition Gallery of the Fine Arts Center at the State University College of New York at Geneseo.

Merritt, Howard. *Thomas Cole*. Rochester: University of Rochester, 1969. Catalogue for the Memorial Art Gallery at the University of Rochester.

Mumford, Louis. *The Brown Decades: A Study of the Arts in America, 1865–1895*. New York: Dover, 1955.

Public Education Association. *The American Vision: Paintings, 1825–1875*. New York: 1968. Catalogue to Exhibits at the Knoedler, Rosenberg, Hirschl & Adler Galleries.

Richardson, E. P. *Painting in America*. New York: Crowell, 1965.

Shelley, Donald. "William Guy Wall and his Watercolors for the Historic Hudson River Portfolio." *New York Historical Society Quarterly*, 31 (1947): 25–45.

Smithsonian Institution. "Scenes . . . From Which the Hand of Nature has Never Been Lifted." The *Smithsonian*, August 1972, pp.34–40.

Sweet, Frederick A. *The Hudson River School and the Early American Landscape Tradition.* New York: Whitney Museum of American Art, 1945.

Vessell, Elliot S., ed. *The Life and Works of Thomas Cole . . . by Louis Legrand Noble.* Cambridge: Harvard University Press, 1964.

Literary Sources

Arden, Eugene. "The Evil City in American Fiction." *New York History,* July 1954, pp.259–79.

Auser, Cortland. *Nathaniel P. Willis.* New York: Twayne, 1969.

Beers, Henry. *Nathaniel Parker Willis.* Boston: Houghton, Mifflin, 1885.

Hommell, Pauline. *Teacup Tales: Folklore of the Hudson River.* New York: Vantage Press, 1958.

Irving, Washington. *Knickerbocker's History of New York.* New York: Capricorn Books, 1965 (originally published in 1809).

—— *The Sketch Book.* New York: New American Library, 1961 (originally published in 1819–20).

—— *A Book of the Hudson.* New York: Putnam, 1849.

Murphy, Henry C. *Anthology of New Netherland or Translations from the Early Dutch Poets of New York With Memoirs of Their Lives.* New York: the Bradford Club, 1865.

Willis, Nathaniel P. *American Scenery.* 2 vols. London: Geo. Virtue, 1840. (Willis was responsible for only the textual portions).

—— *Hurry-Graphs, or, Sketches of Scenery . . .* New York: Scribner, 1851.

—— *Outdoors at Idlewild or the Shaping of a Home on the Banks of the Hudson.* New York: Scribner, 1855.

Winslow, Elizabeth, ed. *Jonathan Edwards: Basic Writings.* New York: The New American Library, 1966.

Wynkoop, P., pub. *Legends and Poetry of the Hudson.* New York: P. Wynkoop & Sons, 1868.

Hudson River Histories

Bacon, Edgar Mayhew. *The Hudson River from Ocean to Source, Historical, Legendary, Picturesque.* New York: Putnam, 1902.

Boyle, Robert H. *The Hudson River: A Natural and Unnatural History.* New York: Norton, expanded edition, 1979.

Brown, Henry C. *The Lordly Hudson.* New York: Scribner, 1937.

Bruce, Wallace. *The Hudson.* Boston: Houghton Mifflin, 1881.

—— *The Hudson, Three Centuries of History, Romance and Invention.* New York: Bryant Union Co., 1907.

Carmer, Carl. *The Hudson.* New York: Rinehart, 1939.

Goodwin, Maud. *Dutch and English on the Hudson*. New Haven: Yale University Press, 1921.

Greene, Nelson, ed. *History of the Valley of the Hudson, River of Destiny, 1609–1930*. 5 vols. Chicago: S. J. Clarke Pubs., 1931.

Johnson, Clifton. *The Picturesque Hudson*. New York: Macmillan, 1909.

Lossing, Benson J. *The Hudson from the Wilderness to the Sea*. New York: Virtue & Yorston, 1866.

Mylod, John. *Biography of a River, The People and Legends of the Hudson Valley*. New York: Hawthorn, 1969.

New York News-Letter. "The Hudson River, Part I—The Palisades"; "Part II—The Highlands." New York: Wm. Van Wart, 33, no.6 (November–December 1900) and 34, no.1 (January–February 1901).

Reed, John. *The Hudson River Valley*. New York: Clarkson N. Potter, 1960.

Van Vorst, Marie. "The Hudson River." *Harpers Magazine*, March 1905, pp.543–55.

Wilstach, Paul. *Hudson River Landings*. Indianapolis: Bobbs-Merrill, 1933.

County and Local Histories

Ackerman, D. "Historic Closter." *Proceedings*, Bergen County Historical Society, no.7 (1910–11), pp.21ff.

Bannerman, Charles S. *The Story of Bannerman Island*. Blue Point, N.Y.: Francis Bannerman Sons, Inc., 1962. p.46.

Bedell, C. F. *Now and Then and Long Ago in Rockland County*. Suffern: private printing, The Ramapo Valley Independent, 1941.

Carr, William and Richard Koke. *Twin Forts of the Popolopen: Forts Clinton and Montgomery, N.Y. 1775–1777*. Historical Bulletin no.1, Bear Mountain: Bear Mountain Trailside Museums, July 1937.

Clayton, W. Woodford. *History of Bergen and Passaic Counties, New Jersey, with Biographical Sketches*. Philadelphia: Evarts & Peck, 1882.

Cole, David, ed. *History of Rockland County, New York*. New York: J. B. Beers, 1884.

Corning, A. Elwood. "Orange County." In Louise Zimm, ed. *Southeastern New York, A History*. 3 vols. New York: Lewis Historical Pub. Co., 1946, 3:453–604; "Rockland County," 3:609–775.

Eager, Samuel. *An Outline History of Orange County*. Newburgh: S. T. Callahan, 1846–47.

Gilman, Winthrop. *Essays on the History of Palisade, New York*. Palisades: The Palisades Library, 1903.

Greco, James J. *The Story of Englewood Cliffs*. Englewood Cliffs: Published by the Tercentenary Committee, 1964, p.245.

Green, Frank B. *The History of Rockland County*. New York: A. S. Barnes, 1886.

Headley, Russell, ed. *The History of Orange County, New York.* Middletown: Van Deusen & Elms, 1908.

Jewell, Willitt C. "Putnam County." In Louise Zimm, ed. *Southeastern New York, A History.* New York: Lewis Historical Publishing Co., 1946, vol. 2.

Jones, H. Crampton. "History of Constitution Island." *New York History,* July 1952, pp.279–93.

Maples, S. S., ed. *Closter, the First 285 Years.* Closter: The Fiftieth Anniversary Committee, 1954. p.50.

Ruttenber, E. M. and L. H. Clark, *History of Orange County, New York.* Philadelphia: Evarts & Peck, 1881.

Sterling, Adaline W. *The Book of Englewood.* Englewood: The Committee on the History of Englewood, 1922.

Upper Nyack Centennial Committee. *1872–1972, Centennial: Village of Upper Nyack, N.Y.* Printed by Print Sprint Inc., 1972.

Van Valen, J.M. *History of Bergen County, New Jersey.* New York: New Jersey [*sic*] Pub. and Engraving Co., 1900, p. 691.

Westervelt, Frances A., ed. *History of Bergen County, New Jersey, 1630–1923.* 3 vols. New York: Lewis Historical Pub. Co., 1923.

Hudson River Guidebooks

Bartlett, William H. *American Scenery, or Land, Lake, and River, Illustrations of Transatlantic Nature.* 2 vols. London: Geo. Virtue, 1840.

Bruce, Wallace. *The Hudson River by Daylight etc.* New York: American News Company, 1875. p.151.

—— *The Hudson River Guide and Map.* New York: Bryant Union, 1903.

—— [Thursty McQuill]. *The Hudson River by Daylight.* New York: J. Featherson, 1882.

Colt, Mrs. S. S., ed. *The Tourist's Guide through the Empire State . . . by Hudson River and New York Central Route.* Albany: author, 1871.

Colton, J. H. *A Guide Book to West Point.* New York: author, 1844. p. 112.

Cranston, Henry. *The Hudson Highlands.* New York: New York Hotel (specially printed for the owner of "Cranston's Hotel" or the New York Hotel), 1883.

Hines, Charles C. *Hine's Annual, 1906, The West Bank of the Hudson, Albany to Tappan.* New York: author, 1907.

Hudson River Day Line Co. *The Most Charming Inland Water Route on the American Continent.* New York: L. Stillson Co., 1903.

——. *Snapshots on the Upper Hudson.* n.p., n.d.

Hudson River Railroad Corporation. *Woodcut Views of the Principal Objects of Interest Upon the Line.* New York: Locke & Co., 1851.

Ingersoll, Ernest. *Illustrated Guide to the Hudson River and Catskill Mountains.* New York: Rand McNally, 1909.

Knapp, Samuel. *The Picturesque Beauties of the Hudson River and its Vicinity Illustrated in a Series of Views from Original Drawings.* New York: J. Disturnell, 1835.

Link, William F. *The Hudson by Daylight.* New York: Hudson River Day Line, 1878.

McDannald, Alexander H. *The Storied Hudson.* New York: Hudson River Night Line, 1927.

Munsell, Joel. *Guide to the Hudson River by Railroad and Steamboat.* Albany: author, 1863.

Nelson, T. *American Views, Views of the Hudson.* New York: T. Nelson & Sons, 1878 (?).

Sears, Robert, ed. *A New and Popular Pictorial Description of the United States etc.* New York: Robert Sears, 1848.

Strong, T. W. *The Hudson* (Illustrated With Pen and Pencil). New York: T. W. Strong, 1852.

Taintor, Charles N. *The Hudson River Route, New York to West Point . . . Scenery and Objects of Interest Along the Route.* New York: Taintor Brothers, 1887.

Travellers Steamboat and Railroad Guide to the Hudson. New York: Gaylord Watson, 1857.

Wilson, Henry. *Illustrated Guide to the Hudson River.* New York: author, 1849.

Travel Accounts

Beltrami, Giacomo. *A Pilgrimage in Europe and America.* London: Hunt & Clarke, 1828.

Chastellux, François-Jean. *Voyage de Newport a Philadelphie, Albany, . . .* Newport: The Press of the French Fleet, 1781.

Child, Mrs. L. *Letters from New York.* New York: C. S. Francis, 1850.

Codman, John. *Winter Sketches from the Saddle by a Septuagenarian.* New York: Putnam, 1888.

Crèvecoeur, St. Jean de. *Letters from an American Farmer.* London: Printed for T. Davies, 1782.

—— *Voyage dans la Haute Pennsylvanie et dans l'état de New-York, par un membre adoptif de la Nation Oneida.* 3 vols. Paris: Chez Maradan, 1801.

Danckaerts, Jasper. *Journal of 1679–80.* New York: Scribner, 1909.

Dwight, Timothy. *Travels in New England and New York.* 4 vols. New Haven: S. Converse, 1822.

Fowler, John. *Journal of a Tour in the State of New York in the Year 1830.* London: Whittaker, Treacher & Arnot, 1831.

Greene, Asa. [George Fibbleton] *Travels in America.* New York: Wm. Pearson, 1833.

Halsey, F. W., ed. *A Tour of Four Great Rivers etc., Being the Journal of Richard*

Smith of Burlington, New Jersey. Port Washington, N.Y.: Ira Freidman, 1964 (reprint of 1906 edition).

Hunt, Freeman. *Letters About the Hudson River and its Vicinity Written in 1835–1837*. New York: author, 1837.

James, Henry. "New York and the Hudson: A Spring Impression." *North American Review*, 181 (1905): 801–33.

Kalm, Peter. *Travels in North America*. 2 vols. New York: Dover, 1964 (original English version, 1770).

LaRochefoucauld-Liancourt, François. *Voyage dans les Etats-Unis de l'Amerique fait en 1795, 1796 et 1797*. 8 vols. Paris: Chez DuPont, 1798.

Milbert, Jacques. *Picturesque Itinerary of the Hudson River and Travels in North America*. 2 vols. Upper Saddle River, N.J.: the Gregg Press, 1969 (translated by Constance Sherman from the 1828–29 Paris edition).

Monaghan, Frank. *Franch Travellers in the United States, 1765–1932, A Bibliography*. New York: Antiquarian Press, 1961 (first published in 1933 by the New York Public Library).

Montulé, Edouard de. *Travels in America, 1816–17*. Bloomington: Indiana University Press, 1950 (translated from the 1821 Paris edition).

New York Historical Society. *Collections*. 2nd series. vol. 1, 1841 (travel accounts contained herein: Verrazano, Van der Donck, and Hudson's mate, Robert Juet).

Olmsted, Frederick Law. *A Journey in the Back Country*. New York: Mason Bros., 1860.

Patten, Edmund. *A Glimpse of the United States and the Northern States of America . . . During the Autumn of 1852*. London: Effingham Wilson Pub., 1853.

Sarmiento. *Travels in the United States in 1847*. Princeton: Princeton University Press, 1970 (translated by M. A. Rockland).

Todd, C. Lafayette. "Some Nineteenth-Century European Travellers in New York State." *New York History*, October 1962, pp. 336–70.

Van Zandt, Roland, ed. *Chronicles of the Hudson: Three Centuries of Travellers' Accounts*. New Brunswick, N.J.: Rutgers University Press, 1971.

Volney, C. F. *A View of the Soil and Climate of the United States of America*. Philadelphia: J. Conrad & Co., 1804. p. 446 (translated with occasional remarks by C. B. Brown).

Wallace, D. H., ed. "From the Windows of a Mail Coach, A Scotsman (J. B. Dunlop) Looks at New York State in 1811." *New York Historical Society Quarterly*, January 1956, p. 272.

Diaries and Memoirs

Clinton, Charles. *The Marble Covered Field Book*. Dated 1771 and contained in New York Public Library uncatalogued collection of materials, Local History Division (the field notes and journal relate to the surveying of the Cheesecocks Patent in 1735–47).

Gesner, Nicholas. "Diary, 1830–1850." Original and Handwritten, contained in Palisades Free Library, Palisades, N.Y.

Lydenberg, H. M., ed. *Archibald Robertson, Diaries and Sketches in America, 1762–1780.* New York: New York Public Library, 1930.

Nevins, Allan and M. H. Thomas, eds. *The Diary of George Templeton Strong, 1835–1875,* 4 vols. New York: the Macmillan Co., 1952.

Thacher, James. *Military Journal During the American Revolutionary War, From 1775 to 1783.* Hartford: Silas Andrus & Son, 1854.

Tilghman, Tench. *Memoirs of Lieutenant Colonel Tench Tilghman . . . Containing Revolutionary Journals and Letters.* Albany: J. Munsell, 1876.

Theses

Collins, Stephen. "The Biotic Communities of Greenbrook Sanctuary." Ph.D. Dissertation, New Brunswick: Rutgers University, 1956.

Kury, Theodore. "Historical Geography of the Iron Industry in the New York–New Jersey Highlands, 1700–1900." Ph.D. Dissertation, Baton Rouge: Louisiana State University, 1968.

LaBuddle, Kenneth. "The Mind of Thomas Cole." Ph.D. Dissertation, University of Minnesota, 1954.

Matros, Ronald. "Geography and the Aesthetic Landscape." M. A. Thesis, University of Minnesota, 1963.

Maps and Atlases

1776

Romans, Bernard. *American Military Pocket Atlas.* London: Sayer & Bennet.

Lewis, S. "A Plan of the Northern Part of New Jersey." Map 66 in Emerson Fite and Archibald Freeman. *A Book of Old Maps.* Cambridge: Harvard University Press, 1926.

Sauthier, C. J. "A Topographic Map of the Northern Part of New York Island." London: Wm. Faden.

1777

DesBarres, J. F. W. "A Sketch of the Operations of His Majesty's Fleet and Army." London: DesBarres, January 17.

Erskine, Robert. "Map of the Northern Part of New Jersey and Southern New York State."

1779

Sauthier, C. J. "A Chorological Map of the Province of New York." London: Wm. Faden.

1781

Erskine, Robert. "West of the Hudson." In *Magazine of American History*, 5 (1880):8.

1812

Aaron, Arrowsmith and Lewis. "New Jersey." In *A New and Elegant General Atlas*. Boston: Thomas and Andrews, 1812.

1818(?)

Eddy, John. "The State of New York with Parts of the Adjacent States." New York: Samuel Maverick.

1820

"Map of the State of New York with Part of the State of Northeastern New Jersey." New York: Amos Lay Pub.

1828

Gordon, Thomas. "A Map of the State of New Jersey With Rockland County." Trenton: The author.

Tanner, H. A. "A Map of the State of New Jersey." Trenton.

1829

Cammeyer, William. "A New Map of the Hudson River." Albany: William Cammeyer Jr.

DeWitt, Simeon, Surveyor General. *An Atlas of the State of New York*. New York: David Burr.

1831

"Topographical Map of Northern New Jersey." New York: Pendleton.

1854

"Rockland County, New York." New York: Surveyed and Published by R. F. O'Connor.

1859

Seymour and Tower. "Map of the Northern Railroad of New Jersey." New York: Robertson, Seibert and Shearn.

"Map of Orange and Rockland Counties, New York." From actual surveys by F. F. French, W. E. Wood and S. N. Beers. Philadelphia: Corey & Bachman, Pubs.

1861

"Map of the Counties of Bergen and Passaic, New Jersey." From actual surveys by G. M. Hopkins. Philadelphia: G. H. Corey, Pub.

1864

"Lloyd's Topographical Map of the Hudson River From Troy to Sandy Hook etc." New York & London: J. T. Lloyd.

1865

Bacot, R. C. "Map Showing the Survey of Lands Under the Waters of the Hudson River and Bay of New York." Accompanying a report of commissioners to the Legislature of the State of New Jersey. New York: J. Seymour & Co.

1875

Beers, F. W. *County Atlas of Rockland, New York. From recent and actual surveys and records.* New York: Walker & Jewett.

1876

Davis, F. A. *New Historical Atlas of Rockland County.* Philadelphia: F. A. Davis and H. L. Kochensperger.

Walker, A. H. *Atlas of Bergen County, New Jersey.* Reading, Pa.: Reading Pub. House.

1880

"Map of the Highlands of the Hudson, Orange County." Newburgh, N.Y.: James P. Kirby.

1881

"Map of Orange County." In Ruttenber and Clark, *History of Orange County, New York* (q.v.).

1891

"Road Map of the Counties of Rockland and Orange." New York: Colton.

Beers, F. W. *Atlas of the Hudson River Valley.* New York: Watson & Co.

1900

"Map of Palisades Park and Palisades Heights." New York: Palisades Park Company.

1903

Lathrop, J. M. *Atlas of Orange County, New York.* Philadelphia: A. H. Mueller.

Handy Guide (and Map) to the Hudson River. New York: Rand McNally Co.

1909

Potter, H. B. "Bergen County." New York: R. A. Welcke.

Other Materials

American Scenic and Historical Preservation Society. "Hook Mountain, Point-no-Point, or Rockland Point on the Hudson River, now being Destroyed by Stone Crushing Works." Being a Souvenir Postcard issued in 1905 (?).

Anderson, Maxwell. *High Tor.* A play appearing in B. Mantle, ed. *Best Plays of 1936–37.* New York: Dodd, 1937.

Department of Earth, Space and Graphic Sciences. *Field Trip Guide to the Hudson Highlands and Fortress West Point.* U.S. Military Academy, West Point, N.Y. 1976.

Hudson River Valley Commission. *Historic Resources of the Hudson.* New York: Georgian Lithographers, 1969. p. 96.

Lobeck, A. K. *Panoramic View of the New York Region.* Scenic Folder no. 1. New York: The Geographical Press, 1952.

New Jersey Historical Society. "Iconography of New Jersey." An unpublished collection of historical views of New Jersey. Book no. 3, "Bergen County, the Palisades."

New York Public Library. "A Retrospective Collection of Paintings from the Palisades by V. D. Perrine." 1904. Manuscript Division.

—— "List of Prints, Books, Manuscripts etc. relating to the Hudson River." 1909. Astor, Lennox and Tilden Foundations.

—— "Eno Collection of New York City Views." A Collection of Photostatic reproductions of Original Prints, 1954.

—— "Uncatalogued Collection of pamphlets and books pertaining to the Hudson River and Valley." 6 vols. Local History Division. Catalogued: IRM (Hudson River) n.c. 1–6.

—— "Views of New York State." A Scrapbook of Postcard and other views contained in the Local History Division.

Rockefeller, Laurence. "Palisades Interstate Park." A Speech delivered in 1957 to the Garden Clubs of New Jersey at the Greenbrook Sanctuary.

Index

Note: pages containing illustrations are set in italics.